Java XML and JSON

Document Processing for Java SE

Second Edition

Jeff Friesen

Apress®

Java XML and JSON: Document Processing for Java SE

Jeff Friesen
Dauphin, MB, Canada

ISBN-13 (pbk): 978-1-4842-4329-9
https://doi.org/10.1007/978-1-4842-4330-5

ISBN-13 (electronic): 978-1-4842-4330-5

Library of Congress Control Number: 2018968598

Managing Director, Apress Media LLC: Welmoed Spahr
Acquisitions Editor: Jonathan Gennick
Development Editor: Laura Berendson
Coordinating Editor: Jill Balzano

Cover image designed by Freepik (www.freepik.com)

Distributed to the book trade worldwide by Springer Science+Business Media New York, 233 Spring Street, 6th Floor, New York, NY 10013. Phone 1-800-SPRINGER, fax (201) 348-4505, e-mail orders-ny@springer-sbm.com, or visit www.springeronline.com. Apress Media, LLC is a California LLC and the sole member (owner) is Springer Science + Business Media Finance Inc (SSBM Finance Inc). SSBM Finance Inc is a Delaware corporation.

For information on translations, please e-mail rights@apress.com, or visit http://www.apress.com/rights-permissions.

Apress titles may be purchased in bulk for academic, corporate, or promotional use. eBook versions and licenses are also available for most titles. For more information, reference our Print and eBook Bulk Sales web page at http://www.apress.com/bulk-sales.

Any source code or other supplementary material referenced by the author in this book is available to readers on GitHub via the book's product page, located at www.apress.com/978-1-4842-4329-9. For more detailed information, please visit http://www.apress.com/source-code.

Printed on acid-free paper

To my parents.

Table of Contents

About the Author

Jeff Friesen is a freelance teacher and software developer with an emphasis on Java. In addition to authoring *Java I/O, NIO and NIO.2* (Apress), *Java Threads and the Concurrency Utilities* (Apress), and the first edition of this book, Jeff has written numerous articles on Java and other technologies (such as Android) for JavaWorld (`JavaWorld.com`), informIT (`InformIT.com`), `Java.net`, SitePoint (`SitePoint.com`), and other web sites. Jeff can be contacted via his web site at `JavaJeff.ca` or via his LinkedIn (`LinkedIn.com`) profile (`www.linkedin.com/in/javajeff`).

About the Technical Reviewer

Massimo Nardone has more than 24 years of experiences in Security, web/mobile development, Cloud, and IT architecture. His true IT passions are Security and Android.

He has been programming and teaching how to program with Android, Perl, PHP, Java, VB, Python, C/C++, and MySQL for more than 20 years.

He holds a Master of Science degree in Computing Science from the University of Salerno, Italy.

He has worked as a Project Manager, Software Engineer, Research Engineer, Chief Security Architect, Information Security Manager, PCI/SCADA Auditor, and Senior Lead IT Security/Cloud/SCADA Architect for many years.

His technical skills include Security, Android, Cloud, Java, MySQL, Drupal, Cobol, Perl, web and mobile development, MongoDB, D3, Joomla, Couchbase, C/C++, WebGL, Python, Pro Rails, Django CMS, Jekyll, Scratch, etc.

He worked as visiting lecturer and supervisor for exercises at the Networking Laboratory of the Helsinki University of Technology (Aalto University). He holds four international patents (PKI, SIP, SAML, and Proxy areas).

He currently works as Chief Information Security Officer (CISO) for Cargotec Oyj, and he is member of ISACA Finland Chapter Board.

Massimo has been reviewing more than 45 IT books for different publishing companies, and he is the coauthor of *Pro Android Games* (Apress, 2015), *Pro JPA 2 in Java EE 8* (APress 2018), and *Beginning EJB in Java EE 8* (Apress, 2018).

Acknowledgments

I thank Apress Acquisition Editor Jonathan Gennick and the Apress Editorial Board for giving me the opportunity to create this second edition. I also thank Editor Jill Balzano for guiding me through the book development process. Finally, I thank my technical reviewer and copy editor for catching mistakes and making the book look great.

Introduction

XML and (the more popular) JSON let you organize data in textual formats. This book introduces you to these technologies along with Java APIs for integrating them into your Java code. This book introduces you to XML and JSON as of Java 11.

Chapter 1 introduces XML, where you learn about basic language features (such as the XML declaration, elements and attributes, and namespaces). You also learn about well-formed XML documents and how to validate them via the Document Type Definition and XML Schema grammar languages.

Chapter 2 focuses on Java's SAX API for parsing XML documents. You learn how to obtain a SAX 2 parser; you then tour XMLReader methods along with handler and entity resolver interfaces. Finally, you explore a demonstration of this API and learn how to create a custom entity resolver.

Chapter 3 addresses Java's DOM API for parsing and creating XML documents. After discovering the various nodes that form a DOM document tree, you explore the DOM API, where you learn how to obtain a DOM parser/document builder and how to parse and create XML documents. You then explore the Java DOM APIs related to the Load and Save, and Traversal and Range specifications.

Chapter 4 places the spotlight on Java's StAX API for parsing and creating XML documents. You learn how to use StAX to parse XML documents with stream-based and event-based readers and to create XML documents with stream-based and event-based writers.

Moving on, Chapter 5 presents Java's XPath API for simplifying access to a DOM tree's nodes. You receive a primer on the XPath language, learning about location path expressions and general expressions. You also explore advanced features starting with namespace contexts.

Chapter 6 completes my coverage of XML by targetting Java's XSLT API. You learn about transformer factories and transformers, and much more. You also go beyond the XSLT 1.0 and XPath 1.0 APIs supported by Java.

Chapter 7 switches gears to JSON. You receive an introduction to JSON, take a tour of its syntax, explore a demonstration of JSON in a JavaScript context (because Java doesn't yet officially support JSON), and learn how to validate JSON objects in the context of JSON Schema.

You'll need to work with third-party libraries to parse and create JSON documents. Chapter 8 introduces you to the mJson library. After learning how to obtain and use mJson, you explore the Json class, which is the entry point for working with mJSon.

Google has released an even more powerful library for parsing and creating JSON documents. The Gson library is the focus of Chapter 9. In this chapter, you learn how to parse JSON objects through deserialization, how to create JSON objects through serialization, and much more.

Chapter 10 focuses on the JsonPath API for performing XPath-like operations on JSON documents.

Chapter 11 introduces you to Jackson, a popular suite of APIs for parsing and creating JSON documents.

Chapter 12 introduces you to JSON-P, an Oracle API that was planned for inclusion in Java SE, but was made available to Java EE instead.

Each chapter ends with assorted exercises that are designed to help you master the content. Along with long answers and true/false questions, you are often confronted with programming exercises. Appendix A provides the answers and solutions.

Thanks for purchasing this book. I hope you find it helpful in understanding XML and JSON in a Java context.

Jeff Friesen (October 2018)

Note You can download this book's source code by pointing your web browser to www.apress.com/9781484243299 and clicking the Source Code tab followed by the Download Now link.

PART I

Exploring XML

CHAPTER 1

Introducing XML

Applications commonly use XML documents to store and exchange data. XML defines rules for encoding documents in a format that is both human-readable and machine-readable. Chapter 1 introduces XML, tours the XML language features, and discusses well-formed and valid documents.

What Is XML?

XML (eXtensible Markup Language) is a *meta-language* (a language used to describe other languages) for defining *vocabularies* (custom markup languages), which is the key to XML's importance and popularity. XML-based vocabularies (such as XHTML) let you describe documents in a meaningful way.

XML vocabulary documents are like HTML (see `http://en.wikipedia.org/wiki/HTML`) documents in that they are text-based and consist of *markup* (encoded descriptions of a document's logical structure) and *content* (document text not interpreted as markup). Markup is evidenced via *tags* (angle bracket–delimited syntactic constructs), and each tag has a name. Furthermore, some tags have *attributes* (name/value pairs).

Note XML and HTML are descendants of *Standard Generalized Markup Language* (*SGML*), which is the original meta-language for creating vocabularies—XML is essentially a restricted form of SGML, while HTML is an *application* of SGML. The key difference between XML and HTML is that XML invites you to create your own vocabularies with their own tags and rules, whereas HTML gives you a single pre-created vocabulary with its own fixed set of tags and rules. XHTML and other XML-based vocabularies are *XML applications*. XHTML was created to be a cleaner implementation of HTML.

© Jeff Friesen 2019
J. Friesen, *Java XML and JSON*, https://doi.org/10.1007/978-1-4842-4330-5_1

If you haven't previously encountered XML, you might be surprised by its simplicity and how closely its vocabularies resemble HTML. You don't need to be a rocket scientist to learn how to create an XML document. To prove this to yourself, check out Listing 1-1.

Listing 1-1. XML-Based Recipe for a Grilled Cheese Sandwich

```
<recipe>
   <title>
      Grilled Cheese Sandwich
   </title>
   <ingredients>
      <ingredient qty="2">
         bread slice
      </ingredient>
      <ingredient>
         cheese slice
      </ingredient>
      <ingredient qty="2">
         margarine pat
      </ingredient>
   </ingredients>
   <instructions>
      Place frying pan on element and select medium heat.
      For each bread slice, smear one pat of margarine on
      one side of bread slice. Place cheese slice between
      bread slices with margarine-smeared sides away from
      the cheese. Place sandwich in frying pan with one
      margarine-smeared side in contact with pan. Fry for
      a couple of minutes and flip. Fry other side for a
      minute and serve.
   </instructions>
</recipe>
```

Listing 1-1 presents an XML document that describes a recipe for making a grilled cheese sandwich. This document is reminiscent of an HTML document in that it consists of tags, attributes, and content. However, that's where the similarity ends. Instead of presenting HTML tags such as <html>, <head>, <img>, and <p>, this informal recipe language presents its own <recipe>, <ingredients>, and other tags.

Note   Although Listing 1-1's <title> and </title> tags are also found in HTML, they differ from their HTML counterparts. Web browsers typically display the content between these tags in their title bars or tab headers. In contrast, the content between Listing 1-1's <title> and </title> tags might be displayed as a recipe header, spoken aloud, or presented in some other way, depending on the application that parses this document.

Language Features Tour

XML provides several language features for use in defining custom markup languages: XML declaration, elements and attributes, character references and CDATA sections, namespaces, and comments and processing instructions. You will learn about these language features in this section.

XML Declaration

An XML document usually begins with the *XML declaration*, special markup telling an XML parser that the document is XML. The absence of the XML declaration in Listing 1-1 reveals that this special markup isn't mandatory. When the XML declaration is present, nothing can appear before it.

The XML declaration minimally looks like <?xml version="1.0"?> in which the nonoptional version attribute identifies the version of the XML specification to which the document conforms. The initial version of this specification (1.0) was introduced in 1998 and is widely implemented.

Note   The World Wide Web Consortium (W3C), which maintains XML, released version 1.1 in 2004. This version mainly supports the use of line-ending characters used on EBCDIC platforms (see `http://en.wikipedia.org/wiki/EBCDIC`) and the use of scripts and characters that are absent from Unicode (see `http://en.wikipedia.org/wiki/Unicode`) 3.2. Unlike XML 1.0, XML 1.1 isn't widely implemented and should be used only when its unique features are needed.

XML supports Unicode, which means that XML documents consist entirely of characters taken from the Unicode character set. The document's characters are encoded into bytes for storage or transmission, and the encoding is specified via the XML declaration's optional encoding attribute. One common encoding is *UTF-8* (see `http://en.wikipedia.org/wiki/UTF-8`), which is a variable-length encoding of the Unicode character set. UTF-8 is a strict superset of ASCII (see `http://en.wikipedia.org/wiki/ASCII`), which means that pure ASCII text files are also UTF-8 documents.

Note   In the absence of the XML declaration or when the XML declaration's `encoding` attribute isn't present, an XML parser typically looks for a special character sequence at the start of a document to determine the document's encoding. This character sequence is known as the *byte-order-mark* (*BOM*) and is created by an editor program (such as Microsoft Windows Notepad) when it saves the document according to UTF-8 or some other encoding. For example, the hexadecimal sequence EF BB BF signifies UTF-8 as the encoding. Similarly, FE FF signifies UTF-16 (see `http://en.wikipedia.org/wiki/UTF-16`) big endian, FF FE signifies UTF-16 little endian, 00 00 FE FF signifies UTF-32 (see `http://en.wikipedia.org/wiki/UTF-32`) big endian, and FF FE 00 00 signifies UTF-32 little endian. UTF-8 is assumed when no BOM is present.

If you'll never use characters apart from the ASCII character set, you can probably forget about the encoding attribute. However, when your native language isn't English or when you're called to create XML documents that include non-ASCII characters, you need to properly specify encoding. For example, when your document contains ASCII plus characters from a non-English Western European language (such as ç, the cedilla used in French, Portuguese, and other languages), you might want to choose ISO-8859-1 as the encoding attribute's value—the document will probably have a smaller size when encoded in this manner than when encoded with UTF-8. Listing 1-2 shows you the resulting XML declaration.

Listing 1-2. An Encoded Document Containing Non-ASCII Characters

```
<?xml version="1.0" encoding="ISO-8859-1"?>
<movie>
    <name>Le Fabuleux Destin d'Amélie Poulain</name>
    <language>français</language>
</movie>
```

The final attribute that can appear in the XML declaration is standalone. This optional attribute, which is only relevant with DTDs (discussed later), determines whether or not there are external markup declarations that affect the information passed from an *XML processor* (a parser) to the application. Its value defaults to no, implying that there are or may be such declarations. A yes value indicates that there are no such declarations. For more information, check out "The standalone pseudo-attribute is only relevant if a DTD is used" (www.xmlplease.com/xml/standalone/).

Elements and Attributes

Following the XML declaration is a *hierarchical* (tree) structure of elements, where an *element* is a portion of the document delimited by a *start tag* (such as <name>) and an *end tag* (such as </name>), or is an *empty-element tag* (a standalone tag whose name ends with a forward slash [/], such as <break/>). Start tags and end tags surround content and possibly other markup, whereas empty-element tags don't surround anything. Figure 1-1 reveals Listing 1-1's XML document tree structure.

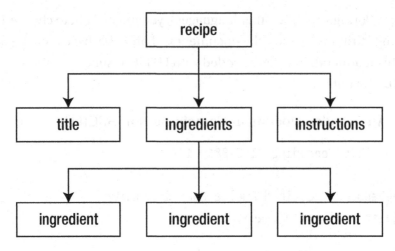

Figure 1-1. *Listing 1-1's tree structure is rooted in the* recipe *element*

As with HTML document structure, the structure of an XML document is anchored in a *root element* (the topmost element). In HTML, the root element is html (the <html> and </html> tag pair). Unlike in HTML, you can choose the root element for your XML documents. Figure 1-1 shows the root element to be recipe.

Unlike the other elements, which have parent elements, recipe has no parent. Also, recipe and ingredients have child elements: recipe's children are title, ingredients, and instructions; and ingredients' children are three instances of ingredient. The title, instructions, and ingredient elements don't have child elements.

Elements can contain child elements, content, or *mixed content* (a combination of child elements and content). Listing 1-2 reveals that the movie element contains name and language child elements and also reveals that each of these child elements contains content (e.g., language contains français). Listing 1-3 presents another example that demonstrates mixed content along with child elements and content.

Listing 1-3. An Abstract Element Containing Mixed Content

```
<?xml version="1.0"?>
<article title="The Rebirth of JavaFX" lang="en">
    <abstract>
        JavaFX 2 marks a significant milestone in the history
        of JavaFX. Now that Sun Microsystems has passed the
        torch to Oracle, JavaFX Script is gone and
        JavaFX-oriented Java APIS (such as
```

```
<code>javafx.application.Application</code>) have
emerged for interacting with this technology. This
article introduces you to this refactored JavaFX,
where you learn about JavaFX 2 architecture and key
APIs.
    </abstract>
    <body>
    </body>
</article>
```

This document's root element is article, which contains abstract and body child elements. The abstract element mixes content with a code element, which contains content. In contrast, the body element is empty.

Note   As with Listings 1-1 and 1-2, Listing 1-3 also contains *whitespace* (invisible characters such as spaces, tabs, carriage returns, and line feeds). The XML specification permits whitespace to be added to a document. Whitespace appearing within content (such as spaces between words) is considered part of the content. In contrast, the parser typically ignores whitespace appearing between an end tag and the next start tag. Such whitespace isn't considered part of the content.

An XML element's start tag can contain one or more attributes. For example, Listing 1-1's <ingredient> tag has a qty (quantity) attribute, and Listing 1-3's <article> tag has title and lang attributes. Attributes provide additional details about elements. For example, qty identifies the amount of an ingredient that can be added, title identifies an article's title, and lang identifies the language in which the article is written (en for English). Attributes can be optional. For example, when qty isn't specified, a default value of 1 is assumed.

Note   Element and attribute names may contain any alphanumeric character from English or another language and may also include the underscore (_), hyphen (-), period (.), and colon (:) punctuation characters. The colon should only be used with namespaces (discussed later in this chapter), and **names cannot contain whitespace**.

Character References and CDATA Sections

Certain characters cannot appear literally in the content that appears between a start tag and an end tag or within an attribute value. For example, you cannot place a literal < character between a start tag and an end tag because doing so would confuse an XML parser into thinking that it had encountered another tag.

One solution to this problem is to replace the literal character with a *character reference*, which is a code that represents the character. Character references are classified as numeric character references or character entity references:

- A *numeric character reference* refers to a character via its Unicode code point and adheres to the format &#*nnnn*; (not restricted to four positions) or &#x*hhhh*; (not restricted to four positions), where *nnnn* provides a decimal representation of the code point and *hhhh* provides a hexadecimal representation. For example, Σ and Σ represent the Greek capital letter sigma. Although XML mandates that the x in &#x*hhhh*; be lowercase, it's flexible in that the leading zero is optional in either format and in allowing you to specify an uppercase or lowercase letter for each *h*. As a result, Σ, Σ, and Σ are also valid representations of the Greek capital letter sigma.

- A *character entity reference* refers to a character via the name of an *entity* (aliased data) that specifies the desired character as its replacement text. Character entity references are predefined by XML and have the format &*name*;, in which *name* is the entity's name. XML predefines five character entity references: < (<), > (>), & (&), ' ('), and " (").

Consider <expression>6 < 4</expression>. You could replace the < with numeric reference <, yielding <expression>6 < 4</expression>, or better yet with <, yielding <expression>6 < 4</expression>. The second choice is clearer and easier to remember.

Suppose you want to embed an HTML or XML document within an element. To make the embedded document acceptable to an XML parser, you would need to replace each literal < (start of tag) and & (start of entity) character with its < and & predefined character entity reference, a tedious and possibly error-prone undertaking—you might forget to replace one of these characters. To save you from tedium and potential errors, XML provides an alternative in the form of a CDATA (character data) section.

A *CDATA section* is a section of literal HTML or XML markup and content surrounded by the <![CDATA[prefix and the]]> suffix. You don't need to specify predefined character entity references within a CDATA section, as demonstrated in Listing 1-4.

Listing 1-4. Embedding an XML Document in Another Document's CDATA Section

```
<?xml version="1.0"?>
<svg-examples>
   <example>
      The following Scalable Vector Graphics document
      describes a blue-filled and black-stroked
      rectangle.
      <![CDATA[<svg width="100%" height="100%"
           version="1.1"
           xmlns="http://www.w3.org/2000/svg">
         <rect width="300" height="100"
               style="fill:rgb(0,0,255);stroke-width:1;
                       stroke:rgb(0,0,0)"/>
      </svg>]]>
   </example>
</svg-examples>
```

Listing 1-4 embeds a Scalable Vector Graphics (SVG) [see http://en.wikipedia. org/wiki/Scalable_Vector_Graphics] XML document within the example element of an SVG examples document. The SVG document is placed in a CDATA section, obviating the need to replace all < characters with < predefined character entity references.

Namespaces

It's common to create XML documents that combine features from different XML languages. Namespaces are used to prevent name conflicts when elements and other XML language features appear. Without namespaces, an XML parser couldn't distinguish between same-named elements or other language features that mean different things, for example, two same-named `title` elements from two different languages.

Note   Namespaces aren't part of XML 1.0. They arrived about a year after this specification was released. To ensure backward compatibility with XML 1.0, namespaces take advantage of colon characters, which are legal characters in XML names. Parsers that don't recognize namespaces return names that include colons.

A *namespace* is a Uniform Resource Identifier (URI)-based container that helps differentiate XML vocabularies by providing a unique context for its contained identifiers. The namespace URI is associated with a *namespace prefix* (an alias for the URI) by specifying, typically on an XML document's root element, either the `xmlns` attribute by itself (which signifies the default namespace) or the `xmlns:`*prefix* attribute (which signifies the namespace identified as *prefix*), and assigning the URI to this attribute.

Note   A namespace's scope starts at the element where it's declared and applies to all of the element's content unless overridden by another namespace declaration with the same prefix name.

When *prefix* is specified, the prefix and a colon character are prepended to the name of each element tag that belongs to that namespace—see Listing 1-5.

Listing 1-5.   Introducing a Pair of Namespaces

```
<?xml version="1.0"?>
<h:html xmlns:h="http://www.w3.org/1999/xhtml"
        xmlns:r="http://www.javajeff.ca/">
   <h:head>
      <h:title>
```

```
    Recipe
  </h:title>
</h:head>
<h:body>
<r:recipe>
  <r:title>
    Grilled Cheese Sandwich
  </r:title>
  <r:ingredients>
    <h:ul>
    <h:li>
    <r:ingredient qty="2">
      bread slice
    </r:ingredient>
    </h:li>
    <h:li>
    <r:ingredient>
      cheese slice
    </r:ingredient>
    </h:li>
    <h:li>
    <r:ingredient qty="2">
      margarine pat
    </r:ingredient>
    </h:li>
    </h:ul>
  </r:ingredients>
  <h:p>
  <r:instructions>
    Place frying pan on element and select medium
    heat. For each bread slice, smear one pat of
    margarine on one side of bread slice. Place
    cheese slice between bread slices with
    margarine-smeared sides away from the cheese.
    Place sandwich in frying pan with one
```

```
            margarine-smeared side in contact with pan.
            Fry for a couple of minutes and flip. Fry
            other side for a minute and serve.
        </r:instructions>
        </h:p>
      </r:recipe>
      </h:body>
</h:html>
```

Listing 1-5 describes a document that combines elements from the XHTML (see http://en.wikipedia.org/wiki/XHTML) language with elements from the recipe language. All element tags that associate with XHTML are prefixed with h:, and all element tags that associate with the recipe language are prefixed with r:.

The h: prefix associates with the www.w3.org/1999/xhtml URI, and the r: prefix associates with the www.javajeff.ca URI. XML doesn't mandate that URIs point to document files. It only requires that they be unique to guarantee unique namespaces.

This document's separation of the recipe data from the XHTML elements makes it possible to preserve this data's structure while also allowing an XHTML-compliant web browser (such as Mozilla Firefox) to present the recipe via a web page (see Figure 1-2).

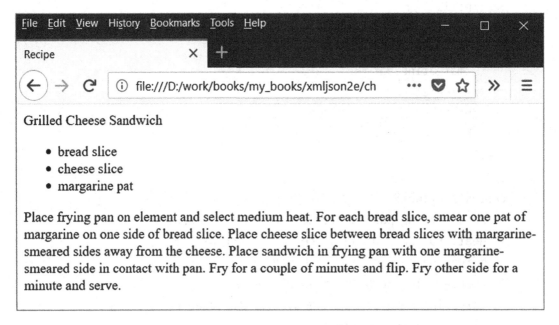

Figure 1-2. *Mozilla Firefox presents the recipe data via XHTML tags*

A tag's attributes don't need to be prefixed when those attributes belong to the element. For example, qty isn't prefixed in `<r:ingredient qty="2">`. However, a prefix is required for attributes belonging to other namespaces. For example, suppose you want to add an XHTML `style` attribute to the document's `<r:title>` tag to provide styling for the recipe title when displayed via an application. You can accomplish this task by inserting an XHTML attribute into the `title` tag, as follows:

```
<r:title h:style="font-family: sans-serif;">
```

The XHTML `style` attribute has been prefixed with `h:` because this attribute belongs to the XHTML language namespace and not to the recipe language namespace.

When multiple namespaces are involved, it can be convenient to specify one of these namespaces as the default namespace to reduce the tedium in entering namespace prefixes. Consider Listing 1-6.

Listing 1-6. Specifying a Default Namespace

```
<?xml version="1.0"?>
<html xmlns="http://www.w3.org/1999/xhtml"
      xmlns:r="http://www.javajeff.ca/">
   <head>
      <title>
         Recipe
      </title>
   </head>
   <body>
   <r:recipe>
      <r:title>
         Grilled Cheese Sandwich
      </r:title>
      <r:ingredients>
         <ul>
         <li>
         <r:ingredient qty="2">
            bread slice
         </r:ingredient>
         </li>
```

```
            <li>
            <r:ingredient>
               cheese slice
            </r:ingredient>
            </li>
            <li>
            <r:ingredient qty="2">
               margarine pat
            </r:ingredient>
            </li>
            </ul>
         </r:ingredients>
         <p>
         <r:instructions>
            Place frying pan on element and select medium
            heat. For each bread slice, smear one pat of
            margarine on one side of bread slice. Place
            cheese slice between bread slices with
            margarine-smeared sides away from the cheese.
            Place sandwich in frying pan with one
            margarine-smeared side in contact with pan.
            Fry for a couple of minutes and flip. Fry
            other side for a minute and serve.
         </r:instructions>
         </p>
      </r:recipe>
      </body>
</html>
```

Listing 1-6 specifies a default namespace for the XHTML language. No XHTML element tag needs to be prefixed with h:. However, recipe language element tags must still be prefixed with the r: prefix.

Comments and Processing Instructions

XML documents can contain *comments*, which are character sequences beginning with `<!--` and ending with `-->`. For example, you might place `<!-- Todo -->` in Listing 1-3's body element to remind yourself that you need to finish coding this element.

Comments are used to clarify portions of a document. They can appear anywhere after the XML declaration except within tags, cannot be nested, cannot contain a double hyphen (`--`) because doing so might confuse an XML parser that the comment has been closed, shouldn't contain a hyphen (`-`) for the same reason, and are typically ignored during processing. Comments are not content.

XML also permits processing instructions to be present. A *processing instruction* is an instruction that's made available to the application parsing the document. The instruction begins with `<?` and ends with `?>`. The `<?` prefix is followed by a name known as the *target*. This name typically identifies the application to which the processing instruction is intended. The rest of the processing instruction contains text in a format appropriate to the application. Two examples of processing instructions are `<?xml-stylesheet href="modern.xsl" type="text/xml"?>` (associate an eXtensible Stylesheet Language [XSL] [see `http://en.wikipedia.org/wiki/XSL`] stylesheet with an XML document) and `<?php /* PHP code */ ?>` (pass a PHP [see `http://en.wikipedia.org/wiki/PHP`] code fragment to the application). Although the XML declaration looks like a processing instruction, this isn't the case.

Note   The XML declaration isn't a processing instruction.

Well-Formed Documents

HTML is a sloppy language in which elements can be specified out of order, end tags can be omitted, and so on. The complexity of a web browser's page layout code is partly due to the need to handle these special cases. In contrast, XML is a much stricter language. To make XML documents easier to parse, XML mandates that XML documents follow certain rules:

- *All elements must either have start and end tags or consist of empty-element tags.* For example, unlike the HTML `<p>` tag that's often specified without a `</p>` counterpart, `</p>` must also be present from an XML document perspective.

- *Tags must be nested correctly.* For example, while you'll probably get away with specifying `<b><i>XML</b></i>` in HTML, an XML parser would report an error. In contrast, `<b><i>XML</i></b>` doesn't result in an error, because the nested tag pairs mirror each other.

- *All attribute values must be quoted.* Either single quotes (') or double quotes (") are permissible (although double quotes are the more commonly specified quotes). It's an error to omit these quotes.

- *Empty elements must be properly formatted.* For example, HTML's `<br>` tag would have to be specified as `<br/>` in XML. You can specify a space between the tag's name and the / character although the space is optional.

- *Be careful with case.* XML is a **case-sensitive** language in which tags differing in case (such as `394211_2_En` and `394211_2_En`) are considered different. It's an error to mix start and end tags of different cases, for example, `394211_2_En` with `</Author>`.

XML parsers that are aware of namespaces enforce two additional rules:

- Each element and attribute name must not include more than one colon character.

- No entity names, processing instruction targets, or notation names (discussed later) can contain colons.

An XML document that conforms to these rules is *well formed*. The document has a logical and clean appearance and is much easier to process. XML parsers will only parse well-formed XML documents.

Valid Documents

It's not always enough for an XML document to be well formed; in many cases the document must also be valid. A *valid* document adheres to constraints. For example, a constraint could be placed upon Listing 1-1's recipe document to ensure that the `ingredients` element always precedes the `instructions` element; perhaps an application must first process `ingredients`.

Note   XML document validation is similar to a compiler analyzing source code to make sure that the code makes sense in a machine context. For example, each of int, count, =, 1, and ; is a valid Java character sequence, but 1 `count` `;` `int` `=` isn't a valid Java construct (whereas int `count` `=` `1;` is a valid Java construct).

Some XML parsers perform validation, whereas other parsers don't because validating parsers are harder to write. A parser that performs validation compares an XML document to a *grammar document*. Any deviation from the grammar document is reported as an error to the application—the XML document isn't valid. The application may choose to fix the error or reject the XML document. Unlike well-formedness errors, validity errors aren't necessarily fatal and the parser can continue to parse the XML document.

Note   Validating XML parsers often don't validate by default because validation can be time consuming. They must be instructed to perform validation.

Grammar documents are written in a special language. Two commonly used grammar languages are Document Type Definition and XML Schema.

Document Type Definition

Document Type Definition (*DTD*) is the oldest grammar language for specifying an XML document's *grammar*. DTD grammar documents (known as DTDs) are written in accordance to a strict syntax that states what elements may be present and in what parts of a document, and also what is contained within elements (child elements, content, or mixed content) and what attributes may be specified. For example, a DTD may specify that a recipe element must have an ingredients element followed by an instructions element.

Listing 1-7 presents a DTD for the recipe language that was used to construct Listing 1-1's document.

Listing 1-7. The Recipe Language's DTD

```
<!ELEMENT recipe (title, ingredients, instructions)>
<!ELEMENT title (#PCDATA)>
<!ELEMENT ingredients (ingredient+)>
<!ELEMENT ingredient (#PCDATA)>
<!ELEMENT instructions (#PCDATA)>
<!ATTLIST ingredient qty CDATA "1">
```

This DTD first declares the recipe language's elements. Element declarations take the form `<!ELEMENT` *name content-specifier*`>`, where *name* is any legal XML name (e.g., it cannot contain whitespace), and *content-specifier* identifies what can appear within the element.

The first element declaration states that exactly one `recipe` element can appear in the XML document—this declaration doesn't imply that `recipe` is the root element. Furthermore, this element must include exactly one each of the `title`, `ingredients`, and `instructions` child elements, and in that order. Child elements must be specified as a comma-separated list. Furthermore, a list is always surrounded by parentheses.

The second element declaration states that the `title` element contains *parsed character data* (nonmarkup text). The third element declaration states that at least one `ingredient` element must appear in `ingredients`. The + character is an example of a regular expression that means one or more. Other expressions that may be used are * (zero or more) and ? (once or not at all). The fourth and fifth element declarations are similar to the second by stating that `ingredient` and `instructions` elements contain parsed character data.

Note   Element declarations support three other content specifiers. You can specify `<!ELEMENT` *name* `ANY>` to allow any type of element content or `<!ELEMENT` *name* `EMPTY>` to disallow any element content. To state that an element contains mixed content, you would specify #PCDATA and a list of element names, separated by vertical bars (|). For example, `<!ELEMENT ingredient (#PCDATA | measure | note)*>` states that the `ingredient` element can contain a mix of parsed character data, zero or more `measure` elements, and zero or more `note` elements. It doesn't specify the order in which the parsed character data and these elements occur. However, #PCDATA must be the first item specified in the list. When a regular expression is used in this context, it must appear to the right of the closing parenthesis.

Listing 1-7's DTD lastly declares the recipe language's attributes, of which there is only one: qty. Attribute declarations take the form <!ATTLIST *ename aname type default-value*>, where *ename* is the name of the element to which the attribute belongs, *aname* is the name of the attribute, *type* is the attribute's type, and *default-value* is the attribute's default value.

The attribute declaration identifies qty as an attribute of ingredient. It also states that qty's type is CDATA (any string of characters not including the ampersand, less than or greater than signs, or double quotes may appear; these characters may be represented via &, <, >, and ", respectively) and that qty is optional, assuming default value 1 when absent.

MORE ABOUT ATTRIBUTES

DTD lets you specify additional attribute types: ID (create a unique identifier for an attribute that identifies an element), IDREF (an attribute's value is an element located elsewhere in the document), IDREFS (the value consists of multiple IDREFs), ENTITY (you can use external binary data or unparsed entities), ENTITIES (the value consists of multiple entities), NMTOKEN (the value is restricted to any valid XML name), NMTOKENS (the value is composed of multiple XML names), NOTATION (the value is already specified via a DTD notation declaration), and enumerated (a list of possible values to choose from; values are separated with vertical bars).

Instead of specifying a default value verbatim, you can specify #REQUIRED to mean that the attribute must always be present with some value (<!ATTLIST *ename aname type* #REQUIRED>), #IMPLIED to mean that the attribute is optional and no default value is provided (<!ATTLIST *ename aname type* #IMPLIED>), or #FIXED to mean that the attribute is optional and must always take on the DTD-assigned default value when used (<!ATTLIST *ename aname type* #FIXED "value">).

You can specify a list of attributes in one ATTLIST declaration. For example, <!ATTLIST *ename aname1 type1 default-value1 aname2 type2 default-value2*> declares two attributes identified as *aname1* and *aname2*.

A DTD-based validating XML parser requires that a document include a *document type declaration* identifying the DTD that specifies the document's grammar before it will validate the document.

Note   Document Type Definition and document type declaration are two different things. The DTD acronym identifies a Document Type Definition and never identifies a document type declaration.

A document type declaration appears immediately after the XML declaration and is specified in one of the following ways:

- `<!DOCTYPE` *root-element-name* `SYSTEM` *uri*`>` references an external but private DTD via *uri*. The referenced DTD isn't available for public scrutiny. For example, I might store my recipe language's DTD file (`recipe.dtd`) in a private `dtds` directory on my `www.javajeff. ca` website, and use `<!DOCTYPE recipe SYSTEM "http://www. javajeff.ca/dtds/recipe.dtd">` to identify this DTD's location via *system identifier* `http://www.javajeff.ca/dtds/recipe.dtd`.

- `<!DOCTYPE` *root-element-name* `PUBLIC` *fpi uri*`>` references an external but public DTD via *fpi*, a *formal public identifier* (see `http:// en.wikipedia.org/wiki/Formal_Public_Identifier`), and *uri*. If a validating XML parser cannot locate the DTD via public identifier *fpi*, it can use system identifier *uri* to locate the DTD. For example, `<!DOCTYPE html PUBLIC "-//W3C//DTD XHTML 1.0 Transitional//EN" "http://www.w3.org/TR/xhtml1/DTD/xhtml1- transitional.dtd">` references the XHTML 1.0 DTD first via public identifier `-//W3C//DTD XHTML 1.0 Transitional//EN` and second via system identifier `http://www.w3.org/TR/xhtml1/DTD/xhtml1- transitional.dtd`.

- `<!DOCTYPE` *root-element* `[` *dtd* `]>` references an internal DTD, one that is embedded within the XML document. The internal DTD must appear between square brackets.

Listing 1-8 presents Listing 1-1 (minus the child elements between the `<recipe>` and `</recipe>` tags) with an internal DTD.

Listing 1-8. The Recipe Document with an Internal DTD

```
<?xml version="1.0"?>
<!DOCTYPE recipe [
   <!ELEMENT recipe (title, ingredients, instructions)>
   <!ELEMENT title (#PCDATA)>
   <!ELEMENT ingredients (ingredient+)>
   <!ELEMENT ingredient (#PCDATA)>
   <!ELEMENT instructions (#PCDATA)>
   <!ATTLIST ingredient qty CDATA "1">
]>
<recipe>
   <!-- Child elements removed for brevity. -->
</recipe>
```

Note   A document can have internal and external DTDs, for example, `<!DOCTYPE`
`recipe SYSTEM "http://www.javajeff.ca/dtds/recipe.dtd" [`
`<!ELEMENT ...>]>`. The internal DTD is referred to as the *internal DTD subset*,
and the external DTD is referred to as the *external DTD subset*. Neither subset can
override the element declarations of the other subset.

You can also declare notations and general and parameter entities within DTDs.
A *notation* is an arbitrary piece of data that typically describes the format of unparsed
binary data and typically has the form `<!NOTATION name SYSTEM uri>`, where *name*
identifies the notation and *uri* identifies some kind of plugin that can process the data
on behalf of the application that's parsing the XML document. For example, `<!NOTATION`
`image SYSTEM "psp.exe">` declares a notation named `image` and identifies Windows
executable `psp.exe` as a plugin for processing images.

It's also common to use notations to specify binary data types via media types (see
`http://en.wikipedia.org/wiki/Media_type`). For example, `<!NOTATION image SYSTEM`
`"image/jpeg">` declares an image notation that identifies the `image/jpeg` media type for
Joint Photographic Experts Group images.

General entities are entities referenced from inside an XML document via *general entity references*, syntactic constructs of the form &*name*;. Examples include the predefined lt, gt, amp, apos, and quot character entities, whose <, >, &, ', and " character entity references are aliases for characters <, >, &, ', and ", respectively.

General entities are classified as internal or external. An *internal general entity* is a general entity whose value is stored in the DTD and has the form <!ENTITY *name value*>, where *name* identifies the entity and *value* specifies its value. For example, <!ENTITY copyright "Copyright © 2019 Jeff Friesen. All rights reserved."> declares an internal general entity named copyright. The value of this entity may include another declared entity, such as © (the HTML entity for the copyright symbol), and can be referenced from anywhere in an XML document by specifying &copyright;.

An *external general entity* is a general entity whose value is stored outside the DTD. The value might be textual data (such as an XML document), or it might be binary data (such as a JPEG image). External general entities are classified as external parsed general entity and external unparsed general entity.

An *external parsed general entity* references an external file that stores the entity's textual data, which is subject to being inserted into a document and parsed by a validating parser when a general entity reference is specified in the document, and which has the form <!ENTITY *name* SYSTEM *uri*>, where *name* identifies the entity and *uri* identifies the external file. For example, <!ENTITY chapter-header SYSTEM "http://www.javajeff. ca/entities/chapheader.xml"> identifies chapheader.xml as storing the XML content to be inserted into an XML document wherever &chapter-header; appears in the document. The alternative <!ENTITY *name* PUBLIC *fpi uri*> form can be specified.

Caution   Because the contents of an external file may be parsed, this content must be well formed.

An *external unparsed general entity* references an external file that stores the entity's binary data and has the form <!ENTITY *name* SYSTEM *uri* NDATA *nname*>, where *name* identifies the entity, *uri* locates the external file, and NDATA identifies the notation declaration named *nname*. The notation typically identifies a plugin for processing the binary data or the Internet media type of this data. For example, <!ENTITY photo SYSTEM "photo.jpg" NDATA image> associates name photo with external binary file photo.png and notation image. The alternative <!ENTITY *name* PUBLIC *fpi uri* NDATA *nname*> form can be specified.

Note   XML doesn't allow references to external general entities to appear in attribute values. For example, you cannot specify `&chapter-header;` in an attribute's value.

Parameter entities are entities referenced from inside a DTD via *parameter entity references*, syntactic constructs of the form *%name;*. They're useful for eliminating repetitive content from element declarations. For example, you're creating a DTD for a large company, and this DTD contains three element declarations: `<!ELEMENT salesperson (firstname, lastname)>`, `<!ELEMENT lawyer (firstname, lastname)>`, and `<!ELEMENT accountant (firstname, lastname)>`. Each element contains repeated child element content. If you need to add another child element (such as `middleinitial`), you'll need to make sure that all of the elements are updated; otherwise, you risk a malformed DTD. Parameter entities can help you solve this problem.

Parameter entities are classified as internal or external. An *internal parameter entity* is a parameter entity whose value is stored in the DTD and has the form `<!ENTITY % name value>`, where *name* identifies the entity and *value* specifies its value. For example, `<!ENTITY % person-name "firstname, lastname">` declares a parameter entity named `person-name` with value `firstname, lastname`. Once declared, this entity can be referenced in the three previous element declarations, as follows: `<!ELEMENT salesperson (%person-name;)>`, `<!ELEMENT lawyer (%person-name;)>`, and `<!ELEMENT accountant (%person-name;)>`. Instead of adding `middleinitial` to each of `salesperson`, `lawyer`, and `accountant`, as was done previously, you would now add this child element to `person-name`, as in `<!ENTITY % person-name "firstname, middleinitial, lastname">`, and this change would be applied to these element declarations.

An *external parameter entity* is a parameter entity whose value is stored outside the DTD. It has the form `<!ENTITY % name SYSTEM uri>`, where name identifies the entity and uri locates the external file. For example, `<!ENTITY % person-name SYSTEM "http://www.javajeff.ca/entities/names.dtd">` identifies `names.dtd` as storing the `firstname, lastname` text to be inserted into a DTD wherever `%person-name;` appears in the DTD. The alternative `<!ENTITY % name PUBLIC *fpi uri*>` form can be specified.

> **Note**   This discussion sums up the basics of DTD. One additional topic that wasn't covered (for brevity) is *conditional inclusion*, which lets you specify those portions of a DTD to make available to parsers and is typically used with parameter entity references.

XML Schema

XML Schema is a grammar language for declaring the structure, content, and *semantics* (meaning) of an XML document. This language's grammar documents are known as *schemas* that are themselves XML documents. Schemas must conform to the XML Schema DTD (see `www.w3.org/2001/XMLSchema.dtd`).

XML Schema was introduced by the W3C to overcome limitations with DTD, such as DTD's lack of support for namespaces. Also, XML Schema provides an object-oriented approach to declaring an XML document's grammar. This grammar language provides a much larger set of primitive types than DTD's CDATA and PCDATA types. For example, you'll find integer, floating-point, various date and time, and string types to be part of XML Schema.

> **Note**   XML Schema predefines 19 primitive types, which are expressed via the following identifiers: `anyURI`, `base64Binary`, `boolean`, `date`, `dateTime`, `decimal`, `double`, `duration`, `float`, `hexBinary`, `gDay`, `gMonth`, `gMonthDay`, `gYear`, `gYearMonth`, `NOTATION`, `QName`, `string`, and `time`.

XML Schema provides *restriction* (reducing the set of permitted values through constraints), *list* (allowing a sequence of values), and *union* (allowing a choice of values from several types) derivation methods for creating new *simple types* from these primitive types. For example, XML Schema derives 13 integer types from `decimal` through restriction; these types are expressed via the following identifiers: `byte`, `int`, `integer`, `long`, `negativeInteger`, `nonNegativeInteger`, `nonPositiveInteger`, `positiveInteger`, `short`, `unsignedByte`, `unsignedInt`, `unsignedLong`, and `unsignedShort`. It also provides support for creating *complex types* from simple types.

A good way to become familiar with XML Schema is to follow through an example, such as creating a schema for Listing 1-1's recipe language document. The first step in creating this recipe language schema is to identify all of its elements and attributes. The elements are `recipe`, `title`, `ingredients`, `instructions`, and `ingredient`; qty is the solitary attribute.

The next step is to classify the elements according to XML Schema's *content model*, which specifies the types of child elements and text *nodes* (see `http://en.wikipedia. org/wiki/Node_(computer_science)`) that can be included in an element. An element is considered to be *empty* when the element has no child elements or text nodes, *simple* when only text nodes are accepted, *complex* when only child elements are accepted, and *mixed* when child elements and text nodes are accepted. None of Listing 1-1's elements have empty or mixed content models. However, the `title`, `ingredient`, and `instructions` elements have simple content models; and the `recipe` and `ingredients` elements have complex content models.

For elements that have a simple content model, we can distinguish between elements having attributes and elements not having attributes. XML Schema classifies elements having a simple content model and no attributes as simple types. Furthermore, it classifies elements having a simple content model and attributes, or elements from other content models as complex types. Furthermore, XML Schema classifies attributes as simple types because they only contain text values—attributes don't have child elements. Listing 1-1's `title` and `instructions` elements and its qty attribute are simple types. Its `recipe`, `ingredients`, and `ingredient` elements are complex types.

At this point, we can begin to declare the schema. The following code fragment presents the introductory `schema` element:

```
<xs:schema xmlns:xs="http://www.w3.org/2001/XMLSchema">
```

The `schema` element introduces the grammar. It also assigns the commonly used xs namespace prefix to the standard XML Schema namespace; xs: is subsequently prepended to XML Schema element names.

Next, we use the `element` element to declare the `title` and `instructions` simple type elements, as follows:

```
<xs:element name="title" type="xs:string"/>
<xs:element name="instructions" type="xs:string"/>
```

XML Schema requires that each element have a name and (unlike DTD) be associated with a type, which identifies the kind of data stored in the element. For example, the first element declaration identifies title as the name via its name attribute and string as the type via its type attribute (string or character data appears between the <title> and </title> tags). The xs: prefix in xs:string is required because string is a predefined W3C type.

Continuing, we now use the attribute element to declare the qty simple type attribute, as follows:

```
<xs:attribute name="qty" type="xs:unsignedInt" default="1"/>
```

This attribute element declares an attribute named qty. I've chosen unsignedInt as this attribute's type because quantities are nonnegative values. Furthermore, I've specified 1 as the default value for when qty isn't specified—attribute elements default to declaring optional attributes.

Note   The order of element and attribute declarations isn't significant within a schema.

Now that we've declared the simple types, we can start to declare the complex types. To begin, we'll declare recipe, as follows:

```
<xs:element name="recipe">
    <xs:complexType>
        <xs:sequence>
            <xs:element ref="title"/>
            <xs:element ref="ingredients"/>
            <xs:element ref="instructions"/>
        </xs:sequence>
    </xs:complexType>
</xs:element>
```

This declaration states that recipe is a complex type (via the complexType element) consisting of a sequence (via the sequence element) of one title element followed by one ingredients element followed by one instructions element. Each of these elements is declared by a different element that's referred to by its element's ref attribute.

The next complex type to declare is ingredients. The following code fragment provides its declaration:

```
<xs:element name="ingredients">
   <xs:complexType>
      <xs:sequence>
         <xs:element ref="ingredient"
                     maxOccurs="unbounded"/>
      </xs:sequence>
   </xs:complexType>
</xs:element>
```

This declaration states that ingredients is a complex type consisting of a sequence of one or more ingredient elements. The "or more" is specified by including element's maxOccurs attribute and setting this attribute's value to unbounded.

Note The maxOccurs attribute identifies the maximum number of times that an element can occur. A similar minOccurs attribute identifies the minimum number of times that an element can occur. Each attribute can be assigned 0 or a positive integer. Furthermore, you can specify unbounded for maxOccurs, which means that there's no upper limit on occurrences of the element. Each attribute defaults to a value of 1, which means that an element can appear only one time when neither attribute is present.

The final complex type to declare is ingredient. Although ingredient can contain only text nodes, which implies that it should be a simple type, it's the presence of the qty attribute that makes it complex. Check out the following declaration:

```
<xs:element name="ingredient">
   <xs:complexType>
      <xs:simpleContent>
         <xs:extension base="xs:string">
            <xs:attribute ref="qty"/>
         </xs:extension>
      </xs:simpleContent>
   </xs:complexType>
</xs:element>
```

The element named `ingredient` is a complex type (because of its optional `qty` attribute). The `simpleContent` element indicates that `ingredient` can only contain simple content (text nodes), and the `extension` element indicates that `ingredient` is a new type that extends the predefined `string` type (specified via the `base` attribute), implying that `ingredient` inherits all of `string`'s attributes and structure. Furthermore, `ingredient` is given an additional `qty` attribute.

Listing 1-9 combines the previous examples into a complete schema.

Listing 1-9. The Recipe Document's Schema

```xml
<?xml version="1.0"?>
<xs:schema xmlns:xs="http://www.w3.org/2001/XMLSchema">
<xs:element name="title" type="xs:string"/>
<xs:element name="instructions" type="xs:string"/>
<xs:attribute name="qty" type="xs:unsignedInt" default="1"/>
<xs:element name="recipe">
    <xs:complexType>
        <xs:sequence>
            <xs:element ref="title"/>
            <xs:element ref="ingredients"/>
            <xs:element ref="instructions"/>
        </xs:sequence>
    </xs:complexType>
</xs:element>
<xs:element name="ingredients">
    <xs:complexType>
        <xs:sequence>
            <xs:element ref="ingredient"
                        maxOccurs="unbounded"/>
        </xs:sequence>
    </xs:complexType>
</xs:element>
```

```
<xs:element name="ingredient">
   <xs:complexType>
      <xs:simpleContent>
         <xs:extension base="xs:string">
            <xs:attribute ref="qty"/>
         </xs:extension>
      </xs:simpleContent>
   </xs:complexType>
</xs:element>
```

After creating the schema, you can reference it from a recipe document. Accomplish this task by specifying xmlns:xsi and xsi:schemaLocation attributes on the document's root element start tag (<recipe>), as follows:

```
<recipe xmlns="http://www.javajeff.ca/"
        xmlns:xsi="http://www.w3.org/2001/XMLSchema-instance"
        xsi:schemaLocation="http://www.javajeff.ca/schemas recipe.xsd">
```

The xmlns attribute identifies http://www.javajeff.ca/ as the document's default namespace. Unprefixed elements and their unprefixed attributes belong to this namespace.

The xmlns:xsi attribute associates the conventional xsi (XML Schema Instance) prefix with the standard http://www.w3.org/2001/XMLSchema-instance namespace. The only item in the document that's prefixed with xsi: is schemaLocation.

The schemaLocation attribute is used to locate the schema. This attribute's value can be multiple pairs of space-separated values but is specified as a single pair of such values in this example. The first value (http://www.javajeff.ca/schemas) identifies the target namespace for the schema, and the second value (recipe.xsd) identifies the location of the schema within this namespace.

Note   Schema files that conform to XML Schema's grammar are commonly assigned the .xsd file extension.

If an XML document declares a namespace (xmlns default or xmlns:prefix), that namespace must be made available to the schema so that a validating parser can resolve all references to elements and other schema components for that namespace. We also need to mention which namespace the schema describes, and we do so by including the targetNamespace attribute on the schema element. For example, suppose our recipe document declares a default XML namespace, as follows:

```
<?xml version="1.0"?>
<recipe xmlns="http://www.javajeff.ca/">
```

At minimum, we would need to modify Listing 1-9's schema element to include targetNameSpace and the recipe document's default namespace as targetNameSpace's value, as follows:

```
<xs:schema targetNamespace="http://www.javajeff.ca/"
           xmlns:xs="http://www.w3.org/2001/XMLSchema">
```

EXERCISES

The following exercises are designed to test your understanding of Chapter 1's content:

1. Define XML.

2. True or false: XML and HTML are descendants of SGML.

3. What language features does XML provide for use in defining custom markup languages?

4. What is the XML declaration?

5. Identify the XML declaration's three attributes. Which attribute is nonoptional?

6. True or false: An element always consists of a start tag followed by content followed by an end tag.

7. Following the XML declaration, an XML document is anchored in what kind of element?

8. What is mixed content?

9. What is a character reference? Identify the two kinds of character references.

10. What is a CDATA section? Why would you use it?

11. Define namespace.

12. What is a namespace prefix?

13. True or false: A tag's attributes don't need to be prefixed when those attributes belong to the element.

14. What is a comment? Where can it appear in an XML document?

15. Define processing instruction.

16. Identify the rules that an XML document must follow to be considered well formed.

17. What does it mean for an XML document to be valid?

18. A parser that performs validation compares an XML document to a grammar document. Identify the two common grammar languages.

19. What is the general syntax for declaring an element in a DTD?

20. Which grammar language lets you create complex types from simple types?

21. Create a `books.xml` document file with a `books` root element. The `books` element must contain one or more `book` elements, where a `book` element must contain one `title` element, one or more `author` elements, and one `publisher` element (and in that order). Also, the `book` element's `<book>` tag must contain `isbn` and `pubyear` attributes. Record `Advanced C++`/`James Coplien`/`Addison Wesley`/`0201548550`/`1992` in the first book element, `Beginning Groovy and Grails`/`Christopher M. Judd`/`Joseph Faisal Nusairat`/`James Shingler`/`Apress`/`9781430210450`/`2008` in the second book element, and `Effective Java`/`Joshua Bloch`/`Addison Wesley`/`0201310058`/`2001` in the third book element.

22. Modify `books.xml` to include an internal DTD that satisfies the previous exercise's requirements.

Summary

Applications often use XML documents to store and exchange data. XML defines rules for encoding documents in a format that is both human-readable and machine-readable. It's a meta-language for defining vocabularies, which is the key to XML's importance and popularity.

XML provides several language features for use in defining custom markup languages. These features include the XML declaration, elements and attributes, character references and CDATA sections, namespaces, and comments and processing instructions.

HTML is a sloppy language where elements can be specified out of order, end tags can be omitted, and so on. In contrast, XML documents are well formed in that they conform to specific rules, which make them easier to process. XML parsers only parse well-formed XML documents.

In many cases, an XML document must also be valid. A valid document adheres to constraints as described by a grammar document. Grammar documents are written in a grammar language, such as the commonly used Document Type Definition and XML Schema.

Chapter 2 introduces Java's SAX API for parsing XML documents.

CHAPTER 2

Parsing XML Documents with SAX

Java provides several APIs for parsing XML documents. The most basic of these APIs is SAX, which is the focus of Chapter 2.

What Is SAX?

Simple API for XML (SAX) is an event-based Java API for parsing an XML document sequentially from start to finish. As a SAX-oriented parser encounters an item from the document's *infoset* (an abstract data model describing an XML document's information—see `http://en.wikipedia.org/wiki/XML_Information_Set`), it makes this item available to an application as an *event* by calling one of the methods in one of the application's *handlers* (objects whose methods are called by the parser to make event information available), which the application has previously registered with the parser. The application can then *consume* this event by processing the infoset item in some manner.

A SAX parser is more memory efficient than a DOM (see Chapter 3) parser in that it doesn't require the entire document to fit into memory. This benefit becomes a drawback for using XPath (see Chapter 5) and XSLT (see Chapter 6), which require that the entire document be stored in memory.

Note According to its official website (`www.saxproject.org`), SAX originated as an XML parsing API for Java. However, SAX isn't exclusive to Java. SAX is also available for Microsoft's .NET framework (see `http://saxdotnet.sourceforge.net`).

© Jeff Friesen 2019
J. Friesen, *Java XML and JSON*, https://doi.org/10.1007/978-1-4842-4330-5_2

Exploring the SAX API

SAX exists in two major versions: SAX 1 and SAX 2. Java implements both versions through the javax.xml.parsers package's abstract SAXParser and SAXParserFactory classes. The org.xml.sax, org.xml.sax.ext, and org.xml.sax.helpers packages provide various types that augment both Java implementations.

Note   I explore only the SAX 2 implementation because SAX 2 makes available additional infoset items about an XML document (such as comments and CDATA section notifications).

Before Java 9, you could use the org.xml.sax.helpers package's XMLReaderFactory class to obtain a SAX 2 parser. In Java 9, Oracle deprecated XMLReaderFactory and recommends using SAXParserFactory instead.

Obtaining a SAX 2 Parser

Classes that implement the XMLReader interface describe SAX 2-based parsers. Instances of these classes are obtained as follows:

1. Call SAXParserFactory's static SAXParserFactory newInstance() method to obtain a new SAXParserFactory subclass instance. Alternatively, you might want to call the static SAXParserFactory newDefaultInstance() method (introduced by Java 9) to obtain an instance of the system-default SAXParserFactory implementation.

2. Configure the SAXParserFactory object by calling various SAXParserFactory configuration methods, such as void setNamespaceAware(boolean awareness), which results in a parser that supports XML namespaces.

3. Call SAXParserFactory's SAXParser newSAXParser() method to return a SAXParser subclass instance.

4. Call SAXParser's XMLReader getXMLReader() method to return an instance of a class that implements XMLReader.

The following code fragment follows these steps to create and return an XMLReader object whose parser is aware of namespaces:

```
SAXParserFactory spf = SAXParserFactory.newInstance();
spf.setNamespaceAware(true);
SAXParser sp = spf.newSAXParser();
XMLReader xmlr = sp.getXMLReader();
```

Note   SAXParserFactory's newInstance() method follows an ordered lookup procedure to identify the SAXParserFactory implementation class to load. First, it looks for a javax.xml.parsers.SAXParserFactory system property and, when present, uses its value as the implementation class name. Lastly, it invokes newDefaultInstance() to return the system-default implementation.

The newSAXParser() method creates a new SAXParser subclass object using the currently configured factory parameters. It throws javax.xml.parsers. ParserConfigurationException when a parser cannot be created that satisfies the requested configuration. It throws org.xml.sax.SAXException when a SAX-oriented error occurs.

Touring XMLReader Methods

The returned XMLReader object makes available several methods for configuring the parser and parsing a document's content. These methods are described as follows:

- ContentHandler getContentHandler() returns the current content handler, which is an instance of a class that implements the org. xml.sax.ContentHandler interface, or null when none has been registered.

- DTDHandler getDTDHandler() returns the current DTD handler, which is an instance of a class that implements the org.xml.sax. DTDHandler interface, or null when none has been registered.

- `EntityResolver getEntityResolver()` returns the current entity resolver, which is an instance of a class that implements the `org.xml.sax.EntityResolver` interface, or `null` when none has been registered.

- `ErrorHandler getErrorHandler()` returns the current error handler, which is an instance of a class that implements the `org.xml.sax.ErrorHandler` interface, or `null` when none has been registered.

- `boolean getFeature(String name)` returns the Boolean value that corresponds to the feature identified by `name`, which must be a fully qualified URI. This method throws `org.xml.sax.SAXNotRecognizedException` when the name isn't recognized as a feature, and throws `org.xml.sax.SAXNotSupportedException` when the name is recognized but the associated value cannot be determined when `getFeature()` is called. `SAXNotRecognizedException` and `SAXNotSupportedException` are subclasses of `SAXException`.

- `Object getProperty(String name)` returns the `java.lang.Object` instance that corresponds to the property identified by name, which must be a fully qualified URI. This method throws `SAXNotRecognizedException` when the name isn't recognized as a property, and throws `SAXNotSupportedException` when the name is recognized but the associated value cannot be determined when `getProperty()` is called.

- `void parse(InputSource input)` parses an XML document and doesn't return until the document has been parsed. The `input` parameter stores a reference to an `org.xml.sax.InputSource` object, which describes the document's source (such as a `java.io.InputStream` object, or even a `java.lang.String`-based system identifier URI). This method throws `java.io.IOException` when the source cannot be read and `SAXException` when parsing fails, probably due to a well-formedness violation.

- `void parse(String systemId)` parses an XML document by executing `parse(new InputSource(systemId));`.

- `void setContentHandler(ContentHandler handler)` registers the content handler identified by `handler` with the parser. The `ContentHandler` interface provides 11 callback methods that are called to report various parsing events (such as the start and end of an element).

- `void setDTDHandler(DTDHandler handler)` registers the DTD handler identified by `handler` with the parser. The `DTDHandler` interface provides a pair of callback methods for reporting on notations and external unparsed entities.

- `void setEntityResolver(EntityResolver resolver)` registers the entity resolver identified by `resolver` with the parser. The `EntityResolver` interface provides a single callback method for resolving entities.

- `void setErrorHandler(ErrorHandler handler)` registers the error handler identified by `handler` with the parser. The `ErrorHandler` interface provides three callback methods that report *fatal errors* (problems that prevent further parsing, such as well-formedness violations), *recoverable errors* (problems that don't prevent further parsing, such as validation failures), and *warnings* (nonerrors that need to be addressed, such as prefixing an element name with the W3C-reserved `xml` prefix).

- `void setFeature(String name, boolean value)` assigns `value` to the feature identified by `name`, which must be a fully qualified URI. This method throws `SAXNotRecognizedException` when the name isn't recognized as a feature, and throws `SAXNotSupportedException` when the name is recognized but the associated value cannot be set when `setFeature()` is called.

- `void setProperty(String name, Object value)` assigns `value` to the property identified by `name`, which must be a fully qualified URI. This method throws `SAXNotRecognizedException` when the name isn't recognized as a property, and throws `SAXNotSupportedException` when the name is recognized but the associated value cannot be set when `setProperty()` is called.

When a handler isn't installed, all events pertaining to that handler are silently ignored. Not installing an error handler can be problematic because normal processing might not continue and the application wouldn't be aware that anything had gone wrong. When an entity resolver isn't installed, the parser performs its own default resolution. I'll have more to say about entity resolution later in this chapter.

Note   You typically install a new content handler, DTD handler, entity resolver, or error handler before a document is parsed, but can also do so while parsing the document. The parser starts using the handler when the next event occurs.

Setting Features and Properties

After obtaining an XMLReader object, you can configure that object by setting its features and properties. A *feature* is a name/value pair that describes a parser mode, such as validation. In contrast, a *property* is a name/value pair that describes some other aspect of the parser interface, such as a lexical handler that augments the content handler by providing callback methods for reporting on comments, CDATA delimiters, and a few other syntactic constructs.

Features and properties have names, which must be absolute URIs beginning with the http:// prefix. A feature's value is always a Boolean true/false value. In contrast, a property's value is an arbitrary object. The following code fragment demonstrates setting a feature and a property:

```
String FEAT_VAL = "http://xml.org/sax/features/validation";
xmlr.setFeature(FEAT_VAL, true);
String PROP_LH = "http://xml.org/sax/properties/lexical-handler";
xmlr.setProperty(PROP_LH, new LexicalHandler() { /* ... */ });
```

The setFeature() call enables the validation feature so that the parser will perform validation. Feature names are prefixed with http://xml.org/sax/features/.

Note   Parsers must support the namespaces and namespace-prefixes
features. namespaces decides whether URIs and local names are passed to
ContentHandler's startElement() and endElement() methods. It defaults
to true—these names are passed. The parser can pass empty strings when
false. namespace-prefixes decides whether a namespace declaration's
xmlns and xmlns:prefix attributes are included in the org.xml.sax.
Attributes list passed to startElement(), and also decides whether qualified
names are passed as the method's third argument—a *qualified name* is a prefix
plus a local name. It defaults to false, meaning that xmlns and xmlns:prefix
aren't included and meaning that parsers don't have to pass qualified names. No
properties are mandatory. The JDK documentation's org.xml.sax package page
lists standard SAX 2 features and properties.

The setProperty() call assigns an instance of a class that implements the org.xml.
sax.ext.LexicalHandler interface to the lexical-handler property so that interface
methods can be called to report on comments, CDATA sections, and so on. Property
names are prefixed with http://xml.org/sax/properties/.

Note   Unlike ContentHandler, DTDHandler, EntityResolver, and
ErrorHandler, LexicalHandler is an extension (it's not part of the core SAX
API), which is why XMLReader doesn't declare a void setLexicalHandler
(LexicalHandler handler) method. If you want to install a lexical handler,
you must use XMLReader's setProperty() method to install the handler as the
value of the http://xml.org/sax/properties/lexical-handler property.

Features and properties can be read-only or read-write. (In some rare cases, a
feature or property might be write-only.) When setting or reading a feature or property,
SAXNotSupportedException or SAXNotRecognizedException might be thrown.
For example, if you try to modify a read-only feature/property, an instance of the
SAXNotSupportedException class is thrown. Also, this exception could be thrown if
you call setFeature() or setProperty() during parsing. Trying to set the validation
feature for a parser that doesn't perform validation is a scenario where an instance of the
SAXNotRecognizedException class is thrown.

Touring the Handler and Resolver Interfaces

The interface-based handlers installed by setContentHandler(), setDTDHandler(), and setErrorHandler(); the entity resolver installed by setEntityResolver(); and the handler described by the lexical-handler property provide various callback methods. You need to understand these methods before you can codify them to respond effectively to parsing events.

Touring ContentHandler

ContentHandler declares the following content-oriented informational callback methods:

- void characters(char[] ch, int start, int length) reports an element's character data via the ch array. The arguments that are passed to start and length identify that portion of the array that's relevant to this method call. Characters are passed via a char[] array instead of via a String object as a performance optimization. Parsers commonly store a large amount of the document in an array and repeatedly pass a reference to this array along with updated start and length values to characters().

- void endDocument() reports that the end of the document has been reached. An application might use this method to close an output file or perform some other cleanup.

- void endElement(String uri, String localName, String qName) reports that the end of an element has been reached. uri identifies the element's namespace URI or is empty when there is no namespace URI or namespace processing hasn't been enabled. localName identifies the element's local name, which is the name without a prefix (e.g., the html in html or h:html). qName references the qualified name, for example, h:html or html when there is no prefix. endElement() is invoked when an end tag is detected, or immediately following startElement() when an empty-element tag is detected.

- `void endPrefixMapping(String prefix)` reports that the end of a namespace prefix mapping (e.g., `xmlns:h`) has been reached, and prefix reports this prefix (e.g., h).

- `void ignorableWhitespace(char[] ch, int start, int length)` reports *ignorable whitespace* (whitespace located between tags where the DTD doesn't allow mixed content). This whitespace is often used to indent tags. The parameters serve the same purpose as those in the `characters()` method.

- `void processingInstruction(String target, String data)` reports a processing instruction, in which `target` identifies the application to which the instruction is directed and `data` provides the instruction's data (the null reference when there is no data).

- `void setDocumentLocator(Locator locator)` reports an `org.xml.sax.Locator` object (an instance of a class implementing the `Locator` interface) whose `int getColumnNumber()`, `int getLineNumber()`, `String getPublicId()`, and `String getSystemId()` methods can be called to obtain location information at the end position of any document-related event, even when the parser isn't reporting an error. This method is called before `startDocument()` and is a good place to save the `Locator` object so that it can be accessed from other callback methods.

- `void skippedEntity(String name)` reports all skipped entities. Validating parsers resolve all general entity references, but nonvalidating parsers have the option of skipping them because nonvalidating parsers don't read DTDs where these entities are declared. If the nonvalidating parser doesn't read a DTD, it will not know if an entity is properly declared. Instead of attempting to read the DTD and report the entity's replacement text, the nonvalidating parser calls `skippedEntity()` with the entity's name.

- `void startDocument()` reports that the start of the document has been reached. An application might use this method to create an output file or perform some other initialization.

- void startElement(String uri, String localName, String qName, Attributes attributes) reports that the start of an element has been reached. uri identifies the element's namespace URI or is empty when there is no namespace URI or namespace processing hasn't been enabled. localName identifies the element's local name, qName references its qualified name, and attributes references a list of the element's attributes—this list is empty when there are no attributes. startElement() is invoked when a start tag or an empty-element tag is detected.

- void startPrefixMapping(String prefix, String uri) reports that the start of a namespace prefix mapping (e.g., xmlns:h="http://www.w3.org/1999/xhtml") has been reached, in which prefix reports this prefix (such as h) and uri reports the URI to which the prefix is mapped (e.g., http://www.w3.org/1999/xhtml).

Each method except for setDocumentLocator() is declared to throw SAXException, which an overriding callback method might choose to throw when it detects a problem.

Touring DTDHandler

DTDHandler declares the following DTD-oriented informational callback methods:

- void notationDecl(String name, String publicId, String systemId) reports a notation declaration, in which name provides this declaration's name attribute value, publicId provides this declaration's public attribute value (the null reference when this value isn't available), and systemId provides this declaration's system attribute value.

- void unparsedEntityDecl(String name, String publicId, String systemId, String notationName) reports an external unparsed entity declaration, in which name provides the value of this declaration's name attribute, publicId provides the value of the public attribute (the null reference when this value isn't available), systemId provides the value of the system attribute, and notationName provides the NDATA name.

Each method is declared to throw SAXException, which an overriding callback method might choose to throw when it detects a problem.

Touring ErrorHandler

`ErrorHandler` declares the following error-oriented informational callback methods:

- `void error(SAXParseException exception)` reports that a recoverable parser error (typically the document isn't valid) has occurred; the details are specified via the argument passed to `exception`. This method is typically overridden to report the error via a command window or to log it to a file or a database.

- `void fatalError(SAXParseException exception)` reports that an unrecoverable parser error (the document isn't well formed) has occurred; the details are specified via the argument passed to `exception`. This method is typically overridden so that the application can log the error before it stops processing the document (because the document is no longer reliable).

- `void warning(SAXParseException e)` reports that a nonserious error (such as an element name beginning with the reserved `xml` character sequence) has occurred; the details are specified via the argument passed to `exception`. This method is typically overridden to report the warning via a console or to log it to a file or a database.

Each method is declared to throw `SAXException`, which an overriding callback method might choose to throw when it detects a problem.

Touring EntityResolver

`EntityResolver` declares the following callback method:

- `InputSource resolveEntity(String publicId, String systemId)` is called to let the application resolve an external entity (such as an external DTD subset) by returning a custom `InputSource` object that's based on a different URI. This method is declared to throw `SAXException` when it detects a SAX-oriented problem and is also declared to throw `IOException` when it encounters an I/O error, possibly in response to creating an `InputStream` object or a `java.io.Reader` object for the `InputSource` being created.

Touring LexicalHandler

LexicalHandler declares the following additional content-oriented informational callback methods:

- void comment(char[] ch, int start, int length) reports a comment via the ch array. The arguments that are passed to start and length identify that portion of the array that's relevant to this method call.

- void endCDATA() reports the end of a CDATA section.

- void endDTD() reports the end of a DTD.

- void endEntity(String name) reports the end of the entity identified by name.

- void startCDATA() reports the start of a CDATA section.

- void startDTD(String name, String publicId, String systemId) reports the start of the DTD identified by name. publicId specifies the declared public identifier for the external DTD subset or is the null reference when none was declared. Similarly, systemId specifies the declared system identifier for the external DTD subset or is the null reference when none was declared.

- void startEntity(String name) reports the start of the entity identified by name.

Each method is declared to throw SAXException, which an overriding callback method might choose to throw when it detects a problem.

Because it can be tedious to implement all of the methods in each interface, the SAX API conveniently provides the org.xml.sax.helpers.DefaultHandler adapter class to relieve you of this tedium. DefaultHandler implements ContentHandler, DTDHandler, EntityResolver, and ErrorHandler. SAX also provides org.xml.sax. ext.DefaultHandler2, which subclasses DefaultHandler and which also implements LexicalHandler.

Demonstrating the SAX API

Listing 2-1 presents the source code to SAXDemo, an application that demonstrates the SAX API. The application consists of a SAXDemo entry-point class and a Handler subclass of DefaultHandler2.

Listing 2-1. SAXDemo

```
import java.io.FileReader;
import java.io.IOException;

import javax.xml.parsers.ParserConfigurationException;
import javax.xml.parsers.SAXParser;
import javax.xml.parsers.SAXParserFactory;

import org.xml.sax.InputSource;
import org.xml.sax.SAXException;
import org.xml.sax.XMLReader;

import static java.lang.System.*;

public class SAXDemo
{
   final static String FEAT_NSP =
      "http://xml.org/sax/features/namespace-prefixes";

   final static String FEAT_VAL =
      "http://xml.org/sax/features/validation";

   final static String PROP_LH =
      "http://xml.org/sax/properties/lexical-handler";

   public static void main(String[] args)
   {
      if (args.length < 1 || args.length > 2)
      {
         err.println("usage: java SAXDemo xmlfile [v]");
         return;
      }
      try
```

47

```java
      {
          SAXParserFactory spf =
              SAXParserFactory.newInstance();
          spf.setNamespaceAware(true);
          SAXParser sp = spf.newSAXParser();
          XMLReader xmlr = sp.getXMLReader();
          if (args.length == 2 && args[1].equals("v"))
              xmlr.setFeature(FEAT_VAL, true);
          xmlr.setFeature(FEAT_NSP, true);
          Handler handler = new Handler();
          xmlr.setContentHandler(handler);
          xmlr.setDTDHandler(handler);
          xmlr.setEntityResolver(handler);
          xmlr.setErrorHandler(handler);
          xmlr.setProperty(PROP_LH, handler);
          FileReader fr = new FileReader(args[0]);
          xmlr.parse(new InputSource(fr));
      }
      catch (IOException ioe)
      {
          err.printf("IOE: %s%n", ioe.toString());
      }
      catch (ParserConfigurationException pce)
      {
          err.printf("PCE: %s%n", pce.toString());
      }
      catch (SAXException saxe)
      {
          err.printf("SAXE: %s%n", saxe.toString());
      }
   }
}
```

SAXDemo's main() method first verifies that one or two command-line arguments (the name of an XML document optionally followed by lowercase letter v, which tells SAXDemo to create a validating parser) have been specified. It then creates an XMLReader object; conditionally enables the validation feature and enables the namespace-prefixes feature; instantiates the companion Handler class; installs this Handler object as the parser's content handler, DTD handler, entity resolver, and error handler; installs this Handler object as the value of the lexical-handler property; creates an input source to read the document from a file; and parses the document.

The Handler class's source code is presented in Listing 2-2.

Listing 2-2. Handler

```
import org.xml.sax.Attributes;
import org.xml.sax.InputSource;
import org.xml.sax.Locator;
import org.xml.sax.SAXParseException;

import org.xml.sax.ext.DefaultHandler2;

import static java.lang.System.*;

public class Handler extends DefaultHandler2
{
   private Locator locator;

   @Override
   public void characters(char[] ch, int start, int length)
   {
      out.print("characters() [");
      for (int i = start; i < start + length; i++)
         out.print(ch[i]);
      out.println("]");
   }

   @Override
   public void comment(char[] ch, int start, int length)
   {
      out.print("characters() [");
      for (int i = start; i < start + length; i++)
```

```java
         out.print(ch[i]);
      out.println("]");
   }

   @Override
   public void endCDATA()
   {
      out.println("endCDATA()");
   }

   @Override
   public void endDocument()
   {
      out.println("endDocument()");
   }

   @Override
   public void endDTD()
   {
      out.println("endDTD()");
   }

   @Override
   public void endElement(String uri, String localName,
                          String qName)
   {
      out.print("endElement() ");
      out.printf("uri=[%s], ", uri);
      out.printf("localName=[%s], ", localName);
      out.printf("qName=[%s]%n", qName);
   }

   @Override
   public void endEntity(String name)
   {
      out.print("endEntity() ");
      out.printf("name=[%s]%n", name);
   }
```

```java
@Override
public void endPrefixMapping(String prefix)
{
   out.print("endPrefixMapping() ");
   out.printf("prefix=[%s]%n", prefix);
}

@Override
public void error(SAXParseException saxpe)
{
   out.printf("error() %s%n", saxpe.toString());
}

@Override
public void fatalError(SAXParseException saxpe)
{
   out.printf("fatalError() %s%n", saxpe.toString());
}

@Override
public void ignorableWhitespace(char[] ch, int start, int length)
{
   out.print("ignorableWhitespace() [");
   for (int i = start; i < start + length; i++)
      out.print(ch[i]);
   out.println("]");
}

@Override
public void notationDecl(String name, String publicId,
                         String systemId)
{
   out.print("notationDecl() ");
   out.printf("name=[%s], ", name);
   out.printf("publicId=[%s], ", publicId);
   out.printf("systemId=[%s]%n", systemId);
}
```

```java
@Override
public void processingInstruction(String target, String data)
{
    out.print("processingInstruction() ");
    out.printf("target=[%s], ", target);
    out.printf("data=[%s]%n", data);
}

@Override
public InputSource resolveEntity(String publicId, String systemId)
{
    out.print("resolveEntity() ");
    out.printf("publicId=[%s], ", publicId);
    out.printf("systemId=[%s]%n", systemId);
    // Do not perform a remapping.
    InputSource is = new InputSource();
    is.setPublicId(publicId);
    is.setSystemId(systemId);
    return is;
}

@Override
public void setDocumentLocator(Locator locator)
{
    out.print("setDocumentLocator() ");
    out.printf("locator=[%s]%n", locator);
    this.locator = locator;
}

@Override
public void skippedEntity(String name)
{
    out.print("skippedEntity() ");
    out.printf("name=[%s]%n", name);
}
```

```java
@Override
public void startCDATA()
{
   out.println("startCDATA()");
}

@Override
public void startDocument()
{
   out.println("startDocument()");
}

@Override
public void startDTD(String name, String publicId, String systemId)
{
   out.print("startDTD() ");
   out.printf("name=[%s], ", name);
   out.printf("publicId=[%s], ", publicId);
   out.printf("systemId=[%s]%n", systemId);
}

@Override
public void startElement(String uri, String localName, String qName,
                         Attributes attributes)
{
   out.print("startElement() ");
   out.printf("uri=[%s], ", uri);
   out.printf("localName=[%s], ", localName);
   out.printf("qName=[%s]%n", qName);
   for (int i = 0; i < attributes.getLength(); i++)
      out.printf("  Attribute: %s, %s%n", attributes.getLocalName(i),
                         attributes.getValue(i));
   out.printf("Column number=[%d]%n", locator.getColumnNumber());
   out.printf("Line number=[%d]%n", locator.getLineNumber());
}
```

```java
@Override
public void startEntity(String name)
{
    out.print("startEntity() ");
    out.printf("name=[%s]%n", name);
}

@Override
public void startPrefixMapping(String prefix, String uri)
{
    out.print("startPrefixMapping() ");
    out.printf("prefix=[%s], ", prefix);
    out.printf("uri=[%s]%n", uri);
}

@Override
public void unparsedEntityDecl(String name,
                              String publicId,
                              String systemId,
                              String notationName)
{
    out.print("unparsedEntityDecl() ");
    out.printf("name=[%s], ", name);
    out.printf("publicId=[%s], ", publicId);
    out.printf("systemId=[%s], ", systemId);
    out.printf("notationName=[%s]%n", notationName);
}

@Override
public void warning(SAXParseException saxpe)
{
    out.printf("warning() %s%n", saxpe.toString());
}
}
```

The Handler subclass is pretty straightforward; it outputs every possible piece of information about an XML document, subject to feature and property settings. You'll find this class handy for exploring the order in which events occur along with various features and properties.

Assuming that files based on Listings 2-1 and 2-2 are located in the same directory, compile them as follows:

```
javac SAXDemo.java
```

Execute the following command to parse Listing 1-4's svg-examples.xml document:

```
java SAXDemo svg-examples.xml
```

SAXDemo responds by presenting the following output (the hashcode will probably be different):

```
setDocumentLocator() locator=[com.sun.org.apache.xerces.internal.parsers.Ab
stractSAXParser$LocatorProxy@53b32d7]
startDocument()
startElement() uri=[], localName=[svg-examples], qName=[svg-examples]
Column number=[15]
Line number=[2]
characters() [
    ]
startElement() uri=[], localName=[example], qName=[example]
Column number=[13]
Line number=[3]
characters() [
    The following Scalable Vector Graphics document ]
characters() [
    describes a blue-filled and black-stroked
    rectangle.]
characters() [
    ]
startCDATA()
```

```
characters() [<svg width="100%" height="100%"
         version="1.1"
         xmlns="http://www.w3.org/2000/svg">
      <rect width="300" height="100"
            style="fill:rgb(0,0,255);stroke-width:1;
                  stroke:rgb(0,0,0)"/>
   </svg>]
endCDATA()
characters() [
   ]
endElement() uri=[], localName=[example], qName=[example]
characters() [
]
endElement() uri=[], localName=[svg-examples], qName=[svg-examples]
endDocument()
```

The first output line proves that setDocumentLocator() is called first. The second and third lines also identify the Locator object whose getColumnNumber() and getLineNumber() methods are called to output the parser location when startElement() is called—these methods return column and line numbers starting at 1.

Perhaps you're curious about the four instances of the following output:

```
characters() [
   ]
```

The instance of this output that follows the endCDATA() output is reporting a carriage return/line feed combination that wasn't included in the preceding characters() method call, which passed the contents of the CDATA section minus these line terminator characters. This is also the case for the instance of this output that follows the rectangle.] output. In contrast, the instances of this output that follow the startElement() call for svg-examples and follow the endElement() call for example are somewhat curious. There's no content between <svg-examples> and <example>, and between </example> and </svg-examples>, or is there?

You can satisfy this curiosity by modifying svg-examples.xml to include an internal DTD. Place the following DTD (which indicates that an svg-examples element contains one or more example elements and that an example element contains parsed character data) between the XML declaration and the <svg-examples> start tag:

```
<!DOCTYPE svg-examples [
<!ELEMENT svg-examples (example+)>
<!ELEMENT example (#PCDATA)>
]>
```

Continuing, execute the following command:

```
java SAXDemo svg-examples.xml
```

This time, you should see the following output (although the hashcode will probably differ):

```
setDocumentLocator() locator=[com.sun.org.apache.xerces.internal.parsers.Ab
stractSAXParser$LocatorProxy@53b32d7]
startDocument()
startDTD() name=[svg-examples], publicId=[null], systemId=[null]
endDTD()
startElement() uri=[], localName=[svg-examples], qName=[svg-examples]
Column number=[15]
Line number=[6]
ignorableWhitespace() [
    ]
startElement() uri=[], localName=[example], qName=[example]
Column number=[13]
Line number=[7]
characters() [
    The following Scalable Vector Graphics document
    describes a blue-filled and black-stroked ]
characters() [
    rectangle.
    ]
startCDATA()
characters() [<svg width="100%" height="100%"
        version="1.1"
        xmlns="http://www.w3.org/2000/svg">
      <rect width="300" height="100"
          style="fill:rgb(0,0,255);stroke-width:1;
```

```
                        stroke:rgb(0,0,0)"/>
       </svg>]
endCDATA()
characters() [
   ]
endElement() uri=[], localName=[example], qName=[example]
ignorableWhitespace() [
]
endElement() uri=[], localName=[svg-examples], qName=[svg-examples]
endDocument()
```

This output reveals that the `ignorableWhitespace()` method was called after `startElement()` for `svg-examples` and after `endElement()` for `example`. The former two calls to `characters()` that produced the strange output were reporting ignorable whitespace.

Recall that I previously defined *ignorable whitespace* as whitespace located between tags where the DTD doesn't allow mixed content. For example, the DTD indicates that `svg-examples` shall contain only `example` elements, not `example` elements and parsed character data. However, the line terminator following the `<svg-examples>` tag and the leading whitespace before `<example>` are parsed character data. The parser now reports these characters by calling `ignorableWhitespace()`.

This time, there are only two occurrences of the following output:

```
characters() [
   ]
```

The first occurrence reports the line terminator separately from the `example` element's text (before the CDATA section); it didn't do so previously, which proves that `characters()` is called with either all or part of an element's content. Once again, the second occurrence reports the line terminator that follows the CDATA section.

Let's validate `svg-examples.xml` without the previously presented internal DTD. We'll do so by executing the following command—don't forget to include the `v` command-line argument or the document won't validate:

```
java SAXDemo svg-examples.xml v
```

Among its output are the following error()-prefixed lines:

```
error() org.xml.sax.SAXParseException; lineNumber: 2; columnNumber: 14;
Document is invalid: no grammar found.
error() org.xml.sax.SAXParseException; lineNumber: 2; columnNumber: 14;
Document root element "svg-examples", must match DOCTYPE root "null".
```

These lines reveal that a DTD grammar hasn't been found. Furthermore, the parser reports a mismatch between svg-examples (it considers the first encountered element to be the root element) and null (it considers null to be the name of the root element in the absence of a DTD). Neither violation is considered to be fatal, which is why error() is called instead of fatalError().

Add the internal DTD to svg-examples.xml and reexecute java SAXDemo svg-examples.xml v. This time, you should see no error()-prefixed lines in the output.

Tip   SAX 2 validation defaults to validating against a DTD. To validate against an XML Schema-based schema instead, add the schemaLanguage property with the http://www.w3.org/2001/XMLSchema value to the XMLReader object. Accomplish this task for SAXDemo by specifying xmlr.setProperty("http://java.sun.com/xml/jaxp/properties/schemaLanguage", "http://www.w3.org/2001/XMLSchema"); before xmlr.parse(new InputSource(new FileReader(args[0])));.

Creating a Custom Entity Resolver

While exploring XML in Chapter 1, I introduced you to the concept of *entities*, which are aliased data. I then discussed general entities and parameter entities in terms of their internal and external variants.

Unlike internal entities, whose values are specified in a DTD, the values of external entities are specified outside of a DTD and are identified via public and/or system identifiers. The system identifier is a URI, whereas the public identifier is a formal public identifier.

An XML parser reads an external entity (including the external DTD subset) via an InputSource object that's connected to the appropriate system identifier. In many cases, you pass a system identifier or InputSource object to the parser and let it discover where to find other entities that are referenced from the current document entity.

However, for performance or other reasons, you might want the parser to read the external entity's value from a different system identifier, such as a local DTD copy's system identifier. You can accomplish this task by creating an *entity resolver* that uses the public identifier to choose a different system identifier. Upon encountering an external entity, the parser calls the custom entity resolver to obtain this identifier.

Consider Listing 2-3's formal specification of Listing 1-1's grilled cheese sandwich recipe.

Listing 2-3. XML-Based Recipe for a Grilled Cheese Sandwich Specified in Recipe Markup Language

```
<?xml version="1.0" encoding="UTF-8"?>
<!DOCTYPE recipeml PUBLIC
    "-//FormatData//DTD RecipeML 0.5//EN"
    "http://www.formatdata.com/recipeml/recipeml.dtd">
<recipeml version="0.5">
    <recipe>
        <head>
            <title>Grilled Cheese Sandwich</title>
        </head>
        <ingredients>
            <ing>
                <amt><qty>2</qty><unit>slice</unit></amt>
                <item>bread</item>
            </ing>
            <ing>
                <amt><qty>1</qty><unit>slice</unit></amt>
                <item>cheese</item>
            </ing>
            <ing>
                <amt><qty>2</qty><unit>pat</unit></amt>
                <item>margarine</item>
            </ing>
```

```
    </ingredients>
    <directions>
        <step>Place frying pan on element and select
        medium heat.</step>
        <step>For each bread slice, smear one pat of
        margarine on one side of bread slice.</step>
        <step>Place cheese slice between bread slices with
        margarine-smeared sides away from the
        cheese.</step>
        <step>Place sandwich in frying pan with one
        margarine-smeared size in contact with pan.</step>
        <step>Fry for a couple of minutes and flip.</step>
        <step>Fry other side for a minute and
        serve.</step>
    </directions>
  </recipe>
</recipeml>
```

Listing 2-3 specifies the grilled cheese sandwich recipe in *Recipe Markup Language* (*RecipeML*), an XML-based language for marking up recipes. (A company named FormatData [see www.formatdata.com] released this format in 2000.)

The document type declaration reports -//FormatData//DTD RecipeML 0.5// EN as the formal public identifier and http://www.formatdata.com/recipeml/ recipeml.dtd as the system identifier. Instead of keeping the default mapping, let's map this formal public identifier to recipeml.dtd, a system identifier for a local copy of this DTD file.

To create a custom entity resolver to perform this mapping, we declare a class that implements the EntityResolver interface in terms of its InputSource resolveEntity(String publicId, String systemId) method. We then use the supplied publicId value as a key into a map that points to the desired systemId value, and then use this value to create and return a custom InputSource. Listing 2-4 presents the resulting class.

Listing 2-4. LocalRecipeML

```java
import java.util.HashMap;
import java.util.Map;

import org.xml.sax.EntityResolver;
import org.xml.sax.InputSource;
import org.xml.sax.SAXException;

import static java.lang.System.*;

public class LocalRecipeML implements EntityResolver
{
   private Map<String, String> mappings = new HashMap<>();

   LocalRecipeML()
   {
     mappings.put("-//FormatData//DTD RecipeML 0.5//EN", "recipeml.dtd");
   }

   @Override
   public InputSource resolveEntity(String publicId, String systemId)
   {
     if (mappings.containsKey(publicId))
     {
       out.println("obtaining cached recipeml.dtd");
       systemId = mappings.get(publicId);
       InputSource localSource =
           new InputSource(systemId);
       return localSource;
     }
     return null;
   }
}
```

Listing 2-4 declares `LocalRecipeML`. This class's constructor stores the formal public identifier for the RecipeML DTD and the system identifier for a local copy of this DTD's document in a map.

Note   Although it's unnecessary to use a map in this example (an `if (publicId.equals("-//FormatData//DTD RecipeML 0.5//EN"))` `return new InputSource("recipeml.dtd") else return null;` statement would suffice), I've chosen to use a map in case I want to expand the number of mappings in the future. In another scenario, you would probably find a map to be very convenient. For example, it's easier to use a map than to use a series of `if` statements in a custom entity resolver that maps XHTML's strict, transitional, and frameset formal public identifiers and also maps its various entity sets to local copies of these document files.

The overriding `resolveEntity()` method uses `publicId`'s argument to locate the corresponding system identifier in the map—the `systemId` parameter value is ignored because it never refers to the local copy of `recipeml.dtd`. When the mapping is found, an `InputSource` object is created and returned. If the mapping couldn't be found, `null` would be returned.

To install this custom entity resolver in SAXDemo, specify `xmlr.` `setEntityResolver(new LocalRecipeML());` before the `parse()` method call. After recompiling the source code, execute the following command:

```
java SAXDemo gcs.xml
```

Here, `gcs.xml` stores Listing 2-3's text. In the resulting output, you should observe the message "obtaining cached recipeml.dtd" before the call to `startEntity()`.

Tip   The SAX API includes an `org.xml.sax.ext.EntityResolver2` interface that provides improved support for resolving entities. If you prefer to implement `EntityResolver2` instead of `EntityResolver`, replace the `setEntityResolver()` call to install the entity resolver with a `setFeature()` call whose feature name is `use-entity-resolver2` (don't forget the `http://` `xml.org/sax/features/prefix`).

EXERCISES

The following exercises are designed to test your understanding of Chapter 2's content:

1. Define SAX.

2. How do you obtain a SAX 2-based parser?

3. What is the purpose of the XMLReader interface?

4. How do you tell a SAX parser to perform validation?

5. Identify the four kinds of SAX-oriented exceptions that can be thrown when working with SAX.

6. What interface does a handler class implement to respond to content-oriented events?

7. Identify the three other core interfaces that a handler class is likely to implement.

8. Define ignorable whitespace.

9. True or false: void error(SAXParseException exception) is called for all kinds of errors.

10. What is the purpose of the DefaultHandler class?

11. What is an entity? What is an entity resolver?

12. *Apache Tomcat* is an open-source web server developed by the Apache Software Foundation. Tomcat stores usernames, passwords, and roles (for authentication purposes) in its tomcat-users.xml configuration file. Create a DumpUserInfo application that uses SAX to parse the user elements in the following example tomcat-users.xml file and, for each user element, dump its username, password, and roles attribute values to standard output in a *key* = *value* format:

```xml
<?xml version='1.0' encoding='utf-8'?>
<tomcat-users>
    <role rolename="dbadmin"/>
    <role rolename="manager"/>
    <user username="JohnD" password="password1"
          roles="dbadmin,manager"/>
    <user username="JillD" password="password2"
          roles="manager"/>
</tomcat-users>
```

13.   Create a SAXSearch application that searches Exercise 1-21's books.xml file for those book elements whose publisher child elements contain text that equals the application's single command-line publisher name argument. Once there is a match, output the title element's text followed by the book element's isbn attribute value. For example, java SAXSearch Apress should output title = Beginning Groovy and Grails, isbn = 9781430210450, whereas java SAXSearch "Addison Wesley" should output title = Advanced C++, isbn = 0201548550 followed by title = Effective Java, isbn = 0201310058 on separate lines. Nothing should output when the command-line publisher name argument doesn't match a publisher element's text.

14.   Use Listing 2-1's SAXDemo application to validate Exercise 1-22's books.xml content against its DTD. Execute java SAXDemo books.xml -v to perform the validation.

Summary

SAX is an event-based Java API for parsing an XML document sequentially from start to finish. As a SAX-oriented parser encounters an item from the document's infoset, it makes this item available to an application as an event by calling one of the methods in one of the application's handlers, which the application has previously registered with the parser. The application can then consume this event by processing the infoset item in some manner.

SAX exists in two major versions: SAX 1 and SAX 2. Java implements both versions through the javax.xml.parsers package's abstract SAXParser and SAXParserFactory classes. The org.xml.sax, org.xml.sax.ext, and org.xml.sax.helpers packages provide various types that augment both Java implementations.

XMLReader makes available several methods for configuring the parser and parsing a document's content. Some of these methods get and set the content handler, DTD handler, entity resolver, and error handler, which are described by the ContentHandler, DTDHandler, EntityResolver, and ErrorHandler interfaces. After learning about XMLReader's methods and these interfaces, you learned about the nonstandard LexicalHandler interface and how to create a custom entity resolver.

Chapter 3 introduces Java's DOM API for parsing/creating XML documents.

CHAPTER 3

Parsing and Creating XML Documents with DOM

SAX can parse XML documents but cannot create them. In contrast, DOM can parse and create XML documents. Chapter 3 introduces you to DOM.

What Is DOM?

Document Object Model (DOM) is a Java API for parsing an XML document into an in-memory tree of nodes and for creating an XML document from a node tree. After a DOM parser creates a tree, an application uses the DOM API to navigate over and extract infoset items from the tree's nodes.

DOM has two big advantages over SAX:

- DOM permits random access to a document's infoset items, whereas SAX only permits serial access.

- DOM lets you also create XML documents, whereas you can only parse documents with SAX.

However, SAX is advantageous over DOM in that it can parse documents of arbitrary size, whereas the size of documents parsed or created by DOM is limited by the amount of available memory for storing the document's node-based tree structure.

© Jeff Friesen 2019
J. Friesen, *Java XML and JSON*, https://doi.org/10.1007/978-1-4842-4330-5_3

Note   DOM originated as an object model for the Netscape Navigator 3 and Microsoft Internet Explorer 3 web browsers. Collectively, these implementations are known as DOM Level 0. Because each vendor's DOM implementation was only slightly compatible with the other, the W3C subsequently took charge of DOM's development to promote standardization and has so far released DOM Levels 1, 2, 3, and 4. Java 11 supports the first three DOM levels through its DOM API.

A Tree of Nodes

DOM views an XML document as a tree that's composed of several kinds of nodes. This tree has a single *root node*, and all nodes except for the root have a *parent node*. Also, each node has a list of *child nodes*. When this list is empty, the child node is known as a *leaf node*.

Note   DOM permits nodes to exist that are not part of the tree structure. For example, an element node's attribute nodes are not regarded as child nodes of the element node. Also, nodes can be created but not inserted into the tree; they can also be removed from the tree.

Each node has a *node name*, which is the complete name for nodes that have names (such as an element's or an attribute's prefixed name), and #*node-type* for unnamed nodes, where *node-type* is one of `cdata-section`, `comment`, `document`, `document-fragment`, or `text`. Nodes also have *local names* (names without prefixes), prefixes, and namespace URIs (although these attributes may be null for certain kinds of nodes, such as comments). Finally, nodes have string values, which happen to be the content of text nodes, comment nodes, and similar text-oriented nodes; normalized values for attributes; and null for everything else.

DOM classifies nodes into 12 types; most of them can be considered part of a *DOM tree*. All of these types are described as follows:

- *Attribute node*: one of an element's attributes. It has a name, a local name, a prefix, a namespace URI, and a normalized string value. The value is *normalized* by resolving any entity references and by converting sequences of whitespace to a single whitespace character.

An attribute node has children, which are the text and any entity reference nodes that form its value. Attribute nodes are not regarded as children of their associated element nodes.

- *CDATA section node*: the contents of a CDATA section. Its name is #cdata-section and its value is the CDATA section's text.

- *Comment node*: a document comment. Its name is #comment and its value is the comment text. A comment node has a parent, which is the node that contains the comment.

- *Document node*: the root of a DOM tree. Its name is #document, it always has a single element child node, and it will also have a document type child node when the document has a document type declaration. Furthermore, it can have additional child nodes describing comments or processing instructions that appear before or after the root element's start tag. There can be only one document node in the tree.

- *Document fragment node*: an alternative root node. Its name is #document-fragment and it contains anything that an element node can contain (such as other element nodes and even comment nodes). A parser never creates this kind of a node. However, an application can create a document fragment node when it extracts part of a DOM tree to be moved somewhere else. Document fragment nodes let you work with subtrees.

- *Document type node*: a document type declaration. Its name is the name specified by the document type declaration for the root element. Also, it has a (possibly null) public identifier, a required system identifier, an internal DTD subset (which is possibly null), a parent (the document node that contains the document type node), and lists of DTD-declared notations and general entities. Its value is always set to null.

- *Element node*: a document's element. It has a name, a local name, a (possibly null) prefix, and a namespace URI, which is null when the element doesn't belong to any namespace. An element node contains children, including text nodes, and even comment and processing-instruction nodes.

- *Entity node*: the parsed and unparsed entities that are declared in a document's DTD. When a parser reads a DTD, it attaches a map of entity nodes (indexed by entity name) to the document type node. An entity node has a name and a system identifier and can also have a public identifier if one appears in the DTD. Finally, when the parser reads the entity, the entity node is given a list of read-only child nodes that contain the entity's replacement text.

- *Entity reference node*: a reference to a DTD-declared entity. Each entity reference node has a name and is included in the tree when the parser doesn't replace entity references with their values. The parser never includes entity reference nodes for character references (such as & or Σ) because they're replaced by their respective characters and included in a text node.

- *Notation node*: a DTD-declared notation. A parser that reads the DTD attaches a map of notation nodes (indexed by notation name) to the document type node. Each notation node has a name and a public identifier or a system identifier, whichever identifier was used to declare the notation in the DTD. Notation nodes don't have children.

- *Processing-instruction node*: a processing instruction that appears in the document. It has a name (the instruction's target), a string value (the instruction's data), and a parent (its containing node).

- *Text node*: document content. Its name is #text and it represents a portion of an element's content when an intervening node (such as a comment) must be created. Characters such as < and & that are represented in the document via character references are replaced by the literal characters they represent. When these nodes are written to a document, these characters must be escaped.

Although these node types store considerable information about an XML document, there are limitations, such as not exposing whitespace outside of the root element. Also, most DTD or schema information, such as element types (`<!ELEMENT...>`) and attribute types (`<xs:attribute...>`), cannot be accessed through the DOM.

DOM Level 3 addresses some of the DOM's various limitations. For example, although DOM doesn't provide a node type for the XML declaration, DOM Level 3 makes it possible to access the XML declaration's version, encoding, and standalone attribute values via attributes of the document node.

Note   Nonroot nodes never exist in isolation. For example, it's never the case for an element node to not belong to a document or to a document fragment. Even when such nodes are disconnected from the main tree, they remain aware of the document or document fragment to which they belong.

Exploring the DOM API

Java implements DOM through the javax.xml.parsers package's abstract DocumentBuilder and DocumentBuilderFactory classes and the nonabstract FactoryConfigurationError and ParserConfigurationException classes. The org. w3c.dom, org.w3c.dom.bootstrap, org.w3c.dom.events, org.w3c.dom.ls, org.w3c. dom.ranges, org.w3c.dom.traversal, and org.w3c.dom.views packages provide various types that augment this implementation.

Obtaining a DOM Parser/Document Builder

A DOM parser is also known as a *document builder* because of its dual role in parsing and creating XML documents. You obtain a DOM parser/document builder by first instantiating DocumentBuilderFactory, by calling one of its newInstance() class methods. For example, the following code fragment invokes DocumentBuilderFactory's DocumentBuilderFactory newInstance() class method:

```
DocumentBuilderFactory dbf =
   DocumentBuilderFactory.newInstance();
```

Behind the scenes, newInstance() follows an ordered lookup procedure to identify the DocumentBuilderFactory implementation class to load. This procedure first examines the javax.xml.parsers.DocumentBuilderFactory system property and lastly chooses the Java platform's default DocumentBuilderFactory implementation class when no other class is found. If an implementation class isn't available (perhaps the class identified by the `javax.xml.parsers.DocumentBuilderFactory` system property doesn't exist) or cannot be instantiated, `newInstance()` throws an instance of the `FactoryConfigurationError` class. Otherwise, it instantiates the class and returns its instance.

After obtaining a `DocumentBuilderFactory` instance, you can call various configuration methods to configure the factory. For example, you could call `DocumentBuilderFactory`'s `void setNamespaceAware(boolean awareness)` method with a `true` argument to tell the factory that any returned document builder must provide support for XML namespaces. You can also call `void setValidating(boolean validating)` with `true` as the argument to validate documents against their DTDs or call `void setSchema(Schema schema)` to validate documents against the `javax.xml.validation.Schema` instance identified by `schema`.

VALIDATION API

Schema is a member of Java's Validation API, which decouples document parsing from validation, making it easier for applications to take advantage of specialized validation libraries that support additional schema languages (such as Relax NG—see `http://en.wikipedia.org/wiki/RELAX_NG`), and making it easier to specify the location of a schema.

The Validation API is associated with the `javax.xml.validation` package, which also includes `SchemaFactory`, `SchemaFactoryLoader`, `TypeInfoProvider`, `Validator`, and `ValidatorHandler`. Schema is the central class and represents an immutable in-memory representation of a grammar.

DOM supports the Validation API via `DocumentBuilderFactory`'s `void setSchema(Schema schema)` and `Schema getSchema()` methods. Similarly, SAX supports Validation via `javax.xml.parsers.SAXParserFactory`'s `void setSchema(Schema schema)` and `Schema getSchema()` methods.

The following code fragment demonstrates the Validation API in a DOM context:

```
// Parse an XML document into a DOM tree.
DocumentBuilder parser =
    DocumentBuilderFactory.newInstance().newDocumentBuilder();
Document document = parser.parse(new File("instance.xml"));
```

```
// Create a SchemaFactory capable of understanding W3C XML Schema (WXS).
SchemaFactory factory =
    SchemaFactory.newInstance(XMLConstants.W3C_XML_SCHEMA_NS_URI);
// Load a WXS schema, represented by a Schema instance.
Source schemaFile = new StreamSource(new File("mySchema.xsd"));
Schema schema = factory.newSchema(schemaFile);
// Create a Validator instance, which is used to validate an XML document.
Validator validator = schema.newValidator();
// Validate the DOM tree.
try
{
    validator.validate(new DOMSource(document));
}
catch (SAXException saxe)
{
    // XML document is invalid!
}
```

This example refers to XSLT types such as Source. I explore XSLT in Chapter 6.

After the factory has been configured, call its DocumentBuilder newDocumentBuilder() method to return a document builder that supports the configuration, as demonstrated here:

```
DocumentBuilder db = dbf.newDocumentBuilder();
```

If a document builder cannot be returned (perhaps the factory cannot create a document builder that supports XML namespaces), this method throws a ParserConfigurationException instance.

Parsing and Creating XML Documents

Assuming that you've successfully obtained a document builder, what happens next depends on whether you want to parse or create an XML document.

DocumentBuilder provides several overloaded parse() methods for parsing an XML document into a node tree. These methods differ in how they obtain the document. For example, Document parse(String uri) parses the document that's identified by its string-based URI argument.

Note   Each parse() method throws java.lang.IllegalArgumentException when null is passed as the method's first argument, java.io.IOException when an input/output error occurs, and org.xml.sax.SAXException when the document cannot be parsed. This last exception type indicates that DocumentBuilder's parse() methods rely on SAX to take care of the actual parsing work. Because they are more involved in building the node tree, DOM parsers are commonly referred to as *document builders*.

DocumentBuilder also declares the abstract Document newDocument() method for creating a DOM tree.

The returned org.w3c.dom.Document object provides access to a parsed document through methods such as DocumentType getDoctype(), which makes the document type declaration available through the org.w3c.dom.DocumentType interface. Conceptually, Document is the root of the document's node tree. It also declares various "create" and other methods for creating a node tree. For example, Element createElement(String tagName) creates an element named by tagName, returning a new org.w3c.dom.Element object with the specified name but with its local name, prefix, and namespace URI set to null.

Note   Apart from DocumentBuilder, DocumentBuilderFactory, and a few other classes, DOM is based on interfaces, of which Document and DocumentType are examples. Behind the scenes, DOM methods (such as the parse() methods) return objects whose classes implement these interfaces.

Document and all other org.w3c.dom interfaces that describe different kinds of nodes are subinterfaces of the org.w3c.dom.Node interface. As such, they inherit Node's constants and methods.

Node declares 12 constants that represent the various kinds of nodes; ATTRIBUTE_NODE and ELEMENT_NODE are examples. To identify the kind of node represented by a given Node object, call Node's short getNodeType() method and compare the returned value to one of these constants.

Note   The rationale for using getNodeType() and these constants, instead of using instanceof and a class name, is that DOM (the object model, not the Java DOM API) was designed to be language independent, and languages such as AppleScript don't have the equivalent of instanceof.

Node declares several methods for getting and setting common node properties. These methods include String getNodeName(), String getLocalName(), String getNamespaceURI(), String getPrefix(), void setPrefix(String prefix), String getNodeValue(), and void setNodeValue(String nodeValue), which let you get and (for some properties) set a node's name (such as #text), local name, namespace URI, prefix, and normalized string value.

Note   Various Node methods (such as setPrefix() and getNodeValue()) throw an instance of the org.w3c.dom.DOMException class when something goes wrong. For example, setPrefix() throws this exception when the prefix argument contains an illegal character, the node is read-only, or the argument is malformed. Similarly, getNodeValue() throws DOMException when getNodeValue() would return more characters than can fit into a DOMString (a W3C type) variable on the implementation platform. DOMException declares a series of constants (such as DOMSTRING_SIZE_ERR) that classify the reason for the exception.

Node declares several methods for navigating the node tree. Three of its navigation methods are described here:

- boolean hasChildNodes() returns true when a node has child nodes.
- Node getFirstChild() returns the node's first child.
- Node getLastChild() returns the node's last child.

For nodes with multiple children, you'll find the NodeList getChildNodes() method to be handy. This method returns an org.w3c.dom.NodeList instance whose int getLength() method returns the number of nodes in the list and whose Node item(int index) method returns the node at the indexth position in the list (or null when index's value isn't valid—it's less than zero or greater than or equal to getLength()'s value).

Node declares four methods for modifying the tree by inserting, removing, replacing, and appending child nodes:

- Node insertBefore(Node newChild, Node refChild) inserts newChild before the existing node specified by refChild and returns newChild.

- Node removeChild(Node oldChild) removes the child node identified by oldChild from the tree and returns oldChild.

- Node replaceChild(Node newChild, Node oldChild) replaces oldChild with newChild and returns oldChild.

- Node appendChild(Node newChild) adds newChild to the end of the current node's child nodes and returns newChild.

Finally, Node declares several utility methods, including Node cloneNode(boolean deep) (create and return a duplicate of the current node, recursively cloning its subtree when true is passed to deep), and void normalize() (descend the tree from the given node and merge all adjacent text nodes, deleting those text nodes that are empty).

Tip   To obtain an element node's attributes, first call Node's NamedNodeMap getAttributes() method. This method returns an org.w3c.dom. NamedNodeMap implementation when the node represents an element; otherwise, it returns null. As well as declaring methods for accessing these nodes by name (such as Node getNamedItem(String name)), NamedNodeMap declares int getLength() and Node item(int index) methods for returning all attribute nodes by index. You would then obtain the Node's name by calling a method such as getNodeName().

In addition to inheriting Node's constants and methods, Document declares its own methods. For example, you can call Document's String getXmlEncoding(), boolean getXmlStandalone(), and String getXmlVersion() methods to return the XML declaration's encoding, standalone, and version attribute values, respectively.

Document declares three methods for locating one or more elements:

- Element getElementById(String elementId) returns the element that has an id attribute (as in <img id=...>) matching the value specified by elementId.

- NodeList getElementsByTagName(String tagname) returns a nodelist of a document's elements (in document order) matching the specified tagName.

- NodeList getElementsByTagNameNS(String namespaceURI, String localName) is equivalent to the second method except in adding to the nodelist only those elements matching localName and namespaceURI values. Pass "*" to namespaceURI to match all namespaces; pass "*" to localName to match all local names.

The returned element node and each element node in the list implement the Element interface. This interface declares methods to return nodelists of descendent elements in the tree, attributes associated with the element, and more. For example, String getAttribute(String name) returns the value of the attribute identified by name, whereas Attr getAttributeNode(String name) returns an attribute node by name. The returned node is an implementation of the org.w3c.dom.Attr interface.

Demonstrating the DOM API

You now have enough information to explore applications for parsing and creating XML documents. This section shows you how to accomplish these tasks.

Parsing an XML Document

Listing 3-1 presents the source code to a DOM-based parsing application that briefly demonstrates how to parse an XML document into a DOM tree.

Listing 3-1. DOMDemo (Version 1)

```java
import java.io.IOException;

import javax.xml.parsers.DocumentBuilder;
import javax.xml.parsers.DocumentBuilderFactory;
import javax.xml.parsers.FactoryConfigurationError;
import javax.xml.parsers.ParserConfigurationException;

import org.w3c.dom.Attr;
import org.w3c.dom.Document;
import org.w3c.dom.Element;
import org.w3c.dom.NamedNodeMap;
import org.w3c.dom.Node;
import org.w3c.dom.NodeList;

import org.xml.sax.SAXException;

import static java.lang.System.*;

public class DOMDemo
{
   public static void main(String[] args)
   {
      if (args.length != 1)
      {
         err.println("usage: java DOMDemo xmlfile");
         return;
      }
      try
      {
         DocumentBuilderFactory dbf =
            DocumentBuilderFactory.newInstance();
         dbf.setNamespaceAware(true);
         DocumentBuilder db = dbf.newDocumentBuilder();
         Document doc = db.parse(args[0]);
```

```java
      out.printf("Version = %s%n", doc.getXmlVersion());
      out.printf("Encoding = %s%n", doc.getXmlEncoding());
      out.printf("Standalone = %b%n%n", doc.getXmlStandalone());
      if (doc.hasChildNodes())
      {
         NodeList nl = doc.getChildNodes();
         for (int i = 0; i < nl.getLength(); i++)
         {
            Node node = nl.item(i);
            if (node.getNodeType() == Node.ELEMENT_NODE)
               dump((Element) node);
         }
      }
   }
   catch (IOException ioe)
   {
      err.printf("IOE: %s%n", ioe.toString());
   }
   catch (SAXException saxe)
   {
      err.printf("SAXE: %s%n", saxe.toString());
   }
   catch (FactoryConfigurationError fce)
   {
      err.printf("FCE: %s%n", fce.toString());
   }
   catch (ParserConfigurationException pce)
   {
      err.printf("PCE: %s%n", pce.toString());
   }
}
```

```java
static void dump(Element e)
{
   out.printf("Element: %s, %s, %s, %s%n",
              e.getNodeName(), e.getLocalName(),
              e.getPrefix(), e.getNamespaceURI());
   NamedNodeMap nnm = e.getAttributes();
   if (nnm != null)
      for (int i = 0; i < nnm.getLength(); i++)
      {
         Node node = nnm.item(i) ;
         Attr attr = e.getAttributeNode(node.getNodeName());
         out.printf("  Attribute %s = %s%n",
                    attr.getName(), attr.getValue());
      }
   NodeList nl = e.getChildNodes();
   for (int i = 0; i < nl.getLength(); i++)
   {
      Node node = nl.item(i);
      if (node instanceof Element)
         dump((Element) node);
   }
}
}
```

DOMDemo's main() method first verifies that one command-line argument (the name of an XML document) has been specified. It then creates a document builder factory, informs the factory that it wants a namespace-aware document builder, and has the factory return this document builder.

Continuing, main() parses the document into a node tree; outputs the XML declaration's version number, encoding, and standalone attribute values; and recursively dumps all element nodes (starting with the root node) and their attribute values.

Notice the use of getNodeType() in one part of this listing and instanceof in another part. The getNodeType() method call isn't necessary (it's only present for demonstration) because instanceof can be used instead. However, the cast from Node type to Element type in the dump() method calls is necessary.

Compile Listing 3-1 as follows:

```
javac DOMDemo.java
```

Run the resulting application to dump Listing 1-3's article XML content, as follows:

```
java DOMDemo article.xml
```

You should observe the following output:

```
Version = 1.0
Encoding = null
Standalone = false

Element: article, article, null, null
  Attribute lang = en
  Attribute title = The Rebirth of JavaFX
Element: abstract, abstract, null, null
Element: code, code, null, null
Element: body, body, null, null
```

Each Element-prefixed line presents the node name, followed by the local name, followed by the namespace prefix, followed by the namespace URI. The node and local names are identical because namespaces aren't being used. For the same reason, the namespace prefix and namespace URI are null.

Continuing, execute the following command to dump Listing 1-5's recipe content:

```
java DOMDemo recipe.xml
```

This time, you observe the following output, which includes namespace information:

```
Version = 1.0
Encoding = null
Standalone = false

Element: h:html, html, h, http://www.w3.org/1999/xhtml
  Attribute xmlns:h = http://www.w3.org/1999/xhtml
  Attribute xmlns:r = http://www.javajeff.ca/
Element: h:head, head, h, http://www.w3.org/1999/xhtml
Element: h:title, title, h, http://www.w3.org/1999/xhtml
Element: h:body, body, h, http://www.w3.org/1999/xhtml
```

```
Element: r:recipe, recipe, r, http://www.javajeff.ca/
Element: r:title, title, r, http://www.javajeff.ca/
Element: r:ingredients, ingredients, r, http://www.javajeff.ca/
Element: h:ul, ul, h, http://www.w3.org/1999/xhtml
Element: h:li, li, h, http://www.w3.org/1999/xhtml
Element: r:ingredient, ingredient, r, http://www.javajeff.ca/
  Attribute qty = 2
Element: h:li, li, h, http://www.w3.org/1999/xhtml
Element: r:ingredient, ingredient, r, http://www.javajeff.ca/
Element: h:li, li, h, http://www.w3.org/1999/xhtml
Element: r:ingredient, ingredient, r, http://www.javajeff.ca/
  Attribute qty = 2
Element: h:p, p, h, http://www.w3.org/1999/xhtml
Element: r:instructions, instructions, r, http://www.javajeff.ca/
```

Creating an XML Document

Listing 3-2 presents another version of the DOMDemo application that briefly demonstrates the creation of a DOM tree.

Listing 3-2. DOMDemo (Version 2)

```
import javax.xml.parsers.DocumentBuilder;
import javax.xml.parsers.DocumentBuilderFactory;
import javax.xml.parsers.FactoryConfigurationError;
import javax.xml.parsers.ParserConfigurationException;

import org.w3c.dom.Document;
import org.w3c.dom.Element;
import org.w3c.dom.Node;
import org.w3c.dom.NodeList;
import org.w3c.dom.Text;

import static java.lang.System.*;
```

```java
public class DOMDemo
{
    public static void main(String[] args)
    {
        try
        {
            DocumentBuilderFactory dbf =
                DocumentBuilderFactory.newInstance();
            DocumentBuilder db = dbf.newDocumentBuilder();
            Document doc = db.newDocument();
            // Create the root element.
            Element root = doc.createElement("movie");
            doc.appendChild(root);
            // Create name child element and add it to the
            // root.
            Element name = doc.createElement("name");
            root.appendChild(name);
            // Add a text element to the name element.
            Text text = doc.createTextNode("Le Fabuleux " +
                                           "Destin d'Amélie " +
                                           "Poulain");
            name.appendChild(text);
            // Create language child element and add it to the
            // root.
            Element language = doc.createElement("language");
            root.appendChild(language);
            // Add a text element to the language element.
            text = doc.createTextNode("français");
            language.appendChild(text);
            out.printf("Version = %s%n", doc.getXmlVersion());
            out.printf("Encoding = %s%n",
                        doc.getXmlEncoding());
            out.printf("Standalone = %b%n%n",
                        doc.getXmlStandalone());
            NodeList nl = doc.getChildNodes();
```

```java
      for (int i = 0; i < nl.getLength(); i++)
      {
         Node node = nl.item(i);
         if (node.getNodeType() == Node.ELEMENT_NODE)
            dump((Element) node);
      }
   }
   catch (FactoryConfigurationError fce)
   {
      err.printf("FCE: %s%n", fce.toString());
   }
   catch (ParserConfigurationException pce)
   {
      err.printf("PCE: %s%n", pce.toString());
   }
}

static void dump(Element e)
{
   out.printf("Element: %s, %s, %s, %s%n",
               e.getNodeName(), e.getLocalName(),
               e.getPrefix(), e.getNamespaceURI());
   NodeList nl = e.getChildNodes();
   for (int i = 0; i < nl.getLength(); i++)
   {
      Node node = nl.item(i);
      if (node instanceof Element)
         dump((Element) node);
      else
      if (node instanceof Text)
         out.printf("Text: %s%n", ((Text) node).getWholeText());
   }
}
}
```

DOMDemo creates Listing 1-2's movie document. It uses Document's createElement() method to create the root movie element and movie's name and language child elements. It also uses Document's Text createTextNode(String data) method to create text nodes that are attached to the name and language nodes. Notice the calls to Node's appendChild() method, to append child nodes (such as name) to parent nodes (such as movie).

After creating this tree, DOMDemo outputs the tree's element nodes and other information. This output appears as follows:

```
Version = 1.0
Encoding = null
Standalone = false

Element: movie, null, null, null
Element: name, null, null, null
Text: Le Fabuleux Destin d'Amélie Poulain
Element: language, null, null, null
Text: français
```

There's one problem with the output: the XML declaration's encoding attribute hasn't been set to ISO-8859-1. You cannot accomplish this task via the DOM API. Instead, you need to use the XSLT API. While exploring XSLT in Chapter 6, you'll learn how to set the encoding attribute, and you'll also learn how to output this tree to an XML document file.

Working with Load and Save

Before DOM Level 3, there was no standard way to load XML content into a new DOM tree and save an existing DOM tree to an XML document. The World Wide Web Consortium (W3C) responded to this deficiency by developing the DOM Level 3 Load and Save Specification (www.w3.org/TR/DOM-Level-3-LS/), which adds this support. Although this capability might not seem like much, additional capabilities such as filtering data during a load operation have also been included.

Java supports the DOM Level 3 Load and Save Specification via the org.w3c.dom.ls package and its interface types:

- DOMImplementationLS contains factory methods for creating Load and Save objects.

- LSInput represents an input source for data.

- LSLoadEvent represents a load event object that signals the completion of a document load.

- LSOutput represents an output destination for data.

- LSParser provides an interface to an object that is able to build, or augment, a DOM tree from various input sources.

- LSParserFilter provides applications with the ability to examine nodes as they are being constructed while parsing.

- LSProgressEvent represents a progress event object that notifies the application about progress as a document is parsed.

- LSResourceResolver provides a way for applications to redirect references to external resources.

- LSSerializer provides an API for serializing (writing) a DOM document to an XML document.

- LSSerializerFilter provides applications with the ability to examine nodes as they are being serialized and decide what nodes should be serialized (or not).

This API reveals that load operations rely on a parser and save operations rely on a serializer.

This package also provides the LSException class, which describes an exception that's thrown when processing stops because of a DOM error during a parse or write operation.

Loading an XML Document into a DOM Tree

Listing 3-3 presents a third version of the DOMDemo application that uses Load and Save to load an XML document into a new DOM tree.

Listing 3-3. DOMDemo (Version 3)

```java
import org.w3c.dom.Attr;
import org.w3c.dom.Document;
import org.w3c.dom.Element;
import org.w3c.dom.NamedNodeMap;
import org.w3c.dom.Node;
import org.w3c.dom.NodeList;

import org.w3c.dom.bootstrap.DOMImplementationRegistry;

import org.w3c.dom.ls.DOMImplementationLS;
import org.w3c.dom.ls.LSParser;

import static java.lang.System.*;

public class DOMDemo
{
   public static void main(String[] args) throws Exception
   {
      if (args.length != 1)
      {
         err.println("usage: java DOMDemo xmlfile");
         return;
      }
      DOMImplementationLS ls = (DOMImplementationLS)
         DOMImplementationRegistry.newInstance().
         getDOMImplementation("LS");
      if (ls == null)
      {
         err.println("load and save not supported");
         return;
      }
      LSParser parser =
         ls.createLSParser(DOMImplementationLS.
                           MODE_SYNCHRONOUS, null);
      Document doc = parser.parseURI(args[0]);
      if (doc.hasChildNodes())
```

```java
    {
       NodeList nl = doc.getChildNodes();
       for (int i = 0; i < nl.getLength(); i++)
       {
          Node node = nl.item(i);
          if (node.getNodeType() == Node.ELEMENT_NODE)
             dump((Element) node);
       }
    }
  }

  static void dump(Element e)
  {
     out.printf("Element: %s, %s, %s, %s%n",
                 e.getNodeName(), e.getLocalName(),
                 e.getPrefix(), e.getNamespaceURI());
     NamedNodeMap nnm = e.getAttributes();
     if (nnm != null)
        for (int i = 0; i < nnm.getLength(); i++)
        {
           Node node = nnm.item(i);
           Attr attr =
              e.getAttributeNode(node.getNodeName());
           out.printf("  Attribute %s = %s%n",
                       attr.getName(), attr.getValue());
        }
     NodeList nl = e.getChildNodes();
     for (int i = 0; i < nl.getLength(); i++)
     {
        Node node = nl.item(i);
        if (node instanceof Element)
           dump((Element) node);
     }
  }
}
```

DOMDemo's main() method first validates the command line, which requires that only a single argument (the name of an XML file) be specified. main() then creates a DOMImplementationLS object, as follows:

1. It invokes org.w3c.dom.bootstrap.
   DOMImplementationRegistry's static
   DOMImplementationRegistry newInstance() method to obtain a
   DOMImplementationRegistry object.

2. It invokes DOMImplementationRegistry's DOMImplementation
   getDOMImplementation(String features) method on the
   previously returned DOMImplementationRegistry object to obtain
   an object from a class that implements the DOMImplementation
   interface. The string "LS" is passed to getDOMImplementation()
   because a DOMImplementation instance supporting Load and Save
   (DOMImplementationLS) is required. This method returns null
   when an implementation with the desired features isn't found.
   (For brevity, I omit checking for null in subsequent "Load and
   Save" examples.)

3. It casts the returned org.w3c.dom.DOMImplementation instance
   to a DOMImplementationLS instance, which is allowable because
   getDOMImplementation() returns an object whose class
   implements DOMImplementation and DOMImplementationLS.

main() next invokes DOMImplementationLS's LSParser createLSParser
(short mode, String schemaType) method to create a new LSParser object.
DOMImplementationLS.MODE_SYNCHRONOUS is passed to mode to cause the application
to wait until parsing is finished. null is passed to schemaType so that the created
LSParser can work with any kind of schema (although none is being used in this
example).

LSParser provides a Document parseURI(String uri) method for parsing an XML
document located at the specified uri value. main() calls this method to perform the
parse and return a Document, which is subsequently dumped to the standard output.

Note LSParser also provides Document parse(LSInput input) and
Node parseWithContext(LSInput input, Node contextArg, short
action) methods for parsing. The former method takes an LSInput argument,
which can represent a public identifier, a system identifier, a byte stream (possibly
with a specified encoding), a base URI, or a character stream. The latter method
lets you parse one XML document into another XML document. The value passed
to action determines whether the new content precedes, follows, or replaces
existing content.

Compile Listing 3-3 and run it against Listing 1-1's recipe.xml document. You
should observe the following output:

```
Element: recipe, recipe, null, null
Element: title, title, null, null
Element: ingredients, ingredients, null, null
Element: ingredient, ingredient, null, null
  Attribute qty = 2
Element: ingredient, ingredient, null, null
Element: ingredient, ingredient, null, null
  Attribute qty = 2
Element: instructions, instructions, null, null
```

Configuring a Parser

The LSParser interface declares a DOMConfiguration getDomConfig() method that
returns the org.w3c.dom.DOMConfiguration object used when parsing an input source.
You can use the DOMConfiguration object to configure the parser before parsing an XML
document.

DOMConfiguration declares the void setParameter(String name, Object value)
method for setting the value of a configuration parameter. Supported parameter names
and values are described in DOMConfiguration's Javadoc.

Several parameters deal with validation. For example, validation requires that the
parser validate the document against a schema (such as XML Schema or DTD), but only
when this parameter is set to true (it defaults to false). Listing 3-4 presents a DOMDemo
application that configures the parser to validate.

Listing 3-4. DOMDemo (Version 4)

```java
import org.w3c.dom.Attr;
import org.w3c.dom.Document;
import org.w3c.dom.DOMConfiguration;
import org.w3c.dom.Element;
import org.w3c.dom.NamedNodeMap;
import org.w3c.dom.Node;
import org.w3c.dom.NodeList;

import org.w3c.dom.bootstrap.DOMImplementationRegistry;

import org.w3c.dom.ls.DOMImplementationLS;
import org.w3c.dom.ls.LSParser;

import static java.lang.System.*;

public class DOMDemo
{
    public static void main(String[] args) throws Exception
    {
        if (args.length != 1)
        {
            err.println("usage: java DOMDemo xmlfile");
            return;
        }
        DOMImplementationLS ls = (DOMImplementationLS)
            DOMImplementationRegistry.newInstance().
            getDOMImplementation("LS");
        LSParser parser =
            ls.createLSParser(DOMImplementationLS.
                              MODE_SYNCHRONOUS, null);
        DOMConfiguration config = parser.getDomConfig();
        config.setParameter("validate", Boolean.TRUE);
        Document doc = parser.parseURI(args[0]);
        if (doc.hasChildNodes())
        {
            NodeList nl = doc.getChildNodes();
```

```java
        for (int i = 0; i < nl.getLength(); i++)
        {
            Node node = nl.item(i);
            if (node.getNodeType() == Node.ELEMENT_NODE)
                dump((Element) node);
        }
    }
}

static void dump(Element e)
{
    out.printf("Element: %s, %s, %s, %s%n",
                e.getNodeName(), e.getLocalName(),
                e.getPrefix(), e.getNamespaceURI());
    NamedNodeMap nnm = e.getAttributes();
    if (nnm != null)
        for (int i = 0; i < nnm.getLength(); i++)
        {
            Node node = nnm.item(i);
            Attr attr =
                e.getAttributeNode(node.getNodeName());
            out.printf("  Attribute %s = %s%n",
                        attr.getName(), attr.getValue());
        }
    NodeList nl = e.getChildNodes();
    for (int i = 0; i < nl.getLength(); i++)
    {
        Node node = nl.item(i);
        if (node instanceof Element)
            dump((Element) node);
    }
}
}
```

DOMDemo executes `DOMConfiguration config = parser.getDomConfig();` followed by `config.setParameter("validate", Boolean.TRUE);` to configure the parser to perform validation.

Compile the source code. Before running the application, you'll need a suitable XML file. Listing 3-5 offers a suitable candidate.

Listing 3-5. An Invalid Recipe Document

```
<?xml version="1.0"?>
<!DOCTYPE recipe [
   <!ELEMENT recipe (title, ingredients, instructions)>
   <!ELEMENT title (#PCDATA)>
   <!ELEMENT ingredients (ingredient+)>
   <!ELEMENT ingredient (#PCDATA)>
   <!ELEMENT instructions (#PCDATA)>
   <!ATTLIST ingredient qty CDATA "1">
]>
<recipe>
   <title>
      Grilled Cheese Sandwich
   </title>
   <instructions>
      Place frying pan on element and select medium heat.
      For each bread slice, smear one pat of margarine on
      one side of bread slice. Place cheese slice between
      bread slices with margarine-smeared sides away from
      the cheese. Place sandwich in frying pan with one
      margarine-smeared side in contact with pan. Fry for
      a couple of minutes and flip. Fry other side for a
      minute and serve.
   </instructions>
   <ingredients>
      <ingredient qty="2">
         bread slice
      </ingredient>
      <ingredient>
```

```
      cheese slice
   </ingredient>
   <ingredient qty="2">
      margarine pat
   </ingredient>
   </ingredients>
</recipe>
```

Listing 3-5 presents the contents of a recipe document that's similar to the abbreviated recipe content presented in Listing 1-8 (see Chapter 1). However, there is a crucial difference: I've placed the instructions element before the ingredients element, which violates the document's internal DTD.

Run DOMDemo against a recipe.xml file containing this content, and you should observe the following output:

```
[Error] recipe.xml:35:10: The content of element type "recipe" must match
"(title,ingredients,instructions)".
Element: recipe, recipe, null, null
Element: title, title, null, null
Element: instructions, instructions, null, null
Element: ingredients, ingredients, null, null
Element: ingredient, ingredient, null, null
  Attribute qty = 2
Element: ingredient, ingredient, null, null
  Attribute qty = 1
Element: ingredient, ingredient, null, null
  Attribute qty = 2
```

You can use setParameter() to register a custom error handler with the parser, perhaps to log errors. Start by subclassing the org.w3c.dom.DOMErrorHandler class, overriding its boolean handleError(DOMError error) method:

```
public class ErrHandler implements DOMErrorHandler
{
   @Override
   public boolean handleError(DOMError error)
   {
```

```
      short severity = error.getSeverity();
      if (severity == error.SEVERITY_ERROR)
         System.out.printf("DOM3 error: %s%n",
                               error.getMessage());
      else
      if (severity == error.SEVERITY_FATAL_ERROR)
         System.out.printf("DOM3 fatal error: %s%n",
                               error.getMessage());
      else
      if (severity == error.SEVERITY_WARNING)
         System.out.printf("DOM3 warning: %s%n",
                               error.getMessage());
      return true;
   }
}
```

The org.w3c.dom.DOMError object passed to handleError() describes a DOM error. This interface declares three severity level constants: SEVERITY_ERROR, SEVERITY_FATAL_ ERROR, and SEVERITY_WARNING. It also declares short getSeverity() to return the severity level, and other useful methods.

The handleError() method returns false to inform the parser to stop as soon as possible or true to inform the parser to continue (depending on the error's severity level).

After instantiating the error handler subclass, register it with the parser by invoking setParameter() with "error-handler" as the name and an instance of the error handler subclass as the value:

```
DOMConfiguration config = parser.getDomConfig();
config.setParameter("error-handler", new ErrHandler());
```

Filtering an XML Document While Parsing

You can install a *filter* on an LSParser instance to determine what content to accept and what content to ignore while building a parse tree. A filter is an instance of the LSParserFilter interface and must implement the following methods:

- short acceptNode(Node node): This method is called after the XML content corresponding to node has been parsed. It returns LSParserFilter.FILTER_ACCEPT if the node should be included in the DOM tree, LSParserFilter.FILTER_REJECT if the node (and all of its children) should be rejected, LSParserFilter.FILTER_SKIP if the node should be skipped (all of its children are inserted in its place), or LSParserFilter.INTERRUPT if the filter wants to stop document processing (the node is rejected).

- int getWhatToShow(): Tell the parser what types of nodes to show to acceptNode(). Nodes that are not shown to the filter are automatically included in the DOM tree being built. It returns a bitwise ORed combination of org.w3c.dom.NodeFilter SHOW_-prefixed constants (e.g., SHOW_ELEMENT). Constants SHOW_ATTRIBUTE, SHOW_DOCUMENT, SHOW_DOCUMENT_TYPE, SHOW_NOTATION, SHOW_ENTITY, and SHOW_DOCUMENT_FRAGMENT are meaningless because such nodes are never passed to acceptNode().

- short startElement(Element e): The parser calls this method after element e's start tag is scanned but before the rest of the element is processed. The intent is to allow the element, including any children, to be efficiently skipped. Only element nodes are passed to startElement(), which returns the same constants as acceptNode().

Listing 3-6 presents a DOMDemo application that extends Listing 3-3 with a filter.

Listing 3-6. DOMDemo (Version 5)

```
import org.w3c.dom.Attr;
import org.w3c.dom.Document;
import org.w3c.dom.Element;
import org.w3c.dom.NamedNodeMap;
import org.w3c.dom.Node;
```

```java
import org.w3c.dom.NodeList;

import org.w3c.dom.bootstrap.DOMImplementationRegistry;

import org.w3c.dom.ls.DOMImplementationLS;
import org.w3c.dom.ls.LSParser;
import org.w3c.dom.ls.LSParserFilter;

import org.w3c.dom.traversal.NodeFilter;

import static java.lang.System.*;

class InputFilter implements LSParserFilter
{
    private boolean accept;

    InputFilter(boolean accept)
    {
        this.accept = accept;
    }

    @Override
    public short acceptNode(Node node)
    {
        return (accept) ? FILTER_ACCEPT : FILTER_REJECT;
    }

    @Override
    public int getWhatToShow()
    {
        return NodeFilter.SHOW_ELEMENT;
    }

    @Override
    public short startElement(Element e)
    {
        return LSParserFilter.FILTER_ACCEPT;
    }
}
```

```java
public class DOMDemo
{
   public static void main(String[] args) throws Exception
   {
      if (args.length != 2)
      {
         err.println("usage: java DOMDemo xmlfile " +
                     "accept|reject");
         return;
      }
      DOMImplementationLS ls = (DOMImplementationLS)
         DOMImplementationRegistry.newInstance().
         getDOMImplementation("LS");
      LSParser parser =
         ls.createLSParser(DOMImplementationLS.
                           MODE_SYNCHRONOUS, null);
      LSParserFilter filter =
         new InputFilter(args[1].equals("accept"));
      parser.setFilter(filter);
      Document doc = parser.parseURI(args[0]);
      if (doc.hasChildNodes())
      {
         NodeList nl = doc.getChildNodes();
         for (int i = 0; i < nl.getLength(); i++)
         {
            Node node = nl.item(i);
            if (node.getNodeType() == Node.ELEMENT_NODE)
               dump((Element) node);
         }
      }
   }
```

```
static void dump(Element e)
{
    out.printf("Element: %s, %s, %s, %s%n",
                e.getNodeName(), e.getLocalName(),
                e.getPrefix(), e.getNamespaceURI());
    NamedNodeMap nnm = e.getAttributes();
    if (nnm != null)
        for (int i = 0; i < nnm.getLength(); i++)
        {
            Node node = nnm.item(i);
            Attr attr =
                e.getAttributeNode(node.getNodeName());
            out.printf("  Attribute %s = %s%n",
                        attr.getName(), attr.getValue());
        }
    NodeList nl = e.getChildNodes();
    for (int i = 0; i < nl.getLength(); i++)
    {
        Node node = nl.item(i);
        if (node instanceof Element)
            dump((Element) node);
    }
}
}
```

This version of DOMDemo introduces an InputFilter class that extends
LSParserFilter. Its constructor saves an accept argument that tells the filter to accept
every node (when true) or reject every node (when false). The filter is registered with
the LSParser by calling this interface's void setFilter(LSParserFilter filter)
method.

Compile the listing and run the application with Listing 1-1's recipe.xml document
as follows:

```
java DOMDemo recipe.xml accept
```

You should observe the following output:

```
Element: recipe, recipe, null, null
Element: title, title, null, null
Element: ingredients, ingredients, null, null
Element: ingredient, ingredient, null, null
  Attribute qty = 2
Element: ingredient, ingredient, null, null
Element: ingredient, ingredient, null, null
  Attribute qty = 2
Element: instructions, instructions, null, null
```

Now, run the application as follows:

```
java DOMDemo recipe.xml reject
```

This time, you should observe the following output:

```
Element: recipe, recipe, null, null
```

You might be surprised that there is still some output, which reveals recipe as the element's name. Recall that recipe is the root element of the recipe.xml document. A DOM tree requires a root element, which is why this element isn't discarded.

Saving a DOM Tree to an XML Document

Listing 3-7 presents a sixth version of the DOMDemo application that uses Load and Save to save an existing DOM tree to an XML document.

Listing 3-7. DOMDemo (Version 6)

```
import org.w3c.dom.Document;

import org.w3c.dom.bootstrap.DOMImplementationRegistry;

import org.w3c.dom.ls.DOMImplementationLS;
import org.w3c.dom.ls.LSParser;
import org.w3c.dom.ls.LSSerializer;

import static java.lang.System.*;
```

```java
public class DOMDemo
{
    public static void main(String[] args) throws Exception
    {
        if (args.length != 1)
        {
            err.println("usage: java DOMDemo xmlfile");
            return;
        }
        DOMImplementationLS ls = (DOMImplementationLS)
            DOMImplementationRegistry.newInstance().
            getDOMImplementation("LS");
        LSParser parser =
            ls.createLSParser(DOMImplementationLS.
                            MODE_SYNCHRONOUS, null);
        Document doc = parser.parseURI(args[0]);
        LSSerializer serializer = ls.createLSSerializer();
        if (serializer.writeToURI(doc, "_" + args[0]))
            out.println("serialization successful");
    }
}
```

DOMDemo's main() method invokes DOMImplementationLS's LSSerializer createLSSerializer() method to create a new LSSerializer object.

LSSerializer provides a boolean writeToURI(Node node, String uri) method for serializing a DOM tree anchored in node to the XML document described by uri. This method returns true when serialization is successful.

main() calls writeToURI() to perform the serialization and displays a suitable message when serialization is successful.

Note LSSerializer also provides boolean write(Node node, LSOutput destination) and String writeToString(Node node) methods for serializing a DOM tree. The former method takes an LSOutput argument, which can represent a URI, a byte stream (possibly with a specified encoding), a base URI, or a character stream. The latter method lets you serialize a DOM tree to a string, which is returned.

Compile Listing 3-7 and run it against Listing 1-1's `recipe.xml` document. You should observe the following output:

```
serialization successful
```

You should also observe a `_recipe.xml` file containing a nearly identical version of `recipe.xml`'s content.

Note   You can configure an `LSSerializer` instance in an identical manner to configuring an `LSParser` instance. Also, you can filter what's serialized by installing an `LSSerializerFilter`-based filter instance via `LSSerializer`'s `void setFilter(LSSerializerFilter filter)` method.

Working with Traversal and Range

Iterating over a tree of nodes typically involves calling `Element`'s `getChildNodes()` method and using recursion to move down the tree. Listing 3-1 provides an example. It's also tedious to write code to perform a task on a range of nodes, such as deleting a node and its children. The W3C responded to this tedium by developing the DOM Level 2 Traversal and Range Specification (`www.w3.org/TR/2000/REC-DOM-Level-2-Traversal-Range-20001113/`), which adds this support.

Performing Traversals

Traversal lets you walk through a DOM tree and select specific nodes. Java supports Traversal via the `org.w3c.dom.traversal` package and its four interface types:

- `DocumentTraversal` contains methods that create `NodeIterator`s and `TreeWalker`s to traverse a node and its children.

- `NodeFilter` describes a filter for accepting or rejecting nodes.

- `NodeIterator` steps through a DOM tree's/subtree's nodes.

- `TreeWalker` also steps through a DOM tree's/subtree's nodes.

According to the specification, "NodeIterators and TreeWalkers are two different ways of representing the nodes of a document subtree and a position within the nodes they present. A NodeIterator presents a flattened view of the subtree as an ordered sequence of nodes, presented in document order. Because this view is presented without respect to hierarchy, iterators have methods to move forward and backward, but not to move up and down. Conversely, a TreeWalker maintains the hierarchical relationships of the subtree, allowing navigation of this hierarchy. In general, TreeWalkers are better for tasks in which the structure of the document around selected nodes will be manipulated, while NodeIterators are better for tasks that focus on the content of each selected node."

DocumentTraversal declares a pair of methods for obtaining a NodeIterator and a TreeWalker:

- NodeIterator createNodeIterator(Node root, int whatToShow, NodeFilter filter, boolean entityReferenceExpansion): Create a new NodeIterator over the subtree anchored at the specified root node.

- TreeWalker createTreeWalker(Node root, int whatToShow, NodeFilter filter, boolean entityReferenceExpansion): Create a new TreeWalker over the subtree anchored at the specified root node.

For either method, whatToShow is a bitwise ORed set of SHOW_-prefixed constants declared by the NodeFilter class. These constants determine what node types may appear in the logical view of the tree presented by the NodeIterator or TreeWalker object. Also, filter identifies a NodeFilter object for filtering out nodes, or is passed null when no filtering is desired. Finally, entityReferenceExpansion is passed true to expand entity reference nodes.

A DocumentTraversal object is obtained by casting a Document object to DocumentTraversal.

NodeFilter declares a short acceptNode(Node n) method that determines whether or not node n is visible in the *logical view* (a filtered sequence of nodes) provided by NodeIterator or TreeWalker. This method returns one of NodeFilter's FILTER_ACCEPT, FILTER_REJECT, or FILTER_SKIP constants. It's called by a NodeFilter or TreeWalker implementation.

NodeFilter declares several methods, including Node nextNode() and Node previousNode(), for returning the next or previous node and advancing forward or backward to the node beyond that node. Either method returns null when there are no more nodes to step through.

TreeWalker declares several methods, including Node firstChild() and Node lastChild(), for stepping to the first visible or last visible child, respectively, of the current node.

Listing 3-8 presents a seventh version of the DOMDemo application that uses NodeIterator to traverse an XML document. It's similar to (but shorter than) Listing 3-1.

Listing 3-8. DOMDemo (Version 7)

```
import java.io.IOException;

import javax.xml.parsers.DocumentBuilder;
import javax.xml.parsers.DocumentBuilderFactory;
import javax.xml.parsers.FactoryConfigurationError;
import javax.xml.parsers.ParserConfigurationException;

import org.w3c.dom.Attr;
import org.w3c.dom.Document;
import org.w3c.dom.DOMImplementation;
import org.w3c.dom.Element;
import org.w3c.dom.NamedNodeMap;
import org.w3c.dom.Node;

import org.w3c.dom.traversal.DocumentTraversal;
import org.w3c.dom.traversal.NodeFilter;
import org.w3c.dom.traversal.NodeIterator;

import org.xml.sax.SAXException;

import static java.lang.System.*;
```

```java
public class DOMDemo
{
    public static void main(String[] args)
    {
        if (args.length != 1)
        {
            err.println("usage: java DOMDemo xmlfile");
            return;
        }
        try
        {
            DocumentBuilderFactory dbf =
                DocumentBuilderFactory.newInstance();
            dbf.setNamespaceAware(true);
            DocumentBuilder db = dbf.newDocumentBuilder();
            DOMImplementation di = db.getDOMImplementation();
            if (!di.hasFeature("Traversal", "2.0"))
            {
                err.println("parser doesn't support " + "traversal");
                return;
            }
            Document doc = db.parse(args[0]);
            out.printf("Version = %s%n", doc.getXmlVersion());
            out.printf("Encoding = %s%n", doc.getXmlEncoding());
            out.printf("Standalone = %b%n%n", doc.getXmlStandalone());
            NodeIterator ni =
                ((DocumentTraversal) doc).
                createNodeIterator(doc.getDocumentElement(),
                                   NodeFilter.SHOW_ELEMENT,
                                   null, true);
            Node node = ni.nextNode();
```

```java
            while (node != null)
            {
               dump((Element) node);
               node = ni.nextNode();
            }
         }
         catch (IOException ioe)
         {
            err.printf("IOE: %s%n", ioe.toString());
         }
         catch (SAXException saxe)
         {
            err.printf("SAXE: %s%n", saxe.toString());
         }
         catch (FactoryConfigurationError fce)
         {
            err.printf("FCE: %s%n", fce.toString());
         }
         catch (ParserConfigurationException pce)
         {
            err.printf("PCE: %s%n", pce.toString());
         }
      }

      static void dump(Element e)
      {
         out.printf("Element: %s, %s, %s, %s%n",
                    e.getNodeName(), e.getLocalName(),
                    e.getPrefix(), e.getNamespaceURI());
         NamedNodeMap nnm = e.getAttributes();
         if (nnm != null)
            for (int i = 0; i < nnm.getLength(); i++)
            {
               Node node = nnm.item(i);
```

```
            Attr attr =
                e.getAttributeNode(node.getNodeName());
            out.printf("  Attribute %s = %s%n",
                    attr.getName(), attr.getValue());
        }
    }
}
```

The main() method demonstrates how to determine if the document builder supports Traversal or not. It obtains a DOMImplementation instance and invokes its boolean hasFeature(String feature, String version) method with "Traversal" passed to feature and "2.0" passed to version. This method returns true if the feature is supported. It's a good idea to check for support in case a document builder doesn't support Traversal.

Run this application against the article.xml file that was used with the first version of DOMDemo and you'll observe the same output.

Performing Range Operations

Range provides a convenient way to select, delete, extract, and insert a node into a range of nodes. Java supports Range via the org.w3c.dom.range package:

- DocumentRange is an interface that contains a method for creating a *range* (all of the content between a pair of boundary-points).

- Range is an interface that contains methods for describing a range and performing various range operations.

- RangeException is an exception class that describes range operation failure.

A boundary-point's position in a Document or DocumentFragment tree can be characterized by a node and an offset. The node is called the *container* of the boundary-point and of its position. The container and its ancestors are the *ancestor containers* of the boundary-point and of its position. The offset within the node is called the *offset* of the boundary-point and its position.

DocumentRange declares the Range createRange() method for creating a Range object. The returned Range has both of its boundary-points positioned at the beginning of the corresponding Document (before any content). The Range can be used only to select content associated with this Document or with DocumentFragments and Attrs for which this Document is the owner.

A DocumentRange object is obtained by casting a Document object to DocumentRange.

Range declares Node getEndContainer(), int getEndOffset(), Node getStartContainer(), and int getStartOffset() methods to describe a range. It also declares various operation methods, such as void deleteContents() and void selectNodeContents(Node refNode).

Various methods throw RangeException. For example, selectNodeContents() throws this exception when refNode or one of its ancestor nodes is an Entity, Notation, or DocumentType node.

Listing 3-9 presents a final version of the DOMDemo application that uses Range to delete the contents of the ingredients element in Listing 1-1's recipe.xml file.

Listing 3-9. DOMDemo (Version 8)

```
import javax.xml.parsers.DocumentBuilder;
import javax.xml.parsers.DocumentBuilderFactory;

import org.w3c.dom.Document;
import org.w3c.dom.DOMImplementation;
import org.w3c.dom.Element;

import org.w3c.dom.bootstrap.DOMImplementationRegistry;

import org.w3c.dom.ls.DOMImplementationLS;
import org.w3c.dom.ls.LSSerializer;

import org.w3c.dom.ranges.DocumentRange;
import org.w3c.dom.ranges.Range;

import static java.lang.System.*;

public class DOMDemo
{
    public static void main(String[] args) throws Exception
    {
```

```
DocumentBuilderFactory dbf =
    DocumentBuilderFactory.newInstance();
dbf.setNamespaceAware(true);
DocumentBuilder db = dbf.newDocumentBuilder();
DOMImplementation di = db.getDOMImplementation();
if (!di.hasFeature("Range", "2.0"))
{
    err.println("parser doesn't support range");
    return;
}
Document doc = db.parse("recipe.xml");
Range r = ((DocumentRange) doc).createRange();
Element root = doc.getDocumentElement();
r.selectNodeContents(root.getFirstChild().
                          getNextSibling().
                          getNextSibling().
                          getNextSibling());
r.deleteContents();
DOMImplementationLS ls = (DOMImplementationLS)
    DOMImplementationRegistry.newInstance().
    getDOMImplementation("LS");
LSSerializer serializer = ls.createLSSerializer();
if (serializer.writeToURI(doc, "_recipe.xml"))
    out.println("serialization successful");
    }
}
```

The main() method demonstrates how to determine if the document builder supports Range or not. It obtains a DOMImplementation instance and invokes its hasFeature() method with "Range" passed to feature and "2.0" passed to version. This method returns true if the feature is supported. It's a good idea to check for support in case a document builder doesn't support Range.

Run this application against Listing 1-1's `recipe.xml` file, and you should observe a `_recipe.xml` file with the following contents:

```
<?xml version="1.0" encoding="UTF-8"?><recipe>
   <title>
      Grilled Cheese Sandwich
   </title>
   <ingredients/>
   <instructions>
      Place frying pan on element and select medium heat.
      For each bread slice, smear one pat of margarine on
      one side of bread slice. Place cheese slice between
      bread slices with margarine-smeared sides away from
      the cheese. Place sandwich in frying pan with one
      margarine-smeared side in contact with pan. Fry for
      a couple of minutes and flip. Fry other side for a
      minute and serve.
   </instructions>
</recipe>
```

Notice the `<ingredients/>` empty-element tag, which proves that the `ingredients` element's three ingredient child elements have been deleted.

EXERCISES

The following exercises are designed to test your understanding of Chapter 3's content:

1. Define DOM.

2. True or false: Java 11 supports DOM Levels 1 and 2 only.

3. Identify the 12 types of DOM nodes.

4. How do you obtain a document builder?

5. How do you use a document builder to parse an XML document?

6. True or false: Document and all other `org.w3c.dom` interfaces that describe different kinds of nodes are subinterfaces of the Node interface.

7. How do you use a document builder to create a new XML document?

8. How would you determine if a node has children?

9. True or false: When creating a new XML document, you can use the DOM API to specify the XML declaration's `encoding` attribute.

10. What is the purpose of the Load and Save API?

11. What is the difference between `NodeIterator` and `TreeWalker`?

12. What is the difference between Range's `selectNode()` and `selectNodeContents()` methods?

13. Exercise 2-12 asked you to create a `DumpUserInfo` application that uses SAX to parse the user elements in an `example tomcat-users.xml` file and, for each user element, dump its `username`, `password`, and `roles` attribute values to standard output in a *key = value* format. Recreate this application to use DOM.

14. Create a `DOMSearch` application that's the equivalent of Exercise 2-13's `SAXSearch` application.

15. Create a `DOMValidate` application based on Listing 3-1's DOMDemo source code (plus one new line that enables validation) to validate Exercise 1-22's `books.xml` content against its DTD. Execute `java DOMValidate books.xml` to perform the validation. You should observe no errors. However, if you attempt to validate `books.xml` without the DTD, you should observe errors.

16. Extend Listing 3-4 to also include the custom error handler that was presented while discussing parser configuration.

Summary

Document Object Model (DOM) is a Java API for parsing an XML document into an in-memory tree of nodes and for creating an XML document from a node tree. After a DOM parser creates a tree, an application uses the DOM API to navigate over and extract infoset items from the tree's nodes.

DOM views an XML document as a tree that's composed of several kinds of nodes: attribute, CDATA section, comment, document, document fragment, document type, element, entity, entity reference, notation, processing instruction, and text.

A DOM parser is also known as a document builder because of its dual role in parsing and creating XML documents. You obtain a document builder by first instantiating `DocumentBuilderFactory`. You then invoke the factory's `newDocumentBuilder()` method to return the document builder.

Call one of the document builder's `parse()` methods to parse an XML document into a node tree. Call the various document builder methods that are prefixed with "`create`" (along with a few additional methods) to create an XML document.

Before DOM Level 3, there was no standard way to load XML content into a new DOM tree and save an existing DOM tree to an XML document. The W3C responded to this deficiency by developing the DOM Level 3 Load and Save Specification, which adds this support. Java supports the DOM Level 3 Load and Save Specification via the `org.w3c.dom.ls` package and its interface types.

Iterating over a tree of nodes typically involves calling `Element`'s `getChildNodes()` method and using recursion to move down the tree. It's also tedious to write code to perform a task on a range of nodes, such as deleting a node and its children. The W3C responded to this tedium by developing the DOM Level 2 Traversal and Range Specification. Traversal lets you walk through a DOM tree and select specific nodes. Range provides a convenient way to select, delete, extract, and insert a node into a range of nodes.

Chapter 4 introduces the StAX API for parsing/creating XML documents.

CHAPTER 4

Parsing and Creating XML Documents with StAX

Java also includes the StAX API for parsing and creating XML documents. Chapter 4 introduces you to StAX.

What Is StAX?

Streaming API for XML (StAX) is a Java API for parsing an XML document sequentially from start to finish and also for creating XML documents. StAX was introduced by Java 6 as an alternative to SAX and DOM and is located midway between these "polar opposites."

STAX VERSUS SAX AND DOM

Because Java already supports SAX and DOM for document parsing and DOM for document creation, you might be wondering why another XML API is needed. The following points justify StAX's presence in core Java:

- StAX (like SAX) can be used to parse documents of arbitrary sizes. In contrast, the maximum size of documents parsed by DOM is limited by the available memory, which makes DOM unsuitable for mobile devices with limited amounts of memory.

- StAX (like DOM) can be used to create documents. In contrast to DOM, which can create documents whose maximum size is constrained by available memory, StAX can create documents of arbitrary sizes. SAX cannot be used to create documents.

J. Friesen, *Java XML and JSON*, https://doi.org/10.1007/978-1-4842-4330-5_4

- StAX (like SAX) makes infoset items available to applications almost immediately. In contrast, these items are not made available by DOM until after it finishes building the tree of nodes.

- StAX (like DOM) adopts the *pull model,* in which the application tells the parser when it's ready to receive the next infoset item. This model is based on the iterator design pattern (see `http://sourcemaking.com/design_patterns/iterator`), which results in an application that's easier to write and debug. In contrast, SAX adopts the *push model,* in which the parser passes infoset items via events to the application, whether or not the application is ready to receive them. This model is based on the observer design pattern (see `http://sourcemaking.com/design_patterns/observer`), which results in an application that's often harder to write and debug.

Summing up, StAX can parse or create documents of arbitrary size, makes infoset items available to applications almost immediately, and uses the pull model to put the application in charge. Neither SAX nor DOM offers all of these advantages.

Exploring StAX

Java implements StAX through types stored in the `javax.xml.stream`, `javax.xml.stream.events`, and `javax.xml.stream.util` packages. This section introduces you to various types from the first two packages while showing you how to use StAX to parse and create XML documents.

STREAM-BASED VERSUS EVENT-BASED READERS AND WRITERS

StAX parsers are known as *document readers,* and StAX document creators are known as *document writers.* StAX classifies document readers and document writers as stream-based or event-based.

A *stream-based reader* extracts the next infoset item from an input stream via a *cursor* (infoset item pointer). Similarly, a *stream-based writer* writes the next infoset item to an output stream at the cursor position. The cursor can point to only one item at a time, and always moves forward, typically by one infoset item.

Stream-based readers and writers are appropriate when writing code for memory-constrained environments such as Java ME Embedded, because you can use them to create smaller and more efficient code. They also offer better performance for low-level libraries, where performance is important.

An *event-based reader* extracts the next infoset item from an input stream by obtaining an event. Similarly, an *event-based writer* writes the next infoset item to the stream by adding an event to the output stream. In contrast to stream-based readers and writers, event-based readers and writers have no concept of a cursor.

Event-based readers and writers are appropriate for creating XML processing *pipelines* (sequences of components that transform the previous component's input and pass the transformed output to the next component in the sequence), for modifying an event sequence, and more.

Parsing XML Documents

Document readers are obtained by calling the various "create" methods that are declared in the javax.xml.stream.XMLInputFactory class. These creational methods are organized into two categories: methods for creating stream-based readers and methods for creating event-based readers.

Before you can obtain a stream-based or an event-based reader, you need to obtain an instance of the factory by calling one of the newFactory() static methods, such as XMLInputFactory newFactory():

```
XMLInputFactory xmlif = XMLInputFactory.newFactory();
```

Note   You can also call the XMLInputFactory newInstance() static method but might not want to do so because its same-named but parameterized companion method has been deprecated to maintain API consistency, and it's possible that newInstance() will be deprecated as well.

The newFactory() methods follow an ordered lookup procedure to locate the XMLInputFactory implementation class. This procedure first examines the javax. xml.stream.XMLInputFactory system property and lastly returns the system-default implementation (returned from XMLInputFactory newDefaultFactory()). If there is a service configuration error, or if the implementation is not available or cannot be instantiated, the method throws an instance of the javax.xml.stream. FactoryConfigurationError class.

After creating the factory, call XMLInputFactory's void setProperty(String name, Object value) method to set various features and properties as necessary. For example, you might execute xmlif.setProperty(XMLInputFactory.IS_VALIDATING, true); (true is passed as a java.lang.Boolean object via *autoboxing*—see http://docs.oracle.com/ javase/tutorial/java/data/autoboxing.html) to request a DTD-validating stream-based reader. However, the default StAX factory implementation throws java.lang. IllegalArgumentException because it doesn't support DTD validation. Similarly, you might execute xmlif.setProperty(XMLInputFactory.IS_NAMESPACE_AWARE, true); to request a namespace-aware event-based reader, which is supported.

Parsing Documents with Stream-Based Readers

A stream-based reader is created by calling one of XMLInputFactory's createXMLStreamReader() methods, such as XMLStreamReader createXMLStreamReader(Reader reader). These methods throw javax.xml.stream. XMLStreamException when the stream-based reader cannot be created.

The following code fragment creates a stream-based reader whose source is a file named recipe.xml:

```
Reader reader = new FileReader("recipe.xml");
XMLStreamReader xmlsr = xmlif.createXMLStreamReader(reader);
```

The low-level javax.xml.stream.XMLStreamReader interface offers the most efficient way to read XML data with StAX. This interface's boolean hasNext() method returns true when there is a next infoset item to obtain; otherwise, it returns false. The int next() method advances the cursor by one infoset item and returns an integer code that identifies this item's type.

Instead of comparing next()'s return value with an integer value, you would compare this value against a javax.xml.stream.XMLStreamConstants infoset constant, such as START_ELEMENT or DTD—XMLStreamReader extends the XMLStreamConstants interface.

Note You can also obtain the type of the infoset item that the cursor is pointing to by calling XMLStreamReader's int getEventType() method. Specifying "Event" in the name of this method is unfortunate because it confuses stream-based readers with event-based readers.

The following code fragment uses the hasNext() and next() methods to codify a parsing loop that detects the start and end of each element:

```
while (xmlsr.hasNext())
{
   switch (xmlsr.next())
   {
      case XMLStreamReader.START_ELEMENT:
         // Do something at element start.
         break;

      case XMLStreamReader.END_ELEMENT:
         // Do something at element end.
   }
}
```

XMLStreamReader also declares various methods for extracting infoset information. For example, QName getName() returns the qualified name (as a javax.xml. namespace.QName instance) of the element at the cursor position when next() returns XMLStreamReader.START_ELEMENT or XMLStreamReader.END_ELEMENT.

Note QName describes a qualified name as a combination of namespace URI, local part, and prefix components. After instantiating this immutable class (via a constructor such as QName(String namespaceURI, String localPart, String prefix)), you can return these components by calling QName's String getNamespaceURI(), String getLocalPart(), and String getPrefix() methods.

Listing 4-1 presents the source code to a StAXDemo application that reports an XML document's start and end elements via a stream-based reader.

Listing 4-1. StAXDemo (Version 1)

```java
import java.io.FileNotFoundException;
import java.io.FileReader;

import javax.xml.stream.FactoryConfigurationError;
import javax.xml.stream.XMLInputFactory;
import javax.xml.stream.XMLStreamException;
import javax.xml.stream.XMLStreamReader;

import static java.lang.System.*;

public class StAXDemo
{
   public static void main(String[] args)
   {
      if (args.length != 1)
      {
         err.println("usage: java StAXDemo xmlfile");
         return;
      }
      try
      {
         XMLInputFactory xmlif = XMLInputFactory.newFactory();
         FileReader fr = new FileReader(args[0]);
         XMLStreamReader xmlsr = xmlif.createXMLStreamReader(fr);
         while (xmlsr.hasNext())
         {
            switch (xmlsr.next())
            {
               case XMLStreamReader.START_ELEMENT:
                  out.println("START_ELEMENT");
                  out.printf("  Qname = %s%n",
                             xmlsr.getName());
                  break;
```

```
         case XMLStreamReader.END_ELEMENT:
            out.println("END_ELEMENT");
            out.printf("   Qname = %s%n", xmlsr.getName());
      }
   }
}
catch (FactoryConfigurationError fce)
{
   err.printf("FCE: %s%n", fce.toString());
}
catch (FileNotFoundException fnfe)
{
   err.printf("FNFE: %s%n", fnfe.toString());
}
catch (XMLStreamException xmlse)
{
   err.printf("XMLSE: %s%n", xmlse.toString());
}
   }
}
```

After verifying the number of command-line arguments, Listing 4-1's main() method creates a factory, uses the factory to create a stream-based reader that obtains its XML data from the file identified by the solitary command-line argument, and enters a parsing loop. Whenever next() returns XMLStreamReader.START_ELEMENT or XMLStreamReader.END_ELEMENT, XMLStreamReader's getName() method is called to return the element's qualified name.

Compile Listing 4-1 as follows:

```
javac StAXDemo.java
```

Run the resulting application to dump Listing 1-2's movie XML content, as follows:

```
java StAXDemo movie.xml
```

You should observe the following output:

```
START_ELEMENT
  Qname = movie
START_ELEMENT
  Qname = name
END_ELEMENT
  Qname = name
START_ELEMENT
  Qname = language
END_ELEMENT
  Qname = language
END_ELEMENT
  Qname = movie
```

Note   XMLStreamReader declares a void close() method that you will want to call to free any resources associated with this stream-based reader when your application is designed to run for an extended period of time. Calling this method doesn't close the underlying input source.

Parsing Documents with Event-Based Readers

An event-based reader is created by calling one of XMLInputFactory's createXMLEventReader() methods, such as XMLEventReader createXMLEventReader(Reader reader). These methods throw XMLStreamException when the event-based reader cannot be created.

The following code fragment creates an event-based reader whose source is a file named recipe.xml:

```
Reader reader = new FileReader("recipe.xml");
XMLEventReader xmler = xmlif.createXMLEventReader(reader);
```

The high-level javax.xml.stream.XMLEventReader interface offers a somewhat less efficient but more object-oriented way to read XML data with StAX. This interface's boolean hasNext() method returns true when there is an event to obtain; otherwise, it returns false. The XMLEvent nextEvent() method returns the next event as an object whose class implements a subinterface of the javax.xml.stream.events.XMLEvent interface.

Note   XMLEvent is the base interface for handling markup events. It declares methods that apply to all subinterfaces; for example, Location getLocation() (return a javax.xml.stream.Location object whose int getCharacterOffset() and other methods return location information about the event) and int getEventType() (return the event type as an XMLStreamConstants infoset constant, such as START_ELEMENT and PROCESSING_INSTRUCTION—XMLEvent extends XMLStreamConstants). XMLEvent is subtyped by other javax.xml.stream.events interfaces that describe different kinds of events (such as Attribute) in terms of methods that return infoset item-specific information (such as Attribute's QName getName() and String getValue() methods).

The following code fragment uses the hasNext() and nextEvent() methods to codify a parsing loop that detects the start and end of an element:

```
while (xmler.hasNext())
{
   switch (xmler.nextEvent().getEventType())
   {
      case XMLEvent.START_ELEMENT:
         // Do something at element start.
         break;

      case XMLEvent.END_ELEMENT:
         // Do something at element end.
   }
}
```

Listing 4-2 presents the source code to a StAXDemo application that reports an XML document's start and end elements via an event-based reader.

Listing 4-2. StAXDemo (Version 2)

```java
import java.io.FileNotFoundException;
import java.io.FileReader;

import javax.xml.stream.FactoryConfigurationError;
import javax.xml.stream.XMLEventReader;
import javax.xml.stream.XMLInputFactory;
import javax.xml.stream.XMLStreamException;

import javax.xml.stream.events.EndElement;
import javax.xml.stream.events.StartElement;
import javax.xml.stream.events.XMLEvent;

import static java.lang.System.*;

public class StAXDemo
{
    public static void main(String[] args)
    {
        if (args.length != 1)
        {
            err.println("usage: java StAXDemo xmlfile");
            return;
        }
        try
        {
            XMLInputFactory xmlif = XMLInputFactory.newFactory();
            FileReader fr = new FileReader(args[0]);
            XMLEventReader xmler = xmlif.createXMLEventReader(fr);
            while (xmler.hasNext())
            {
                XMLEvent xmle = xmler.nextEvent();
                switch (xmle.getEventType())
                {
                    case XMLEvent.START_ELEMENT:
```

```
                out.println("START_ELEMENT");
                out.printf("   Qname = %s%n",
                                ((StartElement) xmle). getName());
                break;
              case XMLEvent.END_ELEMENT:
                out.println("END_ELEMENT");
                out.printf("   Qname = %s%n",
                                ((EndElement) xmle). getName());
          }
        }
      }
      catch (FactoryConfigurationError fce)
      {
         err.printf("FCE: %s%n", fce.toString());
      }
      catch (FileNotFoundException fnfe)
      {
         err.printf("FNFE: %s%n", fnfe.toString());
      }
      catch (XMLStreamException xmlse)
      {
         err.printf("XMLSE: %s%n", xmlse.toString());
      }
   }
}
```

After verifying the number of command-line arguments, Listing 4-2's main() method
creates a factory, uses the factory to create an event-based reader that obtains its XML
data from the file identified by the solitary command-line argument, and enters a
parsing loop. Whenever nextEvent() returns XMLEvent.START_ELEMENT or XMLEvent.
END_ELEMENT, StartElement's or EndElement's getName() method is called to return the
element's qualified name.

After compiling Listing 4-2, run the resulting application to dump Listing 1-3's article XML content, as follows:

```
java StAXDemo article.xml
```

You should observe the following output:

```
START_ELEMENT
  Qname = article
START_ELEMENT
  Qname = abstract
START_ELEMENT
  Qname = code
END_ELEMENT
  Qname = code
END_ELEMENT
  Qname = abstract
START_ELEMENT
  Qname = body
END_ELEMENT
  Qname = body
END_ELEMENT
  Qname = article
```

Note   You can also create a filtered event-based reader to accept or reject various events by calling one of XMLInputFactory's createFilteredReader() methods, such as XMLEventReader createFilteredReader(XMLEventReader reader, EventFilter filter). The javax.xml.stream. EventFilter interface declares a boolean accept(XMLEvent event) method that returns true when the specified event is part of the event sequence; otherwise, it returns false.

Creating XML Documents

Document writers are obtained by calling the various "create" methods that are declared in the javax.xml.stream.XMLOutputFactory class. These creational methods are organized into two categories: methods for creating stream-based writers and methods for creating event-based writers.

Before you can obtain a stream-based or an event-based writer, you need to obtain an instance of the factory by calling one of the newFactory() static methods, such as XMLOutputFactory newFactory():

XMLOutputFactory xmlof = XMLOutputFactory.newFactory();

Note   You can also call the XMLOutputFactory newInstance() static method but might not want to do so because its same-named but parameterized companion method has been deprecated to maintain API consistency, and it's possible that newInstance() will be deprecated as well.

The newFactory() methods follow an ordered lookup procedure to locate the XMLOutputFactory implementation class. This procedure first examines the javax. xml.stream.XMLOutputFactory system property and lastly returns the system-default implementation (returned from XMLOutputFactory newDefaultFactory()). If there is a service configuration error, or if the implementation is not available or cannot be instantiated, the method throws an instance of the FactoryConfigurationError class.

After creating the factory, call XMLOutputFactory's void setProperty(String name, Object value) method to set various features and properties as necessary. The only property currently supported by all writers is XMLOutputFactory.IS_REPAIRING_ NAMESPACES. When enabled (by passing true or a Boolean object, such as Boolean.TRUE, to value), the document writer takes care of all namespace bindings and declarations, with minimal help from the application. The output is always well formed with respect to namespaces. However enabling this property adds some overhead to the job of writing the XML.

Creating Documents with Stream-Based Writers

A stream-based writer is created by calling one of `XMLOutputFactory`'s `createXMLStreamWriter()` methods, such as `XMLStreamWriter createXMLStreamWriter(Writer writer)`. These methods throw `XMLStreamException` when the stream-based writer cannot be created.

The following code fragment creates a stream-based writer whose destination is a file named `recipe.xml`:

```
Writer writer = new FileWriter("recipe.xml");
XMLStreamWriter xmlsw = xmlof.createXMLStreamWriter(writer);
```

The low-level `XMLStreamWriter` interface declares several methods for writing infoset items to the destination. The following list describes a few of these methods:

- `void close()` closes this stream-based writer and frees any associated resources. The underlying writer is not closed.

- `void flush()` writes any cached data to the underlying writer.

- `void setPrefix(String prefix, String uri)` identifies the namespace `prefix` to which the `uri` value is bound. This `prefix` is used by variants of the `writeStartElement()`, `writeAttribute()`, and `writeEmptyElement()` methods that take namespace arguments but not prefixes. Also, it remains valid until the `writeEndElement()` invocation that corresponds to the last `writeStartElement()` invocation. This method doesn't create any output.

- `void writeAttribute(String localName, String value)` writes the attribute identified by `localName` and having the specified `value` to the underlying writer. A namespace prefix isn't included. This method escapes the &, <, >, and " characters.

- `void writeCharacters(String text)` writes `text`'s characters to the underlying writer. This method escapes the &, <, and > characters.

- `void writeEndDocument()` closes any start tags and writes corresponding end tags to the underlying writer.

- void writeEndElement() writes an end tag to the underlying writer, relying on the internal state of the stream-based writer to determine the tag's prefix and local name.

- void writeNamespace(String prefix, String namespaceURI) writes a namespace to the underlying writer. This method must be called to ensure that the namespace specified by setPrefix() and duplicated in this method call is written; otherwise, the resulting document will not be well formed from a namespace perspective.

- void writeStartDocument() writes the XML declaration to the underlying writer.

- void writeStartElement(String namespaceURI, String localName) writes a start tag with the arguments passed to namespaceURI and localName to the underlying writer.

Listing 4-3 presents the source code to a StAXDemo application that creates a recipe. xml file with many of Listing 1-5's infoset items via a stream-based writer.

Listing 4-3. StAXDemo (Version 3)

```java
import java.io.FileWriter;
import java.io.IOException;

import javax.xml.stream.FactoryConfigurationError;
import javax.xml.stream.XMLOutputFactory;
import javax.xml.stream.XMLStreamException;
import javax.xml.stream.XMLStreamWriter;

import static java.lang.System.*;

public class StAXDemo
{
   final static String NS1 = "http://www.w3.org/1999/xhtml";
   final static String NS2 = "http://www.javajeff.ca/";
```

```java
public static void main(String[] args)
{
    try
    {
        XMLOutputFactory xmlof =
            XMLOutputFactory.newFactory();
        FileWriter fw = new FileWriter("recipe.xml");
        XMLStreamWriter xmlsw =
            xmlof.createXMLStreamWriter(fw);
        xmlsw.writeStartDocument();
        xmlsw.setPrefix("h", NS1);
        xmlsw.writeStartElement(NS1, "html");
        xmlsw.writeNamespace("h", NS1);
        xmlsw.writeNamespace("r", NS2);
        xmlsw.writeStartElement(NS1, "head");
        xmlsw.writeStartElement(NS1, "title");
        xmlsw.writeCharacters("Recipe");
        xmlsw.writeEndElement();
        xmlsw.writeEndElement();
        xmlsw.writeStartElement(NS1, "body");
        xmlsw.setPrefix("r", NS2);
        xmlsw.writeStartElement(NS2, "recipe");
        xmlsw.writeStartElement(NS2, "title");
        xmlsw.writeCharacters("Grilled Cheese Sandwich");
        xmlsw.writeEndElement();
        xmlsw.writeStartElement(NS2, "ingredients");
        xmlsw.setPrefix("h", NS1);
        xmlsw.writeStartElement(NS1, "ul");
        xmlsw.writeStartElement(NS1, "li");
        xmlsw.setPrefix("r", NS2);
        xmlsw.writeStartElement(NS2, "ingredient");
        xmlsw.writeAttribute("qty", "2");
        xmlsw.writeCharacters("bread slice");
        xmlsw.writeEndElement();
        xmlsw.setPrefix("h", NS1);
```

```
            xmlsw.writeEndElement();
            xmlsw.writeEndElement();
            xmlsw.setPrefix("r", NS2);
            xmlsw.writeEndElement();
            xmlsw.writeEndDocument();
            xmlsw.flush();
            xmlsw.close();
        }
        catch (FactoryConfigurationError fce)
        {
            err.printf("FCE: %s%n", fce.toString());
        }
        catch (IOException ioe)
        {
            err.printf("IOE: %s%n", ioe.toString());
        }
        catch (XMLStreamException xmlse)
        {
            err.printf("XMLSE: %s%n", xmlse.toString());
        }
    }
}
```

Although Listing 4-3 is fairly easy to follow, you might be somewhat confused by the duplication of namespace URIs in the setPrefix() and writeStartElement() method calls. For example, you might be wondering about the duplicate URIs in xmlsw. setPrefix("h", NS1); and its xmlsw.writeStartElement(NS1, "html"); successor.

The setPrefix() method call creates a mapping between a namespace prefix (the value) and a URI (the key) without generating any output. The writeStartElement() method call specifies the URI key, which this method uses to access the prefix value, which it then prepends (with a colon character) to the html start tag's name before writing this tag to the underlying writer.

Compile Listing 4-3 and run the resulting application. You should discover a recipe. xml file in the current directory.

Creating Documents with Event-Based Writers

An event-based writer is created by calling one of XMLOutputFactory's createXMLEventWriter() methods, such as XMLEventWriter createXMLEventWriter(Writer writer). These methods throw XMLStreamException when the event-based writer cannot be created.

The following code fragment creates an event-based writer whose destination is a file named recipe.xml:

```
Writer writer = new FileWriter("recipe.xml");
XMLEventWriter xmlew = xmlof.createXMLEventWriter(writer);
```

The high-level XMLEventWriter interface declares the void add(XMLEvent event) method for adding events that describe infoset items to the output stream implemented by the underlying writer. Each argument passed to event is an instance of a class that implements a subinterface of XMLEvent (such as Attribute and StartElement).

To save you the trouble of implementing these interfaces, StAX provides javax.xml.stream.EventFactory. This utility class declares various factory methods for creating XMLEvent subinterface implementations. For example, Comment createComment(String text) returns an object whose class implements the javax.xml.stream.events.Comment subinterface of XMLEvent.

Because these factory methods are declared abstract, you must first obtain an instance of the EventFactory class. You can easily accomplish this task by invoking XMLEventFactory's XMLEventFactory newFactory() static method, as follows:

```
XMLEventFactory xmlef = XMLEventFactory.newFactory();
```

You can then obtain an XMLEvent subinterface implementation, as follows:

```
XMLEvent comment = xmlef.createComment("ToDo");
```

Listing 4-4 presents the source code to a StAXDemo application that creates a recipe.xml file with many of Listing 1-5's infoset items via an event-based writer.

Listing 4-4. StAXDemo (Version 4)

```java
import java.io.FileWriter;
import java.io.IOException;

import java.util.Iterator;

import javax.xml.stream.FactoryConfigurationError;
import javax.xml.stream.XMLEventFactory;
import javax.xml.stream.XMLEventWriter;
import javax.xml.stream.XMLOutputFactory;
import javax.xml.stream.XMLStreamException;

import javax.xml.stream.events.Attribute;
import javax.xml.stream.events.Namespace;
import javax.xml.stream.events.XMLEvent;

import static java.lang.System.*;

public class StAXDemo
{
   final static String NS1 = "http://www.w3.org/1999/xhtml";
   final static String NS2 = "http://www.javajeff.ca/";

   public static void main(String[] args)
   {
      try
      {
         XMLOutputFactory xmlof =
            XMLOutputFactory.newFactory();
         FileWriter fw = new FileWriter("recipe.xml");
         XMLEventWriter xmlew;
         xmlew = xmlof.createXMLEventWriter(fw);
         final XMLEventFactory xmlef =
            XMLEventFactory.newFactory();
         XMLEvent event = xmlef.createStartDocument();
         xmlew.add(event);
         Iterator<Namespace> nsIter;
         nsIter = new Iterator<Namespace>()
```

```
    {
        int index = 0;
        Namespace[] ns;
        {
            ns = new Namespace[2];
            ns[0] = xmlef.createNamespace("h", NS1);
            ns[1] = xmlef.createNamespace("r", NS2);
        }
        @Override
        public boolean hasNext()
        {
            return index != 2;
        }
        @Override
        public Namespace next()
        {
            return ns[index++];
        }
        @Override
        public void remove()
        {
            throw new UnsupportedOperationException();
        }
    };
    event = xmlef.createStartElement("h", NS1, "html", null, nsIter);
    xmlew.add(event);
    event = xmlef.createStartElement("h", NS2, "head");
    xmlew.add(event);
    event = xmlef.createStartElement("h", NS1, "title");
    xmlew.add(event);
    event = xmlef.createCharacters("Recipe");
    xmlew.add(event);
    event = xmlef.createEndElement("h", NS1, "title");
```

```
xmlew.add(event);
event = xmlef.createEndElement("h", NS1, "head");
xmlew.add(event);
event = xmlef.createStartElement("h", NS1, "body");
xmlew.add(event);
event = xmlef.createStartElement("r", NS2, "recipe");
xmlew.add(event);
event = xmlef.createStartElement("r", NS2, "title");
xmlew.add(event);
event = xmlef.createCharacters("Grilled Cheese " + "Sandwich");
xmlew.add(event);
event = xmlef.createEndElement("r", NS2, "title");
xmlew.add(event);
event = xmlef.createStartElement("r", NS2, "ingredients");
xmlew.add(event);
event = xmlef.createStartElement("h", NS1, "ul");
xmlew.add(event);
event = xmlef.createStartElement("h", NS1, "li");
xmlew.add(event);
Iterator<Attribute> attrIter;
attrIter = new Iterator<Attribute>()
{
   int index = 0;
   Attribute[] attrs;
   {
      attrs = new Attribute[1];
      attrs[0] = xmlef.createAttribute("qty", "2");
   }
   @Override
   public boolean hasNext()
   {
      return index != 1;
   }
```

```java
        @Override
        public Attribute next()
        {
            return attrs[index++];
        }
        @Override
        public void remove()
        {
            throw new UnsupportedOperationException();
        }
    };
    event = xmlef.createStartElement("r", NS2, "ingredient",
                                    attrIter, null);
    xmlew.add(event);
    event = xmlef.createCharacters("bread slice");
    xmlew.add(event);
    event = xmlef.createEndElement("r", NS2, "ingredient");
    xmlew.add(event);
    event = xmlef.createEndElement("h", NS1, "li");
    xmlew.add(event);
    event = xmlef.createEndElement("h", NS1, "ul");
    xmlew.add(event);
    event = xmlef.createEndElement("r", NS2, "ingredients");
    xmlew.add(event);
    event = xmlef.createEndElement("r", NS2, "recipe");
    xmlew.add(event);
    event = xmlef.createEndElement("h", NS1, "body");
    xmlew.add(event);
    event = xmlef.createEndElement("h", NS1, "html");
    xmlew.add(event);
    xmlew.flush();
    xmlew.close();
}
```

```
      catch (FactoryConfigurationError fce)
      {
         err.printf("FCE: %s%n", fce.toString());
      }
      catch (IOException ioe)
      {
         err.printf("IOE: %s%n", ioe.toString());
      }
      catch (XMLStreamException xmlse)
      {
         err.printf("XMLSE: %s%n", xmlse.toString());
      }
   }
}
```

Listing 4-4 should be fairly easy to follow; it's the event-based equivalent of Listing 4-3. Notice that this listing includes the creation of java.util.Iterator instances from anonymous classes that implement this interface. These iterators are created to pass namespaces or attributes to XMLEventFactory's StartElement createStartElement (String prefix, String namespaceUri, String localName, Iterator<? extends Attribute> attributes, Iterator<? extends Namespace> namespaces) method. (You can pass null to this parameter when an iterator isn't applicable; for example, when the start tag has no attributes.)

Compile Listing 4-4 and run the resulting application. You should discover a recipe.xml file in the current directory.

XMLEventWriter declares a void add(XMLEventReader reader) convenience method for adding a stream of input events to an output stream in one method call. Listing 4-5 presents the source code to a Copy application that uses this method to copy an XML file to another XML file.

Listing 4-5. Copy

```
import java.io.FileReader;
import java.io.FileWriter;

import javax.xml.stream.XMLEventReader;
import javax.xml.stream.XMLEventWriter;
```

```java
import javax.xml.stream.XMLInputFactory;
import javax.xml.stream.XMLOutputFactory;

import static java.lang.System.*;

public class Copy
{
   public static void main(String[] args) throws Exception
   {
      if (args.length != 2)
      {
         err.println("usage: java copy xmlfile1 xmlfile2");
         return;
      }
      XMLInputFactory xmlif = XMLInputFactory.newFactory();
      FileReader fr = new FileReader(args[0]);
      XMLEventReader xmler = xmlif.createXMLEventReader(fr);
      XMLOutputFactory xmlof = XMLOutputFactory.newFactory();
      FileWriter fw = new FileWriter(args[1]);
      XMLEventWriter xmlew;
      xmlew = xmlof.createXMLEventWriter(fw);
      xmlew.add(xmler);
      xmlew.flush();
      xmlew.close();
   }
}
```

For brevity, I added a throws Exception clause to main()'s header.

Compile Listing 4-5 as follows:

```
javac Copy.java
```

Run the resulting application to copy a recipe.xml file to a _recipe.xml backup file:

```
java Copy recipe.xml _recipe.xml
```

If the source XML file doesn't have an XML declaration, it will be added to the destination XML file.

EXERCISES

The following exercises are designed to test your understanding of Chapter 4's content:

1. Define StAX.

2. What packages make up the StAX API?

3. True or false: A stream-based reader extracts the next infoset item from an input stream by obtaining an event.

4. How do you obtain a document reader? How do you obtain a document writer?

5. What does a document writer do when you call XMLOutputFactory's void setProperty(String name, Object value) method with XMLOutputFactory.IS_REPAIRING_NAMESPACES as the property name and true as the value?

6. Create a ParseXMLDoc application that uses a StAX stream-based reader to parse its single command-line argument, an XML document. After creating this reader, the application should verify that a START_DOCUMENT infoset item has been detected, and then enter a loop that reads the next item and uses a switch statement to output a message corresponding to the item that has been read: ATTRIBUTE, CDATA, CHARACTERS, COMMENT, DTD, END_ELEMENT, ENTITY_DECLARATION, ENTITY_REFERENCE, NAMESPACE, NOTATION_ DECLARATION, PROCESSING_INSTRUCTION, SPACE, or START_ELEMENT. When START_ELEMENT is detected, output this element's name and local name, and output the local names and values of all attributes. The loop ends when the END_DOCUMENT infoset item has been detected. Explicitly close the stream reader followed by the file reader upon which it's based. Test this application with Exercise 1-21's books.xml file.

Summary

StAX is a Java API for parsing an XML document sequentially from start to finish and also for creating XML documents. Java implements StAX through types stored in the `javax.xml.stream`, `javax.xml.stream.events`, and `javax.xml.stream.util` packages.

StAX parsers are known as document readers, and StAX document creators are known as document writers. StAX classifies document readers and document writers as stream-based or event-based.

Document readers are obtained by calling the various "`create`" methods that are declared in the `XMLInputFactory` class. Document writers are obtained by calling the various "`create`" methods that are declared in the `XMLOutputFactory` class.

The low-level `XMLStreamReader` interface offers the most efficient way to read XML data with StAX. This interface's `boolean hasNext()` method returns `true` when there is a next infoset item to obtain; otherwise, it returns `false`. The `int next()` method advances the cursor by one infoset item and returns an integer code that identifies this item's type.

The low-level `XMLStreamWriter` interface declares several methods for writing infoset items to the destination. Examples include `void writeAttribute(String localName, String value)` and `void writeCharacters(String text)`.

The high-level `XMLEventReader` interface offers a somewhat less efficient but more object-oriented way to read XML data with StAX. This interface's `boolean hasNext()` method returns `true` when there is an event to obtain; otherwise, it returns `false`. The `XMLEvent nextEvent()` method returns the next event as an object whose class implements a subinterface of the `XMLEvent` interface.

The high-level `XMLEventWriter` interface declares the `void add(XMLEvent event)` method for adding events that describe infoset items to the output stream implemented by the underlying writer. Each argument passed to `event` is an instance of a class that implements a subinterface of `XMLEvent` (such as `Attribute` and `StartElement`).

Chapter 5 introduces Java's XPath API for simplifying DOM node access.

CHAPTER 5

Selecting Nodes with XPath

Java includes an XPath API for simplifying access to a DOM tree's nodes. Chapter 5 introduces you to XPath.

What Is XPath?

XPath is a nonXML declarative query language (defined by the W3C) for selecting an XML document's infoset items as one or more nodes. For example, you can use XPath to locate Listing 1-1's third `ingredient` element and return this element node.

As well as simplifying access to a DOM tree's nodes, XPath is commonly used in the context of XSLT (discussed in Chapter 6) where it's typically employed to select (via XPath expressions) those input document elements that are to be copied to an output document.

Note   Java 11 supports XPath 1.0, which is assigned package `javax.xml.xpath`.

XPath Language Primer

XPath regards an XML document as a tree of nodes that starts from a root node. This language recognizes seven kinds of nodes: element, attribute, text, namespace, processing instruction, comment, and document. It doesn't recognize CDATA sections, entity references, or document type declarations.

© Jeff Friesen 2019
J. Friesen, *Java XML and JSON*, https://doi.org/10.1007/978-1-4842-4330-5_5

Note   A DOM tree's root node (an `org.w3c.dom.Document` object) isn't the same as a document's root element. The DOM tree's root node contains the entire document, including the root element, any comments or processing instructions that appear before the root element's start tag, and any comments or processing instructions that appear after the root element's end tag.

Location Path Expressions

XPath provides location path expressions for selecting nodes. A *location path expression* locates nodes via a sequence of *steps* starting from the *context node* (the root node or some other document node that's the current node). The returned set of nodes, which is known as a *nodeset*, might be empty, or it might contain one or more nodes.

The simplest location path expression selects the document's root node and consists of a single forward slash character (`/`). The next simplest location path expression is the name of an element, which selects all child elements of the context node that have that name. For example, `ingredient` refers to all `ingredient` child elements of the context node in Listing 1-1's recipe document. This XPath expression returns a set of three `ingredient` nodes when the context node is `ingredients`. However, if `recipe` or `instructions` happened to be the context node, `ingredient` wouldn't return any nodes (`ingredient` is a child of `ingredients` only). When an expression starts with a forward slash (`/`), the expression represents an absolute path that starts from the root node. For example, expression `/movie` selects all `movie` child elements of the root node in Listing 1-2's movie document.

Attributes are also handled by location path expressions. To select an element's attribute, specify `@` followed by the attribute's name. For example, `@qty` selects the `qty` attribute node of the context node.

In most cases, you'll work with root nodes, element nodes, and attribute nodes. However, you might also need to work with namespace nodes, text nodes, processing-instruction nodes, and comment nodes. Unlike namespace nodes, which are typically handled by XSLT, you'll more likely need to process comments, text, and processing instructions. XPath provides `comment()`, `text()`, and `processing-instruction()` functions for selecting comment, text, and processing-instruction nodes.

The `comment()` and `text()` functions don't require arguments because comment and text nodes don't have names. Each comment is a separate comment node, and each text node specifies the longest run of text not interrupted by a tag. The `processing-instruction()` function may be called with an argument that identifies the target of the processing instruction. If called with no argument, all of the context node's processing-instruction child nodes are selected.

XPath provides three wildcards for selecting unknown nodes:

- `*` matches any element node regardless of the node's type. It doesn't match attributes, text nodes, comments, or processing-instruction nodes. When you place a namespace prefix before the `*`, only elements belonging to that namespace are matched.

- `node()` is a function that matches all nodes.

- `@*` matches all attribute nodes.

Note   XPath lets you perform multiple selections by using the vertical bar (`|`). For example, `author/*|publisher/*` selects the children of `author` and the children of `publisher`, and `*|@*` matches all elements and attributes, but doesn't match text, comment, or processing-instruction nodes.

XPath lets you combine steps into *compound paths* by using the / character to separate them. For paths beginning with /, the first path step is relative to the root node; otherwise, the first path step is relative to another context node. For example, `/movie/name` starts with the root node, selects all `movie` element children of the root node, and selects all `name` children of the selected `movie` nodes. If you wanted to return all text nodes of the selected `name` elements, you would specify `/movie/name/text()`.

Compound paths can include // to select nodes from all descendants of the context node (including the context node). When placed at the start of an expression, // selects nodes from the entire tree. For example, `//ingredient` selects all `ingredient` nodes in the tree.

As with file systems that let you identify the current directory with a single period (`.`) and its parent directory with a double period (`..`), you can specify a single period to represent the current node and a double period to represent the parent of the current node. (You would typically use a single period in XSLT to indicate that you want to access the value of the currently matched element.)

It might be necessary to narrow the selection of nodes returned by an XPath expression. For example, expression `/recipe/ingredients/ingredient` returns all ingredient nodes, but perhaps you only want to return the first `ingredient` node. You can narrow the selection by including predicates in the location path.

A *predicate* is a square bracket-delimited Boolean expression that's tested against each selected node. If the expression evaluates to `true`, that node is included in the set of nodes returned by the XPath expression; otherwise, the node isn't included in the set. For example, `/recipe/ingredients/ingredient[1]` selects the first `ingredient` element that's a child of the `ingredients` element.

Predicates can include predefined functions (such as `last()` and `position()`), operators (such as `-`, `<`, and `=`), and other items. Consider the following examples:

- `/recipe/ingredients/ingredient[last()]` selects the last ingredient element that's a child of the `ingredients` element.

- `/recipe/ingredients/ingredient[last() - 1]` selects the next-to-last ingredient element that's a child of the `ingredients` element.

- `/recipe/ingredients/ingredient[position() < 3]` selects the first two ingredient elements that are children of the `ingredients` element.

- `//ingredient[@qty]` selects all ingredient elements (no matter where they're located) that have qty attributes.

- `//ingredient[@qty='1']` or `//ingredient[@qty="1"]` selects all ingredient elements (no matter where they're located) that have qty attributes with value 1.

Note   XPath predefines several functions for use with nodesets: `last()` returns a number identifying the last node, `position()` returns a number identifying a node's position, `count()` returns the number of nodes in its nodeset argument, `id()` selects elements by their unique IDs and returns a nodeset of these elements, `local-name()` returns the local part of the qualified name of the first node in its nodeset argument, `namespace-uri()` returns the namespace part of the qualified name of the first node in its nodeset argument, and `name()` returns the qualified name of the first node in its nodeset argument.

Although predicates are supposed to be Boolean expressions, the predicate might not evaluate to a Boolean value. For example, it could evaluate to a number or a string—XPath supports Boolean, number (IEEE 754 double precision floating-point values), and string expression types as well as a location path expression's nodeset type. If a predicate evaluates to a number, XPath converts that number to true when it equals the context node's position; otherwise, XPath converts that number to false. If a predicate evaluates to a string, XPath converts that string to true when the string isn't empty; otherwise, XPath converts that string to false. Finally, if a predicate evaluates to a nodeset, XPath converts that nodeset to true when the nodeset is nonempty; otherwise, XPath converts that nodeset to false.

Note   The previously presented location path expression examples demonstrate XPath's abbreviated syntax. However, XPath also supports an unabbreviated syntax that's more descriptive of what's happening and is based on an *axis specifier*, which indicates the navigation direction within the XML document's tree representation. For example, where /movie/name selects all movie child elements of the root node followed by all name child elements of the movie elements using the abbreviated syntax, /child::movie/child::name accomplishes the same task with the expanded syntax. Check out Wikipedia's "XPath" entry (https:// en.wikipedia.org/wiki/XPath) for more information.

General Expressions

Location path expressions (which return nodesets) are one kind of XPath expression. XPath also supports general expressions that evaluate to Boolean (such as predicates), number, or string type; for example, position() = 2, 6.8, and "Hello". General expressions are often used in XSLT.

XPath Boolean values can be compared via relational operators <, <=, >, >=, =, and != . Boolean expressions can be combined by using operators and and or. Also, XPath predefines the following Boolean functions:

- boolean() returns a Boolean value for a number, string, or nodeset.

- not() returns true when its Boolean argument is false and vice versa.

- `true()` returns `true`.

- `false()` returns `false`.

- `lang()` returns `true` or `false` depending on whether the language of the context node (as specified by `xml:lang` attributes) is the same as or is a sublanguage of the language specified by the argument string.

XPath numeric values can be manipulated via operators +, -, *, `div`, and `mod` (remainder)—forward slash cannot be used for division because it's used to separate location steps. All five operators behave like their Java language counterparts. XPath also predefines the following numeric functions:

- `number()` converts its argument to a number.

- `sum()` returns the sum of the numeric values represented by the nodes in its nodeset argument.

- `floor()` returns the largest (closest to positive infinity) number that's not greater than its number argument and that's an integer.

- `ceiling()` returns the smallest (closest to negative infinity) number that's not less than its number argument and that's an integer.

- `round()` returns the number that's closest to the argument and that's an integer. When there are two such numbers, the one closest to positive infinity is returned.

XPath strings are ordered character sequences that are enclosed in single quotes or double quotes. A string literal cannot contain the same kind of quote that's also used to delimit the string. For example, a string that contains a single quote cannot be delimited with single quotes. XPath provides the = and != operators for comparing strings. XPath also predefines the following string functions:

- `string()` converts its argument to a string.

- `concat()` returns a concatenation of its string arguments.

- `starts-with()` returns `true` when its first argument string starts with its second argument string (and otherwise returns `false`).

- `contains()` returns `true` when its first argument string contains its second argument string (and otherwise returns `false`).

144

- `substring-before()` returns the substring of its first argument string that precedes the first occurrence of its second argument string in its first argument string or the empty string when its first argument string doesn't contain its second argument string.

- `substring-after()` returns the substring of its first argument string that follows the first occurrence of its second argument string in its first argument string or the empty string when its first argument string doesn't contain its second argument string.

- `substring()` returns the substring of its first (string) argument starting at the position specified in its second (number) argument with length specified in its third (number) argument.

- `string-length()` returns the number of characters in its string argument (or the length of the context node when converted to a string in the absence of an argument).

- `normalize-space()` returns the argument string with whitespace normalized by stripping leading and trailing whitespace and replacing sequences of whitespace characters by a single space (or performing the same action on the context node when converted to a string in the absence of an argument).

- `translate()` returns its first argument string with occurrences of characters in its second argument string replaced by the character at the corresponding position in its third argument string.

XPath and DOM

Suppose you need someone in your home to purchase a bag of sugar. You can tell this person to "Please buy me some sugar." Alternatively, you could say the following: "Please open the front door. Walk down to the sidewalk. Turn left. Walk up the sidewalk for three blocks. Turn right. Walk up the sidewalk one block. Enter the store. Go to aisle 7. Walk two meters down the aisle. Pick up a bag of sugar. Walk to a checkout counter. Pay for the sugar. Retrace your steps home." Most people would expect to receive the shorter instruction and would probably have you committed to an institution if you made a habit out of providing the longer set of instructions.

Traversing a DOM tree of nodes is similar to providing the longer sequence of instructions. In contrast, XPath lets you traverse this tree via a succinct instruction. To see this difference for yourself, consider a scenario where you have an XML-based contacts document that lists your various professional contacts. Listing 5-1 presents a trivial example of such a document.

Listing 5-1. XML-Based Contacts Database

```
<?xml version="1.0"?>
<contacts>
   <contact>
      <name>John Doe</name>
      <city>Chicago</city>
      <city>Denver</city>
   </contact>
   <contact>
      <name>Jane Doe</name>
      <city>New York</city>
   </contact>
   <contact>
      <name>Sandra Smith</name>
      <city>Denver</city>
      <city>Miami</city>
   </contact>
   <contact>
     <name>Bob Jones</name>
     <city>Chicago</city>
   </contact>
</contacts>
```

Listing 5-1 reveals a simple XML grammar consisting of a contacts root element that contains a sequence of contact elements. Each contact element contains one name element and one or more city elements (various contacts travel frequently and spend a lot of time in each city). (To keep the example simple, I'm not providing a DTD or a schema.)

CHAPTER 5   SELECTING NODES WITH XPATH

Suppose you want to locate and output the names of all contacts that live at least part of each year in Chicago. Listing 5-2 presents the source code to a DOMSearch application that accomplishes this task with the DOM API.

Listing 5-2. Locating Chicago Contacts with the DOM API

```java
import java.io.IOException;

import java.util.ArrayList;
import java.util.List;

import javax.xml.parsers.DocumentBuilder;
import javax.xml.parsers.DocumentBuilderFactory;
import javax.xml.parsers.FactoryConfigurationError;
import javax.xml.parsers.ParserConfigurationException;

import org.w3c.dom.Document;
import org.w3c.dom.Element;
import org.w3c.dom.Node;
import org.w3c.dom.NodeList;

import org.xml.sax.SAXException;

import static java.lang.System.*;

public class DOMSearch
{
   public static void main(String[] args)
   {
      try
      {
         DocumentBuilderFactory dbf = DocumentBuilderFactory.newInstance();
         DocumentBuilder db = dbf.newDocumentBuilder();
         Document doc = db.parse("contacts.xml");
         List<String> contactNames = new ArrayList<String>();
         NodeList contacts = doc.getElementsByTagName("contact");
```

```java
        for (int i = 0; i < contacts.getLength(); i++)
        {
            Element contact = (Element) contacts.item(i);
            NodeList cities = contact.getElementsByTagName("city");
            boolean chicago = false;
            for (int j = 0; j < cities.getLength(); j++)
            {
                Element city = (Element) cities.item(j);
                NodeList children = city.getChildNodes();
                StringBuilder sb = new StringBuilder();
                for (int k = 0; k < children.getLength(); k++)
                {
                    Node child = children.item(k);
                    if (child.getNodeType() == Node.TEXT_NODE)
                        sb.append(child.getNodeValue());
                }
                if (sb.toString().equals("Chicago"))
                {
                    chicago = true;
                    break;
                }
            }
            if (chicago)
            {
                NodeList names = contact.getElementsByTagName("name");
                contactNames.add(names.item(0). getFirstChild().
                                getNodeValue());
            }
        }
        for (String contactName: contactNames)
            out.println(contactName);
    }
```

```
catch (IOException ioe)
{
   err.printf("IOE: %s%n", ioe.toString());
}
catch (SAXException saxe)
{
   err.printf("SAXE: %s%n", saxe.toString());
}
catch (FactoryConfigurationError fce)
{
   err.printf("FCE: %s%n", fce.toString());
}
catch (ParserConfigurationException pce)
{
   err.printf("PCE: %s%n", pce.toString());
}
   }
}
```

After parsing contacts.xml and building the DOM tree, main() uses Document's getElementsByTagName() method to return an org.w3c.dom.NodeList of contact element nodes. For each member of this list, main() extracts the contact element node and uses this node with getElementsByTagName() to return a NodeList of the contact element node's city element nodes.

For each member of the cities list, main() extracts the city element node and uses this node with getElementsByTagName() to return a NodeList of the city element node's child nodes—there's only a single child text node in this example, but the presence of a comment or processing instruction would increase the number of child nodes. For example, <city>Chicago<!--The windy city--></city> increases the number of child nodes to 2.

If the child's node type indicates that it's a text node, the child node's value (obtained via getNodeValue()) is stored in a string builder—only one child node is stored in the string builder in this example. If the builder's contents indicate that Chicago has been found, the chicago flag is set to true and execution leaves the cities loop.

If the chicago flag is set when the cities loop exits, the current contact element node's getElementsByTagName() method is called to return a NodeList of the contact element node's name element nodes (of which there should only be one, and which I could enforce through a DTD or schema). It's now a simple matter to extract the first item from this list, call getFirstChild() on this item to return the text node (I assume that only text appears between <name> and </name>), and call getNodeValue() on the text node to obtain its value, which is then added to the contactNames list.

Compile Listing 5-2 as follows:

```
javac DOMSearch.java
```

Run the resulting application as follows:

```
java DOMSearch
```

You should observe the following output:

```
John Doe
Bob Jones
```

Traversing the DOM's tree of nodes is a tedious exercise at best and is error-prone at worst. Fortunately, XPath can greatly simplify this situation.

Before writing the XPath equivalent of Listing 5-2, it helps to define a location path expression. For this example, that expression is //contact[city = "Chicago"]/name/text(), which uses a predicate to select all contact nodes that contain a Chicago city node, then select all child name nodes from these contact nodes, and finally select all child text nodes from these name nodes.

Listing 5-3 presents the source code to an XPathSearch application that uses this XPath expression and Java's XPath API, which consists of various types in the javax.xml.xpath package, to locate Chicago contacts.

Listing 5-3. Locating Chicago Contacts with the XPath API

```
import java.io.IOException;

import javax.xml.parsers.DocumentBuilder;
import javax.xml.parsers.DocumentBuilderFactory;
import javax.xml.parsers.FactoryConfigurationError;
import javax.xml.parsers.ParserConfigurationException;
```

```
import javax.xml.xpath.XPath;
import javax.xml.xpath.XPathConstants;
import javax.xml.xpath.XPathException;
import javax.xml.xpath.XPathExpression;
import javax.xml.xpath.XPathFactory;

import org.w3c.dom.Document;
import org.w3c.dom.NodeList;

import org.xml.sax.SAXException;

import static java.lang.System.*;

public class XPathSearch
{
    public static void main(String[] args)
    {
        try
        {
            DocumentBuilderFactory dbf =
                DocumentBuilderFactory.newInstance();
            DocumentBuilder db = dbf.newDocumentBuilder();
            Document doc = db.parse("contacts.xml");
            XPathFactory xpf = XPathFactory.newInstance();
            XPath xp = xpf.newXPath();
            XPathExpression xpe;
            xpe = xp.compile("//contact[city = 'Chicago']/" +
                             "name/text()");
            Object result =
                xpe.evaluate(doc, XPathConstants.NODESET);
            NodeList nl = (NodeList) result;
            for (int i = 0; i < nl.getLength(); i++)
                out.println(nl.item(i).getNodeValue());
        }
        catch (IOException ioe)
        {
```

```
               err.printf("IOE: %s%n", ioe.toString());
         }
         catch (SAXException saxe)
         {
               err.printf("SAXE: %s%n", saxe.toString());
         }
         catch (FactoryConfigurationError fce)
         {
               err.printf("FCE: %s%n", fce.toString());
         }
         catch (ParserConfigurationException pce)
         {
               err.printf("PCE: %s%n", pce.toString());
         }
         catch (XPathException xpe)
         {
               err.printf("XPE: %s%n", xpe.toString());
         }
     }
}
```

After parsing contacts.xml and building the DOM tree, main() instantiates javax.
xml.xpath.XPathFactory by calling its XPathFactory newInstance() method. The
resulting XPathFactory instance can be used to set features (such as secure processing,
to process XML documents securely) by calling its void setFeature(String name,
boolean value) method, create a javax.xml.xpath.XPath object by calling its XPath
newXPath() method, and more.

XPath declares an XPathExpression compile(String expression) method
for compiling the specified expression (an XPath expression) and returning
the compiled expression as an instance of a class that implements the javax.
xml.xpath.XPathExpression interface. This method throws javax.xml.xpath.
XPathExpressionException (a subclass of javax.xml.xpath.XPathException) when the
expression cannot be compiled.

XPath also declares several overloaded `evaluate()` methods for immediately evaluating an expression and returning the result. Because it can take time to evaluate an expression, you might choose to compile a complex expression first (to boost performance) when you plan to evaluate this expression many times.

After compiling the expression, `main()` calls `XPathExpression`'s `Object evaluate(Object item, QName returnType)` method to evaluate the expression. The first argument is the context node for the expression, which happens to be a `Document` instance in the example. The second argument specifies the kind of object returned by `evaluate()` and is set to `javax.xml.xpath.XPathConstants.NODESET`, a qualified name for the XPath 1.0 nodeset type, which is implemented via DOM's `NodeList` interface.

Note   The XPath API maps XPath's Boolean, number, string, and nodeset types to Java's `java.lang.Boolean`, `java.lang.Double`, `java.lang.String`, and `NodeList` types, respectively. When calling an `evaluate()` method, you specify XPath types via `XPathConstants` constants (BOOLEAN, NUMBER, STRING, and NODESET), and the method takes care of returning an object of the appropriate type. `XPathConstants` also declares a NODE constant, which doesn't map to a Java type. Instead, it's used to tell `evaluate()` that you only want the resulting nodeset to contain a single node.

After casting `Object` to `NodeList`, `main()` uses this interface's `getLength()` and `item()` methods to traverse the nodelist. For each item in this list, `getNodeValue()` is called to return the node's value, which is subsequently output.

Compile Listing 5-3 as follows:

```
javac XPathSearch.java
```

Run the resulting application as follows:

```
java XPathSearch
```

You should observe the following output:

```
John Doe
Bob Jones
```

Advanced XPath

The XPath API provides three advanced features to overcome limitations with the XPath 1.0 language. These features are namespace contexts, extension functions and function resolvers, and variables and variable resolvers.

Namespace Contexts

When an XML document's elements belong to a namespace (including the default namespace), any XPath expression that queries the document must account for this namespace. For nondefault namespaces, the expression doesn't need to use the same namespace prefix; it only needs to use the same URI. However, when a document specifies the default namespace, the expression must use a prefix even though the document doesn't use a prefix.

To appreciate this situation, suppose Listing 5-1's `<contacts>` tag was declared as follows to introduce a default namespace: `<contacts xmlns="http://www.javajeff.ca/">`. Furthermore, suppose that Listing 5-3 included `dbf.setNamespaceAware(true);` after the line that instantiates `DocumentBuilderFactory`. If you were to run the revised `XPathSearch` application against the revised `contacts.xml` file, you wouldn't see any output.

You can correct this problem by implementing `javax.xml.namespace.NamespaceContext` to map an arbitrary prefix to the namespace URI and then registering this namespace context with the `XPath` instance. Listing 5-4 presents a minimal implementation of the `NamespaceContext` interface.

Listing 5-4. *Minimally Implementing* `NamespaceContext`

```
import java.util.Iterator;

import javax.xml.XMLConstants;

import javax.xml.namespace.NamespaceContext;

public class NSContext implements NamespaceContext
{
   @Override
   public String getNamespaceURI(String prefix)
   {
```

154

```
    if (prefix == null)
        throw new
            IllegalArgumentException("prefix is null");
    else
    if (prefix.equals("tt"))
        return "http://www.javajeff.ca/";
    else
        return null;
}

@Override
public String getPrefix(String uri)
{
    return null;
}

@Override
public Iterator<String> getPrefixes(String uri)
{
    return null;
}
}
```

The getNamespaceURI() method is passed a prefix argument that must be mapped
to a URI. When this argument is null, a java.lang.IllegalArgumentException object
must be thrown (according to the Java documentation). When the argument is the
desired prefix value, the namespace URI is returned.

After instantiating the XPath class, you would instantiate NSContext and register
this object with the XPath object by calling XPath's void setNamespaceContext
(NamespaceContext nsContext) method. For example, you would specify xp.
setNamespaceContext(new NSContext()); after XPath xp = xpf.newXPath(); to
register the NSContext object with xp.

All that's left to accomplish is to apply the prefix to the XPath expression, which now
becomes //tt:contact[tt:city='Chicago']/tt:name/text() because the contact,
city, and name elements are now part of the default namespace, whose URI is mapped to
arbitrary prefix tt in the NSContext instance's getNamespaceURI() method.

Compile and run the revised XPathSearch application and you'll see John Doe
followed by Bob Jones on separate lines.

Extension Functions and Function Resolvers

The XPath API lets you define functions (via Java methods) that extend XPath's predefined function repertoire by offering new features not already provided. These Java methods cannot have side effects because XPath functions can be evaluated multiple times and in any order. Furthermore, they cannot override predefined functions; a Java method with the same name as a predefined function is never executed.

Suppose you modify Listing 5-1's XML document to include a birth element that records a contact's date of birth information in YYYY-MM-DD format. Listing 5-5 shows the resulting XML file.

Listing 5-5. XML-Based Contacts Database with Birth Information

```
<?xml version="1.0"?>
<contacts xmlns="http://www.javajeff.ca/">
    <contact>
        <name>John Doe</name>
        <birth>1953-01-02</birth>
        <city>Chicago</city>
        <city>Denver</city>
    </contact>
    <contact>
        <name>Jane Doe</name>
        <birth>1965-07-12</birth>
        <city>New York</city>
    </contact>
    <contact>
        <name>Sandra Smith</name>
        <birth>1976-11-22</birth>
        <city>Denver</city>
        <city>Miami</city>
    </contact>
```

```
<contact>
   <name>Bob Jones</name>
   <birth>1958-03-14</birth>
   <city>Chicago</city>
</contact>
</contacts>
```

Now suppose that you want to select contacts based on birth information. For example, you only want to select contacts whose date of birth is greater than 1960-01-01. Because XPath doesn't provide this function for you, you decide to declare a date() extension function. Your first step is to declare a Date class that implements the javax.xml.xpath.XPathFunction interface—see Listing 5-6.

Listing 5-6. An Extension Function for Returning a Date as a Milliseconds Value

```
import java.text.ParsePosition;
import java.text.SimpleDateFormat;

import java.util.List;

import javax.xml.xpath.XPathFunction;
import javax.xml.xpath.XPathFunctionException;

import org.w3c.dom.Node;
import org.w3c.dom.NodeList;

public class Date implements XPathFunction
{
   private final static ParsePosition POS = new ParsePosition(0);

   private SimpleDateFormat sdf = new SimpleDateFormat("yyyy-mm-dd");

   @Override
   public Object evaluate(List args)
      throws XPathFunctionException
```

```
   {
      if (args.size() != 1)
         throw new XPathFunctionException("Invalid " + "number of " +
                                              "arguments");
      String value;
      Object o = args.get(0);
      if (o instanceof NodeList)
      {
         NodeList list = (NodeList) o;
         value = list.item(0).getTextContent();
      }
      else
      if (o instanceof String)
         value = (String) o;
      else
         throw new XPathFunctionException("Cannot " + "convert " +
                                             "argument " + "type");
      POS.setIndex(0);
      return sdf.parse(value, POS).getTime();
   }
}
```

XPathFunction declares a single Object evaluate(List args) method that XPath calls when it needs to execute the extension function. evaluate() is passed a java. util.List of objects that describe the arguments that were passed to the extension function by the XPath evaluator. Furthermore, this method returns a value of a type appropriate to the extension function (date()'s long integer return type is compatible with XPath's number type).

The date() extension function is intended to be called with a single argument, which is either of type nodeset or of type string. This extension function throws javax. xml.xpath.XPathFunctionException when the number of arguments (as indicated by the list's size) isn't equal to 1.

When the argument is of type NodeList (a nodeset), the textual content of the first node in the nodeset is obtained; this content is assumed to be a date value in YYYY-MM-DD format (for brevity, I'm overlooking error checking). When the argument is of type String, it's assumed to be a date value in this format. Any other type of argument results in a thrown XPathFunctionException object.

Date comparison is simplified by converting the date to a milliseconds value. This task is accomplished with the help of the java.text.SimpleDateFormat and java.text.ParsePosition classes. After resetting the ParsePosition object's index (via setIndex(0)), SimpleDateFormat's Date parse(String text, ParsePosition pos) method is called to parse the string according to the pattern established when SimpleDateFormat was instantiated, and starting from the parse position identified by the ParsePosition index. This index is reset before the parse() method call because parse() updates this object's index.

The parse() method returns a java.util.Date object whose long getTime() method is called to return the number of milliseconds represented by the parsed date.

After implementing the extension function, you need to create a *function resolver*, which is an object whose class implements the javax.xml.xpath. XPathFunctionResolver interface and which tells the XPath evaluator about the extension function (or functions). Listing 5-7 presents the DateResolver class.

Listing 5-7. A Function Resolver for the date() Extension Function

```
import javax.xml.namespace.QName;

import javax.xml.xpath.XPathFunction;
import javax.xml.xpath.XPathFunctionResolver;

public class DateResolver implements XPathFunctionResolver
{
   private static final QName name =
      new QName("http://www.javajeff.ca/", "date", "tt");
```

```
    @Override
    public XPathFunction resolveFunction(QName name, int arity)
    {
        if (name.equals(this.name) && arity == 1)
            return new Date();
        return null;
    }
}
```

XPathFunctionResolver declares a single XPathFunction resolveFunction(QName functionName, int arity) method that XPath calls to identify the name of the extension function and obtain an instance of a Java object whose evaluate() method implements the function.

The functionName parameter identifies the function's qualified name because all extension functions must live in a namespace and must be referenced via a prefix (which doesn't have to match the prefix in the document). As a result, you must also bind a namespace to the prefix via a namespace context (as demonstrated previously). The arity parameter identifies the number of arguments that the extension function accepts and is useful when overloading extension functions. If the functionName and arity values are acceptable, the extension function's Java class is instantiated and returned; otherwise, null is returned.

Finally, the function resolver class is instantiated and registered with the XPath object by calling XPath's void setXPathFunctionResolver(XPathFunctionResolver resolver) method.

The following excerpt from Version 3 of this chapter's XPathSearch application (in this book's code archive) demonstrates all of these tasks in order to use date() in XPath expression //tt:contact[tt:date(tt:birth) > tt:date('1960-01-01')]/tt:name/text(), which returns only those contacts whose date of birth is greater than 1960-01-01 (Jane Doe followed by Sandra Smith):

```
DocumentBuilderFactory dbf = DocumentBuilderFactory.newInstance();
dbf.setNamespaceAware(true);
DocumentBuilder db = dbf.newDocumentBuilder();
Document doc = db.parse("contacts.xml");
XPathFactory xpf = XPathFactory.newInstance();
XPath xp = xpf.newXPath();
```

```
xp.setNamespaceContext(new NSContext());
xp.setXPathFunctionResolver(new DateResolver());
XPathExpression xpe;
String expr;
expr = "//tt:contact[tt:date(tt:birth) > " +
       "tt:date('1960-01-01')]/tt:name/text()";
xpe = xp.compile(expr);
Object result = xpe.evaluate(doc, XPathConstants.NODESET);
NodeList nl = (NodeList) result;
for (int i = 0; i < nl.getLength(); i++)
   out.println(nl.item(i).getNodeValue());
```

Compile and run the revised XPathSearch application and you'll see Jane Doe followed by Sandra Smith on separate lines.

Variables and Variable Resolvers

All of the previously specified XPath expressions have been based on literal text. XPath also lets you specify variables to parameterize these expressions in a similar manner to using variables with SQL prepared statements.

A variable appears in an expression by prefixing its name (which may or may not have a namespace prefix) with a $. For example, /a/b[@c = $d]/text() is an XPath expression that selects all a elements of the root node, and all of a's b elements that have c attributes containing the value identified by variable $d, and returns the text of these b elements. This expression corresponds to Listing 5-8's XML document.

Listing 5-8. A Simple XML Document for Demonstrating an XPath Variable

```
<?xml version="1.0"?>
<a>
   <b c="x">b1</b>
   <b>b2</b>
   <b c="y">b3</b>
   <b>b4</b>
   <b c="x">b5</b>
</a>
```

To specify variables whose values are obtained during expression evaluation, you must register a variable resolver with your XPath object. A *variable resolver* is an instance of a class that implements the javax.xml.xpath.XPathVariableResolver interface in terms of its Object resolveVariable(QName variableName) method and which tells the evaluator about the variable (or variables).

The variableName parameter contains the qualified name of a variable's name. (Remember that a variable name may be prefixed with a namespace prefix.) This method verifies that the qualified name appropriately names the variable and then returns its value.

After creating the variable resolver, you register it with the XPath object by calling XPath's void setXPathVariableResolver(XPathVariableResolver resolver) method.

The following excerpt from Version 4 of this chapter's XPathSearch application (in this book's code archive) demonstrates all of these tasks in order to specify $d in XPath expression /a/b[@c=$d]/text(), which returns b1 followed by b5. It assumes that Listing 5-8 is stored in a file named example.xml:

```
DocumentBuilderFactory dbf =
   DocumentBuilderFactory.newInstance();
DocumentBuilder db = dbf.newDocumentBuilder();
Document doc = db.parse("example.xml");
XPathFactory xpf = XPathFactory.newInstance();
XPath xp = xpf.newXPath();
XPathVariableResolver xpvr =
   new XPathVariableResolver()
   {
      @Override
      public Object resolveVariable(QName varname)
      {
         if (varname.getLocalPart().equals("d"))
            return "x";
         else
            return null;
      }
   };
```

```
xp.setXPathVariableResolver(xpvr);
XPathExpression xpe;
xpe = xp.compile("/a/b[@c = $d]/text()");
Object result = xpe.evaluate(doc, XPathConstants.NODESET);
NodeList nl = (NodeList) result;
for (int i = 0; i < nl.getLength(); i++)
   out.println(nl.item(i).getNodeValue());
```

Compile and run the revised XPathSearch application and you'll see b1 followed by b5 on separate lines.

Caution   When you qualify a variable name with a namespace prefix (as in $ns:d), you must also register a namespace context to resolve the prefix.

EXERCISES

The following exercises are designed to test your understanding of Chapter 5's content:

1. Define XPath.

2. Where is XPath commonly used?

3. Identify the seven kinds of nodes that XPath recognizes.

4. True or false: XPath recognizes CDATA sections.

5. Describe what XPath provides for selecting nodes.

6. True or false: In a location path expression, you must prefix an attribute name with the @ symbol.

7. Identify the functions that XPath provides for selecting comment, text, and processing-instruction nodes.

8. What does XPath provide for selecting unknown nodes?

9. How do you perform multiple selections?

10. What is a predicate?

11. Identify the functions that XPath provides for working with nodesets.

12. Identify the three advanced features that the XPath API provides to overcome limitations with the XPath 1.0 language.

13. True or false: The XPath API maps XPath's number type to `java.lang.Float`.

14. Modify Listing 5-1's contacts document by changing `<name>John Doe</name>` to `<Name>John Doe</Name>`. Because you no longer see John Doe in the output when you run Listing 5-3's `XPathSearch` application (you only see Bob Jones), modify this application's location path expression so that you see John Doe followed by Bob Jones.

Summary

XPath is a nonXML declarative query language for selecting an XML document's infoset items as one or more nodes. It simplifies access to a DOM tree's nodes and is also useful with XSLT where it's typically employed to select those input document elements (via XPath expressions) that are to be copied to an output document.

XPath regards an XML document as a tree of nodes that starts from a root node. This language recognizes seven kinds of nodes: element, attribute, text, namespace, processing instruction, comment, and document. It doesn't recognize CDATA sections, entity references, or document type declarations.

XPath provides location path expressions for selecting nodes. A location path expression locates nodes via a sequence of steps starting from the context node (the root node or some other document node that's the current node). The returned set of nodes, which is known as a nodeset, might be empty, or it might contain one or more nodes.

Location path expressions (which return nodesets) are one kind of XPath expression. XPath also supports general expressions that evaluate to Boolean (such as predicates), number, or string type; for example, `position() = 2`, `6.8`, and `"Hello"`. General expressions are often used in XSLT.

The XPath API provides advanced features to overcome limitations with the XPath 1.0 language: namespace contexts (which map arbitrary namespace prefixes to namespace URIs), extension functions and function resolvers (for defining functions that extend XPath's predefined function repertoire), and variables and variable resolvers (for parameterizing XPath expressions).

Chapter 6 introduces you to XSLT for transforming XML documents.

CHAPTER 6

Transforming XML Documents with XSLT

Along with SAX, DOM, StAX, and XPath, Java includes the XSLT API, for transforming XML documents. Chapter 6 introduces you to XSLT.

What Is XSLT?

Extensible Stylesheet Language (*XSL*) is a family of languages for transforming and formatting XML documents. *XSL Transformation* (*XSLT*) is the XSL language for transforming XML documents to other formats, such as HTML (for presenting an XML document's content via a web browser).

XSLT accomplishes its work by using XSLT processors and stylesheets. An *XSLT processor* is a software component that applies an *XSLT stylesheet* (an XML-based template consisting of content and transformation instructions) to an input document (without modifying the document) and copies the transformed result to a result tree, which can be output to a file or output stream or even piped into another XSLT processor for additional transformations. Figure 6-1 illustrates the transformation process.

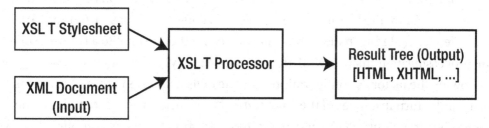

Figure 6-1. *An XSLT processor transforms an XML input document into a result tree*

© Jeff Friesen 2019
J. Friesen, *Java XML and JSON*, https://doi.org/10.1007/978-1-4842-4330-5_6

The beauty of XSLT is that you don't need to develop custom software applications to perform the transformations. Instead, you simply create an XSLT stylesheet and input it along with the XML document needing to be transformed to an XSLT processor.

Exploring the XSLT API

Java implements XSLT through the types in the `javax.xml.transform`, `javax.xml.transform.dom`, `javax.xml.transform.sax`, `javax.xml.transform.stax`, and `javax.xml.transform.stream` packages. The `javax.xml.transform` package defines the generic APIs for processing transformation instructions and for performing a transformation from a *source* (where the XSLT processor's input originates) to a *result* (where the processor's output is sent). The remaining packages define the APIs for obtaining different kinds of sources and results.

The `javax.xml.transform.TransformerFactory` class is the starting point for working with XSLT. You instantiate `TransformerFactory` by calling one of its `newInstance()` methods. For example, the following code fragment uses `TransformerFactory`'s `TransformerFactory newInstance()` class method to create the factory:

```
TransformerFactory tf = TransformerFactory.newInstance();
```

Behind the scenes, `newInstance()` follows an ordered lookup procedure to identify the `TransformerFactory` implementation class to load. This procedure first examines the `javax.xml.transform.TransformerFactory` system property and lastly returns the system-default implementation (returned from `TransformerFactory newDefaultInstance()`). If there is a service configuration error, or if the implementation is not available or cannot be instantiated, this method throws an instance of the `javax.xml.stream.TransformerFactoryConfigurationError` class.

After obtaining a `TransformerFactory` object, you can call various configuration methods to configure the factory. For example, you could call `TransformerFactory`'s `void setFeature(String name, boolean value)` method to enable a feature (such as secure processing, to transform XML documents securely).

Following the factory's configuration, call one of its `newTransformer()` methods to create and return instances of the `javax.xml.transform.Transformer` class. The following code fragment calls `Transformer newTransformer()` to accomplish this task:

```
Transformer t = tf.newTransformer();
```

The noargument `newTransformer()` method copies source input to the destination without making any changes. This kind of transformation is known as the *identity transformation*.

To change input, specify a *stylesheet*. Accomplish this task by calling the factory's `Transformer newTransformer(Source source)` method, where the `javax.xml.transform.Source` interface describes a source for the stylesheet. The following code fragment accomplishes this task:

```
FileReader fr = new FileReader("recipe.xsl");
Transformer t = tf.newTransformer(new StreamSource(fr));
```

This code fragment creates a transformer that obtains a stylesheet from a file named `recipe.xsl` via a `javax.xml.transform.stream.StreamSource` object connected to a file reader. It's customary to use the `.xsl` or `.xslt` extension to identify XSLT stylesheet files.

The `newTransformer()` methods throw `javax.xml.transform.TransformerConfigurationException` when they cannot return a `Transformer` instance that corresponds to the factory configuration.

After obtaining a `Transformer` instance, you can call its `void setOutputProperty(String name, String value)` method to influence a transformation. The `javax.xml.transform.OutputKeys` class declares constants for frequently used keys. For example, `OutputKeys.METHOD` is the key for specifying the method for outputting the result tree (as XML, HTML, plain text, or something else).

Tip   To set multiple properties in a single method call, create a `java.util.Properties` object and pass this object as an argument to `Transformer`'s `void setOutputProperties(Properties prop)` method. Properties set by `setOutputProperty()` and `setOutputProperties()` override the stylesheet's `xsl:output` instruction settings.

Before you can perform a transformation, you need to obtain instances of classes that implement the `Source` and `javax.xml.transform.Result` interfaces. You then pass these instances to `Transformer`'s `void transform(Source xmlSource, Result outputTarget)` method, which throws an instance of the `javax.xml.transform.TransformerException` class when a problem arises during the transformation.

The following code fragment shows you how to obtain a source and a result and perform the transformation:

```
Source source = new DOMSource(doc);
Result result = new StreamResult(System.out);
t.transform(source, result);
```

The first line instantiates the `javax.xml.transform.dom.DOMSource` class, which acts as a holder for a DOM tree rooted in the `org.w3c.dom.Document` object specified by doc. The second line instantiates the `javax.xml.transform.stream.StreamResult` class, which acts as a holder for the standard output stream, to which the transformed data items are sent. The third line reads data from the `Source` object and outputs transformed data to the `Result` object.

TRANSFORMER FACTORY FEATURE DETECTION

Although Java's default transformers support the various `Source` and `Result` implementation classes that are located in the `javax.xml.transform.dom`, `javax.xml.transform.sax`, `javax.xml.transform.stax`, and `javax.xml.transform.stream` packages, a nondefault transformer (perhaps specified via the `javax.xml.transform.TransformerFactory` system property) might be more limited. For this reason, each `Source` and `Result` implementation class declares a FEATURE string constant that can be passed to `TransformerFactory`'s boolean `getFeature(String name)` method. This method returns `true` when the `Source` or `Result` implementation class is supported. For example, `tf.getFeature(StreamSource.FEATURE)` returns `true` when stream sources are supported.

The `javax.xml.transform.sax.SAXTransformerFactory` class provides additional SAX-specific factory methods that can be used only when the `TransformerFactory` object is also an instance of this class. To help you make the determination, `SAXTransformerFactory` also declares a FEATURE string constant that you can pass to `getFeature()`. For example, `tf.getFeature(SAXTransformerFactory.FEATURE)` returns `true` when the transformer factory referenced from `tf` is an instance of `SAXTransformerFactory`.

Most of Java's XML API interface objects and the factories that return them are not thread-safe. This situation also applies to transformers. Although you can reuse the same transformer multiple times on the same thread, you cannot access the transformer from multiple threads.

This problem can be solved for transformers by using instances of classes that implement the javax.xml.transform.Templates interface. The Java documentation for this interface has this to say: *Templates must be threadsafe for a given instance over multiple threads running concurrently, and may be used multiple times in a given session.* As well as promoting thread safety, Templates instances can improve performance because they represent compiled XSLT stylesheets.

The following code fragment shows how you might perform a transformation without a Templates object:

```
TransformerFactory tf = TransformerFactory.newInstance();
FileReader fr = new FileReader("recipe.xsl");
StreamSource ssStyleSheet = new StreamSource(fr);
Transformer t = tf.newTransformer(ssStyleSheet);
t.transform(new DOMSource(doc), new StreamResult(System.out));
```

You cannot access t's transformer from multiple threads. In contrast, the following code fragment shows you how to construct a transformer from a Templates object so that it can be accessed from multiple threads:

```
TransformerFactory tf = TransformerFactory.newInstance();
FileReader fr = new FileReader("recipe.xsl");
StreamSource ssStyleSheet = new StreamSource(fr);
Templates te = tf.newTemplates(ssStylesheet);
Transformer t = te.newTransformer();
t.transform(new DOMSource(doc), new StreamResult(System.out));
```

The differences are the call to Transformerfactory's Templates newTemplates(Source source) method to create and return objects whose classes implement the Templates interface, and the call to this interface's Transformer newTransformer() method to obtain the Transformer object.

Demonstrating the XSLT API

Listing 3-2 presents a DOMDemo application that creates a DOM document tree based on Listing 1-2's movie XML document. Unfortunately, you cannot use the DOM API to assign ISO-8859-1 to the XML declaration's encoding attribute. Also, you cannot use DOM (apart from Load and Save) to output this tree to a file or other destination. However, you can overcome these problems with XSLT, as demonstrated in Listing 6-1.

Listing 6-1. Assigning ISO-8859-1 to the XML Declaration's Encoding Attribute via XSLT

```
import javax.xml.parsers.DocumentBuilder;
import javax.xml.parsers.DocumentBuilderFactory;
import javax.xml.parsers.FactoryConfigurationError;
import javax.xml.parsers.ParserConfigurationException;

import javax.xml.transform.OutputKeys;
import javax.xml.transform.Result;
import javax.xml.transform.Source;
import javax.xml.transform.Transformer;
import javax.xml.transform.TransformerConfigurationException;
import javax.xml.transform.TransformerException;
import javax.xml.transform.TransformerFactory;
import javax.xml.transform.TransformerFactoryConfigurationError;

import javax.xml.transform.dom.DOMSource;

import javax.xml.transform.stream.StreamResult;

import org.w3c.dom.Document;
import org.w3c.dom.Element;
import org.w3c.dom.Text;

import static java.lang.System.*;
```

```java
public class XSLTDemo
{
   final static String KEY_INDENT =
      "{http://xml.apache.org/xslt}indent-amount";

   public static void main(String[] args)
   {
      try
      {
         DocumentBuilderFactory dbf =
            DocumentBuilderFactory.newInstance();
         DocumentBuilder db = dbf.newDocumentBuilder();
         Document doc = db.newDocument();
         doc.setXmlStandalone(true);
         // Create the root element.
         Element root = doc.createElement("movie");
         doc.appendChild(root);
         // Create name child element and add it to the
         // root.
         Element name = doc.createElement("name");
         root.appendChild(name);
         // Add a text element to the name element.
         Text text = doc.createTextNode("Le Fabuleux " +
                                        "Destin d'Amélie " + "Poulain");
         name.appendChild(text);
         // Create language child element and add it to the
         // root.
         Element language = doc.createElement("language");
         root.appendChild(language);
         // Add a text element to the language element.
         text = doc.createTextNode("français");
         language.appendChild(text);
         // Use a transformer to output this tree with
         // ISO-8859-1 encoding to the standard output
```

```
        // stream.
        TransformerFactory tf = TransformerFactory.newInstance();
        Transformer t = tf.newTransformer();
        t.setOutputProperty(OutputKeys.METHOD, "xml");
        t.setOutputProperty(OutputKeys.ENCODING, "ISO-8859-1");
        t.setOutputProperty(OutputKeys.INDENT, "yes");
        t.setOutputProperty(KEY_INDENT, "3");
        Source source = new DOMSource(doc);
        Result result = new StreamResult(out);
        t.transform(source, result);
    }
    catch (FactoryConfigurationError fce)
    {
        err.printf("FCE: %s%n", fce.toString());
    }
    catch (ParserConfigurationException pce)
    {
        err.printf("PCE: %s%n", pce.toString());
    }
    catch (TransformerConfigurationException tce)
    {
        err.printf("TCE: %s%n", tce.toString());
    }
    catch (TransformerException te)
    {
        err.printf("TE: %s%n", te.toString());
    }
    catch (TransformerFactoryConfigurationError tfce)
    {
        err.printf("TFCE: %s%n", tfce.toString());
    }
  }
}
```

Listing 6-1 first creates a DOM tree. It then creates a transformer factory and obtains a transformer from this factory. Four properties are then set on the transformer, and a stream source and result are obtained. Finally, the transform() method is called to transform source content to the result.

The four properties set on the transformer influence the transformation. OutputKeys.METHOD specifies that the result tree will be written out as XML, OutputKeys. ENCODING specifies that ISO-8859-1 will be the value of the XML declaration's encoding attribute, and OutputKeys.INDENT specifies that the transformer can output additional whitespace.

The additional whitespace is used to output the XML across multiple lines instead of on a single line. Because it would be nice to indicate the number of spaces for indenting lines of XML, and because this information cannot be specified via an OutputKeys property, the nonstandard "{http://xml.apache.org/xslt}indent-amount" property (property keys begin with brace-delimited URIs) is used to specify an appropriate value (such as 3 spaces). It's okay to specify this property in this application because Java's default XSLT implementation is based on Apache's XSLT implementation.

Compile Listing 6-1 as follows:

```
javac XSLTDemo.java
```

Run the resulting application as follows:

```
java XSLTDemo
```

You should observe the following output:

```
<?xml version="1.0" encoding="ISO-8859-1"?><movie>
   <name>Le Fabuleux Destin d'Amélie Poulain</name>
   <language>français</language>
</movie>
```

Although this example shows you how to output a DOM tree and also how to specify an encoding value for the XML declaration of the resulting XML document, the example doesn't really demonstrate the power of XSLT because (apart from setting the encoding attribute value) it performs an identity transformation. A more interesting example would take advantage of a stylesheet.

Consider a scenario where you want to convert Listing 1-1's recipe document to an HTML document for presentation via a web browser. Listing 6-2 presents a stylesheet that a transformer can use to perform the conversion.

Listing 6-2. An XSLT Stylesheet for Converting a Recipe Document to an HTML Document

```xml
<?xml version="1.0"?>
<xsl:stylesheet version="1.0"
    xmlns:xsl="http://www.w3.org/1999/XSL/Transform">
<xsl:template match="/recipe">
<html>
    <head>
        <title>Recipes</title>
    </head>

    <body>
        <h2>
            <xsl:value-of select="normalize-space(title)"/>
        </h2>

        <h3>Ingredients</h3>

        <ul>
        <xsl:for-each select="ingredients/ingredient">
          <li>
              <xsl:value-of select="normalize-space(text())"/>
              <xsl:if test="@qty"> (<xsl:value-of
                                    select="@qty"/>)</xsl:if>
          </li>
        </xsl:for-each>
        </ul>

        <h3>Instructions</h3>

        <xsl:value-of select="normalize-space(instructions)"/>
    </body>
</html>
</xsl:template>
</xsl:stylesheet>
```

Listing 6-2 reveals that a stylesheet is an XML document. Its root element is stylesheet, which identifies the standard namespace for stylesheets. It's conventional to specify xsl as the namespace prefix for referring to XSLT instruction elements, although any prefix could be specified.

A stylesheet is based on template elements that control how an element and its content are converted. A template focuses on a single element that's identified via the match attribute. This attribute's value is an XPath location path expression, which matches all recipe child nodes of the root element node. Regarding Listing 1-1, only the single recipe root element will be matched and selected.

A template element can contain literal text and stylesheet instructions. For example, the value-of instruction in <xsl:value-of select="normalize-space(title)"/> specifies that the value of the title element (which is a child of the recipe context node) is to be retrieved and copied to the output. Because this text is surrounded by space and newline characters, XPath's normalize-string() function is called to remove this whitespace before the title is copied.

XSLT is a powerful declarative language that includes control flow instructions such as for-each and if. In the context of <xsl:for-each select="ingredients/ingredient">, for-each causes all of the ingredient child nodes of the ingredients node to be selected and processed one at a time. For each node, <xsl:value-of select="normalize-space(text())"/> is executed to copy the content of the ingredient node, normalized to remove whitespace. Also, the if instruction in <xsl:if test="@qty"> (<xsl:value-of select="@qty"/>) determines whether or not the ingredient node has a qty attribute, and (if so) copies a space character followed by this attribute's value (surrounded by parentheses) to the output.

Listing 6-3 presents the source code to an XSLTDemo application that shows you how to write the Java code to process Listing 1-1 via Listing 6-2's stylesheet.

Listing 6-3. Transforming Recipe XML via a Stylesheet

```
import java.io.FileReader;
import java.io.IOException;

import javax.xml.parsers.DocumentBuilder;
import javax.xml.parsers.DocumentBuilderFactory;
import javax.xml.parsers.FactoryConfigurationError;
import javax.xml.parsers.ParserConfigurationException;
```

```
import javax.xml.transform.OutputKeys;
import javax.xml.transform.Result;
import javax.xml.transform.Source;
import javax.xml.transform.Transformer;
import javax.xml.transform.
      TransformerConfigurationException;
import javax.xml.transform.TransformerException;
import javax.xml.transform.TransformerFactory;
import javax.xml.transform.
      TransformerFactoryConfigurationError;

import javax.xml.transform.dom.DOMSource;

import javax.xml.transform.stream.StreamResult;
import javax.xml.transform.stream.StreamSource;

import org.w3c.dom.Document;

import org.xml.sax.SAXException;

import static java.lang.System.*;

public class XSLTDemo
{
   public static void main(String[] args)
   {
      try
      {
         DocumentBuilderFactory dbf =
            DocumentBuilderFactory.newInstance();
         DocumentBuilder db = dbf.newDocumentBuilder();
         Document doc = db.parse("recipe.xml");
         TransformerFactory tf =
            TransformerFactory.newInstance();
         FileReader fr = new FileReader("recipe.xsl");
         StreamSource ssStyleSheet = new StreamSource(fr);
         Transformer t = tf.newTransformer(ssStyleSheet);
         t.setOutputProperty(OutputKeys.METHOD, "html");
```

```
         t.setOutputProperty(OutputKeys.INDENT, "yes");
         Source source = new DOMSource(doc);
         Result result = new StreamResult(out);
         t.transform(source, result);
      }
      catch (IOException ioe)
      {
         err.printf("IOE: %s%n", ioe.toString());
      }
      catch (FactoryConfigurationError fce)
      {
         err.printf("FCE: %s%n", fce.toString());
      }
      catch (ParserConfigurationException pce)
      {
         err.printf("PCE: %s%n", pce.toString());
      }
      catch (SAXException saxe)
      {
         err.printf("SAXE: %s%n", saxe.toString());
      }
      catch (TransformerConfigurationException tce)
      {
         err.printf("TCE: %s%n", tce.toString());
      }
      catch (TransformerException te)
      {
         err.printf("TE: %s%n", te.toString());
      }
      catch (TransformerFactoryConfigurationError tfce)
      {
         err.printf("TFCE: %s%n", tfce.toString());
      }
   }
}
```

Listing 6-3 is similar in structure to Listing 6-1. It reveals that the output method is set to html, and it also reveals that the resulting HTML should be indented. When run, this application generates the following output:

```
<html>
    <head>
        <META http-equiv="Content-Type" content="text/html; charset=UTF-8">
        <title>Recipes</title>
    </head>
    <body>
        <h2>Grilled Cheese Sandwich</h2>
        <h3>Ingredients</h3>
        <ul>
            <li>bread slice (2)</li>
            <li>cheese slice</li>
            <li>margarine pat (2)</li>
        </ul>
        <h3>Instructions</h3>
        Place frying pan on element and select medium heat. For each bread
        slice, smear one pat of margarine on one side of bread slice. Place
        cheese slice between bread slices with margarine-smeared sides away
        from the cheese. Place sandwich in frying pan with one margarine-
        smeared side in contact with pan. Fry for a couple of minutes and
        flip. Fry other side for a minute and serve.
    </body>
</html>
```

OutputKeys.INDENT and its "yes" value let you output the HTML across multiple lines as opposed to outputting the HTML on a single line. However, the XSLT processor performs no additional indentation and ignores attempts to specify the number of spaces to indent via code such as t.setOutputProperty("{http://xml.apache.org/xslt}indent-amount", "3");.

Note   An XSLT processor outputs a <META> tag when OutputKeys.METHOD is set to "html".

Going Beyond XSLT 1.0 and XPath 1.0

Java 11's XSLT implementation is based on the Apache Xalan Project (https://xalan.apache.org), which supports XSLT 1.0 and XPath 1.0. However, more recent versions of XSLT and XPath have been developed: 2.0, 3.0, and (for XPath) 3.1. The following list identifies some of their new features:

- XSLT 2.0 introduces string manipulation using regular expressions, as well as functions and operators for manipulating dates, times, and durations.

- XPath 2.0 is built around the XQuery and XPath Data Model (https://en.wikipedia.org/wiki/XQuery_and_XPath_Data_Model), which offers a much richer type system.

- XSLT 3.0 supports streaming transformations (www.w3.org/TR/xslt-30/), which is useful for processing documents that are too large to fit in memory, or when transformations are chained in XML Pipelines (https://en.wikipedia.org/wiki/XML_pipeline).

- XPath 3.0 supports functions as first-class values.

- XPath 3.1 adds new map and array data types, largely to underpin support for JSON, which I introduce in the next chapter.

You cannot use Java 11's XSLT and XPath APIs to explore these and other new features until you replace the Xalan implementation. One alternative is SAXON (http://saxon.sourceforge.net). This "XSLT and XQuery Processor" supports XSLT 2.0/3.0 and XPath 2.0/3.1 (and more).

Downloading and Testing SAXON-HE 9.9

SAXON is available in home, professional, enterprise, and JavaScript editions. The home edition is an open-source product available under the Mozilla Public License version 2.0. SAXON 9.9 is its most recent version at the time of writing and is the version we will download.

Download Saxon-HE 9.9 by clicking the "Download for Java (5.4 Mbytes)" link on SAXON's SourceForge home page (http://saxon.sourceforge.net). On subsequent pages, click "Saxon-HE" followed by "9.9" followed by "SaxonHE9-9-0-1J.zip." Save and unzip this file. I unzipped SAXON-HE 9.9 to my C:\unzipped\SaxonHE9-9-0-1J directory, which I'll use as its home directory.

Saxonica (http://saxonica.com/welcome/welcome.xml) is the company behind SAXON. Its "Getting started with Saxon on the Java platform" documentation page (www.saxonica.com/html/documentation/about/gettingstarted/gettingstartedjava.html) shows how to test that the software is working. At the command line, I enter the following command (spread across two lines for readability) to run a simple query:

```
java -cp c:\unzipped\SaxonHE9-9-0-1J\saxon9he.jar
     net.sf.saxon.Query -t -qs:"current-date()"
```

I observed the following output (the time and memory values will typically change from run to run):

```
Saxon-HE 9.9.0.1J from Saxonica
Java version 11
Analyzing query from {current-date()}
Analysis time: 213.068628 milliseconds
<?xml version="1.0" encoding="UTF-8"?>2018-10-08-05:00Execution time:
54.719965ms
Memory used: 5837296
```

Playing with SAXON-HE 9.9

Let's revisit the first XSLTDemo application presented in this chapter (Listing 6-1). We can tell this application to use SAXON by inserting the following System.setProperty() call at the beginning of the main() method:

```
System.setProperty("javax.xml.transform.TransformerFactory",
              "net.sf.saxon.TransformerFactoryImpl");
```

To prove that SAXON is being used, we can also insert the following line after the `Transformer t = tf.newTransformer();` line:

```
System.out.println(t);
```

> **Note**   These code fragments are excerpts from a third version of XSLTDemo that's located in the book's code archive.

The source code would be compiled as previously shown. To run the application, you would need to include the `saxon9he.jar` file in the CLASSPATH, or else you would observe a `TransformerFactoryConfigurationError`:

```
java -cp c:\unzipped\SaxonHE9-9-0-1J\saxon9he.jar;. XSLTDemo
```

If all goes well, you should then see the following output:

```
net.sf.saxon.jaxp.IdentityTransformer@8b96fde
<?xml version="1.0" encoding="ISO-8859-1"?>
<movie>
   <name>Le Fabuleux Destin d'Amélie Poulain</name>
   <language>français</language>
</movie>
```

You can start to move beyond XSLT 1.0. For example, you might want to check out *Beginning XSLT 2.0 From Novice to Professional* (`www.apress.com/9781590593240`), an Apress book written by Jeni Tennison. This book will get you comfortable with XSLT 2.0.

> **Caution**   The SAXON Home Edition doesn't include the following capabilities: schema processing and schema-aware XSLT and XQuery; support for higher-order functions; support for XPath 1.0 (and XSLT 1.0) backward compatibility mode, numerous SAXON extensions; calling out to Java methods; XQuery Update support; and various optimizations including join optimization, streamed processing, multi-threaded execution, and byte code generation.

EXERCISES

The following exercises are designed to test your understanding of Chapter 6's content:

1. Define XSLT.

2. How does XSLT accomplish its work?

3. True or false: Call TransformerFactory's void transform(Source xmlSource, Result outputTarget) method to transform a source to a result.

4. Create a books.xsl stylesheet file and a MakeHTML application with a similar structure to the application that processes Listing 6-2's recipe.xsl stylesheet. MakeHTML uses books.xsl to convert Exercise 1-21's books.xml content to HTML. When viewed in a web browser, the HTML should result in a web page that's similar to the page shown in Figure 6-2.

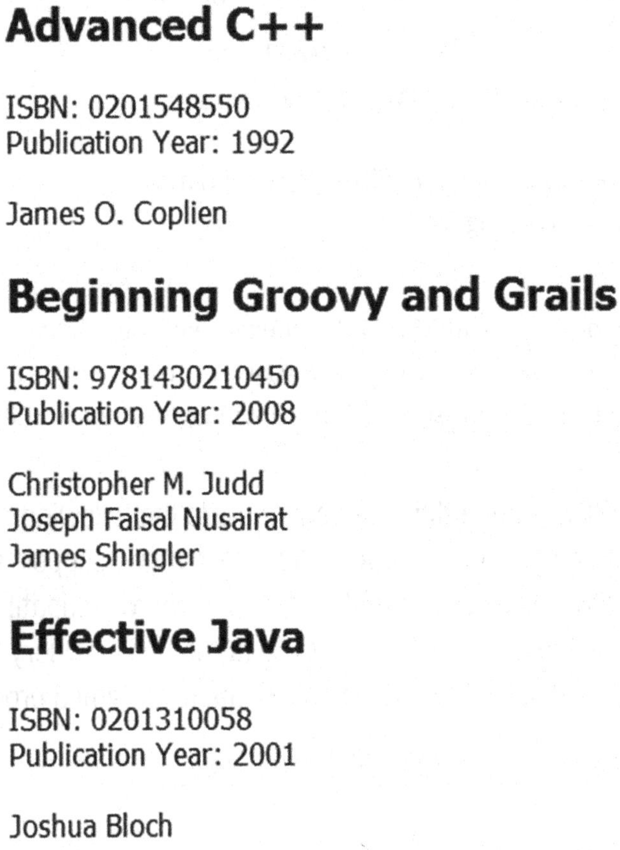

Advanced C++

ISBN: 0201548550
Publication Year: 1992

James O. Coplien

Beginning Groovy and Grails

ISBN: 9781430210450
Publication Year: 2008

Christopher M. Judd
Joseph Faisal Nusairat
James Shingler

Effective Java

ISBN: 0201310058
Publication Year: 2001

Joshua Bloch

Figure 6-2. *Exercise 1-21's books.xml content is presented via a web page*

Summary

XSL is a family of languages for transforming and formatting XML documents. XSLT is the XSL language for transforming XML documents to other formats, such as HTML (for presenting an XML document's content via a web browser).

XSLT accomplishes its work by using XSLT processors and stylesheets. An XSLT processor applies an XSLT stylesheet to an input document (without modifying the document) and copies the transformed result to a result tree, which can be output to a file or output stream or even piped into another XSLT processor for additional transformations.

Java implements XSLT through the types in the `javax.xml.transform`, `javax.xml.transform.dom`, `javax.xml.transform.sax`, `javax.xml.transform.stax`, and `javax.xml.transform.stream` packages. The `javax.xml.transform` package defines the generic APIs for processing transformation instructions and for performing a transformation from a source (where the XSLT processor's input originates) to a result (where the processor's output is sent). The remaining packages define the APIs for obtaining different kinds of sources and results.

Java 11's XSLT implementation is based on the Apache Xalan Project, which supports XSLT 1.0 and XPath 1.0. Because you cannot use Java 11's XSLT and XPath APIs to explore XSLT 2.0/3.0 and XPath 2.0/3.x, you must replace the Xalan implementation. One alternative is SAXON. This "XSLT and XQuery Processor" supports XSLT 2.0/3.0 and XPath 2.0/3.1 (and more).

Chapter 7 introduces you to JSON, a less-verbose alternative to XML.

PART II

Exploring JSON

CHAPTER 7

Introducing JSON

Many applications communicate by exchanging JSON objects instead of XML documents. Chapter 7 introduces JSON, tours its syntax, demonstrates JSON in a JavaScript context, and shows how to validate JSON objects in the context of JSON Schema.

What Is JSON?

JSON (*JavaScript Object Notation*) is a language-independent data format that expresses JSON objects as human-readable lists of *properties* (name/value pairs). Although derived from a nonstrict subset of JavaScript, code to parse JSON objects into equivalent language-dependent objects is available in many programming languages.

Note JSON allows the Unicode U+2028 line separator and U+2029 paragraph separator to appear unescaped in quoted strings. Because JavaScript doesn't support this capability, JSON isn't a proper subset of JavaScript.

JSON is commonly used in asynchronous browser/server communication via AJAX (https://en.wikipedia.org/wiki/Ajax_(programming)). JSON is also used with NoSQL database management systems such as MongoDb and CouchDb; with apps from social media websites such as Twitter, Facebook, LinkedIn, and Flickr; and even with the popular Google Maps API.

Note Many developers prefer JSON to XML because they see JSON as being less verbose and easier to read. Check out "JSON: The Fat-Free Alternative to XML" (www.json.org/xml.html) for more information.

© Jeff Friesen 2019
J. Friesen, *Java XML and JSON*, https://doi.org/10.1007/978-1-4842-4330-5_7

187

JSON Syntax Tour

The JSON data format presents a JSON object as a brace-delimited and comma-separated list of properties (a comma doesn't appear after the final property):

```
{
    property1 ,
    property2 ,
    ...
    propertyN
}
```

For each property, the name is expressed as a string that's typically quoted (and by a pair of double quotes). The name string is followed by a colon character, which is followed by a value of a specific type. Examples include `"name": "JSON"` and `"age": 25`.

JSON supports the following six types:

- *Number*: a signed decimal number that may contain a fractional part and may use exponential (E) notation. JSON doesn't permit nonnumbers (such as NaN), nor does it make any distinction between integer and floating-point. Furthermore, JSON doesn't recognize the octal and hexadecimal formats. (Although JavaScript uses a double precision floating-point format for all numeric values, other languages implementing JSON may encode numbers differently.)

- *String*: a sequence of zero or more Unicode characters. Strings are delimited with double quotes and support a backslash escaping syntax.

- *Boolean*: either of the values `true` or `false`.

- *Array*: an ordered list of zero or more values, each of which may be of any type. Arrays use square bracket notation with elements being comma-separated.

- *Object*: an unordered collection of properties where the names (also called *keys*) are strings. Because objects are intended to represent associative arrays, it's recommended, although not required, that each key be unique within an object. Objects are delimited with braces and use commas to separate each property. Within each property the colon character separates the key from its value.

- *Null*: an empty value, using the keyword `null`.

Note   JSON Schema (discussed later) recognizes a seventh type: integer. This type doesn't include a fraction or exponent and is a subset of number.

Whitespace is allowed and ignored around or between syntactic elements (values and punctuation). Four specific characters are considered whitespace for this purpose: space, horizontal tab, line feed, and carriage return. Also, JSON doesn't support comments.

Using this data format, you can specify a JSON object such as the following anonymous object (excerpted from Wikipedia's JSON page [https://en.wikipedia.org/wiki/JSON]) for describing a person in terms of first name, last name, and other data items:

```
{
    "firstName": "John",
    "lastName": "Smith",
    "isAlive": true,
    "age": 25,
    "address":
    {
        "streetAddress": "21 2nd Street",
        "city": "New York",
        "state": "NY",
        "postalCode": "10021-3100"
    },
    "phoneNumbers":
    [
        {
            "type": "home",
            "number": "212 555-1234"
        },
        {
            "type": "office",
            "number": "646 555-4567"
        }
    ],
```

```
    "children": [],
    "spouse": null
}
```

In this example, the anonymous object consists of eight properties with the following keys:

- firstName identifies a person's first name and is of type string.

- lastName identifies a person's last name and is of type string.

- isAlive identifies a person's alive status and is of type Boolean.

- age identifies how old a person is and is of type number.

- address identifies a person's location and is of type object. Within this object are four properties (of type string): streetAddress, city, state, and postalCode.

- phoneNumbers identifies a person's phone numbers and is of type array. Within the array are two objects; each object consists of type and number properties (of type string).

- children identifies a person's children (if any) and is of type array.

- spouse identifies a person's partner and is empty.

The previous example shows that objects and arrays can be nested, for example, objects placed within arrays that are placed within objects.

Note   By convention, JSON objects are stored in files with the .json file extension.

Demonstrating JSON with JavaScript

Ideally, I'd demonstrate JSON with Java's standard JSON API. However, Java doesn't officially support JSON.

Note   In 2014, Oracle introduced a Java Enhancement Proposal (JEP) for adding a JSON API to Java. Although "JEP 198: Light-Weight JSON API" (`http://openjdk.java.net/jeps/198`) was updated in 2017, it will probably be several more years before this JSON API becomes part of Java.

I'll demonstrate JSON via JavaScript, but in a Java context via Java's Scripting API. (If you're new to Scripting, I'll explain just enough of this API so that you can understand the code.) To get started, Listing 7-1 presents the source code to an application for executing JavaScript code.

Listing 7-1. Executing JavaScript Code with Assistance from Java

```
import java.io.FileReader;
import java.io.IOException;

import javax.script.ScriptEngine;
import javax.script.ScriptEngineManager;
import javax.script.ScriptException;

import static java.lang.System.*;

public class RunScript
{
   public static void main(String[] args)
   {
      if (args.length != 1)
      {
         err.println("usage: java RunScript script");
         return;
      }
      ScriptEngineManager manager =
         new ScriptEngineManager();
      ScriptEngine engine =
         manager.getEngineByName("nashorn");
      try
      {
         engine.eval(new FileReader(args[0]));
```

```
      }
      catch (ScriptException se)
      {
         err.println(se.getMessage());
      }
      catch (IOException ioe)
      {
         err.println(ioe.getMessage());
      }
   }
}
```

Listing 7-1's main() method first verifies that exactly one command-line argument, which names a script file, has been specified. If this isn't the case, it displays usage information and terminates the application.

Assuming that a single command-line argument was specified, the javax.script. ScriptEngineManager class is instantiated. ScriptEngineManager serves as the entry point into the Scripting API.

Next, the ScriptEngineManager object's ScriptEngine getEngineByName(String shortName) method is called to obtain a script engine corresponding to the desired shortName value. Java 11 supports the nashorn script engine (although it has been deprecated), which is returned as an object whose class implements the javax.script. ScriptEngine interface.

ScriptEngine declares several eval() methods for evaluating a script. main() invokes the Object eval(Reader reader) method to read the script from its java.io.FileReader object argument and (assuming that java.io.IOException isn't thrown) then evaluate the script. This method returns any script return value, which I ignore. Also, this method throws javax.script.ScriptException when an error occurs in the script.

Compile Listing 7-1 as follows:

```
javac RunScript.java
```

Before you can run this application, you need a suitable script file. Listing 7-2 presents a script that declares and accesses a JSON object.

Listing 7-2. Declaring and Accessing a Person Object

```
var person =
{
   "firstName": "John",
   "lastName": "Smith",
   "isAlive": true,
   "age": 25,
   "address":
   {
      "streetAddress": "21 2nd Street",
      "city": "New York",
      "state": "NY",
      "postalCode": "10021-3100"
   },
   "phoneNumbers":
   [
      {
         "type": "home",
         "number": "212 555-1234"
      },
      {
         "type": "office",
         "number": "646 555-4567"
      }
   ],
   "children": [],
   "spouse": null
};
print(person.firstName);
print(person.lastName);
print(person.address.city);
print(person.phoneNumbers[1].number);
```

Assuming that Listing 7-2 is stored in `person.js`, run the application as follows:

```
java RunScript person.js
```

You should observe the following output (along with a warning message about Nashorn's planned removal from a future JDK release):

```
John
Smith
New York
646 555-4567
```

A JSON object exists as language-independent text. To convert the text to a language-dependent object, you need to parse the text. JavaScript provides a `JSON` object with a `parse()` method for this task. Pass the text to be parsed as an argument to `parse()` and receive the resulting JavaScript-based object as this method's return value. `parse()` throws `SyntaxError` when the text doesn't conform to the JSON format.

Listing 7-3 presents a script that demonstrates `parse()`.

Listing 7-3. Parsing a JSON Object

```
var creditCardText =
"{ \"number\": \"1234567890123456\", " +
"\"expiry\": \"04/20\", \"type\": " +
"\"visa\" }";
var creditCard = JSON.parse(creditCardText);
print(creditCard.number);
print(creditCard.expiry);
print(creditCard.type);

var creditCardText2 = "{ 'type': 'visa' }";
var creditCard2 = JSON.parse(creditCardText2);
```

Assuming that Listing 7-3 is stored in `cc.js`, run the application as follows:

```
java RunScript cc.js
```

You should observe the following output:

```
1234567890123456
04/20
visa
SyntaxError: Invalid JSON: <json>:1:2 Expected , or } but found '
{ 'type': 'visa' }
  ^ in <eval> at line number 11
```

The syntax error shows that you cannot delimit a name with single quotes (only double quotes are valid).

This is all I have to say about working with JSON in a JavaScript context. Because this book is Java-focused, subsequent chapters will explore various third-party Java APIs for parsing JSON objects into Java-dependent objects and vice versa.

Validating JSON Objects

It's often necessary for applications to validate JSON objects, to ensure that required properties are present and that additional constraints (such as a price never being less than 1 dollar) are met. Validation is typically performed in the context of JSON Schema.

JSON Schema is a grammar language for defining the structure, content, and (to some extent) semantics of JSON objects. It lets you specify *metadata* (data about data) about what an object's properties mean and what values are valid for those properties. The result of applying the grammar language is a *schema* (a blueprint) describing the set of JSON objects that are valid according to the schema.

Note   JSON Schema expresses a schema as a JSON object.

JSON Schema is maintained at the JSON Schema website (http://json-schema. org). This website reveals several advantages for JSON Schema:

- It describes your existing data format.

- If offers clear, human-readable, and machine-readable documentation.

- It provides complete structural validation, which is useful for automated testing and validating client-submitted data.

Note   The JSON Schema website focuses on draft version 7 of the JSON Schema specification. This specification is divided into four parts: JSON Schema Core, JSON Schema Validation, JSON Hyper-Schema, and Relative JSON Pointers.

To understand JSON Schema, consider the following simple JSON object:

```
{
    "name": "John Doe",
    "age": 35
}
```

This object describes a person in terms of a name and an age. Assume that both of these properties must be present, name must be of type string and age must be of type number, and age's value must range from 18 through 64.

The following schema (based on draft version 7 of JSON Schema) provides the necessary constraints for this object:

```
{
    "$schema": "http://json-schema.org/draft-07/schema#",
    "title": "Person",
    "description": "A person",
    "type": "object",
    "properties":
    {
        "name":
        {
            "description": "A person's name",
            "type": "string"
        },
        "age":
        {
            "description": "A person's age",
            "type": "number",
            "minimum": 18,
            "maximum": 64
        }
```

```
    },
    "required": ["name", "age"]
}
```

Reading from top to bottom, you would interpret this JSON-based schema as follows:

- The $schema keyword states that this schema is written according to the draft version 7 specification.

- The title keyword identifies the JSON object being validated by this schema. In this case, a Person object is being validated.

- The description keyword provides a description of the Person object. As with title, description adds no constraint to the data being validated.

- The type keyword signifies that the containing object is a JSON object (via the object value). Also, it identifies property types (such as string and number).

- The properties keyword introduces an array of the properties that can appear in the JSON object. These properties are identified as name and age. Each property is further described by an object that provides a description keyword to describe the property and a type keyword to identify the type of value that can be assigned to the property. This is a constraint: you must assign a string to name and a number to age. For the age property, minimum and maximum keywords are specified to provide additional constraints: the number assigned to age must range from 18 through 64.

- The required keyword introduces an array that identifies those properties that must be present in the JSON object. In the example, both name and age are required properties.

The JSON Schema website provides links to various validator implementations for different programming languages (see http://json-schema.org/implementations. html). You can download an implementation and integrate it into your application, subject to license requirements. For this chapter, I chose to use an online tool called JSON Schema Validator (www.jsonschemavalidator.net) to demonstrate validation.

Figure 7-1 shows the previous JSON object and schema in the appropriate windows of the JSON Schema Validator online tool.

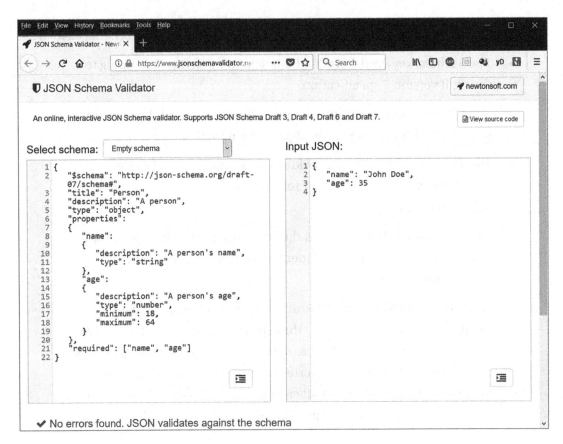

Figure 7-1. *The schema is valid and the JSON object conforms to this schema*

Let's make some changes to the JSON object so that it no longer conforms to the schema, and see how the JSON Schema Validator tool responds. First, we'll assign 65 to age, which exceeds the maximum constraint for the age property. Figure 7-2 shows the result.

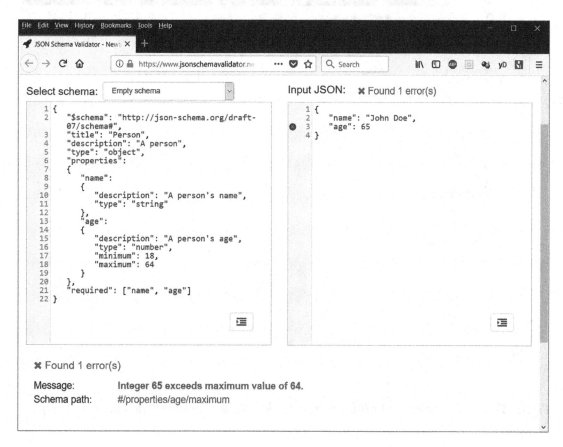

Figure 7-2. *JSON Schema Validator changes its message color to red to signify an error and also identifies the property and constraint that's been violated*

Next, we'll restore age's value to 35, but surround it with double quotes. This changes the type from number to string. See Figure 7-3 for the result.

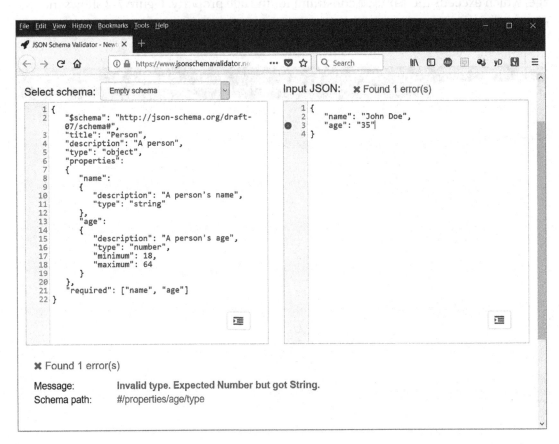

Figure 7-3. JSON Schema Validator reports that the age *property has the wrong type*

Finally, we'll restore age's value to 35, but eliminate the name property. Figure 7-4 shows JSON Schema Validator's response.

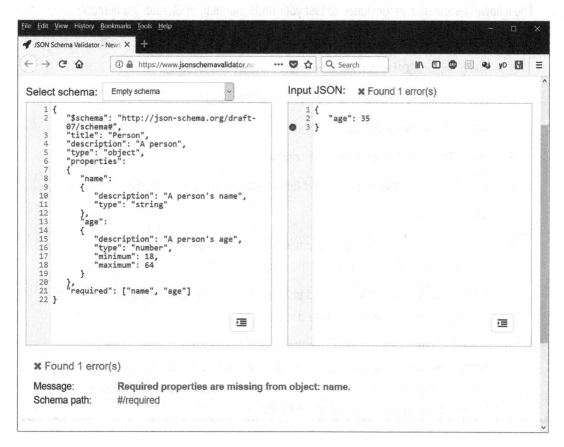

Figure 7-4. *JSON Schema Validator reports that the* name *property is required*

Check out "JSON Schema: A Media Type for Describing JSON Documents" (`https://datatracker.ietf.org/doc/draft-handrews-json-schema/`) and the other Internet-Draft documents accessible from the JSON Schema website (`http://json-schema.org`) to learn more about JSON Schema.

EXERCISES

The following exercises are designed to test your understanding of Chapter 7's content:

1. Define JSON.

2. True or false: JSON is derived from a strict subset of JavaScript.

3. How does the JSON data format present a JSON object?

4. Identify the six types that JSON supports.

5. True or false: JSON doesn't support comments.

6. How would you parse a JSON object into an equivalent JavaScript object?

7. Define JSON Schema.

8. When creating a schema, how do you identify those properties that must be present in those JSON objects that the schema validates?

9. Declare a JSON object for a product in terms of name and price properties. Set the name to "hammer" and the price to 20.

10. Declare a schema for validating the previous JSON object. The schema should constrain name to be a string, price to be a number, price to be at least 1 dollar, and name and price to be present in the object. Use JSON Schema Validator to verify the schema and JSON object.

Summary

JSON is a language-independent data format that expresses JSON objects as human-readable lists of properties. Although derived from JavaScript, code to parse JSON objects into equivalent language-dependent objects is available in many programming languages.

The JSON data format presents a JSON object as a brace-delimited and comma-separated list of properties. For each property, the name is expressed as a doubly quoted string. The name string is followed by a colon character, which is followed by a value of a specific JSON type.

JSON supports six types: number, string, Boolean, array, object, and null. JSON Schema also recognizes an integer type.

Whitespace is allowed and ignored around or between syntactic elements (values and punctuation). Four specific characters are considered whitespace for this purpose: space, horizontal tab, line feed, and carriage return. Also, JSON doesn't support comments.

Java doesn't provide a standard JSON API. One way to explore JSON in a Java context is to leverage Java's Scripting API.

It's often necessary for applications to validate JSON objects, to ensure that required properties are present and that additional constraints (such as a price never being less than 1 dollar) are met. JSON Schema is a grammar language that lets you accomplish validation.

JSON Schema lets you define the structure, content, and (to some extent) semantics of JSON objects. Furthermore, it lets you specify metadata about what an object's properties mean and what values are valid for those properties. The result of applying the grammar language is a schema that describes the set of JSON objects that are valid according to the schema.

Chapter 8 introduces mJson for parsing and creating JSON objects.

Parsing and Creating JSON Objects with mJson

Many third-party APIs are available for parsing and creating JSON objects. Chapter 8 explores one of the simplest of these APIs: mJson.

What Is mJson?

mJson is a small Java JSON library (created by developer Borislav Lordanov) for parsing JSON objects into Java objects and vice versa. This library is documented on GitHub (`http://bolerio.github.io/mjson/`), which reveals the following features:

- Full support for JSON Schema Draft 4 validation

- Single universal type—everything is a `Json` object; there is no type casting

- Single factory method for converting a Java object to a `Json` object; just call `Json.make(`*any Java object here*`)`

- Fast, hand-coded parsing

- Designed as a general purpose data structure for use in Java

- Parent pointers and `up()` method to traverse the JSON structure

- Concise methods to read (`Json.at()`), modify (`Json.set()`, `Json. add()`), duplicate (`Json.dup()`), and merge (`Json.with()`)

- Flexible merging of deep structures (`http://github.com/bolerio/ mjson/wiki/Deep-Merging`)

© Jeff Friesen 2019
J. Friesen, *Java XML and JSON*, https://doi.org/10.1007/978-1-4842-4330-5_8

- Methods for type-checking (e.g., `Json.isString()`) and access to underlying Java value (e.g., `Json.asString()`)

- Method chaining

- Pluggable factory to build your own support for arbitrary Java-Json mapping

- Entire library located in one Java file—no external dependencies

Unlike with other JSON libraries, mJson focuses on manipulating JSON structures in Java without mapping them to strongly typed Java objects. As a result, mJson reduces verbosity and lets you work with JSON in Java as naturally as in JavaScript.

Obtaining and Using mJson

mJson is distributed as a single JAR file; `mjson-1.4.0.jar` is the most recent JAR file at the time of writing. To obtain this JAR file, point your browser to `http://repo1.maven. org/maven2/org/sharegov/mjson/1.4.0/mjson-1.4.0.jar`.

`mjson-1.4.0.jar` contains a `Json` classfile and other classfiles that describe package-private classes nested within the `Json` class. Furthermore, this JAR file reveals that `Json` is located in the `mjson` package.

Note   mJson is licensed according to Apache License Version 2.0 (`www.apache. org/licenses/`).

It's easy to work with `mjson-1.4.0.jar`. Simply include it in the CLASSPATH when compiling source code or running an application, as follows:

```
javac -cp mjson-1.4.0.jar source file
java -cp mjson-1.4.0.jar;. main classfile
```

Exploring the Json Class

The `Json` class describes a JSON object or part of a JSON object. It contains `Schema` and `Factory` interfaces, more than 50 methods, and other members. This section explores many of these methods along with `Schema` and `Factory`.

Note   The API documentation for the `Json` class is located at `http://bolerio.`
`github.io/mjson/apidocs/index.html`.

Creating Json Objects

`Json` declares several `static` methods that create and return `Json` objects. Three of these
methods read and parse an external JSON object:

- `Json read(String s)`: Read a JSON object from the string that was
  passed to s (of type `java.lang.String`) and parse this object.

- `Json read(URL url)`: Read a JSON object from the Uniform Resource
  Locator (URL) passed to url (of type `java.net.URL`) and parse this
  object.

- `Json read(CharacterIterator ci)`: Read a JSON object
  from the character iterator passed to ci (of type `java.text.`
  `CharacterIterator`) and parse this object.

Each method returns a `Json` object that describes the parsed JSON object.

Listing 8-1 presents the source code to an application that demonstrates the
`read(String)` method.

Listing 8-1. Reading and Parsing a String-Based JSON Object

```
import mjson.Json;

import static java.lang.System.*;

public class mJsonDemo
{
   public static void main(String[] args)
   {
      String jsonStr =
      "{" +
      "\"firstName\": \"John\"," +
      "\"lastName\": \"Smith\"," +
      "\"isAlive\": true," +
```

```
            "\"age\": 25," +
            "\"address\":" +
            "{" +
            "\"streetAddress\": \"21 2nd Street\"," +
            "\"city\": \"New York\"," +
            "\"state\": \"NY\"," +
            "\"postalCode\": \"10021-3100\"" +
            "}," +
            "\"phoneNumbers\":" +
            "[" +
            "{" +
            "\"type\": \"home\"," +
            "\"number\": \"212 555-1234\"" +
            "}," +
            "{" +
            "\"type\": \"office\"," +
            "\"number\": \"646 555-4567\"" +
            "}" +
            "]," +
            "\"children\": []," +
            "\"spouse\": null" +
            "}";
            Json json = Json.read(jsonStr);
            out.println(json);
    }
}
```

The main(String[]) method first declares a Java string-based JSON object. It then
invokes Json.read() to read and parse this object, and return the object as a Json object.
Finally, main() outputs a string representation of the Json object (Json's toString()
method is called behind the scenes to convert the Json object to a Java string).

Compile Listing 8-1 as follows:

```
javac -cp mjson-1.4.0.jar mJsonDemo.java
```

Run the resulting application as follows:

```
java -cp mjson-1.4.0.jar;. mJsonDemo
```

You should observe the following output:

```
{"firstName":"John","lastName":"Smith","isAlive":true,"address":{"street
Address":"21 2nd Street","city":"New York","postalCode":"10021-3100","state":
"NY"},"children":[],"age":25,"phoneNumbers":[{"number":"212 555-1234",
"type":"home"},{"number":"646 555-4567","type":"office"}],"spouse":null}
```

The read() methods can also parse smaller JSON fragments, such as an array of different-typed values. See Listing 8-2 for a demonstration.

Listing 8-2. Reading and Parsing a JSON Fragment

```java
import mjson.Json;

import static java.lang.System.*;

public class mJsonDemo
{
   public static void main(String[] args)
   {
      Json json =
         Json.read("[4, 5, {}, true, null, \"ABC\", 6]");
      out.println(json);
   }
}
```

When you run this application, you should observe the following output:

```
[4,5,{},true,null,"ABC",6]
```

In addition to the reading and parsing methods, Json provides static methods for creating Json objects:

- Json array(): Return a Json object representing an empty JSON array.

- Json array(Object... args): Return a Json object (representing a JSON array) filled with args, a variable number of java.lang. Objects.

- `Json make(Object anything)`: Return a `Json` object filled with the contents of anything, which is one of `null`; a value of type `Json`, `String`, `java.util.Collection<?>`, `java.util.Map<?, ?>`, `java.lang.Boolean`, `java.lang.Number`; or an array of one of these types. Maps, collections, and arrays are recursively copied such that each of their elements is converted to a `Json` object. A map's keys are normally strings, but any object with a meaningful `toString()` implementation will work. This method throws `java.lang.IllegalArgumentException` when the concrete type of the argument passed to anything is unknown.

- `Json nil()`: Return a `Json` object that represents `null`.

- `Json object()`: Return a `Json` object representing an empty JSON object.

- `Json object(Object... args)`: Return a `Json` object (representing a JSON object) filled with `args`, a variable number of `Objects`. These objects identify property names and values; the number of objects must be even, with even indexes identifying property names and odd indexes identifying property values. The names are normally of type `String` but can be of any other type that has an appropriate `toString()` method. Each value is first converted to a `Json` object by calling `make(Object)`.

Listing 8-3 presents the source code to an application that demonstrates most of these additional `static` methods.

Listing 8-3. Creating a Person JSON Object

```
import mjson.Json;

import static java.lang.System.*;

public class mJsonDemo
{
   public static void main(String[] args)
   {
      Json jsonAddress =
```

```
        Json.object("streetAddress", "21 2nd Street",
                    "city", "New York",
                    "state", "NY",
                    "postalCode", "10021-3100");
    Json jsonPhone1 =
        Json.object("type", "home",
                    "number", "212 555-1234");
    Json jsonPhone2 =
        Json.object("type", "office",
                    "number", "646 555-4567");
    Json jsonPerson =
        Json.object("firstName", "John",
                    "lastName", "Smith",
                    "isAlive", true,
                    "age", 25,
                    "address", jsonAddress,
                    "phoneNumbers", Json.array(jsonPhone1,
                                                jsonPhone2),
                    "children", Json.array(),
                    "spouse", Json.nil());
    out.println(jsonPerson);
  }
}
```

Listing 8-3 describes an application that creates the same JSON object that's read and parsed in Listing 8-1. Notice that you can pass Json objects to array(Object...) and object(Object...), which lets you build complete JSON objects from smaller fragments. If you run this application, you'll discover the same output as generated by the application described in Listing 8-1.

Listing 8-4 presents the source code to another application that uses make(Object) with Java collections and maps.

Listing 8-4. Making JSON Objects from Java Collections and Maps

```java
import java.util.ArrayList;
import java.util.Arrays;
import java.util.HashMap;
import java.util.List;
import java.util.Map;

import mjson.Json;

import static java.lang.System.*;

public class mJsonDemo
{
    public static void main(String[] args)
    {
        List<String> weekdays =
            Arrays.asList("Sunday", "Monday", "Tuesday",
                            "Wednesday", "Thursday", "Friday",
                            "Saturday");
        out.println(Json.make(weekdays));

        Map<String, Number> people = new HashMap<>();
        people.put("John", 33);
        people.put("Joan", 27);
        out.println(Json.make(people));

        Map<String, String[]> planets = new HashMap<>();
        planets.put("Mercury", null);
        planets.put("Earth", new String[] {"Luna"});
        planets.put("Mars", new String[] {"Phobos",
                                            "Deimos"});
        out.println(Json.make(planets)) ;
    }
}
```

main(String[]) first creates a list of weekday names and then passes this object to make(Object), whose returned Json object is output. Next, a map of people names and ages is created and subsequently passed to make(Object). The resulting JSON object is output. Finally, a map of planet names along with arrays of moon names is created. This map is converted into a more complex JSON object, which is output.

If you compile this source code and run the application, you'll discover the following output:

```
["Sunday","Monday","Tuesday","Wednesday","Thursday","Friday","Saturday"]
{"Joan":27,"John":33}
{"Earth":["Luna"],"Mars":["Phobos","Deimos"],"Mercury":null}
```

Learning About Json Objects

Json offers several methods for learning about the JSON entities described by Json objects. For starters, you can call the Object getValue() method to return the JSON value (as a Java object) of the Json object. The returned value will be Java null or have the Java Boolean, String, Number, Map, java.util.List, or an array type. For objects and arrays, this method performs a deep copy of all nested elements.

To identify the JSON type of the JSON value, call one of the following methods:

- boolean isArray(): Return true for a JSON array value.

- boolean isBoolean(): Return true for a JSON Boolean value.

- boolean isNull(): Return true for the JSON null value.

- boolean isNumber(): Return true for a JSON number value.

- boolean isObject(): Return true for a JSON object value.

- boolean isPrimitive(): Return true for a JSON number, string, or Boolean value.

- boolean isString(): Return true for a JSON string value.

Listing 8-5 presents the source code to an application that demonstrates getValue() and these JSON type-identification methods.

Listing 8-5. Obtaining a Json Object's Value and Identifying Its JSON Type

```
import mjson.Json;

import static java.lang.System.*;

public class mJsonDemo
{
    public static void main(String[] args)
    {
        String jsonStr =
        "{" +
        "\"firstName\": \"John\"," +
        "\"lastName\": \"Smith\"," +
        "\"isAlive\": true," +
        "\"age\": 25," +
        "\"address\":" +
        "{" +
        "\"streetAddress\": \"21 2nd Street\"," +
        "\"city\": \"New York\"," +
        "\"state\": \"NY\"," +
        "\"postalCode\": \"10021-3100\"" +
        "}," +
        "\"phoneNumbers\":" +
        "[" +
        "{" +
        "\"type\": \"home\"," +
        "\"number\": \"212 555-1234\"" +
        "}," +
        "{" +
        "\"type\": \"office\"," +
        "\"number\": \"646 555-4567\"" +
        "}" +
        "]," +
        "\"children\": []," +
```

```java
      "\"spouse\": null" +
      "}";
   Json json = Json.read(jsonStr);
   out.println("Value = " + json.getValue());
   out.println();
   classify(json);
}

static void classify(Json jsonObject)
{
   if (jsonObject.isArray())
      out.println("Array");
   else
   if (jsonObject.isBoolean())
      out.println("Boolean");
   else
   if (jsonObject.isNull())
      out.println("Null");
   else
   if (jsonObject.isNumber())
      out.println("Number");
   else
   if (jsonObject.isObject())
      out.println("Object");
   else
   if (jsonObject.isString())
      out.println("String");
   if (jsonObject.isPrimitive())
      out.println("Primitive");
}
}
```

Compile this source code and run the application, and you'll discover the following output:

```
Value = {firstName=John, lastName=Smith, isAlive=true,
address={streetAddress=21 2nd Street, city=New York, postalCode=10021-3100,
state=NY}, children=[], age=25, phoneNumbers=[{number=212 555-1234,
type=home}, {number=646 555-4567, type=office}], spouse=null}
```

Object

After verifying that a Json object represents the expected JSON type, you can call one of Json's "as" methods to obtain the JSON value as a Java value of an equivalent Java type:

- boolean asBoolean(): Return the JSON value as a Java Boolean.

- byte asByte(): Return the JSON value as a Java byte integer.

- char asChar(): Return the first character of the JSON string value as a Java character.

- double asDouble(): Return the JSON value as a Java double precision floating-point value.

- float asFloat(): Return the JSON value as a Java floating-point value.

- int asInteger(): Return the JSON value as a Java integer.

- List<Json> asJsonList(): Return the underlying list representation of a JSON array. The returned list is the actual array representation so any modifications to it are modifications to the Json object's list.

- Map<String, Json> asJsonMap(): Return the underlying map of properties of a JSON object. The returned map is the actual object representation so any modifications to it are modifications to the Json object's map.

- List<Object> asList(): Return a list of the elements of a Json object that describes a JSON array. The returned list is a copy, and modifications to it don't affect the Json object.

- long asLong(): Return the JSON value as a Java long integer.

- `Map<String, Object> asMap()`: Return a map of the properties of a `Json` object that describes a JSON object. The returned map is a copy, and modifications to it don't affect the `Json` object.

- `short asShort()`: Return the JSON value as a Java short integer.

- `String asString()`: Return the JSON value as a Java string.

Listing 8-6 presents the source code to an application that uses `asMap()` to obtain a map of the `Json` object properties describing a JSON object.

Listing 8-6. Iterating Over a `Json` Object's Properties to Learn About a JSON Object

```
import java.util.Map;

import mjson.Json;

import static java.lang.System.*;

public class mJsonDemo
{
   public static void main(String[] args)
   {
      String jsonStr =
      "{" +
      "\"firstName\": \"John\"," +
      "\"lastName\": \"Smith\"," +
      "\"isAlive\": true," +
      "\"age\": 25," +
      "\"address\":" +
      "{" +
      "\"streetAddress\": \"21 2nd Street\"," +
      "\"city\": \"New York\"," +
      "\"state\": \"NY\"," +
      "\"postalCode\": \"10021-3100\"" +
      "}," +
      "\"phoneNumbers\":" +
      "[" +
      "{" +
```

```
      "\"type\": \"home\"," +
      "\"number\": \"212 555-1234\"" +
      "}," +
      "{" +
      "\"type\": \"office\"," +
      "\"number\": \"646 555-4567\"" +
      "}" +
      "]," +
      "\"children\": []," +
      "\"spouse\": null" +
      "}";
   Json json = Json.read(jsonStr);
   if (json.isObject())
   {
      Map<String, Object> props = json.asMap();
      for (Map.Entry<String, Object> propEntry:
            props.entrySet())
         out.println(propEntry.getKey() + ": " +
                     propEntry.getValue());

   }
}
}
```

main(String[]) declares the same JSON object as presented in Listing 8-1. It then reads and parses this object into a Json object. The isObject() method is called to verify that the Json object represents a JSON object. (It's a good idea to verify first.) Because this should be the case, asMap() is called to return a map of the Json object's properties, which are then iterated over and output.

Caution   If you replace Json json = Json.read(jsonStr); with Json json = Json.make(jsonStr);, you won't see any output because the Json object returned from make() identifies the JSON string type and not the JSON object type.

After studying the source code, compile it and run the application. You'll discover the following output:

```
firstName: John
lastName: Smith
isAlive: true
address: {streetAddress=21 2nd Street, city=New York,
postalCode=10021-3100, state=NY}
children: []
age: 25
phoneNumbers: [{number=212 555-1234, type=home}, {number=646 555-4567,
type=office}]
spouse: null
```

You can access the contents of arrays and objects by calling the following at() methods, which return Json objects that describe array element values or object property values:

- Json at(int index): Return the value (as a Json object) of the array element at the specified index in this Json object's array. This method applies to JSON arrays only. It throws java.lang. IndexOutOfBoundsException when index is out of bounds for the array.

- Json at(String propName): Return the value (as a Json object) of the object property whose name is identified by propName in this Json object's map. Return null when there's no such property. This method applies to JSON objects only.

- Json at(String propName, Json defValue): Return the value (as a Json object) of the object property whose name is identified by propName in this Json object's map. When there's no such property, create a new property whose value is specified by defValue and return defValue. This method applies to JSON objects only.

- Json at(String propName, Object defValue): Return the value (as a Json object) of the object property whose name is identified by propName in this Json object's map. When there's no such property, create a new property whose value is specified by defValue and return defValue. This method applies to JSON objects only.

Listing 8-7 presents the source code to an application that uses the first two at()
methods to access a JSON object's property values.

Listing 8-7. Obtaining and Outputting a JSON Object's Property Values

```java
import mjson.Json;

import static java.lang.System.*;

public class mJsonDemo
{
   public static void main(String[] args)
   {
      String jsonStr =
      "{" +
      "\"firstName\": \"John\"," +
      "\"lastName\": \"Smith\"," +
      "\"isAlive\": true," +
      "\"age\": 25," +
      "\"address\":" +
      "{" +
      "\"streetAddress\": \"21 2nd Street\"," +
      "\"city\": \"New York\"," +
      "\"state\": \"NY\"," +
      "\"postalCode\": \"10021-3100\"" +
      "}," +
      "\"phoneNumbers\":" +
      "[" +
      "{" +
      "\"type\": \"home\"," +
      "\"number\": \"212 555-1234\"" +
      "}," +
      "{" +
      "\"type\": \"office\"," +
      "\"number\": \"646 555-4567\"" +
      "}" +
      "]," +
```

```
            "\"children\": []," +
            "\"spouse\": null" +
            "}";
    Json json = Json.read(jsonStr);
    out.printf("First name = %s%n", json.at("firstName"));
    out.printf("Last name = %s%n", json.at("lastName"));
    out.printf("Is alive = %s%n", json.at("isAlive"));
    out.printf("Age = %d%n", json.at("age").asInteger());
    out.println("Address");
    Json jsonAddr = json.at("address");
    out.printf("   Street address = %s%n", jsonAddr.at("streetAddress"));
    out.printf("   City = %s%n", jsonAddr.at("city"));
    out.printf("   State = %s%n", jsonAddr.at("state"));
    out.printf("   Postal code = %s%n", jsonAddr.at("postalCode"));
    out.println("Phone Numbers");
    Json jsonPhone = json.at("phoneNumbers");
    out.printf("   Type = %s%n", jsonPhone.at(0). at("type"));
    out.printf("   Number = %s%n", jsonPhone.at(0). at("number"));
    out.println();
    out.printf("   Type = %s%n", jsonPhone.at(1). at("type"));
    out.printf("   Number = %s%n", jsonPhone.at(1). at("number"));
    Json jsonChildren = json.at("children");
    out.printf("Children = %s%n", jsonChildren);
    out.printf("Spouse = %s%n", json.at("spouse"));
    }
}
```

Expression json.at("age") returns a Json object describing a JSON number; asInteger() returns this value as a 32-bit Java integer.

Compile this source code and run the application. You'll discover the following output:

```
First name = "John"
Last name = "Smith"
Is alive = true
Age = 25
```

```
Address
    Street address = "21 2nd Street"
    City = "New York"
    State = "NY"
    Postal code = "10021-3100"
Phone Numbers
    Type = "home"
    Number = "212 555-1234"

    Type = "office"
    Number = "646 555-4567"
Children = []
Spouse = null
```

You might be wondering how to detect the empty array that's assigned to the children property name. You can accomplish this task by calling asList() to return a List implementation object, and then calling List's size() method on this object, as follows:

```
System.out.printf("Array length = %d%n", jsonChildren.asList().size());
```

This code fragment will report an array length of zero elements.

Finally, Json provides three methods for verifying that property names exist, and that property names or array elements exist with specified values:

- boolean has(String propName): Return true when this Json object describes a JSON object that has a property identified by propName; otherwise, return false.

- boolean is(int index, Object value): Return true when this Json object describes a JSON array that has the specified value at the specified index; otherwise, return false.

- boolean is(String propName, Object value): Return true when this Json object describes a JSON object that has a property identified by propName and this property has the value identified by value; otherwise, return false.

For example, consider Listing 8-7. Expression json.has("firstName") returns true, whereas expression json.has("middleName") returns false.

Navigating Json Object Hierarchies

When one of the previously discussed at() methods returns a Json object describing a JSON object or JSON array, you can navigate into the object or array by chaining another at() method call to the expression. For example, I used this technique in the previous application to access a phone number:

```
System.out.printf("   Number = %s%n", jsonPhone.at(0).at("number"));
```

Here, jsonPhone.at(0) returns a Json object that represents the first array entry in the phoneNumbers JSON array. Because the array entry happens to be a JSON object, calling at("number") on this Json object causes Json to return the value (as a Json object) of the JSON object's number property.

Each Json object that describes a JSON entity belonging to an array or an object holds a reference to its enclosing array- or object-based Json object. You can call Json's Json up() method to return this enclosing Json object, which is demonstrated in Listing 8-8.

Listing 8-8. Accessing Enclosing Json Objects

```java
import mjson.Json;

import static java.lang.System.*;

public class mJsonDemo
{
   public static void main(String[] args)
   {
      String jsonStr =
      "{" +
      "\"propName\": \"propValue\"," +
      "\"propArray\":" +
      "[" +
      "{" +
      "\"element1\": \"value1\"" +
      "}," +
      "{" +
```

```
            "\"element2\": \"value2\"" +
         "}" +
         "]" +
         "}";
      Json json = Json.read(jsonStr);
      Json jsonElement1 = json.at("propArray").at(0);
      out.println(jsonElement1);
      out.println();
      out.println(jsonElement1.up());
      out.println();
      out.println(jsonElement1.up().up());
      out.println();
      out.println(jsonElement1.up().up().up());
   }
}
```

Compile this source code and run the application, and you'll discover the following output:

```
{"element1":"value1"}

[{"element1":"value1"},{"element2":"value2"}]

{"propArray":[{"element1":"value1"},{"element2":"value2"}],
"propName":"propValue"}

null
```

The first output line describes the first array element in the array assigned to the propArray property. This element is an object consisting of a single element1 property.

jsonElement1.up() returns a Json object describing the array that encloses the JSON object that serves as the array's first element. jsonElement1.up().up() returns a Json object describing the JSON object that encloses the array. Finally, jsonElement1.up().up().up() returns a Json object describing the null value; the JSON object has no parent.

Modifying Json Objects

You'll encounter situations where you'll want to modify existing Json objects' JSON values. For example, you might be creating and saving several similar JSON objects and would like to reuse existing Json objects.

Json lets you modify Json objects that represent JSON arrays and objects. It doesn't let you modify Json objects that represent JSON Boolean, number, or string values because they're regarded as immutable.

Json declares the following set() methods for modifying JSON array elements and JSON object properties:

- Json set(int index, Object value): Set the value of the JSON array element located at index to value.

- Json set(String propName, Json value): Set the value of the JSON object property whose name is specified by propName to value.

- Json set(String property, Object value): Set the value of the JSON object property whose name is specified by propName to value. This method calls make(Object) to convert value to a Json object representing value and then invokes set(String, Json).

Listing 8-9 presents the source code to an application that uses the first and third set() methods to set object property and array element values.

Listing 8-9. Setting Object Property and Array Element Values

```
import mjson.Json;

import static java.lang.System.*;

public class mJsonDemo
{
   public static void main(String[] args)
   {
      String jsonStr =
      "{" +
      "\"name\": null," +
      "\"courses\":" +
```

```
      "[null]" +
      "}";
      Json json = Json.read(jsonStr);
      out.println(json);
      out.println();
      json.set("name", "John Doe");
      Json jsonCourses = json.at("courses");
      jsonCourses.set(0, "English");
      out.println(json);
   }
}
```

Compile this source code and run the application, and you'll discover the following output:

```
{"courses":[null],"name":null}
```

```
{"courses":["English"],"name":"John Doe"}
```

If you attempt to set a value for a property that doesn't exist, Json adds the property. However, if you attempt to set the value for a nonexistent array element, Json throws IndexOutOfBoundsException. For this reason, you might prefer to call one of the following add() methods instead:

- Json add(Json element): Append the specified element to the array represented by this Json object.

- Json add(Object anything): Convert anything to a Json object by calling make(Object) and append the result to the array represented by this Json object.

Listing 8-10 presents the source code to an application that uses the first add() method to append two strings to the empty courses array.

Listing 8-10. Appending Strings to an Empty JSON Array

```
import mjson.Json;

import static java.lang.System.*;

public class mJsonDemo
```

```
{
   public static void main(String[] args)
   {
      String jsonStr =
      "{" +
      "\"name\": null," +
      "\"courses\":" +
      "[]" +
      "}";
      Json json = Json.read(jsonStr);
      out.println(json);
      out.println();
      json.set("name", "John Doe");
      Json jsonCourses = json.at("courses");
      jsonCourses.add("English");
      jsonCourses.add("French");
      out.println(json);
   }
}
```

Compile this source code and run the application. It generates the output shown here:

```
{"courses":[],"name":null}

{"courses":["English","French"],"name":"John Doe"}
```

Json provides a pair of array-oriented remove() methods that take the same arguments as their add() counterparts:

- Json remove(Json element): Remove the specified element from the array represented by this Json object.

- Json remove(Object anything): Convert anything to a Json object by calling make(Object) and remove the result from the array represented by this Json object.

Listing 8-11 presents the source code to an application that uses the second remove() method to remove the "English" string from the courses array.

Listing 8-11. Removing a String from a JSON Array

```java
import mjson.Json;

import static java.lang.System.*;

public class mJsonDemo
{
    public static void main(String[] args)
    {
        String jsonStr =
        "{" +
        "\"name\": null," +
        "\"courses\":" +
        "[]" +
        "}";
        Json json = Json.read(jsonStr);
        out.println(json);
        out.println();
        json.set("name", "John Doe");
        Json jsonCourses = json.at("courses");
        jsonCourses.add("English");
        jsonCourses.add("French");
        out.println(json);
        out.println();
        jsonCourses.remove("English");
        out.println(json);
    }
}
```

Compile this source code and run the application. It generates the output shown here:

```
{"courses":[],"name":null}

{"courses":["English","French"],"name":"John Doe"}

{"courses":["French"],"name":"John Doe"}
```

You can remove an element from an array by index or remove a property from an object by name by calling the following methods:

- `Json atDel(int index)`: Remove the element at the specified `index` from this `Json` object's JSON array and return the element.

- `Json atDel(String propName)`: Remove the property identified by `propName` from this `Json` object's JSON object and return the property value (or `null` when the property doesn't exist).

- `Json delAt(int index)`: Remove the element at the specified `index` from this `Json` object's JSON array.

- `Json delAt(String propName)`: Remove the property identified by `propName` from this `Json` object's JSON object.

Listing 8-12 presents the source code to an application that uses the last two `delAt()` methods to delete a property and an array element.

Listing 8-12. Removing the Last Name and One of the Courses Being Taken

```
import mjson.Json;

import static java.lang.System.*;

public class mJsonDemo
{
   public static void main(String[] args)
   {
      String jsonStr =
      "{" +
      "\"firstName\": \"John\"," +
      "\"lastName\": \"Doe\"," +
      "\"courses\":" +
      "[\"English\", \"French\", \"Spanish\"]" +
      "}";
      Json json = Json.read(jsonStr);
      out.println(json);
      out.println();
      json.delAt("lastName");
```

```
        out.println(json);
        out.println();
        json.at("courses").delAt(1);
        out.println(json);
    }
}
```

To see the results of the delAt() methods, compile this source code and run the application. Its output is shown here:

```
{"firstName":"John","lastName":"Doe","courses":["English","French","Spanish"]}

{"firstName":"John","courses":["English","French","Spanish"]}

{"firstName":"John","courses":["English","Spanish"]}
```

Json provides an additional method for modifying a JSON object:

- Json with(Json objectorarray): Combine this Json object's
  JSON object or JSON array with the argument passed to
  objectorarray. The JSON type of this Json object and the JSON type
  of objectorarray must match. If objectorarray identifies a JSON
  object, all of its properties are appended to this Json object's object.
  If objectorarray identifies a JSON array, all of its elements are
  appended to this Json object's array.

Listing 8-13 presents the source code to an application that uses with(Json) to append properties to an object and elements to an array.

Listing 8-13. Appending Properties to an Object and Elements to an Array

```
import mjson.Json;

import static java.lang.System.*;

public class mJsonDemo
{
    public static void main(String[] args)
    {
        String jsonStr =
```

```
"{" +
"\"firstName\": \"John\"," +
"\"courses\":" +
"[\"English\"]" +
"}";
Json json = Json.read(jsonStr);
out.println(json);
out.println();
Json jsono =
    Json.read("{\"initial\": \"P\", \"lastName\": " + "\"Doe\"}");

Json jsona = Json.read("[\"French\", \"Spanish\"]");
json.with(jsono);
out.println(json);
out.println();
json.at("courses").with(jsona);
out.println(json);
    }
}
```

Compile Listing 8-13 and run the application. Here is the application's output:

```
{"firstName":"John","courses":["English"]}

{"firstName":"John","courses":["English"],"lastName":"Doe","initial":"P"}

{"firstName":"John","courses":["English","French","Spanish"],"lastName":
"Doe","initial":"P"}
```

Note   mJson 1.4.0 overloads with() to customize this method's behavior. See http://github.com/bolerio/mjson/wiki/Deep-Merging for the details.

Validation

Json supports JSON Schema Draft 4 validation via its nested Schema interface and the following static methods:

- Json.Schema schema(Json jsonSchema): Return a Json.Schema object that validates JSON documents according to the schema described by jsonSchema.

- Json.Schema schema(Json jsonSchema, URI uri): Return a Json. Schema object that validates JSON documents according to the schema described by jsonSchema and also located at the Uniform Resource Identifier (URI) passed to uri, which is of type java.net.URI.

- Json.Schema schema(URI uri): Return a Json.Schema object that validates JSON documents according to the schema located at uri.

Validation is performed by calling Schema's Json validate(Json document) method, which attempts to validate a JSON document according to this Schema object. Validation attempts to proceed even when validation errors are detected. The return value is always a Json object whose JSON object contains the Boolean property named ok. When ok is true, there are no other properties. When it's false, the JSON object also contains a property named errors, which is an array of error messages for all detected schema violations.

I've created two sample applications that demonstrate validation. Listing 8-14 is based on example code at the mJson GitHub "A Tour of the API" page (http://github.com/bolerio/mjson/wiki/A-Tour-of-the-API).

Listing 8-14. Validating JSON Objects That Include the id Property

```
import mjson.Json;

import static java.lang.System.*;

public class mJsonDemo
{
   public static void main(String[] args)
   {
      // A simple schema that accepts only JSON objects
      // with a mandatory property 'id'.
```

```
Json.Schema schema =
    Json.schema(Json.object("type", "object",
                            "required",
                            Json.array("id")));
out.println(schema.validate(Json.object("id", 666,
                                        "name",
                                        "Britlan")));
out.println(schema.validate(Json.object("ID", 666,
                                        "name",
                                        "Britlan")));
    }
}
```

If you compile this source code and run the application, you'll discover the following
output:

```
{"ok":true}
{"ok":false,"errors":["Required property id missing from object {\"name\":\
"Britlan\",\"ID\":666}"]}
```

In Chapter 7, I presented the following JSON object:

```
{
    "name": "John Doe",
    "age": 35
}
```

I also presented the following schema as a JSON object:

```
{
    "$schema": "http://json-schema.org/draft-07/schema#",
    "title": "Person",
    "description": "A person",
    "type": "object",
    "properties":
    {
```

```
    "name":
    {
        "description": "A person's name",
        "type": "string"
    },
    "age":
    {
        "description": "A person's age",
        "type": "number",
        "minimum": 18,
        "maximum": 64
    }
},
"required": ["name", "age"]
}
```

Suppose that I copy this schema to a schema.json file and store it on my website at http://javajeff.ca/schema.json. Listing 8-15 presents the source code to an application that uses Json.Schema schema(URI) to obtain this schema for validating the previous JSON object.

Listing 8-15. Validating JSON Objects via an External Schema

```java
import java.net.URI;
import java.net.URISyntaxException;

import mjson.Json;

import static java.lang.System.*;

public class mJsonDemo
{
    final static String SCHEMA_URI =
        "http://javajeff.ca/schema.json";

    public static void main(String[] args)
        throws URISyntaxException
```

```
    {
        Json.Schema schema = Json.schema(new URI(SCHEMA_URI));
        Json json = Json.read("{\"name\": \"John Doe\", " +
                              "\"age\": 35}");
        out.println(schema.validate(json));
        json = Json.read("{\"name\": \"John Doe\", " +
                         "\"age\": 65}");
        out.println(schema.validate(json));
        json = Json.read("{\"name\": \"John Doe\", " +
                         "\"age\": \"35\"}");
        out.println(schema.validate(json));
        json = Json.read("{\"age\": 35}");
        out.println(schema.validate(json));
    }
}
```

Compile this source code and run the application. You should discover the following output:

```
{"ok":true}
{"ok":false,"errors":["Number 65 is above allowed maximum 64.0"]}
{"ok":false,"errors":["Type mistmatch for \"35\", allowed types:
[\"number\"]"]}
{"ok":false,"errors":["Required property name missing from object
{\"age\":35}"]}
```

Customization via Factories

Json defers the creation of Json objects to a factory, which is an instance of a class that implements the Json.Factory interface's methods:

- Json array()

- Json bool(boolean value)

- Json make(Object anything)

- Json nil()

- Json number(Number value)

- Json object()

- Json string(String value)

The Json.DefaultFactory class provides default implementations of these methods, but you can provide custom implementations when necessary. To avoid implementing all of these methods, you can extend DefaultFactory and override only those methods of interest.

After creating a custom Factory class, you would instantiate it and then install the object by calling one of the following static Json methods:

- void setGlobalFactory(Json.Factory factory)

- void attachFactory(Json.Factory factory)

The first method installs the specified factory as a global factory, which is used by all threads that don't have a specific thread-local factory attached to them. The second method attaches the specified factory to the invoking thread only, which lets you use different thread factories in the same classloader. You can remove a thread-local factory and revert to the global factory for a thread by calling the void dettachFactory() method.

One of the customizations mentioned in the mJson documentation is case-insensitive string comparison. Basically, you customize Json's equals() method to perform case-insensitive string comparisons. Listing 8-16 presents the source code to an application that shows how this is done.

Listing 8-16. Customizing Json to Support Case-Insensitive String Comparisons

```
import java.util.List;

import mjson.Json;

import static java.lang.System.*;

public class mJsonDemo
{
   public static void main(String[] args)
   {
      class MyFactory extends Json.DefaultFactory
      {
```

```java
@Override
public Json string(String x)
{
   // Obtain the StringJson instance.
   final Json json = super.string(x);

   class StringIJson extends Json
   {
      private static final long serialVersionUID
         = 1L;

      String val;

      StringIJson(String val)
      {
         this.val = val;
      }

      @Override
      public byte asByte()
      {
         return json.asByte();
      }

      @Override
      public char asChar()
      {
         return json.asChar();
      }

      @Override
      public double asDouble()
      {
         return json.asDouble();
      }
```

```java
@Override
public float asFloat()
{
    return json.asFloat();
}

@Override
public int asInteger()
{
    return json.asInteger();
}

@Override
public List<Object> asList()
{
    return json.asList();
}

@Override
public long asLong()
{
    return json.asLong();
}

@Override
public short asShort()
{
    return json.asShort();
}

@Override
public String asString()
{
    return json.asString();
}

@Override
public Json dup()
```

```java
    {
        return json.dup();
    }

    @Override
    public boolean equals(Object x)
    {
        return x instanceof StringIJson &&
                ((StringIJson) x).
                val.equalsIgnoreCase(val);
    }

    @Override
    public Object getValue()
    {
        return json.getValue();
    }

    @Override
    public int hashCode()
    {
        return json.hashCode();
    }

    @Override
    public boolean isString()
    {
        return json.isString();
    }

    @Override
    public String toString()
    {
        return json.toString();
    }
}
```

```
            return new StringIJson(x);
        }
    }

    Json.setGlobalFactory(new MyFactory());
    Json json1 = Json.read("\"abc\"");
    Json json2 = Json.read("\"abc\"");
    Json json3 = Json.read("\"Abc\"");
    out.println(json1.equals(json2));
    out.println(json1.equals(json3));
    }
}
```

Listing 8-16's mJsonDemo class declares a nested MyFactory class that extends Json. DefaultFactory. The main() method instantiates this class and registers it with Json via the following method call:

```
Json.setGlobalFactory(new MyFactory());
```

main() proceeds to parse three JSON strings via read() method calls and then perform equality operations on them, outputting the results.

Note   The equals() method that's called is not located in the Json class. Instead, it's located in a nested package-private class, such as StringJson. In the listing, the objects assigned to json1, json2, and json3 have type StringJson or (with the factory installed) StringIJson (discussed shortly).

MyFactory overrides the string(String) method, which is responsible for creating Json objects that represent JSON strings. In the Json.java source code (which you can access from http://bolerio.github.io/mjson/—click the tar.gz or .zip folder link near the top of the page), string(String) executes return new StringJson(x, null);.

StringJson is one of Json's nested package-private static classes. Because it cannot be accessed from outside of the mjson package, MyFactory's overriding string(String) method declares an equivalent StringIJson class (the I is for case-insensitive).

Rather than copy all of the code from StringJson to StringIJson, which is wasteful duplication and won't work anyway because some of the code relies on other package-private types, I chose to use the adapter/wrapper design pattern (http://en.wikipedia.org/wiki/Adapter_pattern).

The idea behind the adapter pattern is to have StringIJson duplicate StringJson methods in terms of their headers, and code the bodies to forward almost all method calls to the StringJson equivalents. This is possible by having MyFactory's string(String) method first invoke DefaultFactory's string(String) method, which returns the StringJson object. It's then a simple matter of forwarding calls to this object.

The exception is the equals() method. StringIJson codifies this method to be nearly identical to its StringJson counterpart. The main difference is the call to String's equalsIgnoreCase() method instead of its equals() method. The result is a case-insensitive equals() method.

Compile the source code and run the application, and you should observe the following output:

```
true
true
```

The first output line shows that abc equals abc. The second output line proves that the factory was installed because it shows that abc equals Abc.

EXERCISES

The following exercises are designed to test your understanding of Chapter 8's content:

1. Define mJson.

2. Describe the Json class.

3. Identify Json's methods for reading and parsing external JSON objects.

4. True or false: The read() methods can also parse smaller JSON fragments, such as an array of different-typed values.

5. Identify the methods that Json provides for creating JSON objects.

6. What does Json's boolean isPrimitive() method accomplish?

7. How do you return a Json object's JSON array?

8. True or false: Json's `Map<String, Json> asJsonMap()` method returns a map of the properties of a `Json` object that describes a JSON object. The returned map is a copy, and modifications to it don't affect the `Json` object.

9. Which `Json` methods let you access the contents of arrays and objects?

10. What does Json's `boolean is(int index, Object value)` method accomplish?

11. What does `Json` do when you attempt to set the value for a nonexistent array element?

12. What is the difference between Json's `atDel()` and `delAt()` methods?

13. What does Json's `Json with(Json objectorarray)` method accomplish?

14. Identify Json's methods for obtaining a `Json.Schema` object.

15. How do you validate a JSON document against a schema?

16. What is the difference between Json's `setGlobalFactory()` and `attachFactory()` methods?

17. Two `Json` methods that were not discussed in this chapter are `Json dup()` and `String pad(String callback)`. What do they do?

18. Write an `mJsonDemo` application that demonstrates `dup()` and `pad()`.

Summary

mJson is a small Java JSON library for parsing JSON objects into Java objects and vice versa. It consists of a `Json` class that describes a JSON object or part of a JSON object. `Json` contains `Schema` and `Factory` interfaces, more than 50 methods, and other members.

After obtaining the mJson library, you learned how to use this library to create `Json` objects, learn about `Json` objects, navigate `Json` object hierarchies, modify `Json` objects, validate JSON documents against a schema, and customize `Json` by installing nondefault factories.

Chapter 9 introduces Gson for parsing and creating JSON objects.

Parsing and Creating JSON Objects with Gson

Gson is another API for parsing and creating JSON objects. Chapter 9 explores the latest version of this open-source Google product.

What Is Gson?

Gson (also known as *Google Gson*) is a small Java-based library for parsing and creating JSON objects. Google developed Gson for its own projects, but later made Gson publicly available, starting with version 1.0. According to Wikipedia (`http://en.wikipedia.org/wiki/Gson`), the latest version (at the time of writing) is 2.8.5.

Gson's GitHub page (`http://github.com/google/gson`) identifies five important design goals for Gson:

- Provide simple `toJson()` and `fromJson()` methods to convert Java objects to JSON objects and vice versa

- Allow pre-existing unmodifiable objects to be converted to and from JSON

- Provide extensive support for Java Generics

- Allow custom representations of objects

- Support arbitrarily complex objects (with deep inheritance hierarchies and extensive use of generic types)

Gson parses JSON objects by deserializing JSON objects into Java objects. Similarly, it creates JSON objects by serializing Java objects into JSON objects. Gson relies on Java's Reflection API to assist with serialization and deserialization.

© Jeff Friesen 2019

J. Friesen, *Java XML and JSON*, https://doi.org/10.1007/978-1-4842-4330-5_9

Obtaining and Using Gson

Gson is distributed as a single JAR file; gson-2.8.5.jar is the most recent JAR file at the time of writing. To obtain this JAR file, point your browser to http://search.maven. org/#artifactdetails|com.google.code.gson|gson|2.8.5|jar, click the downloads link and select "jar" from the drop-down list, and save the gson-2.8.5.jar file when prompted to do so. Also, you might want to download gson-2.8.5-javadoc.jar, which contains this API's Javadoc.

Note   Gson is licensed according to Apache License Version 2.0 (www.apache. org/licenses/).

It's easy to work with gson-2.8.5.jar. Simply include it in the CLASSPATH when compiling source code or running an application, as follows:

```
javac -cp gson-2.8.5.jar source file
java -cp gson-2.8.5.jar;. main classfile
```

Exploring Gson

Gson consists of more than 30 classes and interfaces distributed among four packages:

- com.google.gson: This package provides access to Gson, the main class for working with Gson.

- com.google.gson.annotations: This package provides annotation types for use with Gson.

- com.google.gson.reflect: This package provides a utility class for obtaining type information from a generic type.

- com.google.gson.stream: This package provides utility classes for reading and writing JSON-encoded values.

In this section, I first introduce you to the Gson class. Then, I focus on Gson deserialization (parsing JSON objects), followed by Gson serialization (creating JSON objects). I close by briefly discussing additional Gson features, such as annotations and type adapters.

Introducing the Gson Class

The Gson class handles the conversion between JSON and Java objects. You can instantiate this class by using the Gson() constructor, or you can obtain a Gson instance by working with the com.google.gson.GsonBuilder class. The following code fragment demonstrates both approaches:

```
Gson gson1 = new Gson();
Gson gson2 = new GsonBuilder()
    .registerTypeAdapter(Id.class, new IdTypeAdapter())
    .serializeNulls()
    .setDateFormat(DateFormat.LONG)
    .setFieldNamingPolicy(FieldNamingPolicy.UPPER_CAMEL_CASE)
    .setPrettyPrinting()
    .setVersion(1.0)
    .create();
```

Call Gson() when you want to work with the default configuration, and use GsonBuilder when you want to override the default configuration. Configuration method calls are chained together, with GsonBuilder's Gson create() method being called last to return the resulting Gson object.

Gson supports the following default configuration (the list isn't complete; check the Gson and GsonBuilder documentation for more information):

- Gson provides default serialization and deserialization for java. lang.Enum, java.util.Map, java.net.URL, java.net.URI, java. util.Locale, java.util.Date, java.math.BigDecimal, and java.math.BigInteger instances. You can change the default representation by registering a *type adapter* (discussed later) via GsonBuilder.registerTypeAdapter(Type, Object).

- The generated JSON text omits all null fields. However, it preserves nulls in arrays because an array is an ordered list. Also, if a field isn't null, but its generated JSON text is empty, the field is kept. You can configure Gson to serialize null values by calling GsonBuilder. serializeNulls().

- The default `Date` format is the same as `java.text.DateFormat.DEFAULT`. This format ignores the millisecond portion of the date during serialization. You can change the default format by invoking `GsonBuilder.setDateFormat(int)` or `GsonBuilder.setDateFormat(String)`.

- The default field-naming policy for the output JSON text is the same as in Java. For example, a Java class field named `versionNumber` will be output as `"versionNumber"` in JSON. The same rules are applied for mapping incoming JSON to Java classes. You can change this policy by calling `GsonBuilder.setFieldNamingPolicy(FieldNaming Policy)`.

- The JSON text that's generated by the `toJson()` methods is represented compactly: all unneeded whitespace is removed. You can change this behavior by calling `GsonBuilder.setPrettyPrinting()`.

- By default, `Gson` ignores `@Since` annotations. You can enable `Gson` to use these annotations by calling `GsonBuilder.setVersion(double)`.

- By default, `Gson` ignores `@Expose` annotations. You can enable `Gson` to serialize/deserialize only those fields marked with this annotation by calling `GsonBuilder.excludeFieldsWithoutExposeAnnotation()`.

- By default, `Gson` excludes `transient` or `static` fields from consideration for serialization and deserialization. You can change this behavior by calling `GsonBuilder.excludeFieldsWithModifiers (int...)`.

Once you have a `Gson` object, you can call various `fromJson()` and `toJson()` methods to convert between JSON and Java objects. For example, Listing 9-1 presents a simple application that obtains a pair of `Gson` objects and demonstrates JSON-Java object conversion in terms of JSON primitives.

Listing 9-1. Converting Between JSON Primitives and Their Java Equivalents

```
import com.google.gson.Gson;
import com.google.gson.GsonBuilder;

import static java.lang.System.*;
```

```java
public class GsonDemo
{
   public static void main(String[] args)
   {
      Gson gson = new Gson();
      String name = gson.fromJson("\"John Doe\"",
                                  String.class);
      out.println(name);
      gson.toJson(256, out);
      out.println();
      gson.toJson("<html>", out);
      out.println();
      gson = new GsonBuilder().disableHtmlEscaping().create();
      gson.toJson("<html>", out);
      out.println();
   }
}
```

Listing 9-1 declares a GsonDemo class whose main() method first instantiates Gson, keeping its default configuration. It then invokes Gson's <T> T fromJson(String json, Class<T> classOfT) generic method to deserialize the specified java.lang.String-based JSON text (in json) into an object of the specified class (classOfT), which happens to be String.

JSON string "John Doe" (the double quotes are mandatory), which is expressed as a Java String object, is converted (minus the double quotes) to a Java String object. A reference to this object is assigned to name.

After outputting the returned name, main() calls Gson's void toJson(Object src, Appendable writer) method to convert autoboxed integer 256 (stored by the compiler in a java.lang.Integer object) into a JSON integer and output the result to the standard output stream.

main() reinvokes toJson() to output a Java string containing <html>. By default, Gson escapes the HTML < and > characters, and so these characters are not output. To prevent this escaping, it's necessary to obtain a Gson object via GsonBuilder, invoking GsonBuilder's GsonBuilder disableHtmlEscaping() method, which main() does next. A second attempt to output <html> reveals no escaping.

Compile Listing 9-1 as follows:

```
javac -cp gson-2.8.5.jar GsonDemo.java
```

Run the resulting application as follows:

```
java -cp gson-2.8.5.jar;. GsonDemo
```

You should observe the following output:

```
John Doe
256
"\u003chtml\u003e"
"<html>"
```

The output isn't impressive, but it's a start. In the next two sections, you'll see more useful examples of deserialization and serialization.

Parsing JSON Objects Through Deserialization

Apart from parsing JSON primitives (such as numbers or strings) into their Java equivalents, Gson lets you parse JSON objects into Java objects. For example, suppose you have the following JSON object, which describes a person:

```
{ "name": "John Doe", "age": 45 }
```

Also, suppose you have the following Java class:

```
class Person
{
    String name;
    int age;
}
```

You can use the previous fromJson() method to parse the JSON object into an instance of the Person class, which I demonstrate in Listing 9-2.

Listing 9-2. Parsing a JSON Object into a Java Object

```java
import com.google.gson.Gson;

import static java.lang.System.*;

public class GsonDemo
{
    static class Person
    {
        String name;
        int age;

        Person(String name, int age)
        {
            this.name = name;
            this.age = age;
        }

        @Override
        public String toString()
        {
            return name + ": " + age;
        }
    }

    public static void main(String[] args)
    {
        Gson gson = new Gson();
        String json = "{ name: \"John Doe\", age: 45 }";
        Person person = gson.fromJson(json, Person.class);
        out.println(person);
    }
}
```

Listing 9-2 declares a GsonDemo class with a nested Person class that describes a person in terms of a name and an age.

GsonDemo's main() method first instantiates Gson, keeping its default configuration. It then constructs a String-based JSON object representing a person and passes this object along with Person.class to fromJson(String json, Class<T> classOfT). fromJson() parses the name and age stored in the string passed to json and uses Person.class along with the Reflection API to create a Person object and populate it with the name and age. A reference to the Person object is returned and stored in the person variable, and subsequently passed to System.out.println(). This method ultimately invokes Person's toString() method to return a string representation of the Person object, and then writes this string to the standard output stream.

Compile Listing 9-2 and run the resulting application. You should observe the following output:

```
John Doe: 45
```

Another method that you can use to parse a JSON object into an instance of the Person class is <T> T fromJson(JsonElement json, java.lang.Class<T> classOfT). This method differs from the previous fromJson() method in that the json text is specified as a tree of com.google.gson.JsonElements (numbers, arrays, etc.).

ABOUT JSONELEMENT

The JsonElement class represents a JSON element (such as a number, a Boolean value, or an array). It provides various methods for obtaining an element value, such as double getAsDouble(), boolean getAsBoolean(), and JsonArray getAsJsonArray(). JsonElement is an abstract class that serves as the superclass for the following JSON element classes (in the com.google.gson package):

- JsonArray: A concrete class that represents JSON's array type. An array is a list of JsonElements, each of which can be of a different type. This is an ordered list, meaning that the order in which elements are added is preserved.

- JsonNull: A concrete class that represents a JSON null value.

- **JsonObject**: A concrete class that represents JSON's object type. An object consists of name/value pairs, where names are strings and values are any other type of JsonElement, which leads to a tree of JsonElements. The member elements of this object are maintained in the order they were added.

- **JsonPrimitive**: A concrete class that represents one of JSON's number, string, or Boolean types (expressed via their Java types).

Except for JsonNull, each of these subclasses provides various methods for obtaining element values.

Of course, you need a JsonElement tree before you can call this method. One way to accomplish this task is to invoke Gson's JsonElement toJsonTree(Object o) method, which serializes Java object o to the equivalent JsonElement tree. Listing 9-3 provides an example.

Listing 9-3. Parsing a JSON Object into a Java Object Redux

```
import com.google.gson.Gson;
import com.google.gson.GsonBuilder;
import com.google.gson.JsonElement;

import static java.lang.System.*;

class Address
{
   private String street;
   private String city;
   private String state;
   private int zipcode;

   Address(String street, String city, String state,
           int zipcode)
   {
      this.street = street;
      this.city = city;
      this.state = state;
```

```
    this.zipcode = zipcode;
  }

  @Override
  public String toString()
  {
    return street + " " + city + " " + state + " " +
          zipcode;
  }
}

public class GsonDemo
{
  public static void main(String[] args)
  {
    Gson gson = new Gson();
    Address address = new Address(null, "Beverly Hills",
                                  "CA", 90210);
    JsonElement tree = gson.toJsonTree(address);
    out.println(tree);
    out.println(gson.fromJson(tree, Address.class));
    gson = new GsonBuilder().serializeNulls().create();
    tree = gson.toJsonTree(address);
    out.println(tree);
    out.println(gson.fromJson(tree, Address.class));
  }
}
```

Listing 9-3 declares Address and GsonDemo classes. Address describes a US address in terms of street, city, state, and zipcode fields. GsonDemo is the main class.

GsonDemo's main() method first creates a Gson object and then creates an Address object with a null street field. It subsequently invokes Gson's toJsonTree() method to serialize the Address object into an equivalent tree of JsonElements, which is subsequently output.

main() now invokes fromJson(JsonElement json, Class<T> classofT) to deserialize the JsonElement tree into an Address object, which is subsequently output (with assistance from Address's toString() method).

By default, a `null` field (such as `street`) isn't serialized. To serialize a `null` field, it's necessary to work with `GsonBuilder` and invoke its `GsonBuilder serializeNulls()` method, which is what `main()` does next. `main()` then repeats its `fromJson()` and `toJson()` calls, outputting the results.

Compile the source code and run the application, and you should observe the following output:

```
{"city":"Beverly Hills","state":"CA","zipcode":90210}
null Beverly Hills CA 90210
{"street":null,"city":"Beverly Hills","state":"CA","zipcode":90210}
null Beverly Hills CA 90210
```

Customized JSON Object Parsing

The `gson.fromJson(json, Person.class)` and `gson.fromJson(json, Address.class)` method calls rely on Gson's default deserialization mechanism to parse JSON objects. You will often encounter scenarios where you need to parse complex JSON objects into Java objects whose classes don't have the same structure as the JSON objects to be parsed. You can perform this parsing with a custom deserializer, which controls how JSON objects map to Java objects.

The `com.google.gson.JsonDeserializer<T>` interface describes a custom deserializer. The argument passed to `T` identifies the type for which the deserializer is being used. For example, you might pass `Person` to `T` when needing to parse JSON objects with a somewhat different structure.

`JsonDeserializer` declares a single method for handling the deserialization (JSON object parsing):

```
T deserialize(JsonElement json,Type typeOfT,
              JsonDeserializationContext context)
```

`deserialize()` is a callback method that `Gson` calls during deserialization. This method is called with the following arguments:

- `json` identifies the JSON element being deserialized.

- `typeOfT` identifies the type of the Java object in which to deserialize `json`.

- `context` identifies a context in which to perform the deserialization. (I'll have more to say about contexts later.)

253

deserialize() throws com.google.gson.JsonParseException when the JSON element passed to json isn't compatible with the type passed to typeOfT. Because JsonParseException extends java.lang.RuntimeException, you don't have to append a throws clause.

After creating a JsonDeserializer object, you need to register it with Gson. Accomplish this task by calling the following GsonBuilder method:

```
GsonBuilder registerTypeAdapter(Type type, Object typeAdapter)
```

The object passed to type identifies the type of the deserializer and the object passed to typeAdapter identifies the deserializer. Because registerTypeAdapter(Type, Object) returns a GsonBuilder object, you can only use this method in a GsonBuilder context.

To demonstrate customized JSON object parsing, consider an expanded version of the previous JSON object:

```
{ "first-name": "John", "last-name": "Doe", "age": 45, "address": "Box 1 " }
```

This JSON object differs significantly from the previous JSON object, which consisted of name and age fields:

- The name field has been refactored into first-name and last-name fields. Note that the hyphen (-) isn't a legal character for a Java identifier.

- An address field has been added.

If you modify Listing 9-2 by replacing the object assigned to json with this new object, you shouldn't be surprised by the following output:

```
null: 45
```

The parsing is completely messed up. However, we can fix this problem by introducing the following custom deserializer:

```
class PersonDeserializer
    implements JsonDeserializer<Person>
{
    @Override
    public Person
        deserialize(JsonElement json, Type typeOfT,
```

```
                    JsonDeserializationContext context)
{
    JsonObject jsonObject = json.getAsJsonObject();
    String firstName = jsonObject.get("first-name").
                            getAsString();
    String lastName = jsonObject.get("last-name").
                            getAsString();
    int age = jsonObject.getAsJsonPrimitive("age").
                        getAsInt();
    String address = jsonObject.get("address").
                            getAsString();
    return new Person(firstName + " " + lastName,
                45);
}
}
```

When the custom deserializer is used with the previous JSON object, `deserialize()` is called only once, and with an object of type `JsonObject` being passed to `json`. You could cast this value to a `JsonObject`, as in `JsonObject jsonObject = (JsonObject) json;`. Alternatively, you can call `JsonElement`'s `JsonObject getAsJsonObject()` method to obtain the `JsonObject` reference, which is what `deserialize()` first accomplishes.

After obtaining the `JsonObject` reference, `deserialize()` calls its `JsonElement get(String memberName)` method to return a `JsonElement` for the desired `memberName` value. The first call passes `first-name` to `get()`; we want to obtain the value of this JSON field. Because a `JsonPrimitive` is returned in place of `JsonElement`, a call to `JsonPrimitive`'s `String getAsString()` method is chained to the `JsonPrimitive` reference, and `first-name`'s value is obtained. This pattern is followed to obtain the values for the `last-name` and `address` fields.

For variety, I decided to do something different with the age field. I call `JsonObject`'s `JsonPrimitive getAsJsonPrimitive(String memberName)` method to return a `JsonPrimitive` reference corresponding to age. Then, I call `JsonPrimitive`'s `int getAsInt()` method to return the integer value.

After obtaining all field values, a `Person` object is created and then returned. Because I'm reusing the `Person` class shown in Listing 9-2, and because there is no `address` field in this class, I throw `address`'s value away. You might want to modify `Person` to include this field.

The following code fragment shows how you would instantiate `PersonDeserializer` and register it with a `GsonBuilder` instance, which is also used to obtain a `Gson` instance in order to call `fromJson()`, to parse the previous JSON object via the person deserializer:

```
GsonBuilder gsonBuilder = new GsonBuilder();
gsonBuilder.
   registerTypeAdapter(Person.class,
                       new PersonDeserializer());
Gson gson = gsonBuilder.create();
```

I've combined these code fragments into a working application. Listing 9-4 presents the application's source code.

Listing 9-4. Parsing a JSON Object into a Java Object via a Custom Deserializer

```
import java.lang.reflect.Type;

import com.google.gson.Gson;
import com.google.gson.GsonBuilder;
import com.google.gson.JsonDeserializationContext;
import com.google.gson.JsonDeserializer;
import com.google.gson.JsonElement;
import com.google.gson.JsonObject;
import com.google.gson.JsonParseException;

import static java.lang.System.*;

public class GsonDemo
{
   static class Person
   {
      String name;
      int age;
```

```java
    Person(String name, int age)
    {
        this.name = name;
        this.age = age;
    }

    @Override
    public String toString()
    {
        return name + ": " + age;
    }
}

public static void main(String[] args)
{
    class PersonDeserializer
        implements JsonDeserializer<Person>
    {
        @Override
        public Person
            deserialize(JsonElement json, Type typeOfT,
                        JsonDeserializationContext context)
        {
            JsonObject jsonObject = json.getAsJsonObject();
            String firstName = jsonObject.get("first-name").
                                          getAsString();
            String lastName = jsonObject.get("last-name").
                                          getAsString();
            int age = jsonObject.getAsJsonPrimitive("age").
                                 getAsInt();
            String address = jsonObject.get("address").
                                          getAsString();
            return new Person(firstName + " " + lastName,
                              45);
        }
    }
```

```
      GsonBuilder gsonBuilder = new GsonBuilder();
      gsonBuilder.
         registerTypeAdapter(Person.class,
                             new PersonDeserializer());
      Gson gson = gsonBuilder.create();
      String json = "{ first-name: \"John\", " +
                    "last-name: \"Doe\", age: 45, " +
                    "address: \"Box 1\" }";
      Person person = gson.fromJson(json, Person.class);
      out.println(person);
   }
}
```

Compile Listing 9-4 and run the resulting application. You should observe the following output:

```
John Doe: 45
```

Creating JSON Objects Through Serialization

Gson lets you create JSON objects from Java objects by calling one of Gson's toJson() methods. Listing 9-5 provides a simple demonstration.

Listing 9-5. Creating a JSON Object from a Java Object

```
import com.google.gson.Gson;

import static java.lang.System.*;

public class GsonDemo
{
   static class Person
   {
      String name;
      int age;

      Person(String name, int age)
      {
         this.name = name;
```

```
        this.age = age;
    }
}

public static void main(String[] args)
{
    Person p = new Person("Jane Doe", 59);
    Gson gson = new Gson();
    String json = gson.toJson(p);
    out.println(json);
}
}
```

Listing 9-5's main() method first creates a Person object from the nested Person class. It then creates a Gson object and invokes this object's String toJson(Object src) method to serialize the Person object into its equivalent JSON string representation, which toJson(Object) returns.

Compile Listing 9-5 and run the resulting application. You should observe the following output:

```
{"name":"Jane Doe","age":59}
```

If you prefer to write the JSON object to a file, a string buffer, or some other java.lang.Appendable, you can call void toJson(Object src, Appendable writer) to accomplish this task. This toJson() variant sends its output to the specified writer, as demonstrated in Listing 9-6.

Listing 9-6. Creating a JSON Object from a Java Object and Writing the JSON Object to a File

```
import java.io.FileWriter;
import java.io.IOException;

import com.google.gson.Gson;

public class GsonDemo
{
    static class Student
    {
```

```
        String name;
        int id;
        int[] grades;

        Student(String name, int id, int... grades)
        {
            this.name = name;
            this.id = id;
            this.grades = grades;
        }
    }

    public static void main(String[] args) throws IOException
    {
        Student s = new Student("John Doe", 820787, 89, 78,
                                97, 65);
        Gson gson = new Gson();
        FileWriter fw = new FileWriter("student.json");
        gson.toJson(s, fw);
        fw.close();
    }
}
```

Listing 9-6's main() method first creates a Student object from the nested Student class. It then creates Gson and java.io.FileWriter objects and invokes the Gson object's toJson(Object, Appendable) method to serialize the Student object into its equivalent JSON string representation and write the result to student.json. The file writer is then closed so that buffered content can be written to the file (you could specify fw.flush(); instead).

If you run this application, you won't observe any output. However, you should observe a student.json file with the following content:

```
{"name":"John Doe","id":820787,"grades":[89,78,97,65]}
```

Note   void toJson(Object src, Appendable writer) throws the unchecked com.google.gson.JsonIOException when an I/O error arises.

Customized JSON Object Creation

The previous `gson.toJson(p)` and `gson.toJson(s, fw)` method calls rely on Gson's default serialization mechanism to create JSON objects. You will often encounter scenarios where you need to create JSON objects from Java objects whose classes don't have the same structure as the JSON objects to be created. You can perform this creation with a custom serializer, which controls how Java objects map to JSON objects.

The `com.google.gson.JsonSerializer<T>` interface describes a custom serializer. The argument passed to T identifies the type for which the serializer is being used. For example, you might pass `Person` to T when needing to create JSON objects with a somewhat different structure.

`JsonSerializer` declares a single method for handling the serialization (JSON object creation):

```
JsonElement serialize(T src, Type typeOfSrc,
                      JsonSerializationContext context)
```

`serialize()` is a callback method that Gson calls during serialization. This method is called with the following arguments:

- `src` identifies the Java object that needs to be serialized.

- `typeOfSrc` identifies the actual type of the Java object, specified by `src`, to be serialized.

- `context` identifies a context in which to perform the serialization. (I'll have more to say about contexts later.)

After creating a `JsonSerializer` object, you need to register it with Gson. Accomplish this task by calling the following `GsonBuilder` method:

```
GsonBuilder registerTypeAdapter(Type type, Object typeAdapter)
```

The object passed to `type` identifies the type of the serializer and the object passed to `typeAdapter` identifies the serializer. Because `registerTypeAdapter(Type, Object)` returns a `GsonBuilder` object, you can only use this method in a `GsonBuilder` context.

To demonstrate customized JSON object creation, consider the `Book` class that's presented in Listing 9-7.

Listing 9-7. Describing a Book as a Title, List of Authors, and ISBN Numbers

```java
public class Book
{
   private String title;
   private String[] authors;
   private String isbn10;
   private String isbn13;

   public Book(String title, String[] authors,
               String isbn10, String isbn13)
   {
      this.title = title;
      this.authors = authors;
      this.isbn10 = isbn10;
      this.isbn13 = isbn13;
   }

   public String getTitle()
   {
      return title;
   }

   public String[] getAuthors()
   {
      return authors;
   }

   public String getIsbn10()
   {
      return isbn10;
   }

   public String getIsbn13()
   {
      return isbn13;
   }
}
```

Continuing, suppose that Book objects are to be serialized to JSON objects that have the following format:

```
{
   "title": title
   "lead-author": author0
   "other-authors": [ author1, author2, ... ]
   "isbn-10": isbn10
   "isbn-13": isbn13
}
```

You cannot use default serialization because the Book class doesn't declare lead-author, other-authors, isbn-10, and isbn-13 fields. In any case, default serialization creates JSON property names that match a Java class's field names (and the hyphen character is illegal for Java identifiers). To prove that you cannot obtain the desired JSON object with default serialization, suppose you attempt to execute the following code fragment:

```
Book book =
   new Book("PHP and MySQL Web Development, " +
            "Second Edition",
            new String[] { "Luke Welling",
                           "Laura Thomson" },
            "067232525X", "075-2063325254");
Gson gson = new Gson();
System.out.println(gson.toJson(book));
```

This code fragment generates the following output:

```
{"title":"PHP and MySQL Web Development, Second Edition","authors":["Luke Welling","Laura Thomson"],"isbn10":"067232525X","isbn13":"075-2063325254"}
```

The output doesn't match the expected JSON object. However, you can fix this problem by introducing the following custom serializer:

```
class BookSerializer implements JsonSerializer<Book>
{
   @Override
   public JsonElement
      serialize(Book src, Type typeOfSrc,
```

```
                JsonSerializationContext context)
{
    JsonObject jsonObject = new JsonObject();
    jsonObject.addProperty("title", src.getTitle());
    jsonObject.addProperty("lead-author",
                            src.getAuthors()[0]);
    JsonArray jsonOtherAuthors = new JsonArray();
    for (int i = 1; i < src.getAuthors().length;
        i++)
    {
        JsonPrimitive jsonAuthor =
            new JsonPrimitive(src.getAuthors()[i]);
        jsonOtherAuthors.add(jsonAuthor);
    }
    jsonObject.add("other-authors",
                    jsonOtherAuthors);
    jsonObject.addProperty("isbn-10",
                            src.getIsbn10());
    jsonObject.addProperty("isbn-13",
                            src.getIsbn13());
    return jsonObject;
}
}
```

When the custom serializer is used with the previous Java Book object, serialize()
is called only once with the Book object being passed to src. Because a JSON object is
desired as the result of this method, serialize() first creates a JsonObject instance.

JsonObject declares several addProperty() methods for adding properties to the
JSON object that a JsonObject instance represents. serialize() invokes the void
addProperty(String property, String value) method to add the title, lead-author,
isbn-10, and isbn-13 properties.

The other-authors property is handled differently. First, serialize() creates a
JsonArray instance and populates it with all authors except for the first author. Then, it
invokes JsonObject's void add(String property, JsonElement value) method to add
the JsonArray object to the JsonObject.

When serialization finishes, `serialize()` returns the created and populated `JsonObject`.

The following code fragment shows how you would instantiate `BookSerializer` and register it with a `GsonBuilder` instance, which is also used to obtain a `Gson` instance in order to call `toJson()`, to create the desired JSON object via the book serializer:

```
GsonBuilder gsonBuilder = new GsonBuilder();
gsonBuilder.registerTypeAdapter(Book.class,
                                new BookSerializer());
Gson gson = gsonBuilder.create();
```

I've combined these code fragments into a working application. Listing 9-8 presents the application's source code.

Listing 9-8. Creating a JSON Object from a Java Object via a Custom Serializer

```
import java.lang.reflect.Type;

import com.google.gson.Gson;
import com.google.gson.GsonBuilder;
import com.google.gson.JsonArray;
import com.google.gson.JsonElement;
import com.google.gson.JsonObject;
import com.google.gson.JsonPrimitive;
import com.google.gson.JsonSerializationContext;
import com.google.gson.JsonSerializer;

import static java.lang.System.*;

public class GsonDemo
{
   public static void main(String[] args)
   {
      class BookSerializer implements JsonSerializer<Book>
      {
         @Override
         public JsonElement
            serialize(Book src, Type typeOfSrc,
                      JsonSerializationContext context)
```

```java
        {
            JsonObject jsonObject = new JsonObject();
            jsonObject.addProperty("title", src.getTitle());
            jsonObject.addProperty("lead-author",
                                    src.getAuthors()[0]);
            JsonArray jsonOtherAuthors = new JsonArray();
            for (int i = 1; i < src.getAuthors().length;
                i++)
            {
                JsonPrimitive jsonAuthor =
                    new JsonPrimitive(src.getAuthors()[i]);
                jsonOtherAuthors.add(jsonAuthor);
            }
            jsonObject.add("other-authors",
                            jsonOtherAuthors);
            jsonObject.addProperty("isbn-10",
                                    src.getIsbn10());
            jsonObject.addProperty("isbn-13",
                                    src.getIsbn13());
            return jsonObject;
        }
    }
    GsonBuilder gsonBuilder = new GsonBuilder();
    gsonBuilder.registerTypeAdapter(Book.class,
                                    new BookSerializer());
    Gson gson = gsonBuilder.setPrettyPrinting().create();
    Book book =
        new Book("PHP and MySQL Web Development, " +
                "Second Edition",
                new String[] { "Luke Welling",
                "Laura Thomson" },
                "067232525X", "075-2063325254");
    out.println(gson.toJson(book));
    }
}
```

Compile Listings 9-7 and 9-8, and run the resulting application. You should observe the following output, which has been pretty-printed (via the `setPrettyPrinting()` method call on the `GsonBuilder` object) to make the output clearer:

```
{
  "title": "PHP and MySQL Web Development, Second Edition",
  "lead-author": "Luke Welling",
  "other-authors": [
    "Laura Thomson"
  ],
  "isbn-10": "067232525X",
  "isbn-13": "075-2063325254"
}
```

Learning More About Gson

Now that you have a fairly good understanding of Gson library basics, you'll probably want to learn about other features that this library offers. In this section, I introduce you to annotation types, contexts, Gson's support for generics, and type adapters.

Note   My coverage of additional Gson features isn't exhaustive. Check out the "Gson User Guide" (`http://github.com/google/gson/blob/master/UserGuide.md`) to learn about topics that I haven't covered, for example, instance creators.

Annotation Types

Gson offers several annotation types (in the `com.google.gson.annotations` package) for simplifying serialization and deserialization:

- `Expose`: Exposes the annotated field to or hides it from Gson's serialization and/or deserialization mechanisms.

- `JsonAdapter`: Identifies the type adapter to use with a class or field. (I'll discuss this annotation type later when I focus on type adapters.)

- SerializedName: Indicates that the annotated field or method should be serialized to JSON with the provided name value as its name.

- Since: Identifies the starting version number for serializing a field or type. If a Gson object is created with a version number that is less than the value in the @Since annotation, the annotated field/type will not be serialized.

- Until: Identifies the ending version number for serializing a field or type. If a Gson object is created with a version number that equals or exceeds the value in the @Until annotation, the annotated field/type will not be serialized.

Note According to the Gson documentation, Since and Until are useful for managing the versioning of JSON classes in a web service context.

Exposing and Hiding Fields

By default, Gson will not serialize and deserialize fields that are marked transient (or static). You can call GsonBuilder's GsonBuilder excludeFieldsWithModifiers (int... modifiers) method to change this behavior. Also, Gson lets you selectively determine which non-transient fields to serialize and/or deserialize by annotating these fields with instances of the Expose annotation type.

Expose offers the following elements for determining whether a field can be serialized and whether it can be deserialized:

- serialize: When true, the field marked with this @Expose annotation is serialized to JSON text; otherwise, the field isn't serialized. The default value is true.

- deserialize: When true, the field marked with this @Expose annotation is deserialized from JSON text; otherwise, the field isn't deserialized. The default value is true.

The following code fragment shows how to use Expose and these elements so that a field named someField will be serialized and not deserialized:

```
@Expose(serialize = true, deserialize = false)
int someField;
```

By default, Gson ignores Expose. You must configure Gson to expose/hide fields that are annotated with @Expose by calling the following GsonBuilder method:

```
GsonBuilder excludeFieldsWithoutExposeAnnotation()
```

Create a GsonBuilder object and then call GsonBuilder's excludeFieldsWithoutExposeAnnotation() method followed by its Gson create() method on this object to return a configured Gson object:

```
GsonBuilder gsonb = new GsonBuilder();
gsonb.excludeFieldsWithoutExposeAnnotation();
Gson gson = gsonb.create();
```

Listing 9-9 describes an application that demonstrates the Expose annotation type.

Listing 9-9. Exposing and Hiding Fields to and from Serialization and Deserialization

```
import com.google.gson.Gson;
import com.google.gson.GsonBuilder;

import com.google.gson.annotations.Expose;

import static java.lang.System.*;

public class GsonDemo
{
   static class SomeClass
   {
      transient int id;
      @Expose(serialize = true, deserialize = true)
      transient String password;
      @Expose(serialize = false, deserialize = false)
      int field1;
      @Expose(serialize = false, deserialize = true)
      int field2;
      @Expose(serialize = true, deserialize = false)
      int field3;
      @Expose(serialize = true, deserialize = true)
      int field4;
```

269

```java
        @Expose(serialize = true, deserialize = true)
        static int field5;
        static int field6;
    }

    public static void main(String[] args)
    {
        SomeClass sc = new SomeClass();
        sc.id = 1;
        sc.password = "abc";
        sc.field1 = 2;
        sc.field2 = 3;
        sc.field3 = 4;
        sc.field4 = 5;
        sc.field5 = 6;
        sc.field6 = 7;
        GsonBuilder gsonb = new GsonBuilder();
        gsonb.excludeFieldsWithoutExposeAnnotation();
        Gson gson = gsonb.create();
        String json = gson.toJson(sc) ;
        out.println(json);
        SomeClass sc2 = gson.fromJson(json, SomeClass.class);
        out.printf("id = %d%n", sc2.id);
        out.printf("password = %s%n", sc2.password);
        out.printf("field1 = %d%n", sc2.field1);
        out.printf("field2 = %d%n", sc2.field2);
        out.printf("field3 = %d%n", sc2.field3);
        out.printf("field4 = %d%n", sc2.field4);
        out.printf("field5 = %d%n", sc2.field5);
        out.printf("field6 = %d%n", sc2.field6);
    }
}
```

Listing 9-9 demonstrates Expose with transient instance fields along with non-transient instance fields and static fields.

Compile Listing 9-9 and run the resulting application. You should observe the following output:

```
{"field3":4,"field4":5}
id = 0
password = null
field1 = 0
field2 = 0
field3 = 0
field4 = 5
field5 = 6
field6 = 7
```

The first output line shows that only field3 and field4 are serialized. The other fields are not serialized.

The second and third lines show that the transient id and password fields receive default values. transient fields are not serialized/deserialized.

The fourth, fifth, and sixth lines show that default 0 values are assigned to field1, field2, and field3. For field1 and field3, deserialize is assigned false so only default values can be assigned to these fields. Because field2 wasn't serialized, the only value that can be assigned to it is 0.

The seventh line shows that 5 is assigned to field4. This makes sense because the serialize and deserialize elements are assigned true.

Because static fields aren't serialized or deserialized, they keep their initial values, as shown in the eighth and ninth lines (for field5 and field6).

Note   Even if Gson serialized static fields, field6 wouldn't be serialized because it isn't annotated with @Expose, and also because of the gsonb. excludeFieldsWithoutExposeAnnotation() method call, which causes Gson to bypass fields not annotated with @Expose.

Changing Field Names

You don't have to use `JsonSerializer<T>` and `JsonDeserializer<T>` when you only want to change field and/or method names during serialization and deserialization; for example, changing `isbn10` to `isbn-10` and `isbn13` to `isbn-13`. You can use `SerializedName` instead, as shown here:

```
@SerializedName("isbn-10")
String isbn10;
@SerializedName("isbn-13")
String isbn13;
```

The JSON object will present `isbn-10` and `isbn-13` property names, whereas the Java class presents `isbn10` and `isbn13` field names.

Listing 9-10 describes an application that demonstrates the `SerializedName` annotation type.

Listing 9-10. Changing Names

```
import com.google.gson.Gson;

import com.google.gson.annotations.SerializedName;

import static java.lang.System.*;

public class GsonDemo
{
   static class Book
   {
      String title;
      @SerializedName("isbn-10")
      String isbn10;
      @SerializedName("isbn-13")
      String isbn13;
   }
```

```java
public static void main(String[] args)
{
    Book book = new Book();
    book.title = "PHP and MySQL Web Development, " +
                 "Second Edition";
    book.isbn10 = "067232525X";
    book.isbn13 = "075-2063325254";
    Gson gson = new Gson();
    String json = gson.toJson(book);
    out.println(json);
    Book book2 = gson.fromJson(json, Book.class);
    out.printf("title = %s%n", book2.title);
    out.printf("isbn10 = %s%n", book2.isbn10);
    out.printf("isbn13 = %s%n", book2.isbn13);
}
}
```

Compile Listing 9-10 (and Listing 9-7's Book class) and run the resulting application. You should observe the following output:

```
{"title":"PHP and MySQL Web Development, Second Edition",
"isbn-10":"067232525X","isbn-13":"075-2063325254"}
title = PHP and MySQL Web Development, Second Edition
isbn10 = 067232525X
isbn13 = 075-2063325254
```

Versioning

Since and Until are useful for versioning your classes. Using these annotation types, you can determine which fields and/or types are serialized to JSON objects.

Each @Since and @Until annotation receives a double precision floating-point value as its argument. This value specifies a version number, as demonstrated here:

```java
@Since(1.0) private String userID;
@Since(1.0) private String password;
@Until(1.1) private String emailAddress;
```

@Since(1.0) indicates that the field it annotates is to be serialized for all versions greater than or equal to 1.0. Similarly, @Until(1.1) indicates that the field it annotates is to be serialized for all versions less than 1.1.

The version number that's compared to the @Since or @Until version argument is specified by the following GsonBuilder method:

```
GsonBuilder setVersion(double ignoreVersionsAfter)
```

As with Expose, you would first create a GsonBuilder object, then call this method with the desired version number on that object, and finally call create() on the GsonBuilder object to return a newly created Gson object:

```
GsonBuilder gsonb = new GsonBuilder();
gsonb.setVersion(2.0);
Gson gson = gsonb.create();
```

Listing 9-11 describes an application that demonstrates the Since and Until annotation types.

Listing 9-11. Versioning a Class and Its Fields

```
import com.google.gson.Gson;
import com.google.gson.GsonBuilder;

import com.google.gson.annotations.Since;
import com.google.gson.annotations.Until;

import static java.lang.System.*;

public class GsonDemo
{
   @Since(1.0)
   @Until(2.5)
   static class SomeClass
   {
      @Since(1.1)
      @Until(1.5)
      int field;
   }
```

```java
public static void main(String[] args)
{
    SomeClass sc = new SomeClass();
    sc.field = 1;
    GsonBuilder gsonb = new GsonBuilder();
    gsonb.setVersion(0.9);
    Gson gson = gsonb.create();
    out.printf("%s%n%n", gson.toJson(sc));
    gsonb.setVersion(1.0);
    gson = gsonb.create();
    out.printf("%s%n%n", gson.toJson(sc));
    gsonb.setVersion(1.1);
    gson = gsonb.create();
    out.printf("%s%n%n", gson.toJson(sc));
    gsonb.setVersion(1.5);
    gson = gsonb.create();
    out.printf("%s%n%n", gson.toJson(sc));
    gsonb.setVersion(2.5);
    gson = gsonb.create();
    out.printf("%s%n", gson.toJson(sc));
}
}
```

Listing 9-11 presents a nested SomeClass that will be serialized as long as the version number passed to setVersion() ranges from 1.0 to almost 2.5. This class presents a field named field that will be serialized as long as the version number passed to setVersion() ranges from 1.1 to almost 1.5.

Compile Listing 9-11 and run the resulting application. You should observe the following output:

```
null

{}

{"field":1}

{}

null
```

Contexts

The serialize() and deserialize() methods that are declared by the JsonSerializer and JsonDeserializer interfaces are called with com.google.gson.JsonSerializationContext and com.google.gson.JsonDeserializationContext objects, respectively, as their final arguments. These objects provide serialize() and deserialize() methods for performing default serialization and default deserialization on specific Java objects. You'll find them handy when working with nested Java objects that don't require special treatment.

Suppose you have the following Date and Employee classes:

```
class Date
{
   int year;
   int month;
   int day;

   Date(int year, int month, int day)
   {
      this.year = year;
      this.month = month;
      this.day = day;
   }
}

class Employee
{
   String name;
   Date hireDate;
}
```

Now, suppose that you decide to create a custom serializer to add emp-name and hire-date properties (instead of name and hireDate properties) to the resulting JSON object. Because you're not changing the names or the order of Date's fields during serialization, you can leverage the *context* passed to JsonSerializer's serialize() method to handle that part of the serialization for you.

The following code fragment presents a serializer that serializes Employee objects and their nested Date objects:

```java
class EmployeeSerializer
   implements JsonSerializer<Employee>
{
   @Override
   public JsonElement
      serialize(Employee emp, Type typeOfSrc,
               JsonSerializationContext context)
   {
      JsonObject jo = new JsonObject();
      jo.addProperty("emp-name", emp.name);
      jo.add("hire-date",
            context.serialize(emp.hireDate));
      return jo;
   }
}
```

serialize() first creates a JsonObject to describe the serialized JSON object. It then adds an emp-name property with the employee name as the value to this JsonObject. Because default serialization can serialize the hireDate field, serialize() calls context. serialize(emp.hireDate) to generate a property value. This value and the hire-date property name are added to the JsonObject, which is returned from the method.

Listing 9-12 presents the source code to an application that demonstrates this serialize() method.

Listing 9-12. Leveraging a Context to Serialize a Date

```java
import java.lang.reflect.Type;

import com.google.gson.Gson;
import com.google.gson.GsonBuilder;
import com.google.gson.JsonElement;
import com.google.gson.JsonObject;
import com.google.gson.JsonSerializationContext;
import com.google.gson.JsonSerializer;
```

```java
import static java.lang.System.*;

public class GsonDemo
{
   static class Date
   {
      int year;
      int month;
      int day;

      Date(int year, int month, int day)
      {
         this.year = year;
         this.month = month;
         this.day = day;
      }
   }

   static class Employee
   {
      String name;
      Date hireDate;
   }

   public static void main(String[] args)
   {
      Employee e = new Employee();
      e.name = "John Doe";
      e.hireDate = new Date(1982, 10, 12);
      GsonBuilder gb = new GsonBuilder();
      class EmployeeSerializer
         implements JsonSerializer<Employee>
      {
         @Override
         public JsonElement
            serialize(Employee emp, Type typeOfSrc,
                      JsonSerializationContext context)
```

```
    {
        JsonObject jo = new JsonObject();
        jo.addProperty("emp-name", emp.name);
        jo.add("hire-date",
                context.serialize(emp.hireDate));
        return jo;
    }
}
gb.registerTypeAdapter(Employee.class,
                        new EmployeeSerializer());
Gson gson = gb.create();
out.printf("%s%n%n", gson.toJson(e));
    }
}
```

Compile Listing 9-12 and run the resulting application. You should observe the following output (on one line):

```
{"emp-name":"John Doe","hire-date":{"year":1982,"month":10,"day":12}}
```

Generics Support

When you call `String toJson(Object src)` or `void toJson(Object src, Appendable writer)`, Gson calls `src.getClass()` to get `src`'s `java.lang.Class` object so that it can reflectively learn about the fields to serialize. Similarly, when you call a deserialization method such as `<T> T fromJson(String json, Class<T> classOfT)`, Gson uses the `Class` object passed to `classOfT` to help it reflectively build a result Java object. These operations work properly for objects instantiated from nongeneric types. However, when an object is created from a generic type, problems can occur because the generic type information is lost due to *type erasure*. Consider the following code fragment:

```
List<String> weekdays =
    Arrays.asList("Sun", "Mon", "Tue", "Wed", "Thu",
                "Fri", "Sat");
String json = gson.toJson(weekdays);
System.out.printf("%s%n%n", json);
System.out.printf("%s%n%n",
                gson.fromJson(json, weekdays.getClass()));
```

Variable weekdays is an object with generic type `java.util.List<String>`. The `toJson()` method calls `weekdays.getClass()` and discovers, instead, `List` as the type. However, it still successfully serializes weekdays to the following JSON object:

```
["Sun","Mon","Tue","Wed","Thu","Fri","Sat"]
```

Deserialization isn't successful. When `gson.fromJson(json, weekdays.getClass())` is called, this method throws an instance of the `java.lang.ClassCastException` class. Internally, it attempts to cast `java.util.ArrayList` to `java.util.Arrays$ArrayList`, which doesn't work.

The solution to this problem is to specify the correct `List<String>` *parameterized type* (generic type instance) instead of the raw `List` type that's returned from `weekdays.getClass()`. You use the `com.google.gson.reflect.TypeToken<T>` class for this purpose.

`TypeToken<T>` represents a generic type T and enables the retrieval of type information at runtime, which Gson requires. You would instantiate TypeToken using an expression such as the following:

```
Type listType = new TypeToken<List<String>>() {}.getType();
```

This idiom defines an anonymous local inner class whose inherited `getType()` method returns the fully parameterized type as a `java.lang.reflect.Type` object. In this code fragment, the following type is returned:

```
java.util.List<java.lang.String>
```

Pass the resulting Type object to the `<T> T fromJson(String json, Type typeOfT)` method, as follows:

```
gson.fromJson(json, listType)
```

This method call parses and returns the JSON object as a `List<String>`.

You might want to output the result using an expression such as the following:

```
System.out.printf("%s%n%n", gson.fromJson(json, listType));
```

However, you would receive a thrown `ClassCastException` stating that you cannot cast `ArrayList` to `java.lang.Object[]` instead of observing output. The solution to the problem is to introduce a cast to `List`, as follows:

```
System.out.printf("%s%n%n",
                  (List) gson.fromJson(json, listType));
```

After making this change, you would observe the following output:

```
[Sun, Mon, Tue, Wed, Thu, Fri, Sat]
```

Listing 9-13 presents the source code to an application that demonstrates this problem along with other generic-oriented serialization/deserialization problems, and how to solve them.

Listing 9-13. Serializing and Deserializing Objects Based on Generic Types

```java
import java.lang.reflect.Type;

import java.util.ArrayList;
import java.util.List;
import java.util.Map;
import java.util.HashMap;

import com.google.gson.Gson;

import com.google.gson.reflect.TypeToken;

import java.util.Arrays;
import java.util.List;

import static java.lang.System.*;

public class GsonDemo
{
   static
   class Vehicle<T>
   {
      T vehicle;

      T get()
      {
         return vehicle;
      }

      void set(T vehicle)
      {
         this.vehicle = vehicle;
      }
```

```java
        @Override
        public String toString()
        {
           out.printf("Class of vehicle: %s%n",
                       vehicle.getClass());
           return "Vehicle: " + vehicle.toString();
        }
    }

    static
    class Truck
    {
        String make;
        String model;

        Truck(String make, String model)
        {
           this.make = make;
           this.model = model;
        }

        @Override
        public String toString()
        {
           return "Make: " + make + " Model: " + model;
        }
    }

    public static void main(String[] args)
    {
        Gson gson = new Gson();

        // ...

        out.printf("PART 1%n");
        out.printf("------%n%n");
```

```
List<String> weekdays =
   Arrays.asList("Sun", "Mon", "Tue", "Wed", "Thu",
                 "Fri", "Sat");
String json = gson.toJson(weekdays);
out.printf("%s%n%n", json);
try
{
   out.printf("%s%n%n",
              gson.fromJson(json,
                            weekdays.getClass()));
}
catch (ClassCastException cce)
{
   cce.printStackTrace();
   out.println();
}
Type listType =
   new TypeToken<List<String>>() {}.getType();
out.printf("Type = %s%n%n", listType);
try
{
   out.printf("%s%n%n", gson.fromJson(json,
                                      listType));
}
catch (ClassCastException cce)
{
   cce.printStackTrace();
   out.println();
}
out.printf("%s%n%n", (List) gson.fromJson(json,
                                          listType));

// ...

out.printf("PART 2%n");
out.printf("------%n%n");
```

```
Truck truck = new Truck("Ford", "F150");
Vehicle<Truck> vehicle = new Vehicle<>();
vehicle.set(truck);

json = gson.toJson(vehicle);
out.printf("%s%n%n", json);
out.printf("%s%n%n",
            gson.fromJson(json, vehicle.getClass()));

// ...

out.printf("PART 3%n");
out.printf("------%n%n");

Map<String, String> map =
    new HashMap<String, String>()
{
    {
        put("key", "value");
    }
};
out.printf("Map = %s%n%n", map);
out.printf("%s%n%n", gson.toJson(map));
out.printf("%s%n%n", gson.fromJson(gson.toJson(map),
                                    map.getClass()));

// ...

out.printf("PART 4%n");
out.printf("------%n%n");

Type vehicleType =
    new TypeToken<Vehicle<Truck>>() {}.getType();
json = gson.toJson(vehicle, vehicleType);
out.printf("%s%n%n", json);
out.printf("%s%n%n", (Vehicle)
                        gson.fromJson(json,
                                    vehicleType));
```

```
Type mapType =
    new TypeToken<Map<String,String>>() {}.getType();
out.printf("%s%n%n", gson.toJson(map, mapType));
out.printf("%s%n%n", (Map)
            gson.fromJson(gson.toJson(map, mapType),
                          mapType)) ;
   }
}
```

Listing 9-13's GsonDemo class is organized into nested Vehicle and Truck static classes followed by the main() entry-point method. This method is organized into four sections that demonstrate problems and solutions. Here is the output, which I'll refer to during my discussion of main():

```
PART 1
------

["Sun","Mon","Tue","Wed","Thu","Fri","Sat"]

java.lang.ClassCastException: Cannot cast java.util.ArrayList to java.util.
Arrays$ArrayList
      at java.base/java.lang.Class.cast(Class.java:3606)
      at com.google.gson.Gson.fromJson(Gson.java:814)
      at GsonDemo.main(GsonDemo.java:79)

Type = java.util.List<java.lang.String>

java.lang.ClassCastException: class java.util.ArrayList cannot be cast to
class [Ljava.lang.Object; (java.util.ArrayList and [Ljava.lang.Object; are
in module java.base of loader 'bootstrap')
      at GsonDemo.main(GsonDemo.java:92)

[Sun, Mon, Tue, Wed, Thu, Fri, Sat]

PART 2
------

{"vehicle":{"make":"Ford","model":"F150"}}

Class of vehicle: class com.google.gson.internal.LinkedTreeMap
Vehicle: {make=Ford, model=F150}
```

PART 3

Map = {key=value}

null

null

PART 4

{"vehicle":{"make":"Ford","model":"F150"}}

Class of vehicle: class GsonDemo$Truck
Vehicle: Make: Ford Model: F150

{"key":"value"}

{key=value}

Part 1 focuses on the previously discussed List<String> example. The output shows successful serialization via toJson(), followed by unsuccessful deserialization via gson.fromJson(json, weekdays.getClass()), followed by the type stored in the first created TypeToken instance, followed by successful deserialization with a cast problem, followed by successful deserialization with no cast problem.

Part 2 focuses on the serialization and deserialization of a Vehicle<Truck> object named vehicle. This generic object is successfully serialized via a gson.toJson(vehicle) call. Although you can often pass generic objects to toJson(Object src) successfully, this method occasionally fails, as I will show. A subsequent call to gson.fromJson(json, vehicle.getClass()) attempts to deserialize the output, but there is a problem: you observe Vehicle: {make=Ford, model=F150} instead of Vehicle: Make: Ford Model: F150. Because Vehicle is specified instead of the full Vehicle<Truck> generic type, the vehicle field in the Vehicle class is assigned com.google.gson.internal.LinkedTreeMap instead of Truck as its type.

Part 3 attempts to serialize and deserialize a map based on an anonymous subclass of java.util.HashMap. The first null value shows that toJson() wasn't successful: toJson()'s internal map.getClass() call returns a GsonDemo$2 reference, which offers no insight into the object to be serialized. The second null value results from passing null to json in fromJson(String json, Class<T> classOfT).

Part 4 shows how to fix the problems in Parts 2 and 3. This section creates TypeToken<Vehicle<Truck>> and TypeToken<Map<String,String>> objects to store the Vehicle<Truck> and Map<String, String> parameterized types. These objects are then passed to the type parameter of the String toJson(Object src, Type typeOfSrc) and <T> T fromJson(String json, Type typeOfT) methods. (Although gson.toJson(vehicle, vehicleType) isn't necessary because serialization works with gson.toJson(vehicle), you should get into the habit of passing a Type object based on a TypeToken instance as a second argument, just to be safe.)

Note Each of toJson(Object src), <T> T fromJson(String json, Class<T> classOfT), and similar methods works properly when any of the fields of the specified object (src and object derived from classOfT) are based on generic types. The only stipulation is that the specified object should not be generic.

Type Adapters

Previously in this chapter, I showed you how to use JsonSerializer and JsonDeserializer to (respectively) serialize Java objects to JSON strings and vice versa. These interfaces simplify the translation between Java objects and JSON strings, but add an intermediate layer of processing.

The intermediate layer consists of code that converts Java objects and JSON strings to JsonElements. This conversion mitigates the risk of parsing or creating invalid JSON strings, but does take time that can impact performance. You can avoid the intermediate layer and create more efficient code by working with the com.google. gson.TypeAdapter<T> class, where T identifies the Java class serialization source and deserialization target.

Note You should prefer the more efficient TypeAdapter to the less efficient JsonSerializer and JsonDeserializer. In fact, Gson uses an internal TypeAdapter implementation to handle conversions between Java objects and JSON strings.

TypeAdapter is an abstract class that declares several concrete methods along with the following pair of abstract methods:

- `T read(JsonReader in)`: Read a JSON value (array, object, string, number, Boolean, or `null`) and convert it to a Java object, which is returned. The return value may be `null`.

- `void write(JsonWriter out, T value)`: Write a JSON value (array, object, string, number, Boolean, or `null`), which is passed to `value`.

Each method throws `java.io.IOException` when an I/O problem occurs.

The `read()` and `write()` methods read a sequence of JSON *tokens* and write a sequence of JSON tokens, respectively. For `read()`, the source of these tokens is an instance of the concrete `com.google.gson.stream.JsonReader` class. For `write()`, the destination of these tokens is the concrete `com.google.gson.stream.JsonWriter` class. Tokens are described by the `com.google.gson.stream.JsonToken` enum (such as `BEGIN_ARRAY` for open square bracket). They are read and written by calling `JsonReader` and `JsonWriter` methods, such as the following:

- `void beginObject()`: This `JsonReader` method consumes the next token from the JSON stream and asserts that it's the beginning of a new object. A companion `void endObject()` method consumes the next token from the JSON stream and asserts that it's the end of the current object. Either method throws `IOException` when an I/O problem occurs.

- `JsonWriter name(String name)`: This `JsonWriter` method encodes the property name, which cannot be `null`. `IOException` is thrown when an I/O problem occurs.

After creating a TypeAdapter subclass, you instantiate it and register the instance with Gson by calling the `GsonBuilder registerTypeAdapter(Type type, Object typeAdapter)` method, which I previously presented. The object that's passed to `type` represents the class whose objects are serialized or deserialized. The object that's passed to `typeAdapter` is the type adapter instance.

Listing 9-14 presents the source code to an application that demonstrates a type adapter.

Listing 9-14. Serializing and Deserializing a Country Object via a Type Adapter

```java
import java.io.IOException;

import java.util.ArrayList;
import java.util.List;

import com.google.gson.Gson;
import com.google.gson.GsonBuilder;
import com.google.gson.TypeAdapter;

import com.google.gson.stream.JsonReader;
import com.google.gson.stream.JsonWriter;

import static java.lang.System.*;

public class GsonDemo
{
   static
   class Country
   {
      String name;
      int population;
      String[] cities;

      Country() {}

      Country(String name, int population, String... cities)
      {
         this.name = name;
         this.population = population;
         this.cities = cities;
      }
   }

   public static void main(String[] args)
   {
      class CountryAdapter extends TypeAdapter<Country>
      {
```

```java
@Override
public Country read(JsonReader in)
   throws IOException
{

   Country c = new Country();
   List<String> cities = new ArrayList<>();
   in.beginObject();
   while (in.hasNext())
      switch (in.nextName())
      {
         case "name":
            c.name = in.nextString();
               break;

         case "population":
            c.population = in.nextInt();
            break;

         case "cities":
            in.beginArray();
            while (in.hasNext())
               cities.add(in.nextString());
            in.endArray();
            c.cities =
               cities.toArray(new String[0]);
      }
   in.endObject();
   return c;
}

@Override
public void write(JsonWriter out, Country c)
   throws IOException
{
   out.beginObject();
   out.name("name").value(c.name);
   out.name("population").value(c.population);
```

```
            out.name("cities");
            out.beginArray();
            for (int i = 0; i < c.cities.length; i++)
                out.value(c.cities[i]);
            out.endArray();
            out.endObject();
        }
    }
    Gson gson =
        new GsonBuilder().
            registerTypeAdapter(Country.class,
                                new CountryAdapter()).
            create();

    Country c =
        new Country("England", 53012456 /* 2011 census */,
                    "London", "Birmingham", "Cambridge");
    String json = gson.toJson(c);
    out.println(json);
    c = gson.fromJson(json, c.getClass());
    out.printf("Name = %s%n", c.name);
    out.printf("Population = %d%n", c.population);
    out.print("Cities = ");
    for (String city: c.cities)
        out.print(city + " ");
    out.println();
    }
}
```

Listing 9-14's GsonDemo class nests a Country class (which describes a country as a name, a population count, and an array of city names) and also presents a main() entry-point method.

The main() method first declares a local CountryAdapter class that extends TypeAdapter<Country>. CountryAdapter overrides the read() and write() methods to handle the serialization and deserialization tasks.

The `read()` method first creates a new `Country` object, which will store the values being read from the JSON object being deserialized (and accessed from the `JsonReader` argument).

After creating a list to store the array of city names that it will be reading, `read()` calls `beginObject()` to assert that the next token read from the token stream is the beginning of a JSON object.

At this point, `read()` enters a `while` loop. This loop continues while `JsonReader`'s boolean `hasNext()` method returns `true`: there is another object element.

Each `while` loop iteration executes a `switch` statement that calls `JsonReader`'s `String nextName()` method to return the next token, which is a property name in the JSON object. It then compares the token to the three possibilities, `name`, `population`, or `cities`, and executes the associated code to retrieve the property value and assign the value to the appropriate field in the previously created `Country` object.

If the property is `name`, `JsonReader`'s `String nextString()` method is called to return the string value of the next token. If the property is `population`, `JsonReader`'s int `nextInt()` method is called to return the token's `int` value.

Processing the `cities` property is more involved because its value is an array:

- `JsonReader`'s void `beginArray()` method is called to signify that a new array has been detected and to consume the open square bracket token.

- A `while` loop is entered to repeatedly obtain the next array string value and add it to the previously created `cities` list.

- `JsonReader`'s void `endArray()` method is called to signify the end of the current array and to consume the close square bracket token.

- The `cities` list is converted to a Java array, which is assigned to the `Country` object's `cities` member.

After the outer `while` loop ends, `read()` calls `endObject()` to assert that the next token read from the token stream is the end of the current JSON object, and then returns the `Country` object.

The `write()` method is somewhat similar to `read()`. It calls `JsonWriter`'s `JsonWriter name(String name)` method to encode the property name specified by `name` to a JSON property name. Also, it calls `JsonWriter`'s `JsonWriter value(long value)` and `JsonWriter value(String value)` methods to encode `value` as a JSON number or a JSON string.

The main() method proceeds to create a Gson object from a GsonBuilder object, which executes registerTypeAdapter(Country.class, new CountryAdapter()) to instantiate and register CountryAdapter with the Gson object that will be returned. Country.class indicates that Country objects will be serialized and deserialized.

Finally, a Country object is created, serialized to a string, and deserialized to a new Country object.

Compile Listing 9-14 and run the resulting application. You should observe the following output:

```
{"name":"England","population":53012456,"cities":["London","Birmingham",
"Cambridge"]}
Name = England
Population = 53012456
Cities = London Birmingham Cambridge
```

Conveniently Associating Type Adapters with Classes and Fields

The JsonAdapter annotation type is used with a TypeAdapter Class object argument to associate the TypeAdapter instance to use with a class or field. After doing so, you don't need to register the TypeAdapter with Gson, which makes for a bit less coding.

Listing 9-15 refactors Listing 9-14 to demonstrate JsonAdapter.

Listing 9-15. Serializing and Deserializing a Country Object Annotated with a Type Adapter

```
import java.io.IOException;

import java.util.ArrayList;
import java.util.List;

import com.google.gson.Gson;
import com.google.gson.TypeAdapter;

import com.google.gson.annotations.JsonAdapter;

import com.google.gson.stream.JsonReader;
import com.google.gson.stream.JsonWriter;

import static java.lang.System.*;
```

```java
public class GsonDemo
{
    @JsonAdapter(CountryAdapter.class)
    static
    class Country
    {
        String name;
        int population;
        String[] cities;

        Country() {}

        Country(String name, int population, String... cities)
        {
            this.name = name;
            this.population = population;
            this.cities = cities;
        }
    }

    static
    class CountryAdapter extends TypeAdapter<Country>
    {
        @Override
        public Country read(JsonReader in) throws IOException
        {
            out.println("read() called");
            Country c = new Country();
            List<String> cities = new ArrayList<>();
            in.beginObject();
            while (in.hasNext())
                switch (in.nextName())
                {
                    case "name":
                        c.name = in.nextString();
                            break;
```

```java
            case "population":
                c.population = in.nextInt();
                break;

            case "cities":
                in.beginArray();
                while (in.hasNext())
                    cities.add(in.nextString());
                in.endArray();
                c.cities = cities.toArray(new String[0]) ;
        }
    in.endObject();
    return c;
    }

    @Override
    public void write(JsonWriter out, Country c)
        throws IOException
    {
        System.out.println("write() called");
        out.beginObject();
        out.name("name").value(c.name);
        out.name("population").value(c.population);
        out.name("cities");
        out.beginArray();
        for (int i = 0; i < c.cities.length; i++)
            out.value(c.cities[i]);
        out.endArray();
        out.endObject();
    }
}

public static void main(String[] args)
{
    Gson gson = new Gson();
    Country c =
        new Country("England", 53012456 /* 2011 census */,
```

```
                        "London", "Birmingham", "Cambridge");
      String json = gson.toJson(c);
      out.println(json);
      c = gson.fromJson(json, c.getClass());
      out.printf("Name = %s%n", c.name);
      out.printf("Population = %d%n", c.population);
      out.print("Cities = ");
      for (String city: c.cities)
         out.print(city + " ");
      out.println();
   }
}
```

In Listing 9-15, I've bolded the two essential differences from Listing 9-14: the Country type adapter class is annotated @JsonAdapter(CountryAdapter.class), and Gson gson = new Gson(); is specified instead of using a GsonBuilder object and its create() method.

Compile Listing 9-15 and run the resulting application. You should observe the following output:

```
write() called
{"name":"England","population":53012456,"cities":["London","Birmingham",
"Cambridge"]}
read() called
Name = England
Population = 53012456
Cities = London Birmingham Cambridge
```

The read() called and write() called output lines prove that Gson uses the custom type adapter instead of its internal type adapter.

EXERCISES

The following exercises are designed to test your understanding of Chapter 9's content:

1. Define Gson.

2. Identify and describe Gson's packages.

3. What are the two ways to obtain a Gson object?

4. Identify the types for which Gson provides default serialization and deserialization.

5. How would you enable pretty-printing?

6. True or false: By default, Gson excludes `transient` or `static` fields from consideration for serialization and deserialization.

7. Once you have a Gson object, what methods can you call to convert between JSON and Java objects?

8. How do you use Gson to customize JSON object parsing?

9. Describe the `JsonElement` class.

10. Identify the `JsonElement` subclasses.

11. What `GsonBuilder` method do you call to register a serializer or deserializer with a Gson object?

12. What method does `JsonSerializer` provide to serialize a Java object to a JSON object?

13. What annotation types does Gson provide to simplify serialization and deserialization?

14. True or false: To use Expose, it's enough to annotate a field, as in `@Expose(serialize = true, deserialize = false)`.

15. What do `JsonSerializationContext` and `JsonDeserializationContext` provide?

16. True or false: You can call `<T> T fromJson(String json, Class<T> classOfT)` to deserialize any kind of object.

17. Why should you prefer `TypeAdapter` to `JsonSerializer` and `JsonDeserializer`?

18. Modify Listing 9-9 so that the `static` field named `field5` is also serialized and deserialized.

Summary

Gson is a small Java-based library for parsing and creating JSON objects. Google developed Gson for its own projects, but later made Gson publicly available, starting with version 1.0.

Gson parses JSON objects by deserializing JSON objects into Java objects. Similarly, it creates JSON objects by serializing Java objects into JSON objects. Gson relies on Java's Reflection API to assist with these tasks.

Gson consists of more than 30 classes and interfaces distributed among four packages: `com.google.gson` (provides access to `Gson`, the main class), `com.google.gson.annotations` (provides annotation types for use with Gson), `com.google.gson.reflect` (provides a utility class for obtaining type information from a generic type), and `com.google.gson.stream` (provides utility classes for reading and writing JSON-encoded values).

The `Gson` class handles the conversion between JSON and Java objects. You can instantiate this class by using the `Gson()` constructor, or you can obtain a `Gson` instance by working with the `GsonBuilder` class.

Once you have a `Gson` object, you can call various `fromJson()` and `toJson()` methods to convert between JSON and Java objects. These methods rely on Gson's default deserialization and serialization mechanisms, respectively, but you can customize deserialization and serialization by working with the `JsonDeserializer<T>` and `JsonSerializer<T>` interfaces.

Gson offers additional useful features, including annotation types (`Expose`, `JsonAdapter`, `SerializedName`, `Since`, and `Until`) for simplifying serialization and deserialization, contexts for automating the serialization of nested objects and arrays, support for generics, and type adapters.

Chapter 10 introduces JsonPath for extracting JSON values.

CHAPTER 10

Extracting JSON Values with JsonPath

XPath is used to extract values from XML documents. JsonPath performs this task for JSON documents. Chapter 10 introduces you to JsonPath.

Note   If you're unfamiliar with XPath, I recommend that you read Chapter 5 before reading this chapter. JsonPath was derived from XPath.

What Is JsonPath?

JsonPath is a declarative query language (also known as a path-expression-syntax) for selecting and extracting a JSON document's property values. For example, you can use JsonPath to locate "John" in {"firstName": "John"} and return this value. JsonPath is based on XPath 1.0.

JsonPath was created by Stefan Goessner (http://goessner.net). Goessner also created JavaScript-based and PHP-based implementations of JsonPath. For complete documentation, check out Goessner's website (http://goessner.net/articles/JsonPath/index.html).

Swedish software company Jayway (www.jayway.com) subsequently adapted JsonPath to Java. Their Java version of JsonPath is the focus of this chapter. You will find complete documentation on Jayway's implementation of JsonPath at http://github.com/jayway/JsonPath.

© Jeff Friesen 2019
J. Friesen, *Java XML and JSON*, https://doi.org/10.1007/978-1-4842-4330-5_10

Learning the JsonPath Language

JsonPath is a simple language with various features that are similar to their XPath counterparts. This language is used to construct path expressions.

A JsonPath expression begins with the dollar sign ($) character, which refers to the root element of a query. The dollar sign is followed by a sequence of child elements, which are separated via dot (.) notation or via square bracket ([]) notation. For example, consider the following JSON object:

```
{
    "firstName": "John",
    "lastName": "Smith",
    "age": 25,
    "address":
    {
        "streetAddress": "21 2nd Street",
        "city": "New York",
        "state": "NY",
        "postalCode": "10021-3100"
    },
    "phoneNumbers":
    [
        {
            "type": "home",
            "number": "212 555-1234"
        },
        {
            "type": "office",
            "number": "646 555-4567"
        }
    ]
}
```

The following dot notation-based JsonPath expression extracts, from the previous anonymous JSON object, the phone number (212 555-1234) that's assigned to the number field in the anonymous JSON object, which is assigned to the first element in the phoneNumbers array:

```
$.phoneNumbers[0].number
```

The $ character represents the anonymous root JSON object. The leftmost dot character separates the object root from the phoneNumbers property name. The [0] syntax identifies the first element in the array assigned to phoneNumbers.

The first array element stores an anonymous object consisting of "type": "home" and "number": "212 555-1234" properties. The rightmost dot character accesses this object's number child property name, which is assigned the value 212 555-1234. This value is returned from the expression.

Alternatively, I could specify the following square bracket notation to extract the same phone number:

```
$['phoneNumbers'][0]['number']
```

The Jayway documentation identifies $ as an operator and also identifies several other basic operators. Table 10-1 describes these operators.

Table 10-1. *JsonPath Basic Operators*

Operator	Description
$	The root element to query. This operator starts all path expressions. It's equivalent to XPath's / symbol.
@	The current node being processed by a filter predicate. It's equivalent to XPath's . symbol.
*	Wildcard. Available anywhere a name or numeric value is required.
..	Deep scan (also known as recursive descent). Available anywhere a name is required. It's equivalent to XPath's // symbol.
.*name*	Dot-notated child. The dot is equivalent to XPath's / symbol.
['*name*' (, '*name*')]	Bracket-notated child or children.
[*number* (, *number*)]	Array index or indexes.
[*start*:*end*]	Array slice operator.
[?(*expression*)]	Filter operator. The *expression* must evaluate to a Boolean value. In other words, it's a *predicate*.

The Jayway documentation also identifies several functions that can be invoked at the tail end of a path—the input to a function is the output of the path expression; the function output is dictated by the function itself. Table 10-2 describes these functions.

Table 10-2. *JsonPath Functions*

Function	Description
min()	Return the minimum value (as a double) in an array of numbers.
max()	Return the maximum value (as a double) in an array of numbers.
avg()	Return the average value (as a double) of an array of numbers.
stddev()	Return the standard deviation value (as a double) of an array of numbers.
length()	Return the length (as an int) of an array.

Finally, the Jayway documentation identifies various operators for *filters*, which use predicates (Boolean expressions) to restrict returned lists of items. Predicates can use the filter operators in Table 10-3 to determine equality, match regular expressions, and test for inclusion.

Table 10-3. *JsonPath Filter Operators*

Operator	Description
==	Return `true` when the left operand equals the right operand. Note that `1` is not equal to `'1'` (i.e., number `1` and string `1` are two different things).
!=	Return `true` when the left operand doesn't equal the right operand.
<	Return `true` when the left operand is less than the right operand.
<=	Return `true` when the left operand is less than or equal to the right operand.
>	Return `true` when the left operand is greater than the right operand.
>=	Return `true` when the left operand is greater than or equal to the right operand.
=~	Return `true` when the left operand matches the regular expression specified by the right operand; for example, `[?(@.name =~ /foo.*?/i)]`.
in	Return `true` when the left operand exists in the right operand; for example, `[?(@.grade in ['A', 'B'])]`.
nin	Return `true` when the left operand doesn't exist in the right operand.
subsetof	Return `true` when the left operand (an array) is a subset of the right operand (an array); for example, `[?(@.sizes subsetof ['S', 'M', 'L'])]`.
size	Return `true` when the size of the left operand (an array or string) matches the right operand (an integer).
empty	Return `true` when the left operand (an array or string) is empty and the right operand is `true`, or return `true` when the left operand is not empty and the right operand is `false`.

This table reveals `@.name =~ /foo.*?/i` and additional simple predicates. You can create more complex predicates by using the logical AND operator (&&) and the logical OR operator (||). Consider the following example:

```
([?(@.color == 'blue')] || [?(@.color == "red")])
```

You can also use the logical NEGATE operator (!) to negate a predicate:

```
[?(!(@.price < 10 && @.category == 'fiction'))]
```

Within a predicate, you must enclose any string literals with single or double quotes, which both examples demonstrate.

Obtaining and Using the JsonPath Library

As with Chapter 8's mJson and Chapter 9's Gson, you can obtain JsonPath from the Central Maven Repository (http://search.maven.org).

Note   If you're unfamiliar with Maven, think of it as a build tool for Java projects, although Maven developers think of Maven as more than just a build tool—see http://maven.apache.org/background/philosophy-of-maven.html.

If you're familiar with Maven, add the following XML fragment to the Project Object Model (POM) files for your Maven project(s) that will be dependent on JsonPath, and you will be good to go! (To learn about POM, check out http://maven.apache.org/pom.html#What_is_the_POM.)

```
<dependency>
    <groupId>com.jayway.jsonpath</groupId>
    <artifactId>json-path</artifactId>
    <version>2.4.0</version>
</dependency>
```

This XML fragment reveals 2.4.0 as the version of Jayway's JsonPath library that I'm using in this chapter.

Note   It's common for Maven projects to be dependent on other projects. For example, the mJson project (http://search.maven.org/artifact/org.sharegov/mjson/1.4.0/bundle) that I discussed in Chapter 8 and the Gson project (http://search.maven.org/artifact/com.google.code.gson/gson/2.8.5/jar) that I discussed in Chapter 9 are dependent on JUnit (http://en.wikipedia.org/wiki/JUnit). I didn't mention or discuss downloading JUnit in either chapter because this library isn't required for normal use.

Because I'm not currently using Maven, I downloaded the JsonPath JAR file and all of the JAR files on which JsonPath normally depends and then added all of these JAR files to my CLASSPATH. The easiest way for me to accomplish the download task was to point my browser to `https://jar-download.com/artifacts/com.jayway.jsonpath/json-path/2.4.0/source-code` and click the "Download json-path (2.4.0)" button link.

After unarchiving the ZIP file, I discovered a `jar_files` directory with the following files:

- `accessors-smart-1.2.jar`
- `asm-5.0.4.jar`
- `json-path-2.4.0.jar`
- `json-smart-2.3.jar`
- `slf4j-api-1.7.25.jar`

Note   Jayway JsonPath is licensed according to Apache License Version 2.0 (`www.apache.org/licenses/`).

For compiling Java source code that accesses JsonPath, only `json-path-2.4.0.jar` needs to be included in the CLASSPATH:

```
javac -cp json-path-2.4.0.jar source file
```

For running applications that access JsonPath, I use the following command line:

```
java -cp accessors-smart-1.2.jar;asm-5.0.4.jar;json-path-2.4.0.jar;json-smart-2.3.jar;slf4j-api-1.7.25.jar;. main classfile
```

These command lines assume that the JAR files are located in the current directory. To facilitate working with the command lines, place them in a pair of batch files on Windows platforms (substitute %1 for *source file* or *main classfile*) or their counterparts on other platforms.

Note   JsonPath 2.4.0's API reference is available online at `www.javadoc.io/doc/com.jayway.jsonpath/json-path/2.4.0`.

Exploring the JsonPath Library

The JsonPath library is organized into several packages. You will typically interact with the com.jayway.jsonpath package and its types. In this section, I focus exclusively on this package while showing you how to extract values from JSON objects and use predicates to filter items.

Extracting Values from JSON Objects

The com.jayway.jsonpath package provides the JsonPath class as the entry point into using the JsonPath library. Listing 10-1 introduces this class.

Listing 10-1. A First Taste of JsonPath

```
import java.util.HashMap;
import java.util.List;

import com.jayway.jsonpath.JsonPath;

import static java.lang.System.*;

public class JsonPathDemo
{
   public static void main(String[] args)
   {
      String json =
      "{" +
      "    \"store\":" +
      "    {" +
      "       \"book\":" +
      "       [" +
      "          {" +
      "             \"category\": \"reference\"," +
      "             \"author\": \"Nigel Rees\"," +
      "             \"title\": \"Sayings of the Century\"," +
      "             \"price\": 8.95" +
      "          }," +
      "          {" +
```

```
"            \"category\": \"fiction\"," +
"            \"author\": \"Evelyn Waugh\"," +
"            \"title\": \"Sword of Honour\"," +
"            \"price\": 12.99" +
"         }" +
"      ]," +
"      \"bicycle\":" +
"      {" +
"         \"color\": \"red\"," +
"         \"price\": 19.95" +
"      }" +
"   }" +
"}";

JsonPath path = JsonPath.compile("$.store.book[1]");
HashMap books = path.read(json);
out.println(books);
List<Object> authors =
    JsonPath.read(json, "$.store.book[*].author");
out.println(authors);
String author =
    JsonPath.read(json, "$.store.book[1].author");
out.println(author);
   }
}
```

Listing 10-1 provides a JsonPathDemo class whose main() method uses the JsonPath class to extract values from JSON objects. main() first declares a string-based JSON object and assigns its reference to variable json. It then invokes the following static JsonPath method to compile a JsonPath expression (to improve performance) and return the compiled result as a JsonPath object:

```
JsonPath compile(String jsonPath, Predicate... filters)
```

The Predicate varargs list lets you specify an array of filter predicates to match filter predicate place holders (identified as ? characters) in the jsonPath string. I'll demonstrate Predicate and related types later in this chapter.

After compiling the $.store.book[1] JsonPath expression, which identifies the anonymous object in the second element of the array assigned to the book property of the anonymous object assigned to the store property, main() passes this expression to the following JsonPath method:

```
<T> T read(String json)
```

This generic method is called on the previously compiled JsonPath instance. It receives the string-based JSON object (assigned to json) as its argument and applies the JsonPath expression in the compiled JsonPath instance to this argument. The result is the JSON object identified by $.store.book[1].

The read() method is generic because it can return one of several types. In this example, it returns an instance of the java.util.LinkedHashMap class (a subclass of java.util.Hashmap) for storing JSON object property names and their values.

When you intend to reuse JsonPath expressions, it's good to compile them, which improves performance. Because I don't reuse $.store.book[1], I could have used one of JsonPath's static read() methods instead. For example, main() next demonstrates the following read() method:

```
<T> T read(String json, String jsonPath, Predicate... filters)
```

This method creates a new JsonPath object for the jsonPath argument and applies it to the json string. I ignore filters in the example.

The JsonPath expression passed to jsonPath is $.store.book[*].author. This expression includes the * wildcard to match all elements in the book array. It returns the value of the author property for each element in this array.

read() returns this value as an instance of the net.minidev.json.JSONArray class, which is stored in the json-smart-2.3.jar file that you must include in the CLASSPATH. Because JSONArray extends java.util.ArrayList<Object>, it's legal to cast the returned object to List<Object>.

To further demonstrate read(), main() lastly invokes this method with JsonPath expression $.store.book[1].author, which returns the value of the author property in the anonymous object stored in the second element of the book array. This time, read() returns a java.lang.String object.

> **Note**   Regarding the generic `read()` methods, `JsonPath` automatically attempts to cast the result to the type that the method's invoker expects, such as a hashmap for a JSON object, a list of objects for a JSON array, and a string for a JSON string.

Compile Listing 10-1 as follows:

```
javac -cp json-path-2.4.0.jar JsonPathDemo.java
```

Run the resulting application as follows:

```
java -cp accessors-smart-1.2.jar;asm-5.0.4.jar;json-path-2.4.0.jar;json-smart-2.3.jar;slf4j-api-1.7.25.jar;. JsonPathDemo
```

You should observe the following output:

```
{category=fiction, author=Evelyn Waugh, title=Sword of Honour, price=12.99}
["Nigel Rees","Evelyn Waugh"]
Evelyn Waugh
```

You'll probably also observe some messages about SLF4J (Simple Logging Facade for Java) not being able to load the `StaticLoggerBinder` class and defaulting to a no-operation logger implementation. You can safely ignore these messages.

Using Predicates to Filter Items

JsonPath supports *filters* for restricting the nodes that are extracted from a JSON document to those that match the criteria specified by predicates (Boolean expressions). You can work with inline predicates, filter predicates, or custom predicates.

Inline Predicates

An *inline predicate* is a string-based predicate. Listing 10-2 presents the source code to an application that demonstrates several inline predicates.

Listing 10-2. Demonstrating Inline Predicates

```java
import java.util.List;

import com.jayway.jsonpath.JsonPath;

import static java.lang.System.*;

public class JsonPathDemo
{
    public static void main(String[] args)
    {
        String json =
        "{" +
        "    \"store\":" +
        "    {" +
        "        \"book\":" +
        "        [" +
        "            {" +
        "                \"category\": \"reference\"," +
        "                \"author\": \"Nigel Rees\"," +
        "                \"title\": \"Sayings of the Century\"," +
        "                \"price\": 8.95" +
        "            }," +
        "            {" +
        "                \"category\": \"fiction\"," +
        "                \"author\": \"Evelyn Waugh\"," +
        "                \"title\": \"Sword of Honour\"," +
        "                \"price\": 12.99" +
        "            }," +
        "            {" +
        "                \"category\": \"fiction\"," +
        "                \"author\": \"J. R. R. Tolkien\"," +
        "                \"title\": \"The Lord of the Rings\"," +
        "                \"isbn\": \"0-395-19395-8\"," +
        "                \"price\": 22.99" +
        "            }," +
```

```
"          {" +
"              \"category\": \"\"," +
"              \"author\": \"some author\"," +
"              \"title\": \"some title\"," +
"              \"isbn\": \"some isbn\"," +
"              \"price\": 0" +
"          }" +
"      ]," +
"      \"bicycle\":" +
"      [" +
"          {" +
"              \"color\": \"red\"," +
"              \"accessories\": [\"horn\", " +
"              \"bottle\"]," +
"              \"price\": 619.95" +
"          }," +
"          {" +
"              \"color\": \"green\"," +
"              \"accessories\": [\"horn\", " +
"              \"light\"]," +
"              \"price\": 639.95" +
"          }," +
"          {" +
"              \"color\": \"blue\"," +
"              \"accessories\": []," +
"              \"price\": 599.95" +
"          }" +
"      ]" +
"   }" +
"}";

String expr = "$.store.book[?(@.isbn)].title";
List<Object> titles = JsonPath.read(json, expr);
out.println(titles);
expr =
    "$.store.book[?(@.category == 'fiction')].title";
```

```
titles = JsonPath.read(json, expr);
out.println(titles);
expr = "$..book[?(@.author =~ /.*REES/i)].title";
titles = JsonPath.read(json, expr);
out.println(titles);
expr =
    "$..book[?(@.price > 10 && @.price < 20)].title";
titles = JsonPath.read(json, expr);
out.println(titles);
expr = "$..book[?(@.author in ['Nigel Rees'])].title";
titles = JsonPath.read(json, expr);
out.println(titles);
expr =
    "$..book[?(@.author nin ['Nigel Rees'])].title";
titles = JsonPath.read(json, expr);
out.println(titles);
expr = "$.store.bicycle[?(@.accessories " +
        "subsetof ['horn', 'bottle', 'light'])].price";
List<Object> prices = JsonPath.read(json, expr);
out.println(prices);
expr = "$.store.bicycle[?(@.accessories " +
        "subsetof ['horn', 'bottle'])].price";
prices = JsonPath.read(json, expr);
out.println(prices);
expr = "$..book[?(@.author size 12)].title";
titles = JsonPath.read(json, expr);
out.println(titles);
expr = "$..book[?(@.author size 13)].title";
titles = JsonPath.read(json, expr);
out.println(titles);
expr =
    "$..bicycle[?(@.accessories empty true)].price";
titles = JsonPath.read(json, expr);
out.println(titles);
expr =
```

```
    "$..bicycle[?(@.accessories empty false)].price";
  titles = JsonPath.read(json, expr);
  out.println(titles);
  expr = "$..book[?(@.category empty true)].title";
  titles = JsonPath.read(json, expr);
  out.println(titles);
  }
}
```

Listing 10-2's main() method uses the following JsonPath expressions to narrow the list of returned book title strings:

- $.store.book[?(@.isbn)].title: returns the title values for all book elements that contain an isbn property

- $.store.book[?(@.category == 'fiction')].title: returns the title values for all book elements whose category property is assigned the string value fiction

- $..book[?(@.author =~ /.*REES/i)].title: returns the title values for all book elements whose author property value ends with rees (case is insignificant)

- $..book[?(@.price >= 10 && @.price <= 20)].title: returns the title values for all book elements whose price property value lies between 10 and 20

- $..book[?(@.author in ['Nigel Rees'])].title: returns the title values for all book elements whose author property value matches Nigel Rees

- $..book[?(@.author nin ['Nigel Rees'])].title: returns the title values for all book elements whose author property value doesn't match Nigel Rees

- $.store.bicycle[?(@.accessories subsetof ['horn', 'bottle', 'light'])].price: returns the price values for all bicycle elements whose accessories property value (an array) is a subset of the ['horn', 'bottle', 'light'] array

- `$.store.bicycle[?(@.accessories subsetof ['horn', 'bottle'])].price`: returns the price values for all bicycle elements whose accessories property value (an array) is a subset of the `['horn', 'bottle']` array

- `$..book[?(@.author size 12)].title`: returns the title values for all book elements whose author property value (a string) is exactly 12 characters long

- `$..book[?(@.author size 13)].title`: returns the title values for all book elements whose author property value (a string) is exactly 13 characters long

- `$..bicycle[?(@.accessories empty true)].price`: returns the price values for all bicycle elements whose accessories property value (an array) is empty

- `$..bicycle[?(@.accessories empty false)].price`: returns the price values for all bicycle elements whose accessories property value (an array) is not empty

- `$..book[?(@.category empty true)].title`: returns the title values for all book elements whose category property value (a string) has zero length

Compile Listing 10-2 and run the resulting application. You should discover the following output:

```
["The Lord of the Rings","some title"]
["Sword of Honour","The Lord of the Rings"]
["Sayings of the Century"]
["Sword of Honour"]
["Sayings of the Century"]
["Sword of Honour","The Lord of the Rings","some title"]
[619.95,639.95,599.95]
[619.95,599.95]
["Sword of Honour"]
[]
[599.95]
[619.95,639.95]
["some title"]
```

Filter Predicates

A *filter predicate* is a predicate expressed as an instance of the abstract `Filter` class, which implements the `Predicate` interface.

To create a filter predicate, you typically chain together invocations of various fluent methods (`http://en.wikipedia.org/wiki/Fluent_interface`) located in the `Criteria` class, which also implements `Predicate`, and pass the result to `Filter`'s `Filter filter(Predicate predicate)` static method.

```
Filter filter = Filter.filter(Criteria.where("price").lt(20.00));
```

`Criteria`'s `Criteria where(String key)` static method returns a `Criteria` object that stores the provided key, which is `price` in this example. Its `Criteria lt(Object o)` method returns a `Criteria` object for the `<` operator that identifies the value that's compared to the value of the key.

To use the filter predicate, first insert a `?` placeholder for the filter predicate into the path:

```
String expr = "$['store']['book'][?].title";
```

Note   When multiple filter predicates are provided, they are applied in left-to-right order of the placeholders where the number of placeholders must match the number of provided filter predicates. You can specify multiple predicate placeholders in one filter operation [?, ?]; both predicates must match.

Next, because `Filter` implements `Predicate`, you pass the filter predicate to a `read()` method that takes a `Predicate` argument:

```
List<Object> titles = JsonPath.read(json, expr, filter);
```

For each `book` element, the `read()` method executes the filter predicate when it detects the `?` placeholder in the JsonPath expression.

Listing 10-3 presents the source code to an application that demonstrates the previous filter predicate code fragments.

Listing 10-3. Demonstrating Filter Predicates

```java
import java.util.List;

import com.jayway.jsonpath.Criteria;
import com.jayway.jsonpath.Filter;
import com.jayway.jsonpath.JsonPath;

import static java.lang.System.*;

public class JsonPathDemo
{
    public static void main(String[] args)
    {
        String json =
        "{" +
        "    \"store\":" +
        "    {" +
        "        \"book\":" +
        "        [" +
        "            {" +
        "                \"category\": \"reference\"," +
        "                \"author\": \"Nigel Rees\"," +
        "                \"title\": \"Sayings of the Century\"," +
        "                \"price\": 8.95" +
        "            }," +
        "            {" +
        "                \"category\": \"fiction\"," +
        "                \"author\": \"Evelyn Waugh\"," +
        "                \"title\": \"Sword of Honour\"," +
        "                \"price\": 12.99" +
        "            }," +
        "            {" +
        "                \"category\": \"fiction\"," +
        "                \"author\": \"J. R. R. Tolkien\"," +
        "                \"title\": \"The Lord of the Rings\"," +
        "                \"isbn\": \"0-395-19395-8\"," +
```

```
"                    \"price\": 22.99" +
"            }" +
"        ]," +
"        \"bicycle\":" +
"        {" +
"            \"color\": \"red\"," +
"            \"price\": 19.95" +
"        }" +
"    }" +
"}";

    Filter filter =
        Filter.filter(Criteria.where("price").lt(20.00));
    String expr = "$['store']['book'][?].title";
    List<Object> titles = JsonPath.read(json, expr,
                                        filter);
    out.println(titles);
    }
}
```

Compile Listing 10-3 and run the resulting application. You should discover the following output (both books have prices less than 20 dollars):

```
["Sayings of the Century","Sword of Honour"]
```

Custom Predicates

A *custom predicate* is a predicate created from a class that implements the Predicate interface.

To create a custom predicate, instantiate a class that implements Predicate and overrides the following method:

```
boolean apply(Predicate.PredicateContext ctx)
```

PredicateContext is a nested interface whose methods provide information about the context in which apply() is called. For example, Object root() returns a reference to the entire JSON document, and Object item() returns the current item being evaluated by this predicate.

apply() returns the predicate value: true (item is accepted) or false (item is rejected).

The following code fragment creates a custom predicate for returning Book elements containing a price property whose value exceeds 20 dollars:

```
Predicate expensiveBooks =
   new Predicate()
   {
      @Override
      public boolean apply(PredicateContext ctx)
      {
         String value = ctx.item(Map.class).
                        get("price").toString();
         return Float.valueOf(value) > 20.00;
      }
   };
```

PredicateContext's <T> T item(java.lang.Class<T> clazz) generic method maps the JSON object in the Book element to a java.util.Map.

To use the custom predicate, first insert a ? placeholder for the custom predicate into the path:

```
String expr = "$.store.book[?]";
```

Next, pass the custom predicate to a read() method that takes a Predicate argument:

```
List<Map<String, Object>> titles =
   JsonPath.read(json, expr, expensiveBooks);
```

For each book element, read() executes the custom predicate associated with the ? and returns a list of maps (one map per accepted item).

Listing 10-4 presents the source code to an application that demonstrates the previous custom predicate code fragments.

Listing 10-4. Demonstrating Custom Predicates

```
import java.util.List;
import java.util.Map;

import com.jayway.jsonpath.JsonPath;
import com.jayway.jsonpath.Predicate;

import static java.lang.System.*;

public class JsonPathDemo
{
    public static void main(String[] args)
    {
      String json =
      "{" +
      "   \"store\":" +
      "   {" +
      "      \"book\":" +
      "      [" +
      "         {" +
      "            \"category\": \"reference\"," +
      "            \"author\": \"Nigel Rees\"," +
      "            \"title\": \"Sayings of the Century\"," +
      "            \"price\": 8.95" +
      "         }," +
      "         {" +
      "            \"category\": \"fiction\"," +
      "            \"author\": \"Evelyn Waugh\"," +
      "            \"title\": \"Sword of Honour\"," +
      "            \"price\": 12.99" +
      "         }," +
      "         {" +
      "            \"category\": \"fiction\"," +
      "            \"author\": \"J. R. R. Tolkien\"," +
      "            \"title\": \"The Lord of the Rings\"," +
      "            \"isbn\": \"0-395-19395-8\"," +
```

```
"            \"price\": 22.99" +
"          }" +
"        ]," +
"        \"bicycle\":" +
"        {" +
"          \"color\": \"red\"," +
"          \"price\": 19.95" +
"        }" +
"    }" +
"}";

Predicate expensiveBooks =
    new Predicate()
    {
        @Override
        public boolean apply(PredicateContext ctx)
        {
            String value = ctx.item(Map.class).
                            get("price").toString();
            return Float.valueOf(value) > 20.00;
        }
    };
String expr = "$.store.book[?]";
List<Map<String, Object>> titles =
    JsonPath.read(json, expr, expensiveBooks);
out.println(titles);
  }
}
```

Compile Listing 10-4 and run the resulting application. You should discover the following output (one book has a price greater than 20 dollars):

```
[{"category":"fiction","author":"J. R. R. Tolkien","title":"The Lord of the
Rings","isbn":"0-395-19395-8","price":22.99}]
```

```
                        EXERCISES
```

The following exercises are designed to test your understanding of Chapter 10's content:

1. Define JsonPath.

2. True or false: JsonPath is based on XPath 2.0.

3. Identify the operator that represents the root JSON object.

4. In what notations can you specify JsonPath expressions?

5. What operator represents the current node being processed by a filter predicate?

6. True or false: JsonPath's deep scan operator (`..`) is equivalent to XPath's `/` symbol.

7. What does JsonPath's `JsonPath compile(String jsonPath, Predicate... filters)` static method accomplish?

8. What is the return type of the `<T> T read(String json)` generic method that returns JSON object property names and their values?

9. Identify the three predicate categories.

10. Given JSON object `{ "number": [10, 20, 25, 30] }`, write a `JsonPathDemo` application that extracts and outputs the maximum (30), minimum (10), and average (21.25) values.

Summary

JsonPath is a declarative query language (also known as a path-expression-syntax) for selecting and extracting a JSON document's property values.

JsonPath is a simple language with various features that are similar to their XPath counterparts. This language is used to construct path expressions. Each expression begins with the $ operator, which identifies the root element of the query and which corresponds to the XPath / symbol.

As with Chapter 8's mJson and Chapter 9's Gson, you can obtain JsonPath from the Central Maven Repository. Alternatively, if you're not using Maven, you can download the JsonPath JAR file and all of the JAR files on which JsonPath normally depends and then add all of these JAR files to your CLASSPATH.

The JsonPath library is organized into several packages. You will typically interact with the `com.jayway.jsonpath` package and its types. In this chapter, you focused exclusively on this package while learning how to extract values from JSON objects and use predicates to filter items.

Chapter 11 introduces Jackson for parsing and generating JSON content.

Processing JSON with Jackson

Jackson is a popular suite of APIs for parsing and creating JSON objects (and more). Chapter 11 explores the latest version of this "best JSON parser for Java."

What Is Jackson?

Jackson is a suite of data-processing tools for Java. These tools include a streaming JSON parser/generator library, a matching data-binding library (for converting Plain Old Java Objects [POJOs] to and from JSON), and additional data format modules for processing data encoded in XML and other formats.

Note   Jackson was created and is being maintained by Tatu Saloranta (www.linkedin.com/in/tatu-saloranta-b2b36/), who was inspired by the quality and variety of XML tooling available for the Java platform and decided to create something similar for JSON. In 2008, Saloranta founded the company FasterXML (http://fasterxml.com), which distributed Jackson along with other key XML-oriented products. Jackson is currently distributed on GitHub (http://github.com/FasterXML/jackson).

Jackson consists of a core package and two other packages that depend on the core package:

- *Jackson Core*: The core package supports a StAX-like streaming API for reading and writing JSON via sequences of discrete events. This package's name is com.fasterxml.jackson.core. Key classes are JsonParser for reading JSON content and JsonGenerator for writing JSON content.

© Jeff Friesen 2019
J. Friesen, *Java XML and JSON*, https://doi.org/10.1007/978-1-4842-4330-5_11

- *Jackson Databind*: The databind package supports a DOM-like tree model that provides a mutable in-memory tree representation of a JSON document. It also supports reading/writing JSON from/to POJOs. This package's name is `com.fasterxml.jackson.databind`. Key classes are `ObjectMapper` for reading/writing JSON content from/to tree models or POJOs and `JsonNode`, which is the base class for all tree model nodes.

- *Jackson Annotations*: The annotations package provides public core annotation types, most of which are used to configure how data binding (mapping) works. This package's name is `com.fasterxml.jackson.annotation`. Jackson Databind also depends on Jackson Annotations.

Simple and full POJO-oriented data binding are supported. Simple data binding focuses on converting to and from `java.util.Maps`, `java.util.Lists`, `java.lang.Strings`, `java.lang.Numbers`, `java.lang.Booleans`, and the null reference. Full data binding includes simple data binding but also supports converting to and from any Java Beans (`http://en.wikipedia.org/wiki/JavaBeans`) bean type. Conversions are based on property accessor conventions or annotations.

The streaming API performs better than the tree model or POJO-oriented data binding—both APIs leverage the streaming API. However, data binding is the most convenient and the tree model offers the most flexibility.

Obtaining and Using Jackson

The Jackson Core, Jackson Databind, and Jackson Annotations packages can be obtained from Maven (`https://search.maven.org/search?q=jackson-core`). Version 2.9.7 is the latest version at the time of writing.

For each of the *jackson-core*, *jackson-databind*, and *jackson-annotations* artifact IDs, click the "jar" and "javadoc.jar" menu items in the associated drop-down Download menu, and download their referenced JAR files. You should end up with the following JAR file collection:

- `jackson-annotations-2.9.7.jar`

- `jackson-annotations-2.9.7-javadoc.jar`

- jackson-core-2.9.7.jar
- jackson-core-2.9.7-javadoc.jar
- jackson-databind-2.9.7.jar
- jackson-databind-2.9.7-javadoc.jar

I've found it convenient to add all three nonJavadoc JAR files to my CLASSPATH when compiling and running code that uses a combination of Java Core, Java Databind, and Java Annotations:

```
javac -cp jackson-core-2.9.7.jar;jackson-databind-2.9.7.jar;jackson-
annotations-2.9.7.jar source file
```

```
java -cp jackson-core-2.9.7.jar;jackson-databind-2.9.7.jar;jackson-
annotations-2.9.7.jar;. main classfile
```

Working with Jackson's Basic Features

The Jackson Core and Jackson Databind APIs support the consumption and creation of JSON documents. This section introduces various types related to streaming, the tree model, and POJO-oriented data binding.

Streaming

Streaming (also known as *Incremental Processing*) deserializes (reads) and serializes (writes) JSON content as discrete events. Reading is performed by a *parser* that tokenizes JSON content into tokens and associated data; writing is performed by a *generator* that constructs JSON content based on a sequence of calls that output JSON tokens.

Note   Streaming has the lowest memory and processing overhead, making it the most efficient way to process JSON content. It's used mainly by middleware and frameworks because it's harder to use than the tree model or data binding.

Streaming methods throw `java.io.IOException` when an I/O error occurs. When a non-I/O problem is encountered while parsing or generating JSON content, a method throws `JsonProcessingException` (an `IOException` subclass in the `com.fasterxml.jackson.core` package) or one of its subclasses:

- `com.fasterxml.jackson.core.JsonParseException`

- `com.fasterxml.jackson.core.JsonGenerationException`

Stream-Based Parsing

The abstract `com.fasterxml.jackson.core.JsonParser` class describes a low-level JSON parser. It's obtained by calling one of the `com.fasterxml.jackson.core.JsonFactory` class's overloaded `createParser()` methods, which take the JSON content's origin into account.

Note   Parsers can be created to parse content from external sources (such as files or HTTP request streams) or buffered data (such as strings or byte arrays/buffers).

For example, `JsonFactory`'s `JsonParser createParser(String content)` method creates a parser for parsing the JSON content from the string passed to `content`. This method is demonstrated as follows:

```
String truckJSON = "{ \"brand\" : \"Ford F-150\",
                      \"doors\" : 4 }";
JsonFactory factory = new JsonFactory();
JsonParser parser = factory.createParser(truckJSON);
```

After creating a factory and obtaining a parser from the factory, a Java program typically enters a loop that returns a token and does something with it per iteration. This activity continues until the parser is closed:

```
while (!parser.isClosed())
{
   JsonToken token = parser.nextToken();
   System.out.printf("token = %s%n", token);
}
```

JsonParser's boolean isClosed() method returns true when the parser has been closed, perhaps by invoking JsonParser's void close() method.

JsonParser's JsonToken nextToken() method advances the stream enough to determine the type of the next token, returning it as a com.fasterxml.jackson.core. JsonToken instance. When no tokens remain, null is returned.

JsonToken is an enum that identifies the basic token types used for returning the results of parsing JSON content. Examples of its various constants are START_OBJECT ({ was seen) and END_ARRAY (] was seen).

JsonToken also provides various token classification and conversion methods. For example, boolean isBoolean() returns true when the token describes a Boolean value, and boolean isNumeric() returns true when the token describes a number. Also, String asString() returns a string representation of the token (e.g., { for START_ OBJECT) or null when there is no representation (e.g., null for FIELD_NAME—an object's field name has been encountered).

JsonParser provides various getValueAs methods for converting a token's value to the method's return type and returning that value. If conversion fails, null is returned. For example, String getValueAsString() tries to convert the current token's value to a Java String, returning null when the conversion isn't possible. The companion String getValueAsString(String def) method returns a more meaningful default value when conversion fails.

Listing 11-1 presents the source code to an application that demonstrates JsonParser and JsonToken.

Listing 11-1. Learning How to Use JsonParser and JsonToken

```
import java.io.File;

import com.fasterxml.jackson.core.JsonFactory;
import com.fasterxml.jackson.core.JsonParser;
import com.fasterxml.jackson.core.JsonToken;

import static java.lang.System.*;

public class JacksonDemo
{
   public static void main(String[] args) throws Exception
   {
      JsonFactory factory = new JsonFactory();
```

```
        JsonParser parser =
            factory.createParser(new File("person.json"));
        while (!parser.isClosed())
        {
            JsonToken jsonToken = parser.nextToken();
            if (jsonToken == null)
                break;
            out.printf("jsonToken = %s [%s] [%b] [%s]%n",
                        jsonToken, jsonToken.asString(),
                        jsonToken.isNumeric(),
                        parser.getValueAsString());
        }
    }
}
```

Listing 11-1's main() method first creates a factory and then uses it to create a parser for parsing a file named person.json. It then enters the previously described loop to obtain and output tokens.

Listing 11-2 presents the JSON document that's stored in person.json.

Listing 11-2. Describing a Person in JSON

```
{
    "firstName": "John",
    "lastName": "Doe",
    "age": 42,
    "address":
    {
        "street": "400 Some Street",
        "city": "Beverly Hills",
        "state": "CA",
        "zipcode": 90210
    },
    "phoneNumbers":
    [
        {
            "type": "home",
```

```
        "number": "310 555-1234"
    },
    {
        "type": "fax",
        "number": "310 555-4567"
    }
  ]
}
```

Compile Listing 11-1 as follows:

```
javac -cp jackson-core-2.9.7.jar;jackson-databind-2.9.7.jar;jackson-
annotations-2.9.7.jar JacksonDemo.java
```

Run the resulting application as follows:

```
java -cp jackson-core-2.9.7.jar;jackson-databind-2.9.7.jar;jackson-
annotations-2.9.7.jar;. JacksonDemo
```

You should observe the following output:

```
jsonToken = START_OBJECT [{] [false] [null]
jsonToken = FIELD_NAME [null] [false] [firstName]
jsonToken = VALUE_STRING [null] [false] [John]
jsonToken = FIELD_NAME [null] [false] [lastName]
jsonToken = VALUE_STRING [null] [false] [Doe]
jsonToken = FIELD_NAME [null] [false] [age]
jsonToken = VALUE_NUMBER_INT [null] [true] [42]
jsonToken = FIELD_NAME [null] [false] [address]
jsonToken = START_OBJECT [{] [false] [null]
jsonToken = FIELD_NAME [null] [false] [street]
jsonToken = VALUE_STRING [null] [false] [400 Some Street]
jsonToken = FIELD_NAME [null] [false] [city]
jsonToken = VALUE_STRING [null] [false] [Beverly Hills]
jsonToken = FIELD_NAME [null] [false] [state]
jsonToken = VALUE_STRING [null] [false] [CA]
jsonToken = FIELD_NAME [null] [false] [zipcode]
jsonToken = VALUE_NUMBER_INT [null] [true] [90210]
```

```
jsonToken = END_OBJECT [}] [false] [null]
jsonToken = FIELD_NAME [null] [false] [phoneNumbers]
jsonToken = START_ARRAY [[] [false] [null]
jsonToken = START_OBJECT [{] [false] [null]
jsonToken = FIELD_NAME [null] [false] [type]
jsonToken = VALUE_STRING [null] [false] [home]
jsonToken = FIELD_NAME [null] [false] [number]
jsonToken = VALUE_STRING [null] [false] [310 555-1234]
jsonToken = END_OBJECT [}] [false] [null]
jsonToken = START_OBJECT [{] [false] [null]
jsonToken = FIELD_NAME [null] [false] [type]
jsonToken = VALUE_STRING [null] [false] [fax]
jsonToken = FIELD_NAME [null] [false] [number]
jsonToken = VALUE_STRING [null] [false] [310 555-4567]
jsonToken = END_OBJECT [}] [false] [null]
jsonToken = END_ARRAY []] [false] [null]
jsonToken = END_OBJECT [}] [false] [null]
```

Stream-Based Generation

The abstract com.fasterxml.jackson.core.JsonGenerator class describes a low-level JSON generator. It's obtained by calling one of the JsonFactory class's overloaded createGenerator() methods, which take the JSON content's destination into account.

Note   Generators can be created to generate content to external destinations, such as files or networks. Content is sent via output streams or writers.

For example, JsonFactory's JsonGenerator createGenerator(File file, JsonEncoding enc) method creates a generator for writing JSON content to the specified file, overwriting any existing content (or creating the file when it doesn't exist). The value passed to enc determines how the written JSON content is encoded and is one of the constants defined by the com.fasterxml.jackson.core.JsonEncoding enum; for example, JsonEncoding.UTF8. This method is demonstrated as follows:

```
JsonFactory factory = new JsonFactory();
JsonGenerator generator =
   factory.createGenerator(new File("out.json"),
                              JsonEncoding.UTF8);
```

JsonGenerator declares various methods for writing JSON content. For example, void writeStartObject() writes the starting marker ({) for an object.

Listing 11-3 presents the source code to an application that demonstrates JsonGenerator and methods for writing JSON content.

Listing 11-3. Learning How to Use JsonGenerator and Its Methods

```java
import java.io.File;

import com.fasterxml.jackson.core.JsonEncoding;
import com.fasterxml.jackson.core.JsonFactory;
import com.fasterxml.jackson.core.JsonGenerator;

import static java.lang.System.*;

public class JacksonDemo
{
   public static void main(String[] args) throws Exception
   {
      JsonFactory factory = new JsonFactory();
      JsonGenerator generator =
      factory.createGenerator(new File("person.json"),
                                 JsonEncoding.UTF8);
      generator.writeStartObject();
      generator.writeStringField("firstname", "John");
      generator.writeStringField("lastName", "Doe");
      generator.writeNumberField("age", 42);
      generator.writeFieldName("address");
      generator.writeStartObject();
      generator.writeStringField("street",
                                    "400 Some Street");
      generator.writeStringField("city", "Beverly Hills");
      generator.writeStringField("state", "CA");
```

```
generator.writeNumberField("zipcode", 90210);
generator.writeEndObject();
generator.writeFieldName("phoneNumbers");
generator.writeStartArray();
generator.writeStartObject();
generator.writeStringField("type", "home");
generator.writeStringField("number", "310 555-1234");
generator.writeEndObject();
generator.writeStartObject();
generator.writeStringField("type", "fax");
generator.writeStringField("number", "310 555-4567");
generator.writeEndObject();
generator.writeEndArray();
generator.writeEndObject();
generator.close();
out.println("person.json successfully generated");
    }
}
```

writeStartObject() is paired with writeEndObject(), which writes the end-of-object marker (}).

The void writeStringField(String fieldName, String value) method writes the specified fieldName and its value. It's equivalent to calling the void writeFieldName(String value) method followed by the void writeString(String text) method. The writeNumberField(String fileName, int value) method is similar to writeStringField(String fieldName, String value), but writes an integer value instead. It's equivalent to calling writeFieldName(String value) followed by the void writeNumber(int value) method.

The void writeStartArray() method writes the start-of-array marker ([). Its companion void writeEndArray() method writes the end-of-array marker (]).

When no more content needs to be written, the generator is closed by calling its void close() method. The underlying destination is also closed when only the generator has access to the destination.

Compile Listing 11-3 and run the application. You should observe the following output:

```
person.json successfully generated
```

The generated `person.json` file contains the following content:

```
{"firstname":"John","lastName":"Doe","age":42,"address":{"street":"400 Some
Street","city":"Beverly Hills","state":"CA","zipcode":90210},"phoneNumbers"
:[{"type":"home","number":"310 555-1234"},{"type":"fax","number":"310 555-
4567"}]}
```

The output is hard to read but can be improved by installing a pretty printer on the generator. A *pretty printer* is an instance of a class that implements the `com.fasterxml.jackson.core.PrettyPrinter` interface and that formats output to make it easier to read. One such class is `com.fasterxml.jackson.core.util.DefaultPrettyPrinter`, which employs 2-space indentation with platform-default line feeds. An instance of this class is installed on the generator by invoking `JsonGenerator`'s `JsonGenerator useDefaultPrettyPrinter()` method, as follows:

```
generator.useDefaultPrettyPrinter();
```

I excerpted this code fragment from a third version of the `JacksonDemo` application, included in this book's code archive. When run, that application generates a `person.json` file with the following content:

```
{
  "firstname" : "John",
  "lastName" : "Doe",
  "age" : 42,
  "address" : {
    "street" : "400 Some Street",
    "city" : "Beverly Hills",
    "state" : "CA",
    "zipcode" : 90210
  },
  "phoneNumbers" : [ {
    "type" : "home",
    "number" : "310 555-1234"
```

```
}, {
    "type" : "fax",
    "number" : "310 555-4567"
} ]
}
```

Tree Model

The tree model provides a mutable in-memory tree representation of a JSON document. The com.fasterxml.jackson.databind.ObjectMapper class is used to build a tree, whose nodes are instances of classes that descend from the abstract com.fasterxml. jackson.databind.JsonNode class.

ObjectMapper declares several constructors for initializing an object mapper. The noargument ObjectMapper() constructor is the easiest to use:

```
ObjectMapper mapper = new ObjectMapper();
```

Once you have an object mapper, you can use it to read a JSON document into a tree, or create a tree and write it to a JSON document.

Reading a JSON Document into a Tree

After obtaining an ObjectMapper instance, an application can invoke one of its overloaded readTree() methods to read a JSON document into an in-memory tree:

```
JsonNode rootNode = mapper.readTree(new File("person.json"));
```

The JsonNode readTree(File file) method deserializes JSON content from the specified file into a tree expressed as set of JsonNode instances. The root node of this tree is returned.

JsonNode provides various methods for accessing tree nodes. Separate methods exist for basic traversal of JSON objects and arrays. Objects are indexed by field name and arrays are indexed by element index. Additionally, it's possible to use "safe" methods that return dummy com.fasterxml.jackson.databind.node.MissingNode instances instead of the null reference when an object or array doesn't contain an indicated value. Traversal methods include the following:

- `JsonNode get(int index)`: for arrays, returns child element at index (which is 0-based) when the child element exists. If `index` is less than 0 or greater than or equal to the array size, or if the node is not a `com.fasterxml.jackson.databind.node.ArrayNode`, `null` is returned. Note that JSON null values are of type `com.fasterxml.jackson.databind.node.NullNode` and are not represented as the null reference because null indicates that a value doesn't exist.

- `JsonNode get(String fieldName)`: for objects, returns `fieldName`'s value when it exists. If no such field exists or the node is not a `com.fasterxml.jackson.databind.node.ObjectNode`, `null` is returned. Note that JSON null values are of type `NullNode` and are not represented as the null reference because null indicates that a value doesn't exist.

- `JsonNode path(int index)` and `JsonNode path(String fieldName)`: These methods are similar to the `get(int)` and `get(String)` methods. However, instead of returning a Java null reference for missing values, they return a `MissingNode` reference. `MissingNode` is beneficial in that it implements all `JsonNode` methods as expected: it never has any value but can be further traversed (resulting always in a `MissingNode`). It's very useful for safe traversal: if data is there, it will be traversed; if not, it will eventually result in missing data. This can be considered similar to the SQL `NULL` value.

- `JsonNode with(String propertyName)` and `JsonNode withArray(String propertyName)`: The first method is called on object nodes to access a property that has an object value or, when no such property exists, to create, add, and return the created object node. The second method is called on object nodes to access a property that has an array value or, when no such property exists, to create, add, and return the created array node. These methods are very useful for safe modifications: subtrees can be materialized as necessary.

Note   ArrayNode provides an int size() method that returns the number of elements in an array. ObjectNode provides an int size() method that returns the number of properties in an object.

Listing 11-4 presents the source code to an application that demonstrates readTree() and associated methods.

Listing 11-4. Reading a JSON Document into a Tree and Traversing the Tree

```java
import java.io.File;

import com.fasterxml.jackson.databind.JsonNode;
import com.fasterxml.jackson.databind.ObjectMapper;

import static java.lang.System.*;

public class JacksonDemo
{
   public static void main(String[] args) throws Exception
   {
      ObjectMapper mapper = new ObjectMapper();
      JsonNode rootNode =
         mapper.readTree(new File("person.json"));
      out.printf("firstName = %s%n",
                 rootNode.get("firstName"));
      out.printf("lastName = %s%n",
                 rootNode.get("lastName"));
      out.printf("age = %s%n", rootNode.get("age"));
      JsonNode address = rootNode.get("address");
      out.println("address");
      out.printf("   street = %s%n", address.get("street"));
      out.printf("   city = %s%n", address.get("city"));
      out.printf("   state = %s%n", address.get("state"));
      out.printf("   zipcode = %s%n",
                    address.get("zipcode"));
```

```java
        JsonNode phoneNumbers = rootNode.get("phoneNumbers");
        out.println("phoneNumbers");
        for (int i = 0; i < phoneNumbers.size(); i++)
        {
            out.printf("   %d: ", i);
            JsonNode phoneNumber = phoneNumbers.get(i);
            out.printf("type = %s, number = %s%n",
                        phoneNumber.get("type"),
                        phoneNumber.get("number"));
        }
        out.println();
        out.printf("%s%n", rootNode.with("address").
                                    get("street"));
        out.printf("%s%n", rootNode.withArray("phoneNumbers").
                                    get(1).get("type"));
    }
}
```

Compile Listing 11-4 and run the application. Assuming that the current directory also contains Listing 11-2's person.json file, you should observe the following output:

```
firstName = "John"
lastName = "Doe"
age = 42
address
   street = "400 Some Street"
   city = "Beverly Hills"
   state = "CA"
   zipcode = 90210
phoneNumbers
   0: type = "home", number = "310 555-1234"
   1: type = "fax", number = "310 555-4567"

"400 Some Street"
"fax"
```

Creating a Tree and Writing It to a JSON Document

An application can invoke the following `ObjectMapper` methods to begin construction of a tree:

```
ArrayNode createArrayNode()
ObjectNode createObjectNode()
```

JsonNode's `ArrayNode` and `ObjectNode` descendants also provide methods for constructing a tree:

- `ArrayNode` provides several overloaded `add()` methods for appending data to an array. For example, `ArrayNode add(int v)` appends an object containing v to an array. It also provides several overloaded `insert()` methods for inserting data into an array. For example, `ArrayNode insert(int index, int v)` inserts an object containing v at the specified `index` position in the array.

- `ObjectNode` provides several overloaded `put()` methods for updating a property. For example, `ObjectNode put(String fieldName, int v)` sets `fieldName`'s value to an object containing v.

Once the tree has been constructed, it can be written to a JSON document by invoking one of `ObjectMapper`'s overloaded `writeTree()` methods:

```
mapper.writeTree(generator, rootNode);
```

The `void writeTree(JsonGenerator gen, JsonNode rootNode)` method serializes the `rootNode`-anchored tree to a destination via generator gen.

Listing 11-5 presents the source code to an application that demonstrates `writeTree()` and associated methods.

Listing 11-5. Creating a Tree and Writing Its Nodes to a JSON Document

```
import java.io.File;

import com.fasterxml.jackson.core.JsonEncoding;
import com.fasterxml.jackson.core.JsonFactory;
import com.fasterxml.jackson.core.JsonGenerator;

import com.fasterxml.jackson.databind.JsonNode;
```

```java
import com.fasterxml.jackson.databind.ObjectMapper;

import com.fasterxml.jackson.databind.node.ArrayNode;
import com.fasterxml.jackson.databind.node.ObjectNode;

import static java.lang.System.*;

public class JacksonDemo
{
    public static void main(String[] args) throws Exception
    {
        ObjectMapper mapper = new ObjectMapper();
        JsonNode rootNode = mapper.createObjectNode();
        ObjectNode objectNode = (ObjectNode) rootNode;
        objectNode.put("firstName", "John");
        objectNode.put("lastName", "Doe");
        objectNode.put("age", 42);
        ObjectNode addressNode = mapper.createObjectNode();
        addressNode.put("street", "400 Some Street");
        addressNode.put("city", "Beverly Hills");
        addressNode.put("state", "CA");
        addressNode.put("zipcode", 90210);
        objectNode.set("address", addressNode);
        ArrayNode phoneNumbersNode = mapper.createArrayNode();
        ObjectNode phoneNumberNode =
            mapper.createObjectNode();
        phoneNumberNode.put("type", "home");
        phoneNumberNode.put("number", "310 555-1234");
        phoneNumbersNode.add(phoneNumberNode);
        phoneNumberNode = mapper.createObjectNode();
        phoneNumberNode.put("type", "fax");
        phoneNumberNode.put("number", "310 555-4567");
        phoneNumbersNode.add(phoneNumberNode);
        objectNode.set("phoneNumbers", phoneNumbersNode);
        JsonFactory factory = new JsonFactory();
        JsonGenerator generator =
            factory.createGenerator(new File("person.json"),
```

```
                                    JsonEncoding.UTF8);
    generator.useDefaultPrettyPrinter();
    mapper.writeTree(generator, rootNode);
    out.println("person.json successfully generated");
  }
}
```

Compile Listing 11-5 and run the application. You should observe the following output, along with a generated person.json file containing pretty-printed content:

```
person.json successfully generated
```

Data Binding

The ObjectMapper class supports *data binding* in which JSON content is parsed to and from Java objects such as POJOs. JSON content is *deserialized* into Java objects, and Java objects are *serialized* into JSON content.

Deserialization is achieved by calling one of ObjectMapper's overloaded readValue() generic methods, which support deserialization from different sources. For example, the following method deserializes from a file into the given Java type:

```
<T> T readValue(File src, Class<T> valueType)
```

This method doesn't support generic types because of type erasure (http://en.wikipedia.org/wiki/Type_erasure). In contrast, the following method uses the com.fasterxml.jackson.core.type.TypeReference<T> type to support generic types:

```
<T> T readValue(File src, TypeReference valueTypeRef)
```

TypeReference is a generic abstract class that's used to obtain full generic type information via subclassing. I'll show an example shortly.

Serialization is achieved by calling one of ObjectMapper's overloaded writeValue() methods, which support serialization to different destinations. For example, the following method serializes a Java object to a file:

```
writeValue(File resultFile, Object value)
```

Jackson supports simple data binding and full data binding.

Simple Data Binding

Simple data binding converts to and from a limited number of core JDK types. Table 11-1 reveals the JSON types and the core JDK types to which they are mapped.

Table 11-1. *Mapping JSON Types to Java Types*

JSON Type	Java Type
object	`java.util.LinkedHashMap<String,Object>`
array	`java.util.ArrayList<Object>`
string	`java.lang.String`
number (no fraction)	`java.lang.Integer`, `java.lang.Long`, or `java.math.BigInteger` (smallest applicable)
number (fraction)	`java.lang.Double` (configurable to use `java.math.BigDecimal`)
true|false	`java.lang.Boolean`
null	null reference

The following example invokes `readValue()` to read a JSON object into a Java map:

```
Map<?,?> rootAsMap = mapper.readValue(src, Map.class);
```

The `<?,?>` syntax indicates an untyped map. To bind data into a generic map, such as `Map<String,User>`, I would need to specify `TypeReference` as follows:

```
Map<String,User> rootAsMap =
   mapper.readValue(src,
              new TypeReference<Map<String,User>>(){});
```

`TypeReference` is needed only to pass a generic type definition (via an anonymous inner class in this case). What's important is `<Map<String,User>>`, which defines the type to bind to.

Because the range of value types is limited to a few core JDK types, the deserialization type (at the root or lower level) can be defined as `Object.class`. Any value declared to be of `java.lang.Object` type uses simple data binding:

```
Object root = mapper.readValue(src, Object.class);
```

After creating the Java object, it can be serialized to a file or other destination by invoking writeValue(), which is demonstrated as follows:

```
mapper.writeValue(new File("file.json"), rootAsMap);
```

Listing 11-6 presents the source code to an application that demonstrates simple data binding via these code fragments.

Listing 11-6. A Simple Data-Binding Demonstration

```
import java.io.File;

import java.util.List;
import java.util.Map;

import com.fasterxml.jackson.core.type.TypeReference;

import com.fasterxml.jackson.databind.ObjectMapper;

import static java.lang.System.*;

public class JacksonDemo
{
   public static void main(String[] args) throws Exception
   {
      ObjectMapper mapper = new ObjectMapper();
      String ageJson = "65";
      out.println(mapper.readValue(ageJson, Integer.class));
      String planetsJson = "[\"Mercury\", \"Venus\", " +
                           "\"Earth\", \"Mars\"]";
      List<?> list1 = mapper.readValue(planetsJson,
                                       List.class);
      out.println(list1);
//      list1.add("Jupiter");
      List<String> list2 =
         mapper.readValue(planetsJson,
                          new
                          TypeReference<List<String>>(){});
      out.println(list2);
      list2.add("Jupiter");
```

```
        out.println(list2);
        String gradesJson = "{\"John\": 86, \"Jane\": 92}";
        Map<?,?> map = mapper.readValue(gradesJson,
                                        Map.class);
        out.println(map);
        mapper.writeValue(new File("grades.json"), map);
    }
}
```

After creating an `ObjectMapper` instance, Listing 11-6's `main()` method maps a JSON number to a Java `Integer`, which is output.

`main()` now maps a string-based JSON array to a `List`. Because the resulting `list1` object has `List<?>` type, the compiler will not compile `list1.add("Jupiter");`. There's no `add(String)` method when the unbounded wildcard type is specified. Although this problem could be solved by specifying `List list1` (giving `list1` the raw `List` type), any Java object could be stored in the `List`, which would violate type safety. Generics must be used to solve this problem.

The `main()` method next creates a list of strings and uses `TypeReference` to pass `String` to `readValue()`. The compiler is able to compile `list1.add("Jupiter");` because `List<String>` has an `add(String)` method.

`main()` now switches focus to working with `Map`. After creating a grades-oriented map, it outputs the map and uses `writeValue()` to write the map's content to a file named `grades.json`.

Compile Listing 11-6 and run the application. You should observe the following output:

```
65
[Mercury, Venus, Earth, Mars]
[Mercury, Venus, Earth, Mars]
[Mercury, Venus, Earth, Mars, Jupiter]
{John=86, Jane=92}
```

Furthermore, you should observe a `grades.json` file in the current directory. This file should contain the following content:

```
{"John":86,"Jane":92}
```

Full Data Binding

Full data binding converts to and from any Java bean type in addition to Maps, Lists, Strings, Numbers, Booleans, and the null reference. Consider Listing 11-7.

Listing 11-7. A Person Bean

```
/*
{
   "firstName": "John",
   "lastName": "Doe",
   "age": 42,
   "address":
   {
      "street": "400 Some Street",
      "city": "Beverly Hills",
      "state": "CA",
      "zipcode": 90210
   },
   "phoneNumbers":
   [
      {
         "type": "home",
         "number": "310 555-1234"
      },
      {
         "type": "fax",
         "number": "310 555-4567"
      }
   ]
}
*/

public class Person
{
   private String firstName;
   private String lastName;
   private int age;
```

```java
public static class Address
{
    private String street, city, state;
    private int zipcode;
    public String getStreet()
    {
        return street;
    }

    public String getCity()
    {
        return city;
    }

    public String getState()
    {
        return state;
    }

    public int getZipcode()
    {
        return zipcode;
    }

    public void setStreet(String street)
    {
        this.street = street;
    }

    public void setCity(String city)
    {
        this.city = city;
    }

    public void setState(String state)
    {
        this.state = state;
    }
}
```

```java
    private Address address;

    public static class PhoneNumber
    {
        private String type, number;

        public String getType()
        {
            return type;
        }

        public String getNumber()
        {
            return number;
        }

        public void setType(String type)
        {
            this.type = type;
        }

        public void setNumber(String number)
        {
            this.number = number;
        }
    }

    private PhoneNumber[] phoneNumbers;

    public String getFirstName()
    {
        return firstName;
    }

    public String getLastName()
    {
        return lastName;
    }
```

```java
public int getAge()
{
   return age;
}

public Address getAddress()
{
   return address;
}

public PhoneNumber[] getPhoneNumbers()
{
   return phoneNumbers;
}

public void setFirstName(String firstName)
{
   this.firstName = firstName;
}

public void setLastName(String lastName)
{
   this.lastName = lastName;
}

public void setAge(int age)
{
   this.age = age;
}

public void setAddress(Address address)
{
   this.address = address;
}

public void setPhoneNumbers(PhoneNumber[] phoneNumbers)
{
   this.phoneNumbers = phoneNumbers;
}
```

```java
@Override
public String toString()
{
    StringBuffer sb = new StringBuffer();
    sb.append("firstName = " + firstName + "\n");
    sb.append("lastName = " + lastName + "\n");
    sb.append("age = " + age + "\n");
    sb.append("address\n");
    sb.append("   street = " + address.getStreet() +
             "\n");
    sb.append("   city = " + address.getCity() + "\n");
    sb.append("   state = " + address.getState() + "\n");
    sb.append("   zipcode = " + address.getZipcode() +
             "\n");
    sb.append("phoneNumbers\n");
    for (int i = 0; i < phoneNumbers.length; i++)
    {
        sb.append("   type = " +
                 phoneNumbers[i].getType() + "\n");
        sb.append("   number = " +
                 phoneNumbers[i].getNumber() + "\n");
    }
    return sb.toString();
}
}
```

Listing 11-7 describes a Person class that corresponds to Listing 11-2's person.json content. This class adheres to the Java Beans getter/setter method naming conventions.

By default, Jackson maps the fields of a JSON object to fields in a Java object by matching the names of the JSON fields to the getter and setter methods in the Java object. Jackson removes the get and set parts of the names of the getter and setter methods and converts the first character of the remaining name to lowercase. For example, in Listing 11-7, the JSON firstName field matches the Java getFirstName() and setFirstName() getter and setter methods.

Note A getter method makes a non-`public` field serializable and deserializable (once a field has a getter method, it's considered to be a property). In contrast, a setter method makes a non-`public` field deserializable only. For example, in Listing 11-7, commenting out `setAge()` only doesn't affect age's serializability/deserializability. However, commenting out `getAge()` only prevents age from being serialized (e.g., via one of `ObjectMapper`'s `writeValue()` methods).

Listing 11-8 presents the source code to an application that demonstrates full data binding with assistance from the `Person` class.

Listing 11-8. A Full Data-Binding Demonstration

```
import java.io.File;

import com.fasterxml.jackson.databind.ObjectMapper;

import static java.lang.System.* ;

public class JacksonDemo
{
   public static void main(String[] args) throws Exception
   {
      ObjectMapper mapper = new ObjectMapper();
      Person person =
         mapper.readValue(new File("person.json"),
                          Person.class);
      out.println(person);
   }
}
```

Listing 11-8's `main()` method first instantiates `ObjectMapper`. Next, it invokes the mapper's `readValue()` method to read the contents of `person.json` into a `Person` object, which is then printed.

Note   When using full data binding, the deserialization type must be fully specified as something other than `Object.class`, which implies simple data binding. In Listing 11-8, `Person.class` is passed to `readValue()` as the deserialization type.

Compile Listings 11-7 and 11-8 and run the application. Assuming that the current directory also contains Listing 11-2's `person.json` file, you should observe the following output:

```
firstName = John
lastName = Doe
age = 42
address
    street = 400 Some Street
    city = Beverly Hills
    state = CA
    zipcode = 90210
phoneNumbers
    type = home
    number = 310 555-1234
    type = fax
    number = 310 555-4567
```

Working with Jackson's Advanced Features

Jackson provides various advanced features, which focus largely on customization. This section introduces annotation types; custom pretty printers; and factory, parser, and generator features.

Annotation Types

The Jackson Annotations and Jackson Databind packages provide annotation types for influencing how JSON is read into Java objects or what JSON is generated from Java objects. Annotation types are read-only, write-only, or read-write.

Read-Only Annotation Types

Read-only annotation types affect how Jackson deserializes (parses) JSON content into Java objects (i.e., they affect how Jackson reads JSON content). Jackson supports the following read-only annotation types:

- JsonSetter
- JsonAnySetter
- JsonCreator and JsonProperty
- JacksonInject
- JsonDeserialize

JsonSetter

Match the annotated setter method's name to a JSON property name when reading JSON content into Java objects. This annotation type is useful when a Java class's internal property names don't match the JSON document's property names.

Listing 11-9 shows JsonSetter annotating a setter method in a Person class. Because this method isn't present in Person2, JsonSetter annotates the field instead.

Listing 11-9. Using JsonSetter to Match Java Class and JSON Document Property Names

```
import com.fasterxml.jackson.annotation.JsonSetter;

import com.fasterxml.jackson.databind.ObjectMapper;

import static java.lang.System.*;

public class JacksonDemo
{
   public static void main(String[] args) throws Exception
   {
      String jsonContent =
      "{" +
      "   \"id\": 820787," +
      "   \"firstName\": \"Pierre\"" +
      "}";
```

```java
      ObjectMapper mapper = new ObjectMapper();
      Person person = mapper.readValue(jsonContent,
                                       Person.class);
      out.println(person);
      Person2 person2 = mapper.readValue(jsonContent,
                                         Person2.class);
      out.println(person2);
   }
}

class Person
{
   private int personID = 0;
   private String firstName = null;

   public int getPersonID()
   {
      return personID;
   }

   @JsonSetter("id")
   public void setPersonID(int personID)
   {
      this.personID = personID;
   }

   public String getFirstName()
   {
      return firstName;
   }

   public void setFirstName(String firstName)
   {
      this.firstName = firstName;
   }
```

```java
    @Override
    public String toString()
    {
        return personID + ": " + firstName;
    }
}

class Person2
{
    @JsonSetter("id")
    private int personID = 0;
    private String firstName = null;

    public int getPersonID()
    {
        return personID;
    }

    public String getFirstName()
    {
        return firstName;
    }

    public void setFirstName(String firstName)
    {
        this.firstName = firstName;
    }

    @Override
    public String toString()
    {
        return personID + ": " + firstName;
    }
}
```

The value passed to the @JsonSetter annotation is the name of the JSON field to match to this setter method. Here, the name is id because that's the name of the field in the JSON object to be mapped to the setPersonID() setter method.

Person2 doesn't have a `setPersonID()` setter, but this isn't a problem because Person2 contains a `getPersonID()` getter, making `personID` deserializable (via an implicit setter) and serializable (via `getPersonID()`).

Compile Listing 11-9 and run the application. You should observe the following output:

```
820787: Pierre
820787: Pierre
```

JsonAnySetter

Call the same setter method for all unrecognized fields in the JSON object. An unrecognized field is one that isn't already mapped to a property or setter method in the Java object.

Listing 11-10 shows `JsonAnySetter` annotating a setter method in a `PropContainer` class. Without the annotation, the code would fail at runtime.

Listing 11-10. Using `JsonAnySetter` to Install a Setter Method for Unrecognized JSON Object Fields

```java
import java.util.HashMap;
import java.util.Iterator;
import java.util.Map;
import java.util.Map.Entry;

import com.fasterxml.jackson.annotation.JsonAnySetter;

import com.fasterxml.jackson.databind.ObjectMapper;

import static java.lang.System.*;

public class JacksonDemo
{
    public static void main(String[] args) throws Exception
    {
        String jsonContent =
        "{" +
        "   \"id\": 820787," +
        "   \"firstName\": \"Pierre\"," +
```

```
            "   \"lastName\": \"Francois\"" +
            "}";
        ObjectMapper mapper = new ObjectMapper();
        PropContainer pc =
            mapper.readValue(jsonContent, PropContainer.class);
        Iterator<Map.Entry<String, Object>> iter =
            pc.iterator();
        while (iter.hasNext())
        {
            Map.Entry<String, Object> entry = iter.next();
            out.printf("Key: %s, Value: %s%n", entry.getKey(),
                    entry.getValue());
        }
    }
}

class PropContainer
{
    // public String lastName;

    private Map<String, Object> properties;

    PropContainer()
    {
        properties = new HashMap<>();
    }

    @JsonAnySetter
    void addProperty(String fieldName, Object value)
    {
        properties.put(fieldName, value);
    }

    Iterator<Map.Entry<String, Object>> iterator()
    {
        return properties.entrySet().iterator();
    }
}
```

Listing 11-10 introduces a small JSON object with id, firstName, and lastName fields. It also introduces a PropContainer class for storing these property names and their values.

While parsing these fields from the JSON object into the PropContainer object, Jackson would look for setID(), setFirstName(), and setLastName() methods. Because these methods don't exist and there are no public id, firstName, and lastName fields, Jackson would normally output an error message at runtime. However, the presence of addProperty() with its @JsonAnySetter annotation causes Jackson to invoke this method for all three fields.

Compile Listing 11-10 and run the application. You should observe the following output:

```
Key: firstName, Value: Pierre
Key: lastName, Value: Francois
Key: id, Value: 820787
```

Uncomment the line public String lastName;, recompile Listing 11-10, and rerun the application. You should now observe the following output:

```
Key: firstName, Value: Pierre
Key: id, Value: 820787
```

This time, Key: lastName, Value: Francois doesn't appear, because lastName is no longer an unrecognized property—it now exists as a property in PropContainer.

JsonCreator and JsonProperty

JsonCreator tells Jackson that the Java object has a constructor (a "creator") that can match, with help from JsonProperty, the JSON object's fields to the fields of the Java object. These annotation types are useful where it's not possible to use the @JsonSetter annotation. For example, immutable objects cannot have setter methods, so their initial values must be specified in the constructor, which Listing 11-11 demonstrates.

Listing 11-11. Using JsonCreator and JsonProperty to Call a Constructor When Parsing JSON Text

```
import com.fasterxml.jackson.annotation.JsonCreator;
import com.fasterxml.jackson.annotation.JsonProperty;
```

```java
import com.fasterxml.jackson.databind.ObjectMapper;

import static java.lang.System.* ;

public class JacksonDemo
{
    public static void main(String[] args) throws Exception
    {
        String jsonContent =
        "{" +
        "    \"make\": \"Ford\"," +
        "    \"model\": \"F150\"," +
        "    \"year\": 2008" +
        "}";
        ObjectMapper mapper = new ObjectMapper();
        Vehicle vehicle = mapper.readValue(jsonContent,
                                            Vehicle.class);
        out.printf("Make %s, Model %s, Year %d%n",
                    vehicle.getMake(), vehicle.getModel(),
                    vehicle.getYear());
    }
}

class Vehicle
{
    private String make, model;

    private int year;

    @JsonCreator
    Vehicle(@JsonProperty("make") String make,
            @JsonProperty("model") String model,
            @JsonProperty("year") int year)
    {
        this.make = make;
        this.model = model;
        this.year = year;
    }
```

```
String getMake()
{
   return make;
}

String getModel()
{
   return model;
}

int getYear()
{
   return year;
}
}
```

Vehicle's constructor is annotated @JsonCreator to tell Jackson that it should call the constructor when parsing JSON content into a Java object. Furthermore, the constructor's parameters are annotated @JsonProperty to tell Jackson which JSON object fields to pass to which constructor parameters. Note that @JsonProperty receives a single string argument that identifies the JSON object field name.

Compile Listing 11-11 and run the application. You should observe the following output:

```
Make Ford, Model F150, Year 2008
```

JacksonInject

Inject (i.e., set based on an ObjectMapper-configured value) values into the parsed objects instead of reading those values from the JSON content. For example, suppose I add a String webURL field to the previous example's Vehicle class. I can tell Jackson to inject the URL of the vehicle's manufacturer's website into a Vehicle object by performing the following steps:

1. Annotate webURL @JacksonInject.

2. Instantiate com.fasterxml.jackson.databind.
    InjectableValues.Std() and invoke its addValue(Class<?>
    classKey, Object value) method to add the string-based URL
    to an injectable values object.

3. Instantiate `ObjectMapper`.

4. On the `ObjectMapper` instance, invoke `ObjectMapper`'s
    `ObjectReader reader(InjectableValues injectableValues)`
    method to construct a `com.fasterxml.jackson.databind.`
    `ObjectReader` object that will use the specified injectable values.

5. On the `ObjectReader` instance, invoke `ObjectReader`'s
    `ObjectReader forType(Class<?> valueType)` method to
    construct a new reader instance that's configured to data bind into
    the specified `valueType`.

6. On the `ObjectReader` instance that `forType()` returns, invoke
    `ObjectReader`'s `readValue(String src)` method (or a similar
    `readValue()` method) to read the source and perform the
    injection.

Listing 11-12 presents the source code to an application that accomplishes these tasks.

Listing 11-12. Using `JsonInject` to Inject a URL into a Parsed `Vehicle` Object

```
import com.fasterxml.jackson.annotation.JacksonInject;
import com.fasterxml.jackson.annotation.JsonCreator;
import com.fasterxml.jackson.annotation.JsonProperty;

import com.fasterxml.jackson.databind.InjectableValues;
import com.fasterxml.jackson.databind.ObjectMapper;

import static java.lang.System.*;

public class JacksonDemo
{
   public static void main(String[] args) throws Exception
   {
      String jsonContent =
      "{" +
      "   \"make\": \"Ford\"," +
      "   \"model\": \"F150\"," +
      "   \"year\": 2008" +
      "}";
```

```
      InjectableValues inject =
         new InjectableValues.Std()
                              .addValue(String.class,
                                    "ford.com");
      Vehicle vehicle =
         new ObjectMapper().reader(inject)
                           .forType(Vehicle.class)
                           .readValue(jsonContent);
      out.printf("Make %s, Model %s, Year %d, URL %s%n",
               vehicle.getMake(), vehicle.getModel(),
               vehicle.getYear(), vehicle.webURL);
   }
}

class Vehicle
{
   private String make, model;

   private int year;

   @JsonCreator
   Vehicle(@JsonProperty("make") String make,
           @JsonProperty("model") String model,
           @JsonProperty("year") int year)
   {
      this.make = make;
      this.model = model;
      this.year = year;
   }

   String getMake()
   {
      return make;
   }
```

```java
String getModel()
{
    return model;
}

int getYear()
{
    return year;
}

@JacksonInject
String webURL;
}
```

Compile Listing 11-12 and run the application. You should observe the following output:

```
Make Ford, Model F150, Year 2008, URL ford.com
```

JsonDeserialize

Specify a custom deserializer class for a given field in a Java object. For example, suppose a JSON document contains a `color` field with a string-based value such as `black` or `red`. This document is to be deserialized into a `Canvas` class that declares a `color` field of a `Color` enum type. Jackson cannot deserialize this value without help, because it cannot convert a string to an enum instance.

The "help" that Jackson requires starts by adding annotation `@JsonDeserialize` to the `color` field. This annotation type's `using` parameter is assigned the `java.lang.Class` object of the class being used to perform the custom deserialization. Furthermore, that class must subclass the abstract `com.fasterxml.jackson.databind.JsonDeserializer<T>` class, where `T` is the type of the annotated field.

`JsonDeserializer` declares an abstract `T deserialize(JsonParser p, DeserializationContext ctxt)` method that Jackson calls to deserialize JSON content into the value type that this deserializer handles. The `JsonParser` argument identifies the parser of the JSON content, and the `com.fasterxml.jackson.databind.DeserializationContext` argument is used to pass in configuration settings.

Listing 11-13 presents the source code to an application that implements and demonstrates this custom deserialization example.

Listing 11-13. Using `JsonDeserialize` to Deserialize a Color String into a Color Enum Constant

```java
import java.io.IOException;

import com.fasterxml.jackson.core.JsonParser;
import com.fasterxml.jackson.core.JsonProcessingException;

import com.fasterxml.jackson.databind.annotation.
      JsonDeserialize;

import com.fasterxml.jackson.databind.
      DeserializationContext;
import com.fasterxml.jackson.databind.JsonDeserializer;
import com.fasterxml.jackson.databind.ObjectMapper;

import static java.lang.System.*;

public class JacksonDemo
{
   public static void main(String[] args) throws Exception
   {
      String jsonContent =
      "{" +
      "   \"color\": \"black\"" +
      "}";

      Canvas canvas =
         new ObjectMapper().readerFor(Canvas.class)
                           .readValue(jsonContent);
      System.out.printf("Color = %s%n", canvas.color);
   }
}

enum Color
{
   BLACK, UNKNOWN
}

class Canvas
```

```
{
   @JsonDeserialize(using = ColorDeserializer.class)
   public Color color;
}

class ColorDeserializer extends JsonDeserializer<Color>
{
   @Override
   public Color deserialize(JsonParser jsonParser,
                            DeserializationContext
                            deserializationContext)
      throws IOException, JsonProcessingException
   {
      switch (jsonParser.getText().toLowerCase())
      {
         case "black":
            return Color.BLACK;

         default:
            return Color.UNKNOWN;
      }
   }
}
```

Compile Listing 11-13 and run the application. You should observe the following output:

```
Color = BLACK
```

Write-Only Annotation Types

Write-only annotation types affect how Jackson serializes (generates) Java objects into JSON content (i.e., they affect how Jackson writes JSON content). Jackson supports the following write-only annotation types:

- JsonInclude

- JsonGetter

- JsonAnyGetter

- JsonPropertyOrder

- JsonRawValue

- JsonValue

- JsonSerialize

JsonInclude

Include properties for serialization only under certain circumstances. For example, a String property may be included only if its value isn't the null reference.

JsonInclude can be used to annotate a field, a method parameter, a constructor parameter, or an entire class. When a class is annotated, all properties are checked against the annotation's value to see if they can be serialized or not.

JsonInclude's value is specified by assigning one of the JsonInclude.Include enum's constants to its value parameter. Here are three examples:

- ALWAYS: The property is to be included independent of its value. Jackson includes all properties by default (i.e., when JsonInclude isn't used).

- NON_EMPTY: Properties with null values or what are otherwise considered to be empty (e.g., a string has zero length or a Map's isEmpty() method returns true) are not included.

- NON_NULL: Properties with null values are not included.

Listing 11-14 presents the source code to an application that demonstrates JsonInclude with these three enum constants.

Listing 11-14. Using JsonInclude to Skip or Serialize Empty or Null Properties

```
import java.util.ArrayList;
import java.util.List;
import com.fasterxml.jackson.annotation.JsonInclude;

import com.fasterxml.jackson.core.JsonGenerator;

import com.fasterxml.jackson.databind.ObjectMapper;

import static java.lang.System.*;
```

```java
public class JacksonDemo
{
    public static void main(String[] args) throws Exception
    {
        ObjectMapper mapper = new ObjectMapper();
        mapper.disable(JsonGenerator.Feature.
                        AUTO_CLOSE_TARGET);
        Person1 person1 = new Person1();
        mapper.writeValue(out, person1) ;
        out.println();
        Person2 person2 = new Person2();
        mapper.writeValue(out, person2);
        out.println();
        Person3 person3 = new Person3();
        mapper.writeValue(out, person3);
        out.println();
        Person4 person4 = new Person4();
        mapper.writeValue(out, person4);
    }
}

class Person1
{
    public int personID = 0;
    public String firstName = null;
    public String lastName = "Doe";
    public List<String> phoneNumbers = new ArrayList<>();
}

@JsonInclude(JsonInclude.Include.ALWAYS)
class Person2
{
    public int personID = 0;
    public String firstName = null;
    public String lastName = "Doe";
    public List<String> phoneNumbers = new ArrayList<>();
}
```

```
@JsonInclude(JsonInclude.Include.NON_EMPTY)
class Person3
{
   public int personID = 0;
   public String firstName = null;
   public String lastName = "Doe";
   public List<String> phoneNumbers = new ArrayList<>();
}

@JsonInclude(JsonInclude.Include.NON_NULL)
class Person4
{
   public int personID = 0;
   public String firstName = null;
   public String lastName = "Doe";
   public List<String> phoneNumbers = new ArrayList<>();
}
```

`mapper.disable(JsonGenerator.Feature.AUTO_CLOSE_TARGET);` prevents the
`System.out` stream from being closed after `mapper.writeValue()`.

Compile Listing 11-14 and run the application. You should observe the following
output:

```
{"personID":0,"firstName":null,"lastName":"Doe","phoneNumbers":[]}
{"personID":0,"firstName":null,"lastName":"Doe","phoneNumbers":[]}
{"personID":0,"lastName":"Doe"}
{"personID":0,"lastName":"Doe","phoneNumbers":[]}
```

JsonGetter

When serializing a class instance, call the @JsonGetter-annotated method and serialize
the return value as the property's value.

This annotation type is useful for Java classes that follow the jQuery (http://
en.wikipedia.org/wiki/JQuery) style for getter and setter names (such as numDoors()
instead of getNumDoors()). Consider Listing 11-15.

Listing 11-15. Using JSonGetter to Serialize jQuery-Style Properties

```java
import java.io.File;

import com.fasterxml.jackson.annotation.JsonGetter;
import com.fasterxml.jackson.annotation.JsonSetter;

import com.fasterxml.jackson.databind.ObjectMapper;

import static java.lang.System.* ;

public class JacksonDemo
{
    public static void main(String[] args) throws Exception
    {
        String jsonContent =
        "{" +
        "   \"id\": 820787," +
        "   \"firstName\": \"Pierre\"" +
        "}";
        ObjectMapper mapper = new ObjectMapper();
        Person person = mapper.readValue(jsonContent,
                                        Person.class);
        out.println(person);
        mapper.writeValue(new File("pierre.json"), person);
    }
}

class Person
{
    private int personID = 0;
    private String firstName = null;

    @JsonGetter("id")
    public int personID()
    {
        return personID;
    }
```

```java
public void setPersonID(int personID)
{
    this.personID = personID;
}

@JsonGetter("firstName")
public String firstName()
{
    return firstName;
}

public void setFirstName(String firstName)
{
    this.firstName = firstName;
}

@Override
public String toString()
{
    return personID + ": " + firstName;
}
}
```

The personId() and firstName() jQuery-style methods are annotated @JsonGetter. The value set on each @JsonGetter annotation is the property name that Jackson will write to the JSON document.

If @JsonGetter("id") is removed from personID(), Jackson will throw a runtime exception. It will do so because it cannot map the JSON id property to the Java personID property—personID would have to be renamed getId, and setPersonID would have to be renamed setId to remove the exception. If @JsonGetter("firstName") is removed from firstName(), Jackson won't serialize the Java firstName property to JSON.

It isn't necessary to annotate setPersonID() @JsonSetter("id"), which was done in Listing 11-9, because the presence of personID() with its @JsonGetter("id") annotation makes personID deserializable and serializable.

Compile Listing 11-15 and run the application. You should observe the following output:

```
820787: Pierre
```

Furthermore, you should observe a `pierre.json` file with the following content:

```
{"id":820787,"firstName":"Pierre"}
```

JsonAnyGetter

Identify a non-`static`, noargument method that returns a `map` of properties to be serialized to JSON. Each of the map's key/value pairs is serialized along with regular properties. This annotation type is the counterpart to `JsonAnySetter`.

Listing 11-16 presents an application that demonstrates `JsonAnyGetter`. This application extends Listing 11-10, which also demonstrates `JsonAnySetter`.

Listing 11-16. Using JSonAnyGetter to Serialize a Map of Properties

```java
import java.io.File;

import java.util.HashMap;
import java.util.Iterator;
import java.util.Map;
import java.util.Map.Entry;

import com.fasterxml.jackson.annotation.JsonAnyGetter;
import com.fasterxml.jackson.annotation.JsonAnySetter;

import com.fasterxml.jackson.databind.ObjectMapper;

import static java.lang.System.* ;

public class JacksonDemo
{
   public static void main(String[] args) throws Exception
   {
      String jsonContent =
      "{" +
      "   \"id\": 820787," +
      "   \"firstName\": \"Pierre\"," +
      "   \"lastName\": \"Francois\"" +
      "}";
```

```
        ObjectMapper mapper = new ObjectMapper();
        PropContainer pc =
            mapper.readValue(jsonContent, PropContainer.class);
        Iterator<Map.Entry<String, Object>> iter =
            pc.iterator();
        while (iter.hasNext())
        {
            Map.Entry<String, Object> entry = iter.next();
            out.printf("Key: %s, Value: %s%n", entry.getKey(),
                        entry.getValue());
        }
        mapper.writeValue(new File("pierre.json"), pc) ;
    }
}

class PropContainer
{
    public String lastName;

    private Map<String, Object> properties;

    PropContainer()
    {
        properties = new HashMap<>();
    }

    @JsonAnySetter
    void addProperty(String fieldName, Object value)
    {
        properties.put(fieldName, value);
    }

    Iterator<Map.Entry<String, Object>> iterator()
    {
        return properties.entrySet().iterator();
    }

    @JsonAnyGetter
```

```
public Map<String, Object> properties()
{
    return properties;
}
}
```

Compile Listing 11-16 and run the application. You should observe the following output:

```
Key: firstName, Value: Pierre
Key: id, Value: 820787
```

Jackson's deserialization mechanism doesn't add JSON's lastName property to the map because it detects a lastName property of the PropContainer class. It updates lastName instead.

You should also observe a pierre.json file with the following content:

```
{"lastName":"Francois","firstName":"Pierre","id":820787}
```

Jackson's serialization mechanism first writes PropContainer's regular properties (only lastName in this case) and then outputs the properties that are stored in the map.

JsonPropertyOrder

Specify the order in which a Java object's fields should be serialized to JSON content. This annotation type makes it possible to override the default top-down order with a different order. Consider Listing 11-17.

Listing 11-17. Using JSonPropertyOrder to Serialize SomeClass2's Properties in Reverse Order

```
import java.io.File;

import com.fasterxml.jackson.annotation.JsonPropertyOrder;

import com.fasterxml.jackson.databind.ObjectMapper;

import static java.lang.System.*;
```

```java
public class JacksonDemo
{
    public static void main(String[] args) throws Exception
    {
        ObjectMapper mapper = new ObjectMapper();
        SomeClass1 sc1 = new SomeClass1();
        mapper.writeValue(new File("order1.json"), sc1);
        SomeClass2 sc2 = new SomeClass2();
        mapper.writeValue(new File("order2.json"), sc2);
        out.println("serialization successful");
    }
}

class SomeClass1
{
    public int a = 1, b = 2, c = 3, d = 4;
    public String e = "e";
}

@JsonPropertyOrder({"e","d","c","b","a"})
class SomeClass2
{
    public int a = 1, b = 2, c = 3, d = 4;
    public String e = "e";
}
```

Listing 11-17 declares SomeClass1, which isn't annotated with JsonPropertyOrder. Therefore, its fields are serialized in top-down order. In contrast, SomeClass2 is annotated so that its fields are serialized in reverse order.

Note   The @JsonProperty annotation receives an array of quoted field names whose left-to-right order corresponds to the serialized top-to-bottom order.

Compile Listing 11-17 and run the application. You should observe the following output:

```
serialization successful
```

The generated order1.json file contains the following content:

```
{"a":1,"b":2,"c":3,"d":4,"e":"e"}
```

The generated order2.json file contains the following content:

```
{"e":"e","d":4,"c":3,"b":2,"a":1}
```

JsonRawValue

Tell Jackson that the annotated Java method or field should be serialized as is. A string property's value is serialized without the surrounding quote characters. Consider Listing 11-18.

Listing 11-18. Using JSonRawValue to Serialize a Vehicle Field As Is

```java
import java.io.File;

import com.fasterxml.jackson.annotation.JsonRawValue;

import com.fasterxml.jackson.databind.ObjectMapper;

import static java.lang.System.*;

public class JacksonDemo
{
   public static void main(String[] args) throws Exception
   {
      ObjectMapper mapper = new ObjectMapper();
      Driver1 d1 = new Driver1();
      mapper.writeValue(new File("driver1.json"), d1);
      Driver2 d2 = new Driver2();
      mapper.writeValue(new File("driver2.json"), d2);
      out.println("serialization successful");
   }
}
```

```java
class Driver1
{
   public String name = "John Doe";
   public String vehicle = "{ \"make\": \"Ford\", " +
                              "\"model\": \"F150\", " +
                              "\"year\": 2008";
}

class Driver2
{
   public String name = "John Doe";
   @JsonRawValue
   public String vehicle = "{ \"make\": \"Ford\", " +
                              "\"model\": \"F150\", " +
                              "\"year\": 2008";
}
```

Compile Listing 11-18 and run the application. You should observe the following output:

```
serialization successful
```

The generated driver1.json file contains the following content:

```
{"name":"John Doe","vehicle":"{ \"make\": \"Ford\", \"model\": \"F150\",
\"year\": 2008"}
```

The generated driver2.json file contains the following content:

```
{"name":"John Doe","vehicle":{ "make": "Ford", "model": "F150",
"year": 2008}
```

Unlike the previous output, this output reveals that the value of Driver2's vehicle property is serialized as part of the JSON object structure. It's not serialized to a string in the JSON object's vehicle field, as the previous output shows.

JsonValue

Delegate the serialization of a Java object to one of its methods, which must take no arguments and which must return a value of a scalar type (such as String or java.lang. Number) or any serializable type (such as java.util.Collection or Map).

For a noargument method with a String return type, Jackson escapes any double quotation marks inside the returned String, making it impossible to return a full JSON object. However, that task can be accomplished by using @JsonRawValue.

Listing 11-19 demonstrates JsonValue.

Listing 11-19. Using JSonValue to Serialize Props1 and Props2 Objects via Their toJson() Methods

```java
import java.io.File;

import java.util.HashMap;
import java.util.Map;

import com.fasterxml.jackson.annotation.JsonValue;

import com.fasterxml.jackson.databind.ObjectMapper;

import static java.lang.System.*;

public class JacksonDemo
{
   public static void main(String[] args) throws Exception
   {
      ObjectMapper mapper = new ObjectMapper();
      Props1 p1 = new Props1();
      mapper.writeValue(new File("props1.json"), p1);
      Props2 p2 = new Props2();
      mapper.writeValue(new File("props2.json"), p2);
      out.println("serialization successful");
   }
}
```

```java
class Props1
{
    public String a = "A";
    public String b = "B";

    @JsonValue
    public String toJSON()
    {
        return a + "\"-\"" + b;
    }
}

class Props2
{
    private Map<String, String> props = new HashMap<>();

    Props2()
    {
        props.put("a", "A'A'\"A\"");
        props.put("b", "B'B'\"B\"");
    }

    @JsonValue
    public Map<String, String> toJSON()
    {
        return props;
    }
}
```

Compile Listing 11-19 and run the application. You should observe the following output:

```
serialization successful
```

The generated props1.json file contains the following content:

```
"A\"-\"B"
```

The generated props2.json file contains the following content:

```
{"a":"A'A'\"A\"","b":"B'B'\"B\""}
```

This output reveals that double quotation marks are escaped even in noargument methods with return types other than String.

JsonSerialize

Specify a custom serializer class for a given field in a Java object. For example, suppose a Java object contains a color field whose value is an enum instance such as Color.BLACK. This object is to be serialized to a JSON document whose color field is associated with a string-based value such as black or red. Jackson cannot serialize this value without help, because it cannot convert an enum instance to a string.

The "help" that Jackson requires starts by adding a @JsonSerialize annotation to the color field. This annotation type's using parameter is assigned the Class object of the class being used to perform the custom serialization. Furthermore, that class must subclass the abstract com.fasterxml.jackson.databind.JsonSerializer<T> class, where T is the type of the annotated field.

JsonSerializer declares an abstract void serialize(T value, JsonGenerator gen, SerializerProvider serializers) method that Jackson calls to serialize the value type that this serializer handles to JSON content. The JsonGenerator argument identifies the generator of the JSON content, and the com.fasterxml.jackson.databind.SerializerProvider argument is used when serializing complex object graphs.

Listing 11-20 presents the source code to an application that refactors Listing 11-13 to implement and demonstrate this custom serialization example.

Listing 11-20. Using JsonSerialize to Serialize a Color Enum Constant to a Color String

```
import java.io.File;
import java.io.IOException;

import com.fasterxml.jackson.core.JsonGenerator;
import com.fasterxml.jackson.core.JsonParser;
import com.fasterxml.jackson.core.JsonProcessingException;

import com.fasterxml.jackson.databind.annotation.JsonDeserialize;
import com.fasterxml.jackson.databind.annotation.JsonSerialize;
```

```java
import com.fasterxml.jackson.databind.DeserializationContext;
import com.fasterxml.jackson.databind.JsonDeserializer;
import com.fasterxml.jackson.databind.JsonSerializer;
import com.fasterxml.jackson.databind.ObjectMapper;
import com.fasterxml.jackson.databind.SerializerProvider;

import static java.lang.System.*;

public class JacksonDemo
{
   public static void main(String[] args) throws Exception
   {
      String jsonContent =
      "{" +
      "   \"color\": \"black\"" +
      "}";

      Canvas canvas =
         new ObjectMapper().readerFor(Canvas.class)
                           .readValue(jsonContent);
      out.printf("Color = %s%n", canvas.color);
      new ObjectMapper().writeValue(new File("color.json"),
                                    canvas);
   }
}

enum Color
{
   BLACK, UNKNOWN
}

class Canvas
{
   @JsonDeserialize(using = ColorDeserializer.class)
   @JsonSerialize(using = ColorSerializer.class)
   public Color color;
}
```

```java
class ColorDeserializer extends JsonDeserializer<Color>
{
    @Override
    public Color deserialize(JsonParser jsonParser,
                             DeserializationContext
                             deserializationContext)
        throws IOException, JsonProcessingException
    {
        switch (jsonParser.getText().toLowerCase())
        {
            case "black":
                return Color.BLACK;

            default:
                return Color.UNKNOWN;
        }
    }
}

class ColorSerializer extends JsonSerializer<Color>
{
    @Override
    public void serialize(Color color,
                          JsonGenerator jsonGenerator,
                          SerializerProvider
                          serializerProvider)
        throws IOException, JsonProcessingException
    {
        switch (color)
        {
            case BLACK:
                jsonGenerator.writeString("black");
                break;
```

```
      default:
          jsonGenerator.writeString("unknown");
    }
  }
}
```

Compile Listing 11-20 and run the application. You should observe the following output:

```
Color = BLACK
```

Furthermore, you should observe a generated `color.json` file with the following content:

```
{"color":"black"}
```

Read-Write Annotation Types

Read-write annotation types affect the reading of Java objects from JSON content, as well as the writing of Java objects to JSON content. The following read-write annotation types are supported by Jackson:

- `JsonIgnore` and `JsonIgnoreProperties`
- `JsonIgnoreType`
- `JsonAutoDetect`

JsonIgnore and JsonIgnoreProperties

`JsonIgnore` tells Jackson to ignore a certain property (field) of a Java object. The property is ignored when reading JSON content to Java objects and when writing Java objects to JSON content. `JsonIgnoreProperties` tells Jackson to ignore a list of properties of a Java class. The `@JsonIgnoreProperties` annotation is placed above the class declaration instead of above each property (field) to be ignored. These closely related annotation types are demonstrated in Listing 11-21.

Listing 11-21. Using JsonIgnore and JsonIgnoreProperties to Ignore One or More Properties

```java
import java.io.File;

import com.fasterxml.jackson.annotation.JsonIgnore;
import com.fasterxml.jackson.annotation.
      JsonIgnoreProperties;

import com.fasterxml.jackson.databind.ObjectMapper;

import static java.lang.System.*;

public class JacksonDemo
{
   public static void main(String[] args) throws Exception
   {
      ObjectMapper mapper = new ObjectMapper();
      SavingsAccount1 sa1 =
         new SavingsAccount1("101", "John Doe", 50000);
      mapper.writeValue(new File("sa1.json"), sa1);
      SavingsAccount2 sa2 =
         new SavingsAccount2("101", "John Doe", 50000);
      mapper.writeValue(new File("sa2.json"), sa2);
      SavingsAccount3 sa3 =
         new SavingsAccount3("101", "John Doe", 50000);
      mapper.writeValue(new File("sa3.json"), sa3);
      sa1 = mapper.readValue(new File("sa1.json"),
                             SavingsAccount1.class);
      out.printf("bankID = %s%n", sa1.bankID);
      out.printf("accountOwnerName = %s%n",
               sa1.accountOwnerName);
      out.printf("balanceInCents = %d%n",
               sa1.balanceInCents);
      sa2 = mapper.readValue(new File("sa1.json"),
                             SavingsAccount2.class);
      out.printf("bankID = %s%n", sa2.bankID);
      out.printf("accountOwnerName = %s%n",
```

```
                    sa2.accountOwnerName);
        out.printf("balanceInCents = %d%n",
                    sa2.balanceInCents);
        sa3 = mapper.readValue(new File("sa1.json"),
                            SavingsAccount3.class);
        out.printf("bankID = %s%n", sa3.bankID);
        out.printf("accountOwnerName = %s%n",
                    sa3.accountOwnerName);
        out.printf("balanceInCents = %d%n",
                    sa3.balanceInCents);
    }
}

class SavingsAccount1
{
    public String bankID;
    public String accountOwnerName;
    public long balanceInCents;

    SavingsAccount1()
    {
    }

    SavingsAccount1(String bankID, String accountOwnerName,
                    long balanceInCents)
    {
        this.bankID = bankID;
        this.accountOwnerName = accountOwnerName;
        this.balanceInCents = balanceInCents;
    }
}

class SavingsAccount2
{
    @JsonIgnore
    public String bankID;
    public String accountOwnerName;
    public long balanceInCents;
```

```java
    SavingsAccount2()
    {
    }

    SavingsAccount2(String bankID, String accountOwnerName,
                long balanceInCents)
    {
        this.bankID = bankID;
        this.accountOwnerName = accountOwnerName;
        this.balanceInCents = balanceInCents;
    }
}

@JsonIgnoreProperties({"bankID", "accountOwnerName"})
class SavingsAccount3
{
    public String bankID;
    public String accountOwnerName;
    public long balanceInCents;

    SavingsAccount3()
    {
    }

    SavingsAccount3(String bankID, String accountOwnerName,
                long balanceInCents)
    {
        this.bankID = bankID;
        this.accountOwnerName = accountOwnerName;
        this.balanceInCents = balanceInCents;
    }
}
```

The noargument and empty constructors in SavingsAccount1, SavingsAccount2, and SavingsAccount3 are needed to avoid a runtime exception during deserialization.

Compile Listing 11-21 and run the application. You should observe the following output:

```
bankID = 101
accountOwnerName = John Doe
balanceInCents = 50000
bankID = null
accountOwnerName = John Doe
balanceInCents = 50000
bankID = null
accountOwnerName = null
balanceInCents = 50000
```

The null values are the result of bankID and accountOwnerName being set to null because of @JsonIgnore and @jsonIgnoreProperties, even though this information is stored in sa1.json.

The generated sa1.json file contains the following content:

```
{"bankID":"101","accountOwnerName":"John Doe","balanceInCents":50000}
```

The generated sa2.json file contains the following content:

```
{"accountOwnerName":"John Doe","balanceInCents":50000}
```

The generated sa3.json file contains the following content:

```
{"balanceInCents":50000}
```

JsonIgnoreType

All properties of an annotated type are to be ignored during serialization and deserialization. This annotation type is demonstrated in Listing 11-22, where it's used to prevent Address properties from being serialized/deserialized.

Listing 11-22. Using JsonIgnoreType to Ignore Address Properties

```
import java.io.File;

import com.fasterxml.jackson.annotation.JsonIgnoreType;

import com.fasterxml.jackson.databind.ObjectMapper;

import static java.lang.System.*;
```

```java
public class JacksonDemo
{
   public static void main(String[] args) throws Exception
   {
      ObjectMapper mapper = new ObjectMapper();
      Person1 person1 = new Person1();
      person1.name = "John Doe";
      person1.address = new Person1.Address();
      person1.address.street = "100 Smith Street";
      person1.address.city = "SomeCity";
      mapper.writeValue(new File("person1.json"), person1);
      Person2 person2 = new Person2();
      person2.name = "John Doe";
      person2.address = new Person2.Address();
      person2.address.street = "100 Smith Street";
      person2.address.city = "SomeCity";
      mapper.writeValue(new File("person2.json"), person2);
      person1 = mapper.readValue(new File("person1.json"),
                                 Person1.class);
      out.printf("name = %s%n", person1.name);
      out.printf("street = %s%n", person1.address.street);
      out.printf("city = %s%n", person1.address.city);
      person2 = mapper.readValue(new File("person1.json"),
                                 Person2.class);
      out.printf("name = %s%n", person2.name);
      out.printf("street = %s%n", person2.address.street);
      out.printf("city = %s%n", person2.address.city);
   }
}

class Person1
{
   public String name;

   public static class Address
   {
```

```
        public String street;
        public String city;
    }

    public Address address;
}

class Person2
{
    public String name;

    @JsonIgnoreType
    public static class Address
    {
        public String street;
        public String city;
    }

    public Address address;
}
```

Compile Listing 11-22 and run the application. You should observe the following output:

```
name = John Doe
street = 100 Smith Street
city = SomeCity
name = John Doe
Exception in thread "main" java.lang.NullPointerException
        at JacksonDemo.main(JacksonDemo.java:34)
```

The exception is the result of address being set to null because of @JsonIgnoreType, even though the address information is stored in person1.json.

The generated person1.json file contains the following content:

```
{"name":"John Doe","address":{"street":"100 Smith
Street","city":"SomeCity"}}
```

The generated person2.json file contains the following content:

```
{"name":"John Doe"}
```

JsonAutoDetect

Tell Jackson to include non-`public` properties when reading and writing Java objects.

This annotation type declares various visibility elements for determining the minimum visibility level (such as `public` or `protected`) for auto-detection. For example, `fieldVisibility` specifies the minimum visibility required for auto-detecting member fields. One of the `JsonAutoDetect.Visibility` enum constants is assigned to this element. This enum enumerates possible visibility thresholds (minimum visibility) that can be used to limit which methods (and fields) are auto-detected.

Listing 11-23 demonstrates `JsonAutoDetect` and its nested `Visibility` enum.

Listing 11-23. Using `JsonAutoDetect` to Auto-Detect Various Fields

```
import java.io.File;

import com.fasterxml.jackson.annotation.JsonAutoDetect;

import com.fasterxml.jackson.databind.ObjectMapper;

import static java.lang.System.*;

public class JacksonDemo
{
   public static void main(String[] args) throws Exception
   {
      ObjectMapper mapper = new ObjectMapper();
      SomeClass1 sc1 = new SomeClass1(1, 2, 3);
      mapper.writeValue(new File("sc1.json"), sc1);
      SomeClass2 sc2 = new SomeClass2(1, 2, 3);
      mapper.writeValue(new File("sc2.json"), sc2);
      SomeClass3 sc3 = new SomeClass3(1, 2, 3);
      mapper.writeValue(new File("sc3.json"), sc3);
      sc1 = mapper.readValue(new File("sc1.json"),
                          SomeClass1.class);
      sc1.print();
      sc2 = mapper.readValue(new File("sc2.json"),
                          SomeClass2.class);
      sc2.print();
      sc3 = mapper.readValue(new File("sc3.json"),
                          SomeClass3.class);
```

387

```java
        sc3.print();
    }
}

class SomeClass1
{
    public int a;
    private int b;
    protected int c;

    SomeClass1()
    {
    }

    SomeClass1(int a, int b, int c)
    {
        this.a = a;
        this.b = b;
        this.c = c;
    }

    public void print()
    {
        out.printf("a = %d, b = %d, c = %d%n", a, b, c);
    }
}

@JsonAutoDetect(fieldVisibility = JsonAutoDetect.Visibility
                                  .PROTECTED_AND_PUBLIC)
class SomeClass2
{
    public int a;
    private int b;
    protected int c;

    SomeClass2()
    {
    }
```

```java
    SomeClass2(int a, int b, int c)
    {
       this.a = a;
       this.b = b;
       this.c = c;
    }

    public void print()
    {
       out.printf("a = %d, b = %d, c = %d%n", a, b, c);
    }
}

@JsonAutoDetect(fieldVisibility = JsonAutoDetect.Visibility
                                  .ANY)
class SomeClass3
{
    public int a;
    private int b;
    protected int c;

    SomeClass3()
    {
    }

    SomeClass3(int a, int b, int c)
    {
       this.a = a;
       this.b = b;
       this.c = c;
    }

    public void print()
    {
       out.printf("a = %d, b = %d, c = %d%n", a, b, c);
    }
}
```

With Visiblity.PROTECTED_AND_PUBLIC, only access modifiers protected and public are auto-detectable. With Visibility.ANY, protected, public, private, and package access are auto-detectable.

Compile Listing 11-23 and run the application. You should observe the following output:

```
a = 1, b = 0, c = 0
a = 1, b = 0, c = 3
a = 1, b = 2, c = 3
```

The generated sc1.json file contains the following content:

```
{"a":1}
```

The generated sc2.json file contains the following content:

```
{"a":1,"c":3}
```

The generated sc3.json file contains the following content:

```
{"a":1,"b":2,"c":3}
```

Custom Pretty Printers

Jackson supports *pretty printers* to improve the appearance of generated output (making it easier to read). A pretty printer class must implement the PrettyPrinter interface in terms of the following methods:

- void beforeArrayValues(JsonGenerator gen)

- void beforeObjectEntries(JsonGenerator gen)

- void writeArrayValueSeparator(JsonGenerator gen)

- void writeEndArray(JsonGenerator gen, int nrOfValues)

- void writeEndObject(JsonGenerator gen, int nrOfEntries)

- void writeObjectEntrySeparator(JsonGenerator gen)

- void writeObjectFieldValueSeparator(JsonGenerator gen)

- void writeRootValueSeparator(JsonGenerator gen)

- void writeStartArray(JsonGenerator gen)

- void writeStartObject(JsonGenerator gen)

Furthermore, since Jackson 2.1, a stateful implementation of PrettyPrinter must implement the com.fasterxml.jackson.core.util.Instantiatable<T> interface, to allow for the construction of per-generation instances in order to avoid state corruption when sharing the pretty printer instance among threads. Instantiatable declares a T createInstance() method that returns a newly created stateful pretty printer object.

Note A stateless pretty printer class doesn't need to implement Instantiatable. However, if it implements this interface, its createInstance() method should return this to signify the current object.

Earlier in this chapter, I showed the following pretty-printed output:

```
{
  "firstname" : "John",
  "lastName" : "Doe",
  "age" : 42,
  "address" : {
    "street" : "400 Some Street",
    "city" : "Beverly Hills",
    "state" : "CA",
    "zipcode" : 90210
  },
  "phoneNumbers" : [ {
    "type" : "home",
    "number" : "310 555-1234"
  }, {
    "type" : "fax",
    "number" : "310 555-4567"
  } ]
}
```

I'd like to reformat the output to look like this:

```
{
  "firstname" : "John",
  "lastName" : "Doe",
  "age" : 42,
  "address" :
  {
    "street" : "400 Some Street",
    "city" : "Beverly Hills",
    "state" : "CA",
    "zipcode" : 90210
  },
  "phoneNumbers" :
  [
    {
      "type" : "home",
      "number" : "310 555-1234"
    },
    {
      "type" : "fax",
      "number" : "310 555-4567"
    }
  ]
}
```

Listing 11-24 provides the source code to an application with a custom
MyPrettyPrinter class that formats the output as shown in the preceding text.

Listing 11-24. Reformatting Output with a Pretty Printer

```
import java.io.IOException;

import com.fasterxml.jackson.core.JsonEncoding;
import com.fasterxml.jackson.core.JsonFactory;
import com.fasterxml.jackson.core.JsonGenerator;
import com.fasterxml.jackson.core.PrettyPrinter;
```

```java
import com.fasterxml.jackson.core.util.Instantiatable;

import static java.lang.System.*;

public class JacksonDemo
{
    public static void main(String[] args) throws Exception
    {
        JsonFactory factory = new JsonFactory();
        JsonGenerator generator =
        factory.createGenerator(out, JsonEncoding.UTF8);
        generator.setPrettyPrinter(new MyPrettyPrinter());
        generator.writeStartObject();
        generator.writeStringField("firstname", "John");
        generator.writeStringField("lastName", "Doe");
        generator.writeNumberField("age", 42);
        generator.writeFieldName("address");
        generator.writeStartObject();
        generator.writeStringField("street",
                                    "400 Some Street");
        generator.writeStringField("city", "Beverly Hills");
        generator.writeStringField("state", "CA");
        generator.writeNumberField("zipcode", 90210);
        generator.writeEndObject();
        generator.writeFieldName("phoneNumbers");
        generator.writeStartArray();
        generator.writeStartObject();
        generator.writeStringField("type", "home");
        generator.writeStringField("number", "310 555-1234");
        generator.writeEndObject();
        generator.writeStartObject();
        generator.writeStringField("type", "fax");
        generator.writeStringField("number", "310 555-4567");
        generator.writeEndObject();
        generator.writeEndArray();
        generator.writeEndObject();
```

```
        generator.close();
    }
}

class MyPrettyPrinter
    implements PrettyPrinter, Instantiatable<MyPrettyPrinter>
{
    private final String LINE_SEP =
        getProperty("line.separator");

    private int indent = 0;
    private boolean isNewline = true;

    @Override
    public MyPrettyPrinter createInstance()
    {
        return new MyPrettyPrinter();
    }

    @Override
    public void writeStartObject(JsonGenerator jg)
        throws IOException
    {
        if (!isNewline)
            newline(jg);
        jg.writeRaw('{');
        ++indent;
        isNewline = false;
    }

    @Override
    public void beforeObjectEntries(JsonGenerator jg)
        throws IOException
    {
        newline(jg) ;
    }
```

```java
@Override
public void
    writeObjectFieldValueSeparator(JsonGenerator jg)
    throws IOException
{
    jg.writeRaw(" : ");
    isNewline = false;
}

@Override
public void writeObjectEntrySeparator(JsonGenerator jg)
    throws IOException
{

    jg.writeRaw(",");
    newline(jg);
}

@Override
public void writeEndObject(JsonGenerator jg,
                           int nrOfEntries)
    throws IOException
{
    --indent;
    newline(jg);
    jg.writeRaw('}');
    isNewline = indent == 0;
}

@Override
public void writeStartArray(JsonGenerator jg)
    throws IOException
{
    newline(jg);
    jg.writeRaw("[");
    ++indent;
    isNewline = false;
}
```

```java
@Override
public void beforeArrayValues(JsonGenerator jg)
    throws IOException
{
    newline(jg);
}

@Override
public void writeArrayValueSeparator(JsonGenerator jg)
    throws IOException
{
    jg.writeRaw(", ");
    isNewline = false;
}

@Override
public void writeEndArray(JsonGenerator jg,
                          int nrOfValues)
    throws IOException
{
    --indent;
    newline(jg);
    jg.writeRaw(']');
    isNewline = false;
}

@Override
public void writeRootValueSeparator(JsonGenerator jg)
    throws IOException
{
    jg.writeRaw(' ');
}

private void newline(JsonGenerator jg) throws IOException
{
    jg.writeRaw(LINE_SEP);
    for (int i = 0; i < indent; ++i)
```

```
        jg.writeRaw("  ");
      isNewline = true;
   }
}
```

DefaultPrettyPrinter is paired with JsonGenerator's useDefaultPrettyPrinter()
method, which instantiates DefaultPrettyPrinter and installs the instance on the
generator. All other pretty printer classes must be instantiated explicitly, and these
instances must be installed on their generators by using JsonGenerator's JsonGenerator
setPrettyPrinter(PrettyPrinter pp) method, which Listing 11-24 accomplishes as
follows:

```
generator.setPrettyPrinter(new MyPrettyPrinter());
```

Although there's no need to do so, it's possible to explicitly instantiate
DefaultPrettyPrinter and pass the instance to JsonGenerator by calling
setPrettyPrinter().

Note   MyPrettyPrinter's content is based on code found in GitHub issue
"PrettyPrinter Indenter: Ability to insert eol before object and array entries #724"
(http://github.com/FasterXML/jackson-databind/issues/724).

Compile Listing 11-24 and run the application. You should observe the following
output:

```
{
  "firstname" : "John",
  "lastName" : "Doe",
  "age" : 42,
  "address" :
  {
    "street" : "400 Some Street",
    "city" : "Beverly Hills",
    "state" : "CA",
    "zipcode" : 90210
  },
```

```
  "phoneNumbers" :
  [
    {
      "type" : "home",
      "number" : "310 555-1234"
    },
    {
      "type" : "fax",
      "number" : "310 555-4567"
    }
  ]
}
```

For some custom pretty printers, Jackson's `com.fasterxml.jackson.core.util.`
`MinimalPrettyPrinter` class, which adds no indentation but implements everything
necessary for value output to work as expected, might be easier to use.

Factory, Parser, and Generator Features

`JsonFactory`, `JsonFactory`, and `JsonGenerator` instances can be customized by
enabling various *features*, which are constants declared by nested `Feature` enums.

`JsonFactory.Feature` offers the following factory-oriented features (check out the
Javadoc for descriptions):

- CANONICALIZE_FIELD_NAMES

- FAIL_ON_SYMBOL_HASH_OVERFLOW

- INTERN_FIELD_NAMES

- USE_THREAD_LOCAL_FOR_BUFFER_RECYCLING

`JsonFactory` provides four methods to enable, disable, and interrogate the state of
these features:

- JsonFactory configure(JsonFactory.Feature f, boolean state)

- JsonFactory disable(JsonFactory.Feature f)

- JsonFactory enable(JsonFactory.Feature f)

- boolean isEnabled(JsonFactory.Feature f)

`JsonParser.Feature` offers the following parser-oriented features (check out the Javadoc for descriptions):

- `ALLOW_BACKSLASH_ESCAPING_ANY_CHARACTER`
- `ALLOW_COMMENTS`
- `ALLOW_MISSING_VALUES`
- `ALLOW_NON_NUMERIC_NUMBERS`
- `ALLOW_NUMERIC_LEADING_ZEROS`
- `ALLOW_SINGLE_QUOTES`
- `ALLOW_TRAILING_COMMA`
- `ALLOW_UNQUOTED_CONTROL_CHARS`
- `ALLOW_UNQUOTED_FIELD_NAMES`
- `ALLOW_YAML_COMMENTS`
- `AUTO_CLOSE_SOURCE`
- `IGNORE_UNDEFINED`
- `INCLUDE_SOURCE_IN_LOCATION`
- `STRICT_DUPLICATE_DETECTION`

`JsonParser` provides four methods to enable, disable, and interrogate the state of these features:

- `JsonParser configure(JsonParser.Feature f, boolean state)`
- `JsonParser disable(JsonParser.Feature f)`
- `JsonParser enable(JsonParser.Feature f)`
- `boolean isEnabled(JsonParser.Feature f)`

`JsonGenerator.Feature` offers the following generator-oriented features (check out the Javadoc for descriptions):

- `AUTO_CLOSE_JSON_CONTENT`
- `AUTO_CLOSE_TARGET`
- `ESCAPE_NON_ASCII`

- `FLUSH_PASSED_TO_STREAM`

- `IGNORE_UNKNOWN`

- `QUOTE_FIELD_NAMES`

- `QUOTE_NON_NUMERIC_NUMBERS`

- `STRICT_DUPLICATE_DETECTION`

- `WRITE_BIGDECIMAL_AS_PLAIN`

- `WRITE_NUMBERS_AS_STRINGS`

JsonGenerator provides four methods to enable, disable, and interrogate the state of these features:

- `JsonGenerator configure(JsonGenerator.Feature f, boolean state)`

- `JsonGenerator disable(JsonGenerator.Feature f)`

- `JsonGenerator enable(JsonGenerator.Feature f)`

- `boolean isEnabled(JsonGenerator.Feature f)`

Note   For convenience, `JsonFactory` duplicates `JsonParser`'s and `JsonGenerator`'s feature methods, which return, where applicable, `JsonFactory` instead of `JsonParser` or `JsonGenerator`.

Finally, ObjectMapper supports the customization of its JsonParser and JsonGenerator objects by providing the following convenience methods:

- `ObjectMapper configure(JsonGenerator.Feature f, boolean state)`

- `ObjectMapper configure(JsonParser.Feature f, boolean state)`

- `ObjectMapper disable(JsonGenerator.Feature... features)`

- `ObjectMapper disable(JsonParser.Feature... features)`

- `ObjectMapper enable(JsonGenerator.Feature... features)`

- `ObjectMapper enable(JsonParser.Feature... features)`

- boolean isEnabled(JsonFactory.Feature f)

- boolean isEnabled(JsonGenerator.Feature f)

- boolean isEnabled(JsonParser.Feature f)

In Listing 11-14, I disabled JsonGenerator's AUTO_CLOSE_TARGET feature via an ObjectMapper instance by using the following code fragment:

```
mapper.disable(JsonGenerator.Feature.AUTO_CLOSE_TARGET);
```

If you recall, I disabled this feature to prevent mapper.writeValue() from closing the System.out stream.

EXERCISES

The following exercises are designed to test your understanding of Chapter 11's content:

1. Define Jackson.

2. Identify Jackson's packages.

3. True or false: Jackson supports only full data binding and POJO data binding.

4. How does streaming in Jackson work?

5. True or false: Streaming is the least efficient way to process JSON content.

6. How do you create a stream-based parser?

7. After you obtain a parser, how do use the parser to parse JSON content?

8. How do you create a stream-based generator?

9. After you obtain a generator, how do you use the generator to generate JSON content?

10. True or false: The tree model provides a mutable in-memory tree representation of a JSON document.

11. What class is used to start building a tree?

12. How do you read a JSON document into an in-memory tree?

13. What is the difference between JsonNode get(int index) and JsonNode path(int index)?

14. How do you write a tree to a JSON document?

15. Define data binding in Jackson.

16. What is the purpose of the `TypeReference` class?

17. How does simple data binding differ from full data binding?

18. By default, how does Jackson map the fields of a JSON object to fields in a Java object?

19. True or false: A getter method makes a non-`public` field serializable only.

20. List Jackson's read-only annotation types.

21. What does the `JsonPropertyOrder` annotation type accomplish?

22. What's the difference between a stateful and a stateless pretty printer class?

23. How do you prevent `ObjectMapper`'s `writeValue()` methods from closing the `System.out` stream?

24. Modify Listing 11-3 so that numbers are written out as strings.

Summary

Jackson is a suite of data-processing tools for Java. These tools include a streaming JSON parser/generator library, a matching data-binding library (for converting Plain Old Java Objects—POJOs—to and from JSON), and additional data format modules for processing data encoded in XML and other formats.

Jackson consists of core, databind, and annotations packages. The core package supports a StAX-like streaming API for reading and writing JSON via sequences of discrete events. The databind package supports a DOM-like tree model that provides a mutable in-memory tree representation of a JSON document. The annotations package provides public core annotation types, most of which are used to configure how data binding (mapping) works.

The Jackson Core and Jackson Databind packages support the consumption and creation of JSON documents. They offer various types related to streaming, the tree model, and POJO-oriented data binding.

Jackson provides various advanced features, which focus largely on customization in terms of annotation types; custom pretty printers; and factory, parser, and generator features.

The annotation types influence how JSON is read into Java objects or what JSON is generated from Java objects. Annotation types are read-only, write-only, or read-write.

Jackson supports pretty printers to improve the appearance of generated output (making it easier to read). A custom pretty printer class implements the `PrettyPrinter` interface.

`JsonFactory`, `JsonParser`, and `JsonGenerator` instances can be customized by enabling various features, which are constants declared by nested `Feature` enums. Each class provides `configure()`, `enable()`, `disable()`, and `isEnabled()` methods to enable/disable a feature or learn if a feature is enabled.

Chapter 12 introduces JSON-P for parsing and generating JSON content.

CHAPTER 12

Processing JSON with JSON-P

JSON-P is an intriguing API because it was originally considered for inclusion in Java SE, but was made available to Java EE instead. Chapter 12 explores JSON-P.

What Is JSON-P?

JSON Processing (JSON-P) is a Java API for processing (i.e., parsing, generating, querying, and transforming) JSON content.

JSON-P 1.0

JSON-P 1.0 processes JSON content via an object model or a streaming model. The object model lets JSON-P build a tree of objects for JSON text via API classes similarly to Java's DOM API for XML. The streaming model lets JSON-P produce and consume JSON text similarly to Java's StAX API for XML.

JSON-P 1.0 began as "Java Specification Request (JSR) 353: Java API for JSON Processing" (`http://jcp.org/en/jsr/detail?id=353`). It was officially released in May 2013, but only for Java EE 7 and higher. However, it also can be used in a Java SE 6 and higher context.

JSON-P 1.0 consists of 25 types located in package `javax.json`, along with the support packages `javax.json.spi` and `javax.json.stream`. The `javax.json` package mainly contains types that support the object model, the `javax.json.spi` package contains a single type that describes a service provider for JSON processing objects, and the `javax.json.stream` package contains types that support the streaming model. Both models are discussed later.

© Jeff Friesen 2019
J. Friesen, *Java XML and JSON*, https://doi.org/10.1007/978-1-4842-4330-5_12

The `javax.json` package provides the entry-point `Json` factory class for creating JSON processing objects, such as array builders, object builders, readers, writers, parsers, and generators, and additional types that collectively define an object model API for processing JSON text:

- `JsonArray`: an interface that represents an immutable JSON array (an ordered sequence of zero or more values)

- `JsonArrayBuilder`: an interface that describes a builder for creating `JsonArray` models from scratch

- `JsonBuilderFactory`: an interface that describes a factory for creating `JsonArrayBuilder` and `JsonObjectBuilder` objects

- `JsonNumber`: an interface that represents an immutable JSON number value

- `JsonObject`: an interface that represents an immutable JSON object value (an unordered collection of zero or more name/value pairs)

- `JsonObjectBuilder`: an interface that describes a builder for creating `JsonObject` models from scratch

- `JsonReader`: an interface that describes a way to read a JSON object or an array structure from an input source

- `JsonReaderFactory`: an interface that describes a factory for creating `JsonReader` objects

- `JsonString`: an interface that represents an immutable JSON string

- `JsonStructure`: an interface that serves as the direct supertype of `JsonArray` and `JsonObject`

- `JsonValue`: an interface that represents an immutable JSON value, and is also the direct supertype of `JsonNumber`, `JsonString`, and `JsonStructure`

- `JsonWriter`: an interface that describes a way to write a JSON object or an array structure to an output destination

- `JsonWriterFactory`: an interface that describes a factory for creating `JsonWriter` objects

- `JsonValue.ValueType`: an enum of `JsonValue` type constants

- `JsonException`: an exception that identifies some kind of failure during JSON processing

---

JSON VALUE HIERARCHY

`JsonValue` is the superinterface of interface types that represent immutable JSON values. Figure 12-1 shows their hierarchical relationship.

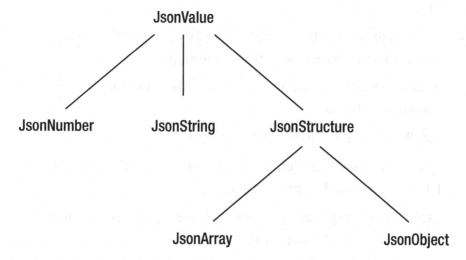

Figure 12-1. *Relating JSON value types*

JSON's Boolean and null types exist as TRUE, FALSE, and NULL constants in `JsonValue`.

The `javax.json.spi` service provider interface package provides a single type for plugging in JSON processing object implementations:

- `JsonProvider`: an abstract class that serves as a service provider for JSON processing objects. The JSON-P libraries include a default Glassfish (http://en.wikipedia.org/wiki/GlassFish) `JsonProvider` implementation.

Finally, the `javax.json.stream` package provides several types that collectively define a streaming API for parsing and generating JSON text:

- `JsonGenerator`: an interface that describes a way to write JSON data to an output destination in a streaming manner

- `JsonGeneratorFactory`: an interface that describes a factory for creating `JsonGenerator` objects

- `JsonLocation`: an interface that describes a way to obtain the location information (e.g., column and line numbers) of a JSON event in an input source

- `JsonParser`: an interface that describes a way to read JSON data from an input source in a streaming (and read-only) manner

- `JsonParserFactory`: an interface that describes a factory for creating `JsonParser` objects

- `JsonParser.EVENT`: an enum of event types

- `JsonGenerationException`: an exception indicating that an incorrect JSON document is being generated

- `JsonParsingException`: an exception indicating that an incorrect JSON document is being parsed

A complete API reference is available by pointing the browser to JSR 353's "JSR-000353 Java API for JSON Processing 1.0 Final Release for Evaluation" (`http://download.oracle.com/otndocs/jcp/json-1_0-fr-eval-spec/index.html`) page, accepting the license agreement, downloading `javax.json-api-1.0-javadoc.zip`, unzipping this archive, and executing `jar xvf javax.json-api-1.0-javadoc.jar` on the resulting `javax.json-api-1.0-javadoc.jar` file. Point the web browser to the unzipped `index.html` file to access the API reference.

JSON-P 1.1

JSON-P 1.1 also supports JSON Pointer, JSON Patch, and JSON Merge Patch. Additionally, the new version introduces editing/transformation operations to JSON array and object builders and updates the API to better support Java SE 8 stream operations (including JSON-specific collectors).

> **Note**   After JSON-P 1.0 was released, JSON Pointer, JSON Patch, and JSON
> Merge Patch specifications were released. *JSON Pointer* defines a string-syntax
> for identifying a specific value in a JSON document. *JSON Patch* defines a JSON
> document structure for expressing a sequence of operations to apply to another
> JSON document (and also makes use of JSON Pointer). *JSON Merge Patch* is
> similar to JSON Patch in that it's also used to change another JSON document's
> structure. However, the syntax of the JSON Merge Patch JSON document more
> closely mimics the syntax of the JSON document that's being changed.

JSON-P 1.1 began as "JSR 374: Java API for JSON Processing 1.1" (http://jcp.org/en/jsr/detail?id=374). It was officially released in May 2017, but only for Java EE 8 and higher. However, it also can be used in a Java SE 8 and higher context.

JSON-P 1.1 consists of 31 types that are located in the main package javax.json, along with the support packages javax.json.spi and javax.json.stream. (No new packages have been added.) The following new types have been added to javax.json:

- JsonMergePatch: an interface that represents an implementation of a JSON Merge Patch as defined by RFC 7386 (http://tools.ietf.org/html/rfc7386)

- JsonPatch: an interface that represents an immutable implementation of a JSON Patch as defined by RFC 6902 (http://tools.ietf.org/html/rfc6902)

- JsonPatchBuilder: an interface that describes a builder for constructing a JSON Patch by adding JSON Patch operations incrementally

- JsonPointer: an interface that represents an immutable implementation of a JSON Pointer as defined by RFC 6901 (http://tools.ietf.org/html/rfc6901)

- JsonPatch.Operation: an enum of valid RFC 6902 JSON Patch operations

The following new type is located in `javax.json.stream`:

- `JsonCollectors`: a class with `java.util.stream.Collector` implementations for accumulating `JsonValues` into `JsonArrays` and `JsonObjects`

Additional changes in the form of new methods have been made to existing classes.

A complete API reference is available by pointing the browser to JSR 374's "JSR-000374 Java API for JSON Processing 1.1 Specification Final Release for Evaluation" (`http://download.oracle.com/otndocs/jcp/json_p-1_1-final-eval-spec/index.html`) page, accepting the license agreement, downloading `javax.json-api-1.1-javadoc.jar`, and executing `jar xvf javax.json-api-1.1-javadoc.jar`. Point the web browser to the unzipped `index.html` file to access the API reference.

Obtaining and Using JSON-P

The latest updates of the JSON-P 1.0 and 1.1 libraries can be obtained from the Maven Repository (`http://mvnrepository.com`). At the time of writing, 1.0.4 is the latest update of JSON-P 1.0, and 1.1.3 is the latest update of JSON-P 1.1.

Obtain version 1.0.4 by pointing your browser to "JSR 374 (JSON Processing) Default Provider » 1.0.4" (`http://mvnrepository.com/artifact/org.glassfish/javax.json/1.0.4`) and clicking the "bundle (83 KB)" link on the Files line. The resulting `javax.json-1.0.4.jar` file contains all of the JSON-P 1.0 classfiles along with the Glassfish default provider classfiles. Add this JAR file to your CLASSPATH when compiling and running code that uses this library:

```
javac -cp javax.json-1.0.4.jar source file
```

```
java -cp javax.json-1.0.4.jar;. main classfile
```

Follow these steps to obtain version 1.1.3:

1. Point your browser to "JSR 374 (JSON Processing) API » 1.1.3" (`http://mvnrepository.com/artifact/javax.json/javax.json-api/1.1.3`) and click the "bundle (30 KB)" link on the Files line.

2. Because the resulting `javax.json-api-1.1.3.jar` file doesn't contain the Glassfish default provider, point your browser to "JSR 374 (JSON Processing) Default Provider » 1.1.3" (`http://mvnrepository.com/artifact/org.glassfish/javax.json/1.1.3`) and click the "bundle (99 KB)" link on the Files line. You should observe a `javax.json-1.1.3.jar` file.

`javax.json-api-1.1.3.jar` contains only the JSON-P 1.1 class files, and `javax.json-1.1.3.jar` contains only the Glassfish class files. Add these JAR files to your CLASSPATH when compiling and running code that uses these libraries:

```
javac -cp javax.json-api-1.1.3.jar;javax.json-1.1.3.jar;. source file
```

```
java -cp javax.json-api-1.1.3.jar;javax.json-1.1.3.jar;. main classfile
```

Working with JSON-P 1.0

JSON-P 1.0 provides object model and streaming model APIs to process JSON text. The object model API represents JSON text in memory via a tree-like structure, which can be navigated and queried in a random-access fashion. The streaming model API represents JSON text as a sequence of events; a parser delivers the next event to an application upon request (the event is "pulled" from the parser). The application can process or discard the event.

The object model is more flexible than the streaming model in that it enables processing that requires random access to the complete content of the tree. However, it's often not as efficient as the streaming model and requires more memory.

Working with the Object Model API

The object model API is similar to Java's DOM API for XML. It's a high-level API that provides immutable object models for JSON object and array structures. These JSON structures are represented as object models using `JsonObject` and `JsonArray`, respectively.

`JsonObject` provides a `java.util.Map` view for accessing an object model's unordered collection of zero or more name/value pairs. Similarly, `JsonArray` provides a `java.util.List` view for accessing an object model's ordered sequence of zero or more values.

411

JsonObject and JsonArray are joined by JsonString and JsonNumber to represent most of JSON's data types. Collectively, they subclass JsonValue, which also defines TRUE, FALSE, and NULL constants for JSON's Boolean and null data types.

Builder patterns are used to create object models from scratch. Applications use interface JsonObjectBuilder to create models that represent JSON objects. The resulting model is of type JsonObject. Similarly, they use interface JsonArrayBuilder to create models that represent JSON arrays. The resulting model is of type JsonArray.

Listing 12-1 presents the source code to an application that demonstrates the builder approach to creating an object model.

Listing 12-1. Using a Builder to Create an Object Model

```
import javax.json.Json;
import javax.json.JsonArray;
import javax.json.JsonObject;

import static java.lang.System.*;

public class JSONPDemo
{
   public static void main(String[] args)
   {
      JsonObject person =
         Json.createObjectBuilder()
             .add("firstName", "John")
             .add("lastName", "Doe")
             .add("age", 42)
             .add("address", Json.createObjectBuilder()
                                  .add("street",
                                       "400 Some Street")
                                  .add("city",
                                       "Beverly Hills")
                                  .add("state", "CA")
             .add("zipcode", 90210))
```

```java
            .add("phoneNumbers",
                Json.createArrayBuilder()
                    .add(Json.createObjectBuilder()
                            .add("type", "home")
                            .add("number",
                                "310 555-1234"))
                        .add(Json.createObjectBuilder()
                                .add("type", "fax")
                                .add("number",
                                    "310 555-4567")))
            .build();
out.printf("First name: %s%n",
            person.getString("firstName"));
out.printf("Last name: %s%n",
            person.getString("lastName"));
out.printf("Age: %d%n", person.getInt("age"));
out.println("Address");
out.println("-------");
JsonObject address = person.getJsonObject("address");
out.printf("   Street: %s%n",
            address.getString("street"));
out.printf("   City: %s%n",
            address.getString("city"));
out.printf("   State: %s%n",
            address.getString("state"));
out.printf("   Zipcode: %d%n",
            address.getInt("zipcode"));
out.println("Phone Numbers");
out.println("-------------");
JsonArray phoneNumbers =
    person.getJsonArray("phoneNumbers");
for (JsonObject phoneNumber:
     phoneNumbers.getValuesAs(JsonObject.class))
```

```
    {
        out.printf("    Type: %s%n",
                    phoneNumber.getString("type"));
        out.printf("    Number: %s%n",
                    phoneNumber.getString("number"));
    }
  }
}
```

Listing 12-1 describes a Java application whose main() method constructs a JsonObject describing a person. It first invokes Json's JsonObjectBuilder createObjectBuilder() method followed by various JsonObjectBuilder add() methods to populate the JsonObject, followed by JsonObjectBuilder's build() method to return the JsonObject.

Constructing the JsonObject requires the use of Json's JsonArrayBuilder createArrayBuilder() method, followed by JsonArrayBuilder's JsonArrayBuilder add(JsonObjectBuilder builder) method to construct the phone numbers JsonArray portion of the JsonObject.

After returning the JsonObject, main() invokes various methods to interrogate the object and output object details.

Compile Listing 12-1 as follows:

```
javac -cp javax.json-1.0.4.jar JSONPDemo.java
```

Run the resulting application as follows:

```
java -cp javax.json-1.0.4.jar;. JSONPDemo
```

You should observe the following output:

```
First name: John
Last name: Doe
Age: 42
Address
-------
    Street: 400 Some Street
    City: Beverly Hills
    State: CA
    Zipcode: 90210
```

Phone Numbers

    Type: home
    Number: 310 555-1234
    Type: fax
    Number: 310 555-4567

Object models also can be created from an input source (such as java. io.InputStream or java.io.Reader) by using interface JsonReader. Similarly, object models can be written to an output destination (such as java.io.OutputStream or java. io.Writer) by using interface JsonWriter.

Listing 12-2 presents the source code to an application that demonstrates the reader approach to creating an object model and also writing this model.

Listing 12-2. Using a Reader to Create an Object Model and a Writer to Write This Model

```
import java.io.File;
import java.io.FileNotFoundException;
import java.io.FileReader;
import java.io.FileWriter;
import java.io.IOException;
import java.io.StringReader;

import javax.json.Json;
import javax.json.JsonArray;
import javax.json.JsonObject;
import javax.json.JsonReader;
import javax.json.JsonWriter;

import static java.lang.System.*;

public class JSONPDemo
{
   public static void main(String[] args)
      throws FileNotFoundException
```

415

```
{
    String json =
    "{" +
    "    \"firstName\": \"John\"," +
    "    \"lastName\": \"Doe\"," +
    "    \"age\": 42," +
    "    \"address\":" +
    "    {" +
    "        \"street\": \"400 Some Street\"," +
    "        \"city\": \"Beverly Hills\"," +
    "        \"state\": \"CA\"," +
    "        \"zipcode\": 90210" +
    "    }," +
    "    \"phoneNumbers\":" +
    "    [" +
    "        {" +
    "            \"type\": \"home\"," +
    "            \"number\": \"310 555-1234\"" +
    "        }," +
    "        {" +
    "            \"type\": \"fax\"," +
    "            \"number\": \"310 555-4567\"" +
    "        }" +
    "    ]" +
    "}";

    File file = new File("person.json");
    JsonReader reader =
        Json.createReader(file.exists() ?
                        new FileReader("person.json") :
                        new StringReader(json));
    JsonObject person = reader.readObject();
    out.printf("First name: %s%n",
            person.getString("firstName"));
    out.printf("Last name: %s%n",
            person.getString("lastName"));
```

```java
out.printf("Age: %d%n", person.getInt("age"));
out.println("Address");
out.println("-------");
JsonObject address = person.getJsonObject("address");
out.printf("   Street: %s%n",
          address.getString("street"));
out.printf("   City: %s%n",
          address.getString("city"));
out.printf("   State: %s%n",
          address.getString("state"));
out.printf("   Zipcode: %d%n",
          address.getInt("zipcode"));
out.println("Phone Numbers");
out.println("-------------");
JsonArray phoneNumbers =
   person.getJsonArray("phoneNumbers");
for (JsonObject phoneNumber:
     phoneNumbers.getValuesAs(JsonObject.class))
{
   out.printf("   Type: %s%n",
             phoneNumber.getString("type"));
   out.printf("   Number: %s%n",
             phoneNumber.getString("number"));
}
try (var fw = new FileWriter("person.json"))
{
   JsonWriter writer = Json.createWriter(fw);
   writer.writeObject(person);
   writer.close();
}
catch (IOException ioe)
{
   out.printf("I/O error: %s%n", ioe.getMessage());
}
   }
}
```

Listing 12-2 describes a Java application whose `main()` method first constructs a `JsonReader` object by invoking `Json`'s `JsonReader createReader(Reader reader)` method with either a `java.io.FileReader` object to read from a `person.json` file or a `java.io.StringReader` object to read from a string when this file doesn't exist. It then creates a `JsonObject` by invoking `JsonReader`'s `JsonObject readObject()` method.

`main()` subsequently invokes various methods to interrogate the object and output object details and then uses `JsonWriter` to write the object to a file named `person.json`.

Compile and run the application as previously shown, and you should observe the same output (and a `person.json` file should be created).

Working with the Streaming Model API

The streaming model API is similar to Java's StAX API for XML. It's a high-level API that provides a stream of events during JSON text parsing, which is represented by interface `JsonParser`. This interface provides `boolean hasNext()` and `Event next()` methods for parsing JSON text from an input source.

Listing 12-3 presents the source code to an application that demonstrates parsing JSON text.

Listing 12-3. Using the Streaming Model to Parse JSON Text

```
import java.io.StringReader;

import javax.json.Json;

import javax.json.stream.JsonParser;

import static javax.json.stream.JsonParser.Event;

import static java.lang.System.*;

public class JSONPDemo
{
   public static void main(String[] args)
   {
      String json =
      "{" +
      "   \"firstName\": \"John\"," +
      "   \"lastName\": \"Doe\"," +
```

```
"    \"age\": 42," +
"    \"address\":" +
"    {" +
"       \"street\": \"400 Some Street\"," +
"       \"city\": \"Beverly Hills\"," +
"       \"state\": \"CA\"," +
"       \"zipcode\": 90210" +
"    }," +
"    \"phoneNumbers\":" +
"    [" +
"       {" +
"          \"type\": \"home\"," +
"          \"number\": \"310 555-1234\"" +
"       }," +
"       {" +
"          \"type\": \"fax\"," +
"          \"number\": \"310 555-4567\"" +
"       }" +
"    ]" +
"}";
JsonParser parser =
   Json.createParser(new StringReader(json));
while (parser.hasNext())
{
   Event event = parser.next();
   if (event == Event.KEY_NAME)
      switch (parser.getString())
      {
         case "firstName":
            parser.next();
            out.printf("First name: %s%n",
                       parser.getString());
            break;
```

```
    case "lastName":
      parser.next();
      out.printf("Last name: %s%n",
                 parser.getString());
      break;

    case "age":
      parser.next();
      out.printf("Age: %d%n", parser.getInt());
      break;

    case "address":
      parser.next();
      out.println("Address");
      out.println("-------");
      break;

    case "street":
      parser.next();
      out.printf("   Street: %s%n",
                 parser.getString());
      break;

    case "city":
      parser.next();
      out.printf("   City: %s%n",
                 parser.getString());
      break;

    case "state":
      parser.next();
      out.printf("   State: %s%n",
                 parser.getString());
      break;
```

```
            case "zipcode":
                parser.next();
                out.printf("   Zipcode: %d%n",
                            parser.getInt());
                break;

            case "phoneNumbers":
                parser.next();
                out.println("Phone Numbers");
                out.println("-------------");
                break;

            case "type":
                parser.next();
                out.printf("   Type: %s%n",
                            parser.getString());
                parser.next();
                parser.next();
                out.printf("   Number: %s%n",
                            parser.getString());
                break;
            }
        }
    }
}
```

Listing 12-3 describes a Java application that constructs a parser by invoking Json's
JsonParser createParser(Reader reader) method with a StringReader object
describing string-based JSON text. It repeatedly invokes JsonParser's hasNext() and
next() methods to respectively test for another event (returning true for an event or
false when there are no more events) and return the event.

next() returns the next event as a JsonParser.Event enum constant. The only event
of interest is the name of an object's key, which is signified by Event.KEY_NAME. This
name is returned by invoking JsonParser's String getString() method. Once a match
is detected, parser.next(); is executed to skip past this name and get to the next event,
typically to return a key's associated value.

Compile and run the application as previously shown, and you should observe the same output.

The streaming model API also supports JSON content generation, which is represented by interface JsonGenerator. This interface provides write-prefixed methods for generating JSON text to an output destination.

Listing 12-4 presents the source code to an application that shows how to generate JSON text.

Listing 12-4. Using the Streaming Model to Generate JSON Text

```java
import java.io.FileWriter;
import java.io.IOException;

import javax.json.Json;

import javax.json.stream.JsonGenerator;

import static java.lang.System.*;

public class JSONPDemo
{
   public static void main(String[] args)
   {
      try (var fw = new FileWriter("person.json"))
      {
         JsonGenerator generator = Json.createGenerator(fw);
         generator.writeStartObject()
                     .write("firstName", "John")
                     .write("lastName", "Doe")
                     .write("age", 42)
                     .writeStartObject("address")
                        .write("street", "400 Some Street")
                        .write("city", "Beverly Hills")
                        .write("state", "CA")
                        .write("zipcode", 90210)
                     .writeEnd()
```

```
                    .writeStartArray("phoneNumbers")
                        .writeStartObject()
                            .write("type", "home")
                            .write("number", "310 555-1234")
                        .writeEnd()
                        .writeStartObject()
                            .write("type", "fax")
                            .write("number", "310 555-4567")
                        .writeEnd()
                    .writeEnd()
                .writeEnd();
        generator.close();
    }
    catch (IOException ioe)
    {
        out.printf("I/O error: %s%n", ioe.getMessage());
    }
    }
}
```

Listing 12-4 describes a Java application whose main() method constructs a generator by invoking Json's JsonGenerator createGenerator(Writer write) method with a FileWriter object describing a file-based destination (person.json). It invokes JsonGenerator's JsonGenerator writeStartObject() method to begin the process of writing the object.

Various write(), writeStartObject(), writeStartArray(), and writeEnd() method calls are chained to the initial writeStartObject() call. Following this sequence, JsonGenerator's close() method is called to close the generator.

Compile and run the application as previously shown, and you should observe no output (although a person.json file is generated) .

Working with JSON-P 1.1's Advanced Features

JSON-P 1.1 builds on JSON-P 1.0 mainly by supporting JSON Pointer, JSON Patch, and JSON Merge Patch; by including editing/transformation operations; and by updating the API to support Java SE 8.

Note   The previous demos work unchanged under JSON-P 1.1. Simply replace
`javax.json-1.0.4.jar` with `javax.json-api-1.1.3.jar;javax.json-1.1.3.jar` in the CLASSPATH.

JSON Pointer

JSON Pointer (http://tools.ietf.org/html/rfc6901) defines a Unicode-string-syntax for identifying a specific value in a JSON document. Essentially, the string contains a sequence of zero or more /-prefixed *reference tokens* (JSON document keys or values).

A JSON Pointer must conform to the following ABNF (http://en.wikipedia.org/wiki/Augmented_Backus-Naur_form) syntax, or the pointer isn't valid:

```
json-pointer    = *( "/" reference-token )
reference-token = *( unescaped / escaped )
unescaped       = %x00-2E / %x30-7D / %x7F-10FFFF
                  ; %x2F ('/') and %x7E ('~') are excluded from 'unescaped'
escaped         = "~" ( "0" / "1" )
                  ; representing '~' and '/', respectively
```

The characters ~ (0x7E) and / (0x2F) have special meanings in JSON Pointer. Therefore, ~ needs to be encoded as ~0 and / needs to be encoded as ~1 when these characters appear in a reference token.

Consider the following JSON document:

```
{
   "name": "Duke",
   "hobbies":
   [
      "reading",
      "surfing",
      "eating pizza"
   ]
}
```

The following list presents four example JSON Pointers for use with this document and (in round brackets) the values of these pointers:

- `""` (the whole document)

- `"/name"` (`"Duke"`)

- `"/hobbies"` (`["reading","surfing","eating pizza"]`)

- `"/hobbies/0"` (`"reading"`)

Array entries are referenced via zero-based digit sequences, where `/0` references the first entry, `/1` references the second entry, and so on.

JSON-P represents a JSON Pointer via the `JsonPointer` interface. An instance of a class that implements this interface is obtained by executing `Json`'s `JsonPointer createPointer(String jsonPointer)` static method.

Assuming that the previous JSON document has been created in memory (and assigned to `duke`), the following code fragment creates a JSON Pointer to the name reference token:

```
JsonPointer pointer = Json.createPointer("/name");
```

After a `JsonPointer` instance has been returned, invoking its `JsonValue getValue(JsonStructure target)` method returns the value at the referenced location in the specified `target`:

```
System.out.printf("%s%n%n",
                  pointer.getValue(duke)); // output: "Duke"
```

`JsonPointer` can be used to add items to, remove items from, and replace items in a JSON document. This interface provides the following methods for this purpose:

- `<T extends JsonStructure> T add(T target, JsonValue value)`

- `<T extends JsonStructure> T remove(T target)`

- `<T extends JsonStructure> T replace(T target, JsonValue value)`

Listing 12-5 presents the source code to an application that demonstrates creating `JsonPointers` along with all of the previous `JsonPointer` methods.

Listing 12-5. Demonstrating JSON Pointer

```java
import javax.json.Json;
import javax.json.JsonArray;
import javax.json.JsonObject;
import javax.json.JsonPointer;

import static java.lang.System.*;

/*
   JsonPointer Demonstration:

   1) Create the following JSON document:

   {
      "firstName": "John",
      "lastName": "Doe",
      "age": 42,
      "address":
      {
         "streetAddress": "400 Some Street",
         "city": "Beverly Hills",
         "state": "CA",
         "zipcode": 90210
      },
      "phoneNumbers":
      [
         {
            "type": "home",
            "number": "310 555-1234"
         },
         {
            "type": "fax",
            "number": "310 555-4567"
         }
      ]
   }
```

2) Use JsonPointer to convert the previous JSON document
   to the following JSON document:

```
{
    "firstName": "John",
    "lastName": "Doe",
    "age": 30,
    "address":
    {
        "streetAddress": "400 Some Street",
        "city": "Beverly Hills",
        "state": "CA",
        "zipcode": 90210
    },
    "phoneNumbers":
    [
        {
            "type": "fax",
            "number": "310 555-4567"
        },
        {
            "type": "cell",
            "number": "123 456-7890"
        }
    ]
}
*/

public class JSONPDemo
{
    public static void main(String[] args)
    {
        JsonObject person;
        person =
            Json.createObjectBuilder()
                .add("firstName", "John")
                .add("lastName", "Doe")
```

427

```
        .add("age", 42)
        .add("address", Json.createObjectBuilder()
                            .add("street",
                                "400 Some Street")
                            .add("city",
                                "Beverly Hills")
                            .add("state", "CA")
                            .add("zipcode", 90210))
    .add("phoneNumbers",
        Json.createArrayBuilder()
            .add(Json.createObjectBuilder()
                        .add("type", "home")
                        .add("number",
                            "310 555-1234"))
            .add(Json.createObjectBuilder()
                        .add("type", "fax")
                        .add("number",
                            "310 555-4567")))
    .build();
JsonPointer pointer = Json.createPointer("/age");
person = pointer.replace(person,
                        Json.createValue(30));
pointer = Json.createPointer("/phoneNumbers/-");
person =
    pointer.add(person,
            Json.createObjectBuilder()
                    .add("type", "cell")
                    .add("number",
                        "123 456-7890").build());
pointer = Json.createPointer("/phoneNumbers/0");
person = pointer.remove(person);
out.printf("First name: %s%n",
        person.getString("firstName"));
out.printf("Last name: %s%n",
        person.getString("lastName"));
```

```java
out.printf("Age: %d%n", person.getInt("age"));
out.println("Address");
out.println("-------");
JsonObject address = person.getJsonObject("address");
out.printf("   Street: %s%n",
           address.getString("street"));
out.printf("   City: %s%n",
           address.getString("city"));
out.printf("   State: %s%n",
           address.getString("state"));
out.printf("   Zipcode: %d%n",
           address.getInt("zipcode"));
out.println("Phone Numbers");
out.println("-------------");
JsonArray phoneNumbers =
    person.getJsonArray("phoneNumbers");
for (JsonObject phoneNumber:
      phoneNumbers.getValuesAs(JsonObject.class))
{
   out.printf("   Type: %s%n",
              phoneNumber.getString("type"));
   out.printf("   Number: %s%n",
              phoneNumber.getString("number"));
}
  }
}
```

Listing 12-5 includes expression Json.createValue(30) for conveniently converting an int to a JsonNumber, which is the appropriate JsonValue subtype to be passed as the second argument to JsonPointer's replace() method. The JsonNumber createValue(int value) method is one of six overloaded static methods added in JSON-P 1.1 for conveniently converting doubles, ints, longs, java.lang.Strings, java.math.BigDecimals, and java.math.BigIntegers to their JSON-P equivalents.

Compile Listing 12-5 as follows:

```
javac -cp javax.json-api-1.1.3.jar;javax.json-1.1.3.jar JSONPDemo.java
```

Run the resulting application as follows:

```
java -cp javax.json-api-1.1.3.jar;javax.json-1.1.3.jar;. JSONPDemo
```

You should observe the following output:

```
First name: John
Last name: Doe
Age: 30
Address
-------
    Street: 400 Some Street
    City: Beverly Hills
    State: CA
    Zipcode: 90210
Phone Numbers
-------------
    Type: fax
    Number: 310 555-4567
    Type: cell
    Number: 123 456-7890
```

The Json class provides a pair of static methods for encoding (escaping) a JSON pointer string and for decoding (unescaping) an encoded pointer string:

- String encodePointer(String pointer)

- String decodePointer(String encPointer)

encodePointer() encodes ~ as ~0 and / as ~1. decodePointer() performs the opposite conversion. Listing 12-6 demonstrates both methods.

Listing 12-6. Demonstrating JSON Pointer Encoding and Decoding

```java
import javax.json.Json;

import static java.lang.System.*;

public class JSONPDemo
{
   public static void main(String[] args)
   {
      if (args.length != 1)
      {
         err.println("usage: java JSONPDemo pointer");
         return;
      }
      String encPointer = Json.encodePointer(args[0]);
      out.printf("Encoded pointer: %s%n\n", encPointer);
      out.printf("Decoded pointer: %s%n\n",
                 Json.decodePointer(encPointer));
   }
}
```

Compile Listing 12-6 and then run the application as follows:

```
java -cp javax.json-1.1.3.jar;javax.json-api-1.1.3.jar;. JSONPDemo /a/b/c~d
```

You should observe the following output:

```
Encoded pointer: ~1a~1b~1c~0d
```

```
Decoded pointer: /a/b/c~d
```

JSON Patch

JSON Patch (http://tools.ietf.org/html/rfc6902) defines a JSON document structure for expressing a sequence of operations to apply to a target JSON document. It's often used with *HTTP PATCH* (http://en.wikipedia.org/wiki/Patch_verb), an HTTP request method for making partial changes to an existing resource.

The JSON Patch document consists of an array of objects where each object denotes a single operation. Consider the following example, for use with JSON document `{"a": {"b": {"c": "val", "d": "val", "e": "val"}}}`:

```
[
  { "op": "test", "path": "/a/b/c", "value": "foo" },
  { "op": "remove", "path": "/a/b/c" },
  { "op": "add", "path": "/a/b/c",
    "value": [ "foo", "bar" ] },
  { "op": "replace", "path": "/a/b/c", "value": 42 },
  { "op": "move", "from": "/a/b/c", "path": "/a/b/d" },
  { "op": "copy", "from": "/a/b/d", "path": "/a/b/e" }
]
```

Each object has an op field that identifies the operation to be performed. Each object also has a path field, which is a JSON Pointer that references a location in the target document.

There are six operations: test, remove, add, replace, move, and copy:

- test: Test that the value at the path location is equal to the value assigned to the value field.

- remove: Remove the value at the path location.

- add: Add a new element to an array or a new field to an object, or replace an existing object field's value.

- replace: Replace the value at the path location with a new value.

- move: Remove the value at the from location and add it to the path location.

- copy: Copy the value at the from location to the path location.

JSON-P's JsonPatch interface represents a JSON Patch. Obtain an instance of a class that implements this interface by executing Json's JsonPatch createPatch(JsonArray patchArray) static method:

```
JsonArray patchops = ...  ;
JsonPatch patch = Json.createPatch(patchops);
```

After obtaining a JsonPatch instance, invoke its <T extends JsonStructure> T apply(t target) generic method to apply the specified patch operations to target:

```
JsonArray result = jsonpatch.apply(target);
```

Listing 12-7 presents the source code to an application that demonstrates creating a JsonPatch object and applying its operations to a JsonObject, to make the same document changes as demonstrated in Listing 12-5.

Listing 12-7. Demonstrating JSON Patch

```
import java.io.StringReader;

import javax.json.Json;
import javax.json.JsonArray;
import javax.json.JsonObject;

import static java.lang.System.*;

/*
   JsonPatch Demonstration:

   1) Create the following JSON document:

   {
      "firstName": "John",
      "lastName": "Doe",
      "age": 42,
      "address":
      {
         "streetAddress": "400 Some Street",
         "city": "Beverly Hills",
         "state": "CA",
         "zipcode": 90210
      },
```

```
    "phoneNumbers":
    [
        {
            "type": "home",
            "number": "310 555-1234"
        },
        {
            "type": "fax",
            "number": "310 555-4567"
        }
    ]
}
```

2) Use JsonPatch to convert the previous JSON document
   to the following JSON document:

```
{
    "firstName": "John",
    "lastName": "Doe",
    "age": 30,
    "address":
    {
        "streetAddress": "400 Some Street",
        "city": "Beverly Hills",
        "state": "CA",
        "zipcode": 90210
    },
    "phoneNumbers":
    [
        {
            "type": "fax",
            "number": "310 555-4567"
        },
        {
            "type": "cell",
            "number": "123 456-7890"
        }
```

```
    ]
  }
*/

public class JSONPDemo
{
    public static void main(String[] args)
    {
        JsonObject person;
        person =
            Json.createObjectBuilder()
                .add("firstName", "John")
                .add("lastName", "Doe")
                .add("age", 42)
                .add("address", Json.createObjectBuilder()
                                    .add("street",
                                        "400 Some Street")
                                    .add("city",
                                        "Beverly Hills")
                                    .add("state", "CA")
                                    .add("zipcode", 90210))
                .add("phoneNumbers",
                    Json.createArrayBuilder()
                        .add(Json.createObjectBuilder()
                                .add("type", "home")
                                .add("number",
                                    "310 555-1234"))
                        .add(Json.createObjectBuilder()
                                .add("type", "fax")
                                .add("number",
                                    "310 555-4567")))
                .build();
        String patch =
        "[" +
        "{" +
        "\"op\": \"replace\"," +
```

```
          "\"path\": \"/age\"," +
          "\"value\": 30" +
          "}," +
          "{" +
          "\"op\": \"add\"," +
          "\"path\": \"/phoneNumbers/-\"," +
          "\"value\": " +
          "{" +
          "\"type\": \"cell\"," +
          "\"number\": \"123 456-7890\"" +
          "}" +
          "}," +
          "{" +
          "\"op\": \"remove\"," +
          "\"path\": \"/phoneNumbers/0\"" +
          "}" +
          "]";
JsonArray patchArray =
    Json.createReader(new StringReader(patch))
        .readArray();
person = Json.createPatch(patchArray).apply(person);
out.printf("First name: %s%n",
            person.getString("firstName"));
out.printf("Last name: %s%n",
            person.getString("lastName"));
out.printf("Age: %d%n", person.getInt("age"));
out.println("Address");
out.println("-------");
JsonObject address = person.getJsonObject("address");
out.printf("   Street: %s%n",
            address.getString("street"));
out.printf("   City: %s%n",
            address.getString("city"));
out.printf("   State: %s%n",
            address.getString("state"));
```

```
    out.printf("   Zipcode: %d%n",
            address.getInt("zipcode"));
    out.println("Phone Numbers");
    out.println("-------------");
    JsonArray phoneNumbers =
        person.getJsonArray("phoneNumbers");
    for (JsonObject phoneNumber:
        phoneNumbers.getValuesAs(JsonObject.class))
    {
        out.printf("   Type: %s%n",
                phoneNumber.getString("type"));
        out.printf("   Number: %s%n",
                phoneNumber.getString("number"));
    }
  }
}
```

Compile Listing 12-7 and run the application. You should observe the following output:

```
First name: John
Last name: Doe
Age: 30
Address
-------
    Street: 400 Some Street
    City: Beverly Hills
    State: CA
    Zipcode: 90210
Phone Numbers
-------------
    Type: fax
    Number: 310 555-4567
    Type: cell
    Number: 123 456-7890
```

It can be tedious to specify all patch operations literally, which is why JSON-P also provides the JsonPatchBuilder interface for constructing a JSON Patch by adding JSON Patch operations incrementally. An instance of a class that implements this interface is obtained by executing either of Json's createPatchBuilder() methods. The builder's add(), remove(), and other methods are called to add patch operations. The build() method returns the resulting JsonPatch:

```
JsonPatchBuilder builder = Json.createPatchBuilder();
JsonPatch patch = builder.replace("/a/b/c", 42)
                         .copy("/a/b/e", "/a/b/d")
                         .build();
```

JSON-P provides a third way to obtain a JSON Patch. Json's JsonPatch createDiff(JsonStructure source, JsonStructure target) static method generates a JSON Patch whose operations describe how to convert from source to target. Note that source and target must have the same types. In other words, they must both be JsonArrays or JsonObjects. The createDiff() method is demonstrated in Listing 12-8.

Listing 12-8. Creating a JSON Patch Based on Differences Between a Source and a Target

```
import javax.json.Json;
import javax.json.JsonObject;

import static java.lang.System.*;

public class JSONPDemo
{
   public static void main(String[] args)
   {
      JsonObject person1;
      person1 =
         Json.createObjectBuilder()
             .add("firstName", "John")
             .add("lastName", "Doe")
             .add("age", 42)
```

```
        .add("address", Json.createObjectBuilder()
                        .add("street",
                                "400 Some Street")
                        .add("city",
                                "Beverly Hills")
                        .add("state", "CA")
                        .add("zipcode", 90210))
        .add("phoneNumbers",
            Json.createArrayBuilder()
                .add(Json.createObjectBuilder()
                        .add("type", "home")
                        .add("number",
                            "310 555-1234"))
                .add(Json.createObjectBuilder()
                        .add("type", "fax")
                        .add("number",
                            "310 555-4567")))
        .build();
JsonObject person2;
person2 =
    Json.createObjectBuilder()
        .add("firstName", "John")
        .add("lastName", "Doe")
        .add("age", 30)
        .add("address", Json.createObjectBuilder()
                        .add("street",
                            "400 Some Street")
                        .add("city",
                            "Beverly Hills")
                        .add("state", "CA")
                        .add("zipcode", 90210))
```

```
            .add("phoneNumbers",
                Json.createArrayBuilder()
                    .add(Json.createObjectBuilder()
                            .add("type", "fax")
                            .add("number",
                                "310 555-4567"))
                    .add(Json.createObjectBuilder()
                            .add("type", "cell")
                            .add("number",
                                "123 456-7890")))
            .build();
        out.println(Json.createDiff(person1, person2));
    }
}
```

Compile Listing 12-8 and run the application. You should observe the following output:

```
[{"op":"replace","path":"/age","value":30},{"op":"remove","path":"/phone
Numbers/0"},{"op":"add","path":"/phoneNumbers/1","value":{"type":"cell",
"number":"123 456-7890"}}]
```

JSON Merge Patch

JSON Merge Patch (http://tools.ietf.org/html/rfc7386) defines a JSON document structure for expressing a sequence of changes to be made to a target JSON document via a syntax that closely mimics that document. Recipients of a JSON Merge Patch document determine the exact set of changes being requested by comparing the content of the provided patch against the current content of the target document. If the patch contains members that don't appear in the target, those members are added. If the target does contain the member, the value is replaced. Null values in the merge patch are given special meaning to indicate the removal of existing values in the target. As with JSON Patch, JSON Merge Patch is often used with HTTP PATCH (http://en.wikipedia.org/wiki/Patch_verb).

For example, consider the following JSON document:

```
{
    "a": "b",
    "c":
    {
        "d": "e",
        "f": "g"
    }
}
```

The following JSON Merge Patch document specifies a change to a's value and the removal of f:

```
{
    "a":"z",
    "c":
    {
        "f": null
    }
}
```

JSON-P's JsonMergePatch interface represents a JSON Merge Patch. Obtain an instance of a class that implements this interface by executing Json's JsonMergePatch createMergePatch(JsonValue patchArray) static method:

```
JsonValue patch = ...;
JsonMergePatch mergePatch = Json.createMergePatch(patch) ;
```

After obtaining a JsonMergePatch instance, invoke its JsonValue apply(JsonValue target) method to apply the specified patch to target:

```
JsonValue result = mergePatch.apply(target);
```

Listing 12-9 presents the source code to an application that demonstrates creating a JsonMergePatch object and applying it to a JsonObject, to make the same document changes as demonstrated in Listing 12-5.

Listing 12-9. Demonstrating JSON Merge Patch

```java
import javax.json.Json;
import javax.json.JsonArray;
import javax.json.JsonMergePatch;
import javax.json.JsonObject;

import static java.lang.System.*;

public class JSONPDemo
{
   public static void main(String[] args)
   {
      JsonObject person;
      person =
         Json.createObjectBuilder()
             .add("firstName", "John")
             .add("lastName", "Doe")
             .add("age", 42)
             .add("address", Json.createObjectBuilder()
                                  .add("street",
                                       "400 Some Street")
                                  .add("city",
                                       "Beverly Hills")
                                  .add("state", "CA")
                                  .add("zipcode", 90210))
             .add("phoneNumbers",
                 Json.createArrayBuilder()
                     .add(Json.createObjectBuilder()
                              .add("type", "home")
                              .add("number",
                                   "310 555-1234"))
                     .add(Json.createObjectBuilder()
                              .add("type", "fax")
                              .add("number",
                                   "310 555-4567")))
             .build();
```

```java
JsonObject patch =
    Json.createObjectBuilder()
        .add("age", 30)
        .add("phoneNumbers",
             Json.createArrayBuilder()
                 .add(Json.createObjectBuilder()
                          .add("type", "fax")
                          .add("number",
                               "310 555-4567"))
                     .add(Json.createObjectBuilder()
                              .add("type", "cell")
                              .add("number",
                                   "123 456-7890")))
              .build();
JsonMergePatch mergePatch =
    Json.createMergePatch(patch);
person = (JsonObject) mergePatch.apply(person);
out.printf("First name: %s%n",
           person.getString("firstName"));
out.printf("Last name: %s%n",
           person.getString("lastName"));
out.printf("Age: %d%n", person.getInt("age"));
out.println("Address");
out.println("-------");
JsonObject address = person.getJsonObject("address");
out.printf("   Street: %s%n",
           address.getString("street"));
out.printf("   City: %s%n",
           address.getString("city"));
out.printf("   State: %s%n",
           address.getString("state"));
out.printf("   Zipcode: %d%n",
           address.getInt("zipcode"));
out.println("Phone Numbers");
out.println("-------------");
```

```
    JsonArray phoneNumbers =
        person.getJsonArray("phoneNumbers");
    for (JsonObject phoneNumber:
            phoneNumbers.getValuesAs(JsonObject.class))
    {
        out.printf("   Type: %s%n",
                    phoneNumber.getString("type"));
        out.printf("   Number: %s%n",
                    phoneNumber.getString("number"));
    }
  }
}
```

Listing 12-9 reveals that an array cannot be manipulated by merge patches. To add an element to an array, or to mutate any of its elements, the entire resulting array must be specified.

It's necessary to cast mergePatch.apply(person) to JsonObject in order to avoid an incompatible-type error: JsonValue cannot be converted to JsonObject.

Compile Listing 12-9 and run the application. You should observe the following output:

```
First name: John
Last name: Doe
Age: 30
Address
-------
    Street: 400 Some Street
    City: Beverly Hills
    State: CA
    Zipcode: 90210
Phone Numbers
-------------
    Type: fax
    Number: 310 555-4567
    Type: cell
    Number: 123 456-7890
```

JSON-P provides another way to obtain a JSON Merge Patch. Json's `JsonMergePatch`
`createMergeDiff(JsonValue source, JsonValue target)` static method generates
a JSON Merge Patch from the source and the target, which yields the target when
applied to the source–source and target don't have to have the same `JsonValue`
subtype. The `createMergeDiff()` method is demonstrated in Listing 12-10.

Listing 12-10. Creating a JSON Merge Patch Based on Differences Between a
Source and a Target

```
import javax.json.Json;
import javax.json.JsonObject;

import static java.lang.System.*;

public class JSONPDemo
{
   public static void main(String[] args)
   {
      JsonObject person1;
      person1 =
         Json.createObjectBuilder()
            .add("firstName", "John")
            .add("lastName", "Doe")
            .add("age", 42)
            .add("address", Json.createObjectBuilder()
                               .add("street",
                                    "400 Some Street")
                               .add("city",
                                    "Beverly Hills")
                               .add("state", "CA")
                               .add("zipcode", 90210))
            .add("phoneNumbers",
                 Json.createArrayBuilder()
                     .add(Json.createObjectBuilder()
                               .add("type", "home")
                               .add("number",
                                    "310 555-1234"))
```

```
                    .add(Json.createObjectBuilder()
                            .add("type", "fax")
                            .add("number",
                                "310 555-4567")))
        .build();
JsonObject person2;
person2 =
    Json.createObjectBuilder()
        .add("firstName", "John")
        .add("lastName", "Doe")
        .add("age", 30)
        .add("address", Json.createObjectBuilder()
                            .add("street",
                                "400 Some Street")
                            .add("city",
                                "Beverly Hills")
                            .add("state", "CA")
                            .add("zipcode", 90210))
        .add("phoneNumbers",
            Json.createArrayBuilder()
                .add(Json.createObjectBuilder()
                        .add("type", "fax")
                        .add("number",
                            "310 555-4567"))
                .add(Json.createObjectBuilder()
                        .add("type", "cell")
                        .add("number",
                            "123 456-7890")))
        .build();
    out.println(Json.createMergeDiff(person1, person2)
                .toJsonValue());
    }
}
```

It's necessary to invoke `toJsonValue()` on the `JsonMergePatch` returned from `createMergeDiff()` in order to see a JSON document as the output.

Compile Listing 12-10 and run the application. You should observe the following output:

```
{"age":30,"phoneNumbers":[{"type":"fax","number":"310 555-4567"},{"type":
"cell","number":"123 456-7890"}]}
```

Editing/Transformation Operations

The JSON object model supports immutable JSON objects and arrays, which makes these entities thread-safe. Because you cannot modify them, you would manually copy each of the properties of the JSON object/array into a `JsonObjectBuilder` or `JsonArrayBuilder` and then modify the entity, which is a rather tedious task. Thankfully, JSON-P 1.1 alleviates the tedium by adding editing/transformation operations to `JsonArrayBuilder` and `JsonObjectBuilder`.

`JsonArrayBuilder` has received several `add(int index, ...)` methods for adding a value between array elements, several `set(int index, ...)` methods for updating an existing element, and a `remove()` method for removing an element. `JsonObjectBuilder` has received a `remove()` method for removing a name/value pair. Listing 12-11 presents the source code to an application that demonstrates some of these methods.

Listing 12-11. Demonstrating Assorted Editing/Transformation Operations

```java
import java.util.ArrayList;
import java.util.Arrays;
import java.util.HashMap;
import java.util.List;
import java.util.Map;

import javax.json.Json;
import javax.json.JsonObject;

import static java.lang.System.*;
```

```java
public class JSONPDemo
{
   public static void main(String[] args)
   {
      List<String> planets =
         Arrays.asList("Mercury", "Venus", "Terra", "Mars",
                       "Jupiter", "Saturn", "Uranus",
                       "Pluto");
      out.println(Json.createArrayBuilder(planets)
                      .remove(7)
                      .set(2, "Earth")
                      .add("Neptune")
                      .build());

      Map<String, Object> employees = new HashMap<>();
      employees.put("John Doe", 42);
      employees.put("Jill Smith", 38);
      employees.put("Bonnie Barnes", 26);
      JsonObject employees_ =
         Json.createObjectBuilder(employees)
            .remove("Jill Smith")
            .build();
      out.println(employees_);
   }
}
```

Listing 12-11 first demonstrates editing/transformation in an array builder context.
A list of planet names is constructed, and this list is passed to Json's JsonArrayBuilder
createArrayBuilder(Collection<?> collection) static method. Various editing/
transformation method calls are chained to createArrayBuilder() to remove Pluto
(which is no longer officially a planet), change Terra to Earth, and add Neptune. The
build() call returns a JsonArray, which is printed to standard output.

Listing 12-11 next demonstrates editing/transformation in an object builder context.
A map of employee names and ages is constructed, and this map is passed to Json's
JsonObjectBuilder createObjectBuilder(Map<String, Object> map) static method.

A remove() method call is chained to createObjectBuilder() to remove Jill Smith. The build() call returns a JsonObject, which is printed to standard output.

Compile Listing 12-11 and run the application. You should observe the following output:

```
["Mercury","Venus","Earth","Mars","Jupiter","Saturn","Uranus","Neptune"]
{"John Doe":42,"Bonnie Barnes":26}
```

Java SE 8 Support

Queries on a JSON object model are currently possible via Java SE 8's stream operations and lambda expressions. To make them truly useful and convenient, JSON-P 1.1 introduced a JsonCollectors class whose static collector methods return JSONObjects or JsonArrays instead of Maps or Lists. For example, consider the following collector method:

```
Collector<JsonValue,JsonObjectBuilder,JsonObject>
   toJsonObject(Function<jsonValue,String> keyMapper,
               Function<JsonValue,JsonValue> valueMapper)
```

This toJsonObject() collector method constructs a java.util.stream.Collector that accumulates the input JsonValue elements into a JsonObject. The name/value pairs of the JsonObject are computed by applying the provided keyMapper and valueMapper mapping functions.

Listing 12-12 presents the source code to an application that demonstrates this collector method.

Listing 12-12. Demonstrating a JSON-P Collector

```
import javax.json.Json;
import javax.json.JsonArray;
import javax.json.JsonObject;

import javax.json.stream.JsonCollectors;

import static java.lang.System.*;
```

```java
public class JSONPDemo
{
   public static void main(String[] args)
   {
      JsonArray employees;
      employees = Json.createArrayBuilder()
                     .add(Json.createObjectBuilder()
                             .add("name", "John")
                             .add("age", 42))
                     .add(Json.createObjectBuilder()
                             .add("name", "Joan")
                             .add("age", 28))
                     .add(Json.createObjectBuilder()
                             .add("name", "Trevor")
                             .add("age", 35))
                     .add(Json.createObjectBuilder()
                             .add("name", "Sally")
                             .add("age", 49))
                     .add(Json.createObjectBuilder()
                             .add("name", "Frank")
                             .add("age", 26))
                     .build();
      out.println(employees);
      out.println();
      JsonObject result =
      employees.getValuesAs(JsonObject.class)
              .stream()
              .filter(x -> x.getInt("age") > 40)
              .collect(JsonCollectors.
                      toJsonObject(x ->
                              x.asJsonObject()
                                .getString("name"),
                              x ->
                              x.asJsonObject()
                                .get("age")));
```

```
      out.println(result);
   }
}
```

Listing 12-12's main() method first creates a JSON array of employee objects where each object consists of a name and an age. After outputting the array, it returns a list view of the array, obtains a stream with the list view as the source, installs (on the stream) a filter that accepts only those entries whose age exceeds 40, and installs (on the stream) a collector that accumulates results into a JSON object. The results are accumulated and output.

asJsonObject() is a JsonValue method that returns the invoking JsonValue as a JsonObject. Although it's possible to invoke getString("name") on the JsonObject, it's not possible to invoke getInt("age") because getInt() returns a primitive int value instead of an Integer object. For this reason, the code invokes JsonObject's inherited get() method from the Map ancestor type.

Note   JsonValue also conveniently provides an asJsonArray() method that returns the invoking JsonValue as a JsonArray.

Compile Listing 12-12 and run the application. You should observe the following output:

```
[{"name":"John","age":42},{"name":"Joan","age":28},{"name":"Trevor",
"age":35},{"name":"Sally","age":49},{"name":"Frank","age":26}]
```

```
{"John":42,"Sally":49}
```

Listing 12-12 reveals JsonArray's <T extends JsonValue> List<T> getValuesAs(Class<T> clazz) method, which returns a list view of the specified type for the array. This method has been present since JSON-P 1.0. However, JSON-P 1.1 introduced the more functional <T,K extends JsonValue> List<T> getValuesAs(Function<K,T> func) default method, which can accept a lambda or method reference argument—Java SE 8 introduced default methods.

JSON-P 1.1's JsonParser class has been upgraded to support Java SE 8 by including the Stream<JsonValue> getArrayStream() and Stream<Map.Entry<String,JsonValue>> getObjectStream() default methods. When called, getArrayStream() returns a stream of JsonArray elements, and getObjectStream() returns a stream of JsonObject name/value pairs.

The combination of JsonParser's parsing methods along with getArrayStream() or getObjectStream() offers an efficient alternative to attempting to read a very large JSON document into memory (which might not fit). For example, suppose a public library contains a JSON document that itemizes all of its books in terms of ISBN, title, and state (available or loaned). Listing 12-13 presents a sample document.

Listing 12-13. A Sample Library JSON Document

```
[
   {
      "isbn": "1234567890",
      "title": "Sample Book 1",
      "state": "avail"
   },
   {
      "isbn": "2342340324",
      "title": "Sample Book 2",
      "state": "loaned"
   },
   {
      "isbn": "2342069340",
      "title": "Sample Book 3",
      "state": "avail"
   },
   {
      "isbn": "5940045033",
      "title": "Sample Book 4",
      "state": "avail"
   },
   {
      "isbn": "2394094699",
      "title": "Sample Book 5",
      "state": "loaned"
   },
```

```
{
    "isbn": "3566433454",
    "title": "Sample Book 6",
    "state": "avail"
},
{
    "isbn": "6990349039",
    "title": "Sample Book 7",
    "state": "avail"
},
{
    "isbn": "5695695690",
    "title": "Sample Book 8",
    "state": "avail"
}
]
```

Suppose it's necessary to print the first five books whose state is avail(able). The entire document, which could grow very large, doesn't need to be read into memory. It's only necessary to read book objects one by one until the first five available books have been printed. Listing 12-14 presents the source code to an application that uses JsonParser along with getArrayStream() and various stream operations to accomplish this task.

Listing 12-14. Efficiently Processing a Potentially Large JSON Document

```java
import java.io.FileReader;
import java.io.FileNotFoundException;

import javax.json.Json;

import javax.json.stream.JsonParser;

import static java.lang.System.*;
```

```java
public class JSONPDemo
{
   public static void main(String[] args)
      throws FileNotFoundException
   {
      if (args.length != 1)
      {
         err.println("usage: java JSONPDemo filespec");
         return;
      }
      JsonParser parser =
         Json.createParser(new FileReader(args[0]));
      while (parser.hasNext())
         if (parser.next() == JsonParser.Event.START_ARRAY)
         {
            parser.getArrayStream()
                  // convert to Stream<JsonObject>
                  .map(v -> v.asJsonObject())
                  .filter(obj -> obj.getString("state")
                                    .equals("avail"))
                  .limit(5)
                  .forEach(obj ->
                           out.printf("ISBN: %s, " +
                                      "TITLE: %s%n%n",
                                      obj.getString("isbn"),
                                      obj.getString("title")));

            // skip the rest of the JsonArray

            parser.skipArray();
         }
   }
}
```

JsonParser offers void skipArray() and void skipObject() methods that skip tokens and advance the parser to END_ARRAY or END_OBJECT, respectively.

Compile Listing 12-14 and run the application. You should observe the following output:

```
ISBN: 1234567890, TITLE: Sample Book 1

ISBN: 2342069340, TITLE: Sample Book 3

ISBN: 5940045033, TITLE: Sample Book 4

ISBN: 3566433454, TITLE: Sample Book 6

ISBN: 6990349039, TITLE: Sample Book 7
```

EXERCISES

The following exercises are designed to test your understanding of Chapter 12's content:

1. Define JSON-P.

2. Describe JSON-P 1.0's package structure.

3. Identify the types for creating `JsonArray` and `JsonObject` models.

4. Which type is the superinterface of interface types that represent immutable JSON values?

5. In what ways does JSON-P 1.1 differ from JSON-P 1.0?

6. True or false: JSON-P 1.0's streaming model is more flexible than its object model.

7. How do you construct a `JsonObject` model?

8. What types does the streaming model provide to read and write JSON content?

9. Describe JSON Merge Patch.

10. Identify the editing/transformation operations that have been added to `JsonArrayBuilder` and `JsonObjectBuilder`.

11. True or false: JSON-P 1.1 introduced a `JsonCollectors` class whose `static` collector methods return `JSONObjects` or `JsonArrays` instead of `Maps` or `Lists`.

12. Write a JSONPDemo application that takes two command-line arguments: the name of a JSON document file and a JSON Pointer. The application should read the file into a JsonObject model (assume that every JSON document file defines an object). The application should then create a JsonPointer for the JSON Pointer argument and apply the JsonPointer instance to the JsonObject, outputting the result. Hint: Refer to the "JSON Pointer" section for an example JSON document and sample JSON Pointers that access different document members.

Summary

JSON Processing (JSON-P) is a Java API for processing (i.e., parsing, generating, querying, and transforming) JSON content.

JSON-P 1.0 processes JSON content via an object model or a streaming model. The object model lets JSON-P build a tree of objects for JSON text via API classes similarly to Java's DOM API for XML. The streaming model lets JSON-P produce and consume JSON text similarly to Java's StAX API for XML.

JSON-P 1.0 consists of 25 types located in package javax.json, along with the support packages javax.json.spi and javax.json.stream. The javax.json package mainly contains types that support the object model, the javax.json.spi package contains a single type that describes a service provider for JSON processing objects, and the javax.json.stream package contains types that support the streaming model.

JSON-P 1.1 also supports JSON Pointer, JSON Patch, and JSON Merge Patch. Additionally, the new version introduces editing/transformation operations to JSON array and object builders and updates the API to better support Java SE 8 stream operations (including JSON-specific collectors).

JSON-P 1.1 consists of the same packages as JSON-P 1.0 but increases the number of types to 31.

JSON Pointer defines a Unicode-string-syntax for identifying a specific value in a JSON document. JSON Patch defines a JSON document structure for expressing a sequence of operations to apply to another JSON document (and also makes use of JSON Pointer). JSON Merge Patch is similar to JSON Patch in that it's also used to change another JSON document's structure. However, the syntax of the JSON Merge Patch JSON document more closely mimics the syntax of the JSON document that's being changed.

Several editing/transformation operations have been introduced to `JsonArrayBuilder` and `JsonObjectBuilder`. `JsonArrayBuilder` has received several `add(int index, ...)` methods for adding a value between array elements, several `set(int index, ...)` methods for updating an existing element, and a `remove()` method for removing an element. `JsonObjectBuilder` has received a `remove()` method for removing a name/value pair.

Queries on a JSON object model are currently possible via Java SE 8's stream operations and lambda expressions. To make them truly useful and convenient, JSON-P 1.1 introduced a `JsonCollectors` class whose `static` collector methods return `JSONObjects` or `JsonArrays` instead of `Maps` or `Lists`.

Appendix A presents the answers to each chapter's exercises.

PART III

Appendixes

APPENDIX A

Answers to Exercises

Each of Chapters 1 through 12 closes with an "Exercises" section that tests your understanding of the chapter's material. The answers to those exercises are presented in this appendix.

Chapter 1: Introducing XML

1. XML (eXtensible Markup Language) is a meta-language for defining vocabularies (custom markup languages), which is the key to XML's importance and popularity.

2. The answer is true: XML and HTML are descendants of SGML.

3. XML provides the XML declaration, elements and attributes, character references and CDATA sections, namespaces, and comments and processing-instruction language features for use in defining custom markup languages.

4. The XML declaration is special markup that informs an XML parser that the document is XML.

5. The XML declaration's three attributes are `version`, `encoding`, and `standalone`. The `version` attribute is nonoptional.

6. The answer is false: an element can consist of the empty-element tag, which is a standalone tag whose name ends with a forward slash (/), such as `<break/>`.

© Jeff Friesen 2019
J. Friesen, *Java XML and JSON*, https://doi.org/10.1007/978-1-4842-4330-5_13

7. Following the XML declaration, an XML document is anchored in a root element.

8. Mixed content is a combination of child elements and content.

9. A character reference is a code that represents a character. The two kinds of character references are numeric character references (such as Σ) and character entity references (such as <).

10. A CDATA section is a section of literal HTML or XML markup and content surrounded by the <![CDATA[prefix and the]]> suffix. You would use a CDATA section when you have a large amount of HTML/XML text and don't want to replace each literal < (start of tag) and & (start of entity) character with its < and & predefined character entity reference, which is a tedious and possibly error-prone undertaking—you might forget to replace one of these characters.

11. A namespace is a Uniform Resource Identifier-based container that helps differentiate XML vocabularies by providing a unique context for its contained identifiers.

12. A namespace prefix is an alias for a URI.

13. The answer is true: a tag's attributes don't need to be prefixed when those attributes belong to the element.

14. A comment is a character sequence beginning with <!-- and ending with -->. It can appear anywhere in an XML document except before the XML declaration, except within tags, and except within another comment.

15. A processing instruction is an instruction that's made available to the application parsing the document. The instruction begins with <? and ends with ?>.

16. The rules that an XML document must follow to be considered well formed are as follows: all elements must either have start and end tags or consist of empty-element tags, tags must be nested correctly, all attribute values must be quoted, empty elements must be properly formatted, and you must be careful with case.

Furthermore, XML parsers that are aware of namespaces enforce two additional rules: all element and attribute names must not include more than one colon character; and no entity names, processing-instruction targets, or notation names can contain colons.

17. For an XML document to be valid, the document must adhere to certain constraints. For example, one constraint might be that a specific element must always follow another specific element.

18. The two common grammar languages are Document Type Definition and XML Schema.

19. The general syntax for declaring an element in a DTD is `<!ELEMENT` *name content-specifier*`>`.

20. XML Schema lets you create complex types from simple types.

21. Listing A-1 presents the `books.xml` document file that was called for in Chapter 1.

Listing A-1. *A Document of Books*

```
<?xml version="1.0"?>
<books>
   <book isbn="0201548550" pubyear="1992">
     <title>
        Advanced C++
     </title>
     394211_2_En
        James O. Coplien
     </author>
     <publisher>
        Addison Wesley
     </publisher>
   </book>
```

```
<book isbn="9781430210450" pubyear="2008">
    <title>
        Beginning Groovy and Grails
    </title>
    394211_2_En
        Christopher M. Judd
    </author>
    394211_2_En
        Joseph Faisal Nusairat
    </author>
    394211_2_En
        James Shingler
    </author>
    <publisher>
        Apress
    </publisher>
</book>
<book isbn="0201310058" pubyear="2001">
    <title>
        Effective Java
    </title>
    394211_2_En
        Joshua Bloch
    </author>
    <publisher>
        Addison Wesley
    </publisher>
</book>
</books>
```

22. Listing A-2 presents the books.xml document file with an internal DTD that was called for in Chapter 1.

Listing A-2. A DTD-Enabled Document of Books

```
<?xml version="1.0"?>
<!DOCTYPE books [
   <!ELEMENT books (book+)>
   <!ELEMENT book (title, author+, publisher)>
   <!ELEMENT title (#PCDATA)>
   <!ELEMENT author (#PCDATA)>
   <!ELEMENT publisher (#PCDATA)>
   <!ATTLIST book isbn CDATA #REQUIRED>
   <!ATTLIST book pubyear CDATA #REQUIRED>
]>
<books>
   <book isbn="0201548550" pubyear="1992">
      <title>
         Advanced C++
      </title>
      394211_2_En
         James O. Coplien
      </author>
      <publisher>
         Addison Wesley
      </publisher>
   </book>
   <book isbn="9781430210450" pubyear="2008">
      <title>
         Beginning Groovy and Grails
      </title>
      394211_2_En
         Christopher M. Judd
      </author>
      394211_2_En
         Joseph Faisal Nusairat
      </author>
```

```
        394211_2_En
           James Shingler
        </author>
        <publisher>
           Apress
        </publisher>
     </book>
     <book isbn="0201310058" pubyear="2001">
        <title>
           Effective Java
        </title>
        394211_2_En
           Joshua Bloch
        </author>
        <publisher>
           Addison Wesley
        </publisher>
     </book>
</books>
```

Chapter 2: Parsing XML Documents with SAX

1. SAX is an event-based Java API for parsing an XML document
    sequentially from start to finish. As a SAX-oriented parser
    encounters an item from the document's infoset, it makes this
    item available to an application as an event by calling one of
    the methods in one of the application's handlers, which the
    application has previously registered with the parser. The
    application can then consume this event by processing the infoset
    item in some manner.

2. You obtain a SAX 2-based parser by obtaining a
    SAXParserFactory instance, then configuring this instance, then
    returning a SAXParser instance from the SAXParserFactory, and
    finally returning an XMLReader instance from the SAXParser.

466

3. The purpose of the `XMLReader` interface is to describe a SAX 2 parser. This interface makes available several methods for configuring the SAX 2 parser and parsing an XML document's content.

4. You tell a SAX parser to perform validation by invoking `XMLReader`'s `setFeature(String name, boolean value)` method, passing `"http://xml.org/sax/features/validation"` to name and `true` to `value`.

5. The four kinds of SAX-oriented exceptions that can be thrown when working with SAX are `SAXException`, `SAXNotRecognizedException`, `SAXNotSupportedException`, and `SAXParseException`.

6. The interface that a handler class implements to respond to content-oriented events is `ContentHandler`.

7. The three other core interfaces that a handler class is likely to implement are `DTDHandler`, `EntityResolver`, and `ErrorHandler`.

8. Ignorable whitespace is whitespace located between tags where the DTD doesn't allow mixed content.

9. The answer is false: `void error(SAXParseException exception)` is called only for recoverable errors.

10. The purpose of the `DefaultHandler` class is to serve as a convenience base class for SAX 2 applications. It provides default implementations for all of the callbacks in the four core SAX 2 handler interfaces: `ContentHandler`, `DTDHandler`, `EntityResolver`, and `ErrorHandler`.

11. An entity is aliased data. An entity resolver is an object that uses the public identifier to choose a different system identifier. Upon encountering an external entity, the parser calls the custom entity resolver to obtain this identifier.

12. Listing A-3 presents the `DumpUserInfo` application that was called for in Chapter 2.

Listing A-3. Using SAX to Dump the Apache `tomcat-users.xml` File's User Information

```java
import java.io.FileReader;
import java.io.IOException;

import javax.xml.parsers.ParserConfigurationException;
import javax.xml.parsers.SAXParser;
import javax.xml.parsers.SAXParserFactory;

import org.xml.sax.Attributes;
import org.xml.sax.InputSource;
import org.xml.sax.SAXException;
import org.xml.sax.XMLReader;

import org.xml.sax.helpers.DefaultHandler;

import static java.lang.System.*;

public class DumpUserInfo
{
   public static void main(String[] args)
   {
      try
      {
         SAXParserFactory spf =
            SAXParserFactory.newInstance();
         spf.setNamespaceAware(true);
         SAXParser sp = spf.newSAXParser();
         XMLReader xmlr = sp.getXMLReader();
         Handler handler = new Handler();
         xmlr.setContentHandler(handler);
         FileReader fr = new FileReader("tomcat-users.xml");
         xmlr.parse(new InputSource(fr));
      }
```

```java
      catch (IOException ioe)
      {
         err.printf("IOE: %s%n", ioe.toString());
      }
      catch (ParserConfigurationException pce)
      {
         err.printf("PCE: %s%n", pce.toString());
      }
      catch (SAXException saxe)
      {
         err.printf("SAXE: %s%n", saxe.toString());
      }
   }
}

class Handler extends DefaultHandler
{
   @Override
   public void startElement(String uri, String localName,
                            String qName,
                            Attributes attributes)
   {
      if (localName.equals("user"))
      {
         for (int i = 0; i < attributes.getLength(); i++)
            out.printf("%s = %s%n",
                       attributes.getLocalName(i),
                       attributes.getValue(i));
         out.println();
      }
   }
}
```

13. Listings A-4 and A-5 present the SAXSearch and Handler classes
     that were called for in Chapter 2.

Listing A-4. A SAX Driver Class for Searching books.xml for a Specific Publisher's Books

```java
import java.io.FileReader;
import java.io.IOException;

import javax.xml.parsers.ParserConfigurationException;
import javax.xml.parsers.SAXParser;
import javax.xml.parsers.SAXParserFactory;

import org.xml.sax.InputSource;
import org.xml.sax.SAXException;
import org.xml.sax.XMLReader;

import static java.lang.System.*;

public class SAXSearch
{
   final static String PROP_LH =
      "http://xml.org/sax/properties/lexical-handler";

   public static void main(String[] args)
   {
      if (args.length != 1)
      {
         err.println("usage: java SAXSearch publisher");
         return;
      }

      try
      {
         SAXParserFactory spf =
            SAXParserFactory.newInstance();
         spf.setNamespaceAware(true);
         SAXParser sp = spf.newSAXParser();
         XMLReader xmlr = sp.getXMLReader();
```

```
      Handler handler = new Handler(args[0]);
      xmlr.setContentHandler(handler);
      xmlr.setErrorHandler(handler);
      xmlr.setProperty(PROP_LH, handler);
      FileReader fr = new FileReader("books.xml");
      xmlr.parse(new InputSource(fr));
   }
   catch (IOException ioe)
   {
      err.printf("IOE: %s%n", ioe.toString());
   }
   catch (ParserConfigurationException pce)
   {
      err.printf("PCE: %s%n", pce.toString());
   }
   catch (SAXException saxe)
   {
      err.printf("SAXE: %s%n", saxe.toString());
   }
}
}
```

Listing A-5. A SAX Callback Class Whose Methods Are Called by the SAX Parser

```
import org.xml.sax.Attributes;
import org.xml.sax.SAXParseException;

import org.xml.sax.ext.DefaultHandler2;

import static java.lang.System.*;

public class Handler extends DefaultHandler2
{
   private boolean isPublisher, isTitle;

   private String isbn, publisher, pubYear, title, srchText;
```

```java
   public Handler(String srchText)
   {
      this.srchText = srchText;
   }

   @Override
   public void characters(char[] ch, int start, int length)
   {
      if (isTitle)
      {
         title = new String(ch, start, length).trim();
         isTitle = false;
      }
      else
      if (isPublisher)
      {
         publisher = new String(ch, start, length).trim();
         isPublisher = false;
      }
   }

   @Override
   public void endElement(String uri, String localName,
                          String qName)
   {
      if (!localName.equals("book"))
         return;
      if (!srchText.equals(publisher))
         return;
      out.printf("title = %s, isbn = %s%n", title, isbn);
   }

   @Override
   public void error(SAXParseException saxpe)
   {
      out.printf("error() %s%n", saxpe.toString());
   }
```

```java
@Override
public void fatalError(SAXParseException saxpe)
{
   out.printf("fatalError() %s%n", saxpe.toString());
}

@Override
public void startElement(String uri, String localName,
                         String qName, Attributes attributes)
{
   if (localName.equals("title"))
   {
      isTitle = true;
      return;
   }
   else
   if (localName.equals("publisher"))
   {
      isPublisher = true;
      return;
   }
   if (!localName.equals("book"))
      return;
   for (int i = 0; i < attributes.getLength(); i++)
      if (attributes.getLocalName(i).equals("isbn"))
         isbn = attributes.getValue(i);
      else
      if (attributes.getLocalName(i).equals("pubyear"))
         pubYear = attributes.getValue(i);
}

@Override
public void warning(SAXParseException saxpe)
{
   out.printf("warning() %s%n", saxpe.toString());
}
}
```

14. When you use Listing 2-1's SAXDemo application to validate
     Exercise A-22's books.xml content against its DTD, you should
     observe no validation errors.

Chapter 3: Parsing and Creating XML Documents with DOM

1. DOM is a Java API for parsing an XML document into an in-
    memory tree of nodes and for creating an XML document from a
    tree of nodes. After a DOM parser has created a document tree, an
    application uses the DOM API to navigate over and extract infoset
    items from the tree's nodes.

2. The answer is false: Java 11 supports DOM Levels 1, 2, and 3.

3. The 12 types of DOM nodes are attribute node, CDATA section
    node, comment node, document node, document fragment node,
    document type node, element node, entity node, entity reference
    node, notation node, processing-instruction node, and text node.

4. You obtain a document builder by first instantiating
    DocumentBuilderFactory via one of its newInstance() methods
    and then invoking newDocumentBuilder() on the returned
    DocumentBuilderFactory object to obtain a DocumentBuilder
    object.

5. You use a document builder to parse an XML document by
    invoking one of DocumentBuilder's parse() methods.

6. The answer is true: Document and all other org.w3c.dom interfaces
    that describe different kinds of nodes are subinterfaces of the Node
    interface.

7. You use a document builder to create a new XML document by
    invoking DocumentBuilder's Document newDocument() method
    and by invoking Document's various "create" methods.

8. You would determine if a node has children by calling Node's boolean hasChildNodes() method, which returns true when a node has child nodes.

9. The answer is false: when creating a new XML document, you cannot use the DOM API to specify the XML declaration's encoding attribute.

10. The purpose of the Load and Save API is to provide a standard way to load XML content into a new DOM tree and save an existing DOM tree to an XML document.

11. The difference between NodeIterator and TreeWalker is as follows: A NodeIterator presents a flattened view of the subtree as an ordered sequence of nodes, presented in document order. Conversely, a TreeWalker maintains the hierarchical relationships of the subtree, allowing navigation of this hierarchy.

12. The difference between Range's selectNode() and selectNodeContents() methods is as follows: selectNode() selects a node and its contents, whereas selectNodeContents() selects the contents within a node (without also selecting the node).

13. Listing A-6 presents the DumpUserInfo application that was called for in Chapter 3.

Listing A-6. Using DOM to Dump the Apache tomcat-users.xml File's User Information

```
import java.io.IOException;

import javax.xml.parsers.DocumentBuilder;
import javax.xml.parsers.DocumentBuilderFactory;
import javax.xml.parsers.FactoryConfigurationError;
import javax.xml.parsers.ParserConfigurationException;

import org.w3c.dom.Attr;
import org.w3c.dom.Document;
import org.w3c.dom.Element;
import org.w3c.dom.NamedNodeMap;
```

```java
import org.w3c.dom.Node;
import org.w3c.dom.NodeList;

import org.xml.sax.SAXException;

import static java.lang.System.*;

public class DumpUserInfo
{
   public static void main(String[] args)
   {
      try
      {
         DocumentBuilderFactory dbf =
            DocumentBuilderFactory.newInstance();
         DocumentBuilder db = dbf.newDocumentBuilder();
         Document doc = db.parse("tomcat-users.xml");
         NodeList nl = doc.getChildNodes();
         for (int i = 0; i < nl.getLength(); i++)
         {
            Node node = nl.item(i);
            if (node.getNodeType() == Node.ELEMENT_NODE)
               dump((Element) node);
         }
      }
      catch (IOException ioe)
      {
         err.printf("IOE: %s%n", ioe.toString());
      }
      catch (SAXException saxe)
      {
         err.printf("SAXE: %s%n", saxe.toString());
      }
      catch (FactoryConfigurationError fce)
      {
         err.printf("FCE: %s%n", fce.toString());
      }
```

```
      catch (ParserConfigurationException pce)
      {
         err.printf("PCE: %s%n", pce.toString());
      }
   }

   static void dump(Element e)
   {
      if (e.getNodeName().equals("user"))
      {
         NamedNodeMap nnm = e.getAttributes();
         if (nnm != null)
            for (int i = 0; i < nnm.getLength(); i++)
            {
               Node node = nnm.item(i);
               Attr attr =
                  e.getAttributeNode(node.getNodeName());
               out.printf("%s = %s%n", attr.getName(),
                          attr.getValue());
            }
         out.println();
      }
      NodeList nl = e.getChildNodes();
      for (int i = 0; i < nl.getLength(); i++)
      {
         Node node = nl.item(i);
         if (node instanceof Element)
            dump((Element) node);
      }
   }
}
```

14. Listing A-7 presents the DOMSearch application that was called for in Chapter 3.

Listing A-7. Using DOM to Search books.xmlfor a Specific Publisher's Books

```java
import java.io.IOException;

import java.util.ArrayList;
import java.util.List;

import javax.xml.parsers.DocumentBuilder;
import javax.xml.parsers.DocumentBuilderFactory;
import javax.xml.parsers.FactoryConfigurationError;
import javax.xml.parsers.ParserConfigurationException;

import org.w3c.dom.Document;
import org.w3c.dom.Element;
import org.w3c.dom.NamedNodeMap;
import org.w3c.dom.Node;
import org.w3c.dom.NodeList;

import org.xml.sax.SAXException;

import static java.lang.System.*;

public class DOMSearch
{
   public static void main(String[] args)
   {
      if (args.length != 1)
      {
         err.println("usage: java DOMSearch publisher");
         return;
      }

      try
      {
         DocumentBuilderFactory dbf =
            DocumentBuilderFactory.newInstance();
         DocumentBuilder db = dbf.newDocumentBuilder();
```

```
Document doc = db.parse("books.xml");
class BookItem
{
   String title;
   String isbn;
}
List<BookItem> bookItems = new ArrayList<>();
NodeList books = doc.getElementsByTagName("book");
for (int i = 0; i < books.getLength(); i++)
{
   Element book = (Element) books.item(i);
   NodeList children = book.getChildNodes();
   String title = "";
   for (int j = 0; j < children.getLength(); j++)
   {
      Node child = children.item(j);
      if (child.getNodeType() == Node.ELEMENT_NODE)
      {
         if (child.getNodeName().equals("title"))
            title = child.getFirstChild().
                         getNodeValue().trim();
         else
         if (child.getNodeName().
             equals("publisher"))
         {
            // Compare publisher name argument
            // (args[0]) with text of publisher's
            // child text node. The trim() method
            // call removes whitespace that would
            // interfere with the comparison.
            if (args[0].
                equals(child.getFirstChild().
                          getNodeValue().trim()))
            {
               BookItem bookItem = new BookItem();
               bookItem.title = title;
```

```java
                        NamedNodeMap nnm =
                           book.getAttributes();
                        Node isbn =
                           nnm.getNamedItem("isbn");
                        bookItem.isbn = isbn.getNodeValue();
                        bookItems.add(bookItem);
                        break;
                  }
               }
            }
         }
      }
      for (BookItem bookItem: bookItems)
         out.printf("title = %s, isbn = %s%n",
                    bookItem.title, bookItem.isbn);
   }
   catch (IOException ioe)
   {
      err.printf("IOE: %s%n", ioe.toString());
   }
   catch (SAXException saxe)
   {
      err.printf("SAXE: %s%n", saxe.toString());
   }
   catch (FactoryConfigurationError fce)
   {
      err.printf("FCE: %s%n", fce.toString());
   }
   catch (ParserConfigurationException pce)
   {
      err.printf("PCE: %s%n", pce.toString());
   }
   }
}
```

15. Listing A-8 presents the `DOMValidate` application that was called
for in Chapter 3.

Listing A-8. Using DOM to Validate XML Content

```java
import java.io.IOException;

import javax.xml.parsers.DocumentBuilder;
import javax.xml.parsers.DocumentBuilderFactory;
import javax.xml.parsers.FactoryConfigurationError;
import javax.xml.parsers.ParserConfigurationException;

import org.w3c.dom.Attr;
import org.w3c.dom.Document;
import org.w3c.dom.Element;
import org.w3c.dom.NamedNodeMap;
import org.w3c.dom.Node;
import org.w3c.dom.NodeList;

import org.xml.sax.SAXException;

import static java.lang.System.*;

public class DOMValidate
{
   public static void main(String[] args)
   {
      if (args.length != 1)
      {
         err.println("usage: java DOMValidate xmlfile");
         return;
      }
      try
      {
         DocumentBuilderFactory dbf =
            DocumentBuilderFactory.newInstance();
         dbf.setNamespaceAware(true);
         dbf.setValidating(true);
         DocumentBuilder db = dbf.newDocumentBuilder();
```

481

```java
        Document doc = db.parse(args[0]);
        out.printf("Version = %s%n", doc.getXmlVersion());
        out.printf("Encoding = %s%n",
                    doc.getXmlEncoding());
        out.printf("Standalone = %b%n%n",
                    doc.getXmlStandalone());
        if (doc.hasChildNodes())
        {
            NodeList nl = doc.getChildNodes();
            for (int i = 0; i < nl.getLength(); i++)
            {
                Node node = nl.item(i);
                if (node.getNodeType() == Node.ELEMENT_NODE)
                    dump((Element) node);
            }
        }
    }
    catch (IOException ioe)
    {
        err.printf("IOE: %s%n", ioe.toString());
    }
    catch (SAXException saxe)
    {
        err.printf("SAXE: %s%n", saxe.toString());
    }
    catch (FactoryConfigurationError fce)
    {
        err.printf("FCE: %s%n", fce.toString());
    }
    catch (ParserConfigurationException pce)
    {
        err.printf("PCE: %s%n", pce.toString());
    }
}
```

```
static void dump(Element e)
{
   out.printf("Element: %s, %s, %s, %s%n",
              e.getNodeName(), e.getLocalName(),
              e.getPrefix(), e.getNamespaceURI());
   NamedNodeMap nnm = e.getAttributes();
   if (nnm != null)
      for (int i = 0; i < nnm.getLength(); i++)
      {
         Node node = nnm.item(i);
         Attr attr =
            e.getAttributeNode(node.getNodeName());
         out.printf("Attribute %s = %s%n",
                    attr.getName(), attr.getValue());
      }
   NodeList nl = e.getChildNodes();
   for (int i = 0; i < nl.getLength(); i++)
   {
      Node node = nl.item(i);
      if (node instanceof Element)
         dump((Element) node);
   }
}
}
```

16. Listing A-9 presents the DOMDemo application that was called for in Chapter 3.

Listing A-9. Installing a Custom Error Handler

```
import org.w3c.dom.Attr;
import org.w3c.dom.Document;
import org.w3c.dom.DOMConfiguration;
import org.w3c.dom.DOMError;
import org.w3c.dom.DOMErrorHandler;
import org.w3c.dom.Element;
```

```java
import org.w3c.dom.NamedNodeMap;
import org.w3c.dom.Node;
import org.w3c.dom.NodeList;

import org.w3c.dom.bootstrap.DOMImplementationRegistry;

import org.w3c.dom.ls.DOMImplementationLS;
import org.w3c.dom.ls.LSParser;

import static java.lang.System.*;

class ErrHandler implements DOMErrorHandler
{
   @Override
   public boolean handleError(DOMError error)
   {
      short severity = error.getSeverity();
      if (severity == error.SEVERITY_ERROR)
         System.out.printf("DOM3 error: %s%n",
                           error.getMessage());
      else
      if (severity == error.SEVERITY_FATAL_ERROR)
         System.out.printf("DOM3 fatal error: %s%n",
                           error.getMessage());
      else
      if (severity == error.SEVERITY_WARNING)
         System.out.printf("DOM3 warning: %s%n",
                           error.getMessage());
      return true;
   }
}

public class DOMDemo
{
   public static void main(String[] args) throws Exception
   {
      if (args.length != 1)
```

```
   {
      err.println("usage: java DOMDemo xmlfile");
      return;
   }
   DOMImplementationLS ls = (DOMImplementationLS)
      DOMImplementationRegistry.newInstance().
      getDOMImplementation("LS");
   LSParser parser =
      ls.createLSParser(DOMImplementationLS.
                        MODE_SYNCHRONOUS, null);
   DOMConfiguration config = parser.getDomConfig();
   config.setParameter("validate", Boolean.TRUE);
   config.setParameter("error-handler",
                        new ErrHandler());
   Document doc = parser.parseURI(args[0]);
   if (doc.hasChildNodes())
   {
      NodeList nl = doc.getChildNodes();
      for (int i = 0; i < nl.getLength(); i++)
      {
         Node node = nl.item(i);
         if (node.getNodeType() == Node.ELEMENT_NODE)
            dump((Element) node);
      }
   }
}

static void dump(Element e)
{
   System.out.printf("Element: %s, %s, %s, %s%n",
                     e.getNodeName(), e.getLocalName(),
                     e.getPrefix(), e.getNamespaceURI());
   NamedNodeMap nnm = e.getAttributes();
```

```
    if (nnm != null)
       for (int i = 0; i < nnm.getLength(); i++)
       {
           Node node = nnm.item(i);
           Attr attr =
               e.getAttributeNode(node.getNodeName());
           out.printf("  Attribute %s = %s%n",
                       attr.getName(), attr.getValue());
       }
    NodeList nl = e.getChildNodes();
    for (int i = 0; i < nl.getLength(); i++)
    {
       Node node = nl.item(i);
       if (node instanceof Element)
           dump((Element) node);
    }
   }
}
```

Chapter 4: Parsing and Creating XML Documents with StAX

1. StAX is a Java API for parsing an XML document sequentially from start to finish and also for creating XML documents.

2. The `javax.xml.stream`, `javax.xml.stream.events`, and `javax.xml.stream.util` packages make up the StAX API.

3. The answer is false: an event-based reader extracts the next infoset item from an input stream by obtaining an event.

4. You obtain a document reader by calling one of the various "create" methods that are declared in the `XMLInputFactory` class. You obtain a document writer by calling one of the various "create" methods that are declared in the `XMLOutputFactory` class.

5. When you call XMLOutputFactory's void setProperty(String name, Object value) method with XMLOutputFactory.IS_ REPAIRING_NAMESPACES as the property name and true as the value, the document writer takes care of all namespace bindings and declarations, with minimal help from the application. The output is always well formed with respect to namespaces.

6. Listing A-10 presents the ParseXMLDoc application that was called for in Chapter 4.

Listing A-10. A StAX Stream-Based Parser for Parsing an XML Document

```java
import java.io.FileReader;
import java.io.IOException;

import javax.xml.stream.XMLEventReader;
import javax.xml.stream.XMLInputFactory;
import javax.xml.stream.XMLStreamException;
import javax.xml.stream.XMLStreamReader;

import static java.lang.System.*;

public class ParseXMLDoc
{
   public static void main(String[] args)
   {
      if (args.length != 1)
      {
         err.println("usage: java ParseXMLDoc pathname");
         return;
      }
      XMLInputFactory xmlif = XMLInputFactory.newFactory();
      XMLStreamReader xmlsr = null;
      try (var fr = new FileReader(args[0]))
      {
         xmlsr = xmlif.createXMLStreamReader(fr);
         int item = xmlsr.getEventType();
```

```
    if (item != XMLStreamReader.START_DOCUMENT)
    {
       err.println("START_DOCUMENT expected");
       return;
    }
    while ((item = xmlsr.next()) !=
           XMLStreamReader.END_DOCUMENT)
       switch (item)
       {
          case XMLStreamReader.ATTRIBUTE:
             out.println("ATTRIBUTE");
             break;
          case XMLStreamReader.CDATA:
             out.println("CDATA");
             break;
          case XMLStreamReader.CHARACTERS:
             out.println("CHARACTERS");
             break;
          case XMLStreamReader.COMMENT:
             out.println("COMMENT");
             break;
          case XMLStreamReader.DTD:
             out.println("DTD");
             break;
          case XMLStreamReader.END_ELEMENT:
             out.println("END_ELEMENT");
             break;
          case XMLStreamReader.ENTITY_DECLARATION:
             out.println("ENTITY_DECLARATION");
             break;
          case XMLStreamReader.ENTITY_REFERENCE:
             out.println("ENTITY_REFERENCE");
             break;
```

```
        case XMLStreamReader.NAMESPACE:
           out.println("NAMESPACE");
           break;
        case XMLStreamReader.NOTATION_DECLARATION:
           out.println("NOTATION_DECLARATION");
           break;
        case XMLStreamReader.PROCESSING_INSTRUCTION:
           out.println("PROCESSING_INSTRUCTION");
           break;
        case XMLStreamReader.SPACE:
           out.println("SPACE");
           break;
        case XMLStreamReader.START_ELEMENT:
           out.println("START_ELEMENT");
           out.printf("Name = %s%n",
                        xmlsr.getName());
           out.printf("Local name = %s%n",
                        xmlsr.getLocalName());
           int nAttrs = xmlsr.getAttributeCount();
           for (int i = 0; i < nAttrs; i++)
              out.printf("Attribute [%s,%s]%n",
                            xmlsr.
                               getAttributeLocalName(i),
                            xmlsr.getAttributeValue(i));
        }
}
catch (IOException ioe)
{
   ioe.printStackTrace();
}
catch (XMLStreamException xmlse)
{
   xmlse.printStackTrace();
}
```

```
    finally
    {
        if (xmlsr != null)
            try
            {
                xmlsr.close();
            }
            catch (XMLStreamException xmlse)
            {
                err.printf("XMLSE: %s%n",
                            xmlse.getMessage());
            }
        }
    }
}
```

When you run this application against Exercise A-21's books.xml file (without an internal DTD) via java ParseXMLDoc books.xml, you should observe the following output:

```
START_ELEMENT
Name = books
Local name = books
CHARACTERS
START_ELEMENT
Name = book
Local name = book
Attribute [isbn,0201548550]
Attribute [pubyear,1992]
CHARACTERS
START_ELEMENT
Name = title
Local name = title
CHARACTERS
END_ELEMENT
CHARACTERS
```

```
START_ELEMENT
Name = author
Local name = author
CHARACTERS
END_ELEMENT
CHARACTERS
START_ELEMENT
Name = publisher
Local name = publisher
CHARACTERS
END_ELEMENT
CHARACTERS
END_ELEMENT
CHARACTERS
START_ELEMENT
Name = book
Local name = book
Attribute [isbn,9781430210450]
Attribute [pubyear,2008]
CHARACTERS
START_ELEMENT
Name = title
Local name = title
CHARACTERS
END_ELEMENT
CHARACTERS
START_ELEMENT
Name = author
Local name = author
CHARACTERS
END_ELEMENT
CHARACTERS
START_ELEMENT
Name = author
Local name = author
```

```
CHARACTERS
END_ELEMENT
CHARACTERS
START_ELEMENT
Name = author
Local name = author
CHARACTERS
END_ELEMENT
CHARACTERS
START_ELEMENT
Name = publisher
Local name = publisher
CHARACTERS
END_ELEMENT
CHARACTERS
END_ELEMENT
CHARACTERS
START_ELEMENT
Name = book
Local name = book
Attribute [isbn,0201310058]
Attribute [pubyear,2001]
CHARACTERS
START_ELEMENT
Name = title
Local name = title
CHARACTERS
END_ELEMENT
CHARACTERS
START_ELEMENT
Name = author
Local name = author
CHARACTERS
END_ELEMENT
CHARACTERS
```

```
START_ELEMENT
Name = publisher
Local name = publisher
CHARACTERS
END_ELEMENT
CHARACTERS
END_ELEMENT
CHARACTERS
END_ELEMENT
```

Chapter 5: Selecting Nodes with XPath

1. XPath is a nonXML declarative query language (defined by the W3C) for selecting an XML document's infoset items as one or more nodes.

2. XPath is commonly used to simplify access to a DOM tree's nodes and in the context of XSLT to select those input document elements (via XPath expressions) that are to be copied to an output document.

3. The seven kinds of nodes that XPath recognizes are element, attribute, text, namespace, processing instruction, comment, and document.

4. The answer is false: XPath doesn't recognize CDATA sections.

5. XPath provides location path expressions for selecting nodes. A location path expression locates nodes via a sequence of steps starting from the context node, which is the root node or some other document node that is the current node. The returned set of nodes might be empty, or it might contain one or more nodes.

6. The answer is true: in a location path expression, you must prefix an attribute name with the @ symbol.

7. The functions that XPath provides for selecting comment, text, and processing-instruction nodes are `comment()`, `text()`, and `processing-instruction()`.

8. XPath provides wildcards for selecting unknown nodes. The `*` wildcard matches any element node regardless of the node's type. It doesn't match attributes, text nodes, comments, or processing-instruction nodes. When you place a namespace prefix before the `*`, only elements belonging to that namespace are matched. The `node()` wildcard is a function that matches all nodes. Finally, the `@*` wildcard matches all attribute nodes.

9. You perform multiple selections by using the vertical bar (`|`). For example, `author/*|publisher/*` selects the children of `author` and the children of `publisher`.

10. A predicate is a square bracket-delimited Boolean expression that's tested against each selected node. If the expression evaluates to `true`, that node is included in the set of nodes returned by the XPath expression; otherwise, the node isn't included in the set.

11. The functions that XPath provides for working with nodesets are `last()`, `position()`, `id()`, `local-name()`, `namespace-uri()`, and `name()`.

12. The three advanced features that the XPath API provides to overcome limitations with the XPath 1.0 language are namespace contexts, extension functions and function resolvers, and variables and variable resolvers.

13. The answer is false: the XPath API maps XPath's number type to `java.lang.Double`.

14. Listings A-11 and A-12 present the `contacts.xml` document file and `XPathSearch` application that were called for in Chapter 5.

Listing A-11. A Contacts Document with a Titlecased Name Element

```
<?xml version="1.0"?>
<contacts>
   <contact>
      <Name>John Doe</Name>
      <city>Chicago</city>
      <city>Denver</city>
   </contact>
   <contact>
      <name>Jane Doe</name>
      <city>New York</city>
   </contact>
   <contact>
      <name>Sandra Smith</name>
      <city>Denver</city>
      <city>Miami</city>
   </contact>
   <contact>
      <name>Bob Jones</name>
      <city>Chicago</city>
   </contact>
</contacts>
```

Listing A-12. Searching for Name or Name Elements via a Multiple Selection

```
import java.io.IOException;

import javax.xml.parsers.DocumentBuilder;
import javax.xml.parsers.DocumentBuilderFactory;
import javax.xml.parsers.FactoryConfigurationError;
import javax.xml.parsers.ParserConfigurationException;

import javax.xml.xpath.XPath;
import javax.xml.xpath.XPathConstants;
import javax.xml.xpath.XPathException;
import javax.xml.xpath.XPathExpression;
import javax.xml.xpath.XPathFactory;
```

```
import org.w3c.dom.Document;
import org.w3c.dom.NodeList;

import org.xml.sax.SAXException;

import static java.lang.System.*;

public class XPathSearch
{
   final static String EXPR =
      "//contact[city = 'Chicago']/name/text()|" +
      "//contact[city = 'Chicago']/Name/text()";

   public static void main(String[] args)
   {
      try
      {
         DocumentBuilderFactory dbf =
            DocumentBuilderFactory.newInstance();
         DocumentBuilder db = dbf.newDocumentBuilder();
         Document doc = db.parse("contacts.xml");
         XPathFactory xpf = XPathFactory.newInstance();
         XPath xp = xpf.newXPath();
         XPathExpression xpe;
         xpe = xp.compile(EXPR);
         Object result =
            xpe.evaluate(doc, XPathConstants.NODESET);
         NodeList nl = (NodeList) result;
         for (int i = 0; i < nl.getLength(); i++)
            out.println(nl.item(i).getNodeValue());
      }
      catch (IOException ioe)
      {
         err.printf("IOE: %s%n", ioe.toString());
      }
```

```
   catch (SAXException saxe)
   {
      err.printf("SAXE: %s%n", saxe.toString());
   }
   catch (FactoryConfigurationError fce)
   {
      err.printf("FCE: %s%n", fce.toString());
   }
   catch (ParserConfigurationException pce)
   {
      err.printf("PCE: %s%n", pce.toString());
   }
   catch (XPathException xpe)
   {
      err.printf("XPE: %s%n", xpe.toString());
   }
}
}
```

Chapter 6: Transforming XML Documents with XSLT

1. XSLT is a family of languages for transforming and formatting XML documents.

2. XSLT accomplishes its work by using XSLT processors and stylesheets. An XSLT processor is a software component that applies an XSLT stylesheet to an input document (without modifying the document), and copies the transformed result to a result tree, which can be output to a file or output stream, or even piped into another XSLT processor for additional transformations.

3. The answer is false: call Transformer's void transform(Source xmlSource, Result outputTarget) method to transform a source to a result.

4.   Listings A-13 and A-14 present the books.xsl document
      stylesheet file and MakeHTML application that were called for in
      Chapter 6.

Listing A-13. A Stylesheet for Converting books.xml Content to HTML

```
<?xml version="1.0"?>
<xsl:stylesheet
    version="1.0"
    xmlns:xsl="http://www.w3.org/1999/XSL/Transform">
<xsl:template match="/books">
<html>
<head>
<title>Books</title>
</head>
<body>
<xsl:for-each select="book">
<h2>
<xsl:value-of select="normalize-space(title/text())"/>
</h2>
ISBN: <xsl:value-of select="@isbn"/><br/>
Publication Year: <xsl:value-of select="@pubyear"/><br/>
<br/><xsl:text>
</xsl:text>
<xsl:for-each select="author">
<xsl:value-of select="normalize-space(text())"/>
<br/><xsl:text>
</xsl:text>
</xsl:for-each>
</xsl:for-each>
</body>
</html>
</xsl:template>
</xsl:stylesheet>
```

Listing A-14. Converting Books XML to HTML via a Stylesheet

```java
import java.io.FileReader;
import java.io.IOException;

import javax.xml.parsers.DocumentBuilder;
import javax.xml.parsers.DocumentBuilderFactory;
import javax.xml.parsers.FactoryConfigurationError;
import javax.xml.parsers.ParserConfigurationException;

import javax.xml.transform.OutputKeys;
import javax.xml.transform.Result;
import javax.xml.transform.Source;
import javax.xml.transform.Transformer;
import javax.xml.transform.TransformerConfigurationException;
import javax.xml.transform.TransformerException;
import javax.xml.transform.TransformerFactory;
import javax.xml.transform.TransformerFactoryConfigurationError;

import javax.xml.transform.dom.DOMSource;

import javax.xml.transform.stream.StreamResult;
import javax.xml.transform.stream.StreamSource;

import org.w3c.dom.Document;

import org.xml.sax.SAXException;

import static java.lang.System.*;

public class MakeHTML
{
   public static void main(String[] args)
   {
      try
      {
         DocumentBuilderFactory dbf =
            DocumentBuilderFactory.newInstance();
         DocumentBuilder db = dbf.newDocumentBuilder();
         Document doc = db.parse("books.xml");
```

```
        TransformerFactory tf =
            TransformerFactory.newInstance();
        StreamSource ssStyleSheet;
        FileReader fr = new FileReader("books.xsl");
        ssStyleSheet = new StreamSource(fr);
        Transformer t = tf.newTransformer(ssStyleSheet);
        t.setOutputProperty(OutputKeys.METHOD, "html");
        t.setOutputProperty(OutputKeys.INDENT, "yes");
        Source source = new DOMSource(doc);
        Result result = new StreamResult(out);
        t.transform(source, result);
    }
    catch (IOException ioe)
    {
        err.printf("IOE: %s%n", ioe.toString());
    }
    catch (FactoryConfigurationError fce)
    {
        err.printf("FCE: %s%n", fce.toString());
    }
    catch (ParserConfigurationException pce)
    {
        err.printf("PCE: %s%n", pce.toString());
    }
    catch (SAXException saxe)
    {
        err.printf("SAXE: %s%n", saxe.toString());
    }
    catch (TransformerConfigurationException tce)
    {
        err.printf("TCE: %s%n", tce.toString());
    }
    catch (TransformerException te)
    {
        err.printf("TE: %s%n", te.toString());
    }
```

```
   catch (TransformerFactoryConfigurationError tfce)
   {
      err.printf("TFCE: %s%n", tfce.toString());
   }
   }
}
```

Chapter 7: Introducing JSON

1. JSON (JavaScript Object Notation) is a language-independent data format that expresses JSON objects as human-readable lists of properties.

2. The answer is false: JSON is derived from a nonstrict subset of JavaScript.

3. The JSON data format presents a JSON object as a brace-delimited and comma-separated list of properties.

4. The six types that JSON supports are number, string, Boolean, array, object, and null.

5. The answer is true: JSON doesn't support comments.

6. You would parse a JSON object into an equivalent JavaScript object by calling the JSON object's `parse()` method with the text to be parsed as this method's argument.

7. JSON Schema is a grammar language for defining the structure, content, and (to some extent) semantics of JSON objects.

8. When creating a schema, you identify those properties that must be present in those JSON objects that the schema validates by placing their names in the array that's assigned to the schema's `required` property name.

9. Listing A-15 presents the JSON object that was called for in Chapter 7.

Listing A-15. A Product in Terms of Name and Price

```
{
   "name": "hammer",
   "price": 20
}
```

10. Listing A-16 presents the schema that was called for in Chapter 7.

Listing A-16. A Schema for Validating Product Objects

```
{
   "$schema": "http://json-schema.org/draft-07/schema#",
   "title": "Product",
   "description": "A product",
   "type": "object",
   "properties":
   {
      "name":
      {
         "description": "A product name",
         "type": "string"
      },
      "price":
      {
         "description": "A product price",
         "type": "number",
         "minimum": 1
      }
   },
   "required": ["name", "price"]
}
```

Chapter 8: Parsing and Creating JSON Objects with mJson

1. mJson is a small Java-based JSON library for parsing JSON objects into Java objects and vice versa.

2. The `Json` class describes a JSON object or part of a JSON object. It contains `Schema` and `Factory` interfaces, more than 50 methods, and other members.

3. `Json`'s methods for reading and parsing external JSON objects are `Json read(String s)`, `Json read(URL url)`, and `Json read(CharacterIterator ci)`.

4. The answer is true: the `read()` methods can also parse smaller JSON fragments, such as an array of different-typed values.

5. The methods that `Json` provides for creating JSON objects are `Json array()`, `Json array(Object... args)`, `Json make(Object anything)`, `Json nil()`, `Json object()`, and `Json object(Object... args)`.

6. `Json`'s `boolean isPrimitive()` method returns `true` when the invoking `Json` object describes a JSON number, string, or Boolean value.

7. You return a `Json` object's JSON array by calling `List<Json> asJsonList()` to return a list of `Json` objects (one per array element) or by calling `List<Object> asList()` to return a list of Java objects (each object describes one of the elements).

8. The answer is false: `Json`'s `Map<String, Object> asMap()` method returns a map of the properties of a `Json` object that describes a JSON object. The returned map is a copy, and modifications to it don't affect the `Json` object.

9. `Json`'s `Json at(int index)`, `Json at(String propName)`, `Json at(String propName, Json defValue)`, and `Json at(String propName, Object defValue)` methods let you access the contents of arrays and objects.

10. `Json`'s `boolean is(int index, Object value)` method returns `true` when this `Json` object describes a JSON array that has the specified `value` at the specified `index`; otherwise, it returns `false`.

11. When you attempt to set the value for a nonexistent array element, `Json` throws `IndexOutOfBoundsException`.

12. The difference between `Json`'s `atDel()` and `delAt()` methods is as follows: the `atDel()` methods return the removed array element or object property, whereas the `delAt()` methods do not return the removed array element or object property.

13. `Json`'s `Json with(Json objectorarray)` method combines this `Json` object's JSON object or JSON array with the argument passed to `objectorarray`. The JSON type of this `Json` object and the JSON type of `objectorarray` must match. If `objectorarray` identifies a JSON object, all of its properties are appended to this `Json` object's object. If `objectorarray` identifies a JSON array, all of its elements are appended to this `Json` object's array.

14. `Json`'s methods for obtaining a `Json.Schema` object are `Json.Schema schema(Json jsonSchema)`, `Json.Schema schema(Json jsonSchema, URI uri)`, and `Json.Schema schema(URI uri)`.

15. You validate a JSON document against a schema by calling `Json.Schema`'s `Json validate(Json document)` method with the JSON document passed as a `Json` argument to this method.

16. The difference between `Json`'s `setGlobalFactory()` and `attachFactory()` methods is that `setGlobalFactory()` installs the specified factory as a global factory, which is used by all threads that don't have a specific thread-local factory attached to them, whereas `attachFactory()` attaches the specified factory to the invoking thread only.

17. The `Json dup()` method returns a clone (a duplicate) of this `Json` entity. The `String pad(String callback)` method wraps a function named `callback` around the JSON object described by the current `Json` object. This is done for the reason explained in Wikipedia's "JSONP" entry (`https://en.wikipedia.org/wiki/JSONP`).

18. Listing A-17 presents the mJsonDemo application that was called for
     in Chapter 8.

Listing A-17. Demonstrating Json's dup() and pad() Methods

```java
import mjson.Json;

import static java.lang.System.*;

public class mJsonDemo
{
   public static void main(String[] args)
   {
      Json json1 = Json.read("{\"name\": \"John Doe\"}");
      Json json2 = json1.dup();
      out.println(json1);
      out.println();
      out.println(json2);
      out.println();
      out.printf("json1 == json2: %b%n", json1 == json2);
      out.printf("json1.equals(json2): %b%n",
                 json1.equals(json2));
      out.println();
      out.println(json1.pad("func"));

      /*
         The following output is generated:

         {"name":"John Doe"}

         {"name":"John Doe"}

         json1 == json2: false
         json1.equals(json2): true

         func({"name":"John Doe"});
      */
   }
}
```

Chapter 9: Parsing and Creating JSON Objects with Gson

1. Gson is a small Java-based library for parsing and creating JSON objects. Google developed Gson for its own projects, but later made Gson publicly available, starting with version 1.0.

2. Gson's packages are `com.google.gson` (provides access to Gson, the main class for working with Gson), `com.google.gson.annotations` (provides annotation types for use with Gson), `com.google.gson.reflect` (provides a utility class for obtaining type information from a generic type), and `com.google.gson.stream` (provides utility classes for reading and writing JSON-encoded values).

3. The two ways to obtain a Gson object are to call the `Gson()` constructor or to invoke the `create()` method on a `GsonBuilder` object.

4. The types for which Gson provides default serialization and deserialization are `java.lang.Enum`, `java.util.Map`, `java.net.URL`, `java.net.URI`, `java.util.Locale`, `java.util.Date`, `java.math.BigDecimal`, and `java.math.BigInteger`.

5. You would enable pretty-printing by calling GsonBuilder's `setPrettyPrinting()` method.

6. The answer is true: by default, Gson excludes `transient` or `static` fields from consideration for serialization and deserialization.

7. Once you have a Gson object, you can call various `fromJson()` and `toJson()` methods to convert between JSON and Java objects.

8. You use Gson to customize JSON object parsing by implementing the `JsonDeserializer<T>` interface, instantiating an object from the implementation, and registering with Gson the deserializer object along with the class object of the Java class whose objects are to be serialized/deserialized.

9. The JsonElement class represents a JSON element (such as
    a number, a Boolean value, or an array). It provides various
    methods for obtaining an element value, such as double
    getAsDouble(), boolean getAsBoolean(), and JsonArray
    getAsJsonArray().

10. The JsonElement subclasses are JsonArray, JsonNull,
    JsonObject, and JsonPrimitive.

11. You call GsonBuilder's GsonBuilder registerTypeAdapter(Type
    type, Object typeAdapter) method to register a serializer or
    deserializer with a Gson object.

12. JsonSerializer provides the JsonElement serialize(T src,
    Type typeOfSrc, JsonSerializationContext context) method
    to serialize a Java object to a JSON object.

13. Gson provides the Expose, JsonAdapter, SerializedName,
    Since, and Until annotation types to simplify serialization and
    deserialization.

14. The answer is false: to use Expose, it's not enough to annotate
    a field, as in @Expose(serialize = true, deserialize =
    false). You also have to call GsonBuilder's GsonBuilder
    excludeFieldsWithoutExposeAnnotation() method.

15. JsonSerializationContext and JsonDeserializationContext
    provide access to methods for performing default serialization
    and default deserialization, which are handy when dealing with
    nested arrays and objects that don't require special treatment.

16. The answer is false: you can call <T> T fromJson(String json,
    Class<T> classOfT) to deserialize nongeneric objects (i.e.,
    objects created from nongeneric classes) only.

17. You should prefer TypeAdapter to JsonSerializer and
    JsonDeserializer because TypeAdapter is more efficient. Unlike
    JsonSerializer and JsonDeserializer, which are associated
    with an intermediate layer of code that converts Java and JSON
    objects to JsonElements, TypeAdapter doesn't perform this
    conversion.

18. Listing A-18 presents the GsonDemo application that was called for in Chapter 9.

Listing A-18. Serializing and Deserializing Properly Exposed Static Fields

```java
import java.lang.reflect.Modifier;

import com.google.gson.Gson;
import com.google.gson.GsonBuilder;

import com.google.gson.annotations.Expose;

import static java.lang.System.*;

public class GsonDemo
{
   static class SomeClass
   {
      transient int id;
      @Expose(serialize = true, deserialize = true)
      transient String password;
      @Expose(serialize = false, deserialize = false)
      int field1;
      @Expose(serialize = false, deserialize = true)
      int field2;
      @Expose(serialize = true, deserialize = false)
      int field3;
      @Expose(serialize = true, deserialize = true)
      int field4;
      @Expose(serialize = true, deserialize = true)
      static int field5;
      static int field6;
   }

   public static void main(String[] args)
   {
      SomeClass sc = new SomeClass();
      sc.id = 1;
      sc.password = "abc";
```

```
        sc.field1 = 2;
        sc.field2 = 3;
        sc.field3 = 4;
        sc.field4 = 5;
        sc.field5 = 6;
        sc.field6 = 7;
        GsonBuilder gsonb = new GsonBuilder();
        gsonb.excludeFieldsWithoutExposeAnnotation();
        gsonb.excludeFieldsWithModifiers(Modifier.TRANSIENT);
        Gson gson = gsonb.create();
        String json = gson.toJson(sc);
        out.println(json);
        SomeClass sc2 = gson.fromJson(json, SomeClass.class);
        out.printf("id = %d%n", sc2.id);
        out.printf("password = %s%n", sc2.password);
        out.printf("field1 = %d%n", sc2.field1);
        out.printf("field2 = %d%n", sc2.field2);
        out.printf("field3 = %d%n", sc2.field3);
        out.printf("field4 = %d%n", sc2.field4);
        out.printf("field5 = %d%n", sc2.field5);
        out.printf("field6 = %d%n", sc2.field6);
    }
}
```

The gsonb.excludeFieldsWithModifiers(Modifier.TRANSIENT); expression prevents only transient fields from being serialized and deserialized: static fields will be serialized and deserialized, by default. Of course, static fields that are not annotated with @Expose have no chance to be serialized and deserialized, because of gsonb.excludeFieldsWithoutExposeAnnotation();.

When you run this application, you should discover the following output:

```
{"field3":4,"field4":5,"field5":6}
id = 0
password = null
field1 = 0
field2 = 0
```

```
field3 = 0
field4 = 5
field5 = 6
field6 = 7
```

The first line shows that the `static` field named `field5` was serialized.

Chapter 10: Extracting JSON Values with JsonPath

1. JsonPath is a declarative query language (also known as a path-expression-syntax) for selecting and extracting a JSON document's property values.

2. The answer is false: JsonPath is based on XPath 1.0.

3. The operator that represents the root JSON object is $.

4. You can specify JsonPath expressions in dot notation and square bracket notation.

5. The @ operator represents the current node being processed by a filter predicate.

6. The answer is false: JsonPath's deep scan operator (..) is equivalent to XPath's // symbol.

7. JsonPath's `JsonPath compile(String jsonPath, Predicate...` `filters)` static method compiles the JsonPath expression stored in the `jsonPath`-referenced string to a `JsonPath` object (to improve performance when JsonPath expressions are reused). The array of predicates is applied to ? placeholders appearing in the string.

8. The return type of the `<T> T read(String json)` generic method that returns JSON object property names and their values is `LinkedHashMap`.

9. The three predicate categories are inline predicates, filter predicates, and custom predicates.

10. Listing A-19 presents the `JsonPathDemo` application that was called for in Chapter 10.

Listing A-19. Extracting and Outputting Maximum, Minimum, and Average
Numeric Values

```java
import com.jayway.jsonpath.JsonPath;

import static java.lang.System.*;

public class JsonPathDemo
{
   public static void main(String[] args)
   {
      String json =
      "{" +
      "   \"numbers\": [10, 20, 25, 30]" +
      "}";

      String expr = "$.numbers.max()";
      double d = JsonPath.read(json, expr);
      out.printf("Max value = %f%n", d);
      expr = "$.numbers.min()";
      d = JsonPath.read(json, expr);
      out.printf("Min value = %f%n", d);
      expr = "$.numbers.avg()";
      d = JsonPath.read(json, expr);
      out.printf("Average value = %f%n", d);
   }
}
```

Chapter 11: Processing JSON with Jackson

1. Jackson is a suite of data-processing tools for Java. These tools
   include a streaming JSON parser/generator library, a matching
   data-binding library (for converting Plain Old Java Objects
   [POJOs] to and from JSON), and additional data format modules
   for processing data encoded in XML and other formats.

2. Jackson's packages include Jackson Core (`com.fasterxml.jackson.core`), Jackson Databind (`com.fasterxml.jackson.databind`), and Jackson Annotations (`com.fasterxml.jackson.annotation`).

3. The answer is false: Jackson supports simple data binding and full (also known as POJO) data binding.

4. Streaming in Jackson deserializes (reads) and serializes (writes) JSON content as discrete events. Reading is performed by a parser that tokenizes JSON content into tokens and associated data; writing is performed by a generator that constructs JSON content based on a sequence of calls that output JSON tokens.

5. The answer is false: streaming is the most efficient way to process JSON content.

6. You create a stream-based parser by instantiating the `JsonFactory` class and invoking one of this class's overloaded `createParser()` methods on the instance to obtain a `JsonParser` instance.

7. After you obtain a parser, you enter a loop that repeats until the parser's `isClosed()` method returns `true`. Each loop iteration invokes `JsonParser`'s `nextToken()` method, which returns a `JsonToken` object that identifies the next token from the JSON content. You can interrogate this object to obtain additional information about the token and then take appropriate action.

8. You create a stream-based generator by instantiating the `JsonFactory` class and invoking one of this class's overloaded `createGenerator()` methods on the instance to obtain a `JsonGenerator` instance.

9. After you obtain a generator, you invoke `JsonGenerator` methods such as `writeStartObject()` and `writeStringField()` to output JSON content. You complete this task by invoking `JsonGenerator`'s `close()` method.

10. The answer is true: the tree model provides a mutable in-memory tree representation of a JSON document.

11. The `ObjectMapper` class is used to start building a tree. The tree's nodes are instances of classes that descend from the abstract `JsonNode` class.

12. You read a JSON document into an in-memory tree by invoking one of `ObjectMapper`'s `readTree()` methods.

13. The difference between `JsonNode get(int index)` and `JsonNode path(int index)` is that `get()` returns `null` for a missing value, whereas `path()` returns a `MissingNode` reference for a missing value.

14. You write a tree to a JSON document by invoking one of `ObjectMapper`'s `writeTree()` methods.

15. Data binding in Jackson is parsing JSON content to and from Java objects such as POJOs. JSON content is deserialized into Java objects, and Java objects are serialized into JSON content.

16. The purpose of the `TypeReference` class is to pass a generic type definition (removed by type erasure) to one of `ObjectMapper`'s `readValue()` methods.

17. Simple data binding differs from full data binding in that simple data binding converts to and from a limited number of core JDK types, whereas full data binding also converts to and from any Java bean type.

18. By default, Jackson maps the fields of a JSON object to fields in a Java object by matching the names of the JSON fields to the getter and setter methods in the Java object. Jackson removes the `get` and `set` parts of the names of the getter and setter methods and converts the first character of the remaining name to lowercase.

19. The answer is false: a getter method makes a non-`public` field serializable and deserializable.

20. Jackson's read-only annotation types are `JsonSetter`, `JsonAnySetter`, `JsonCreator` and `JsonProperty`, `JacksonInject`, and `JsonDeserialize`.

21. The JsonPropertyOrder annotation type specifies the order in which a Java object's fields should be serialized to JSON content.

22. The difference between a stateful and a stateless pretty printer class is that the stateful class must implement the Instantiatable<T> interface, to allow for the construction of per-generation instances in order to avoid state corruption when sharing the pretty printer instance among threads. This is not a requirement for a stateless class.

23. You prevent ObjectMapper's writeValue() methods from closing the System.out stream by executing disable(JsonGenerator. Feature.AUTO_CLOSE_TARGET) on the ObjectMapper instance.

24. Listing A-20 presents the JacksonDemo application that was called for in Chapter 11.

Listing A-20. Writing Numeric Values as Strings

```
import java.io.File;

import com.fasterxml.jackson.core.JsonEncoding;
import com.fasterxml.jackson.core.JsonFactory;
import com.fasterxml.jackson.core.JsonGenerator;

import static java.lang.System.*;

public class JacksonDemo
{
   public static void main(String[] args) throws Exception
   {
      JsonFactory factory = new JsonFactory();
      JsonGenerator generator =
      factory.createGenerator(new File("person.json"),
                              JsonEncoding.UTF8);
      generator.enable(JsonGenerator.Feature.
                    WRITE_NUMBERS_AS_STRINGS);
      generator.writeStartObject();
      generator.writeStringField("firstname", "John");
      generator.writeStringField("lastName", "Doe");
```

```
    generator.writeNumberField("age", 42);
    generator.writeFieldName("address");
    generator.writeStartObject();
    generator.writeStringField("street", "400 Some Street");
    generator.writeStringField("city", "Beverly Hills");
    generator.writeStringField("state", "CA");
    generator.writeNumberField("zipcode", 90210);
    generator.writeEndObject();
    generator.writeFieldName("phoneNumbers");
    generator.writeStartArray();
    generator.writeStartObject();
    generator.writeStringField("type", "home");
    generator.writeStringField("number", "310 555-1234");
    generator.writeEndObject();
    generator.writeStartObject();
    generator.writeStringField("type", "fax");
    generator.writeStringField("number", "310 555-4567");
    generator.writeEndObject();
    generator.writeEndArray();
    generator.writeEndObject();
    generator.close();
    out.println("person.json successfully generated");
  }
}
```

Chapter 12: Processing JSON with JSON-P

1. JSON Processing (JSON-P) is a Java API for processing (i.e., parsing, generating, querying, and transforming) JSON content.

2. JSON-P 1.0 consists of 25 types located in package javax.json, along with the support packages javax.json.spi and javax. json.stream. The javax.json package mainly contains types that support the object model, the javax.json.spi package contains

a single type that describes a service provider for JSON processing objects, and the `javax.json.stream` package contains types that support the streaming model.

3. The types for creating `JsonArray` and `JsonObject` models are `JsonArrayBuilder` and `JsonObjectBuilder`.

4. `JSONValue` is the superinterface of interface types that represent immutable JSON values.

5. JSON-P 1.1 differs from JSON-P 1.0 in that it supports JSON Pointer, JSON Patch, and JSON Merge Patch. Also, the new version adds editing and transformation operations to JSON array and object builders; and it also updates the API to better support Java SE 8 stream operations (including JSON-specific collectors).

6. The answer is false: JSON-P 1.0's object model is more flexible than its streaming model.

7. You construct a `JsonObject` model by invoking `Json`'s `createObjectBuilder()` method to return a `JsonObjectBuilder` instance, invoking a chain of `JsonObjectBuilder`'s `add()` methods on this instance to add a hierarchy of objects, and invoking `JsonObjectBuilder`'s `build()` method on the builder instance to return a `JsonObject` that serves as the root of the tree.

8. The types that the streaming model provides to read and write JSON content are `JsonParser` and `JsonGenerator`.

9. JSON Merge Patch defines a JSON document structure for expressing a sequence of changes to be made to a target JSON document via a syntax that closely mimics that document. Recipients of a JSON Merge Patch document determine the exact set of changes being requested by comparing the content of the provided patch against the current content of the target document. If the patch contains members that don't appear in the target, those members are added. If the target does contain the member, the value is replaced. Null values in the merge patch are given special meaning to indicate the removal of existing values in the target.

10. The editing/transformation operations that have been added to `JsonArrayBuilder` and `JsonObjectBuilder` are as follows: `JsonArrayBuilder` has received several `add(int index, ...)` methods for adding a value between array elements, several `set(int index, ...)` methods for updating an existing element, and a `remove()` method for removing an element. `JsonObjectBuilder` has received a `remove()` method for removing a name/value pair.

11. The answer is true: JSON-P 1.1 introduced a `JsonCollectors` class whose `static` collector methods return `JSONObjects` or `JsonArrays` instead of `Maps` or `Lists`.

12. Listing A-21 presents the `JSONPDemo` application that was called for in Chapter 12.

Listing A-21. Applying a JSON Pointer to a JSON Document

```
import java.io.FileReader;
import java.io.IOException;

import javax.json.Json;
import javax.json.JsonObject;
import javax.json.JsonPointer;
import javax.json.JsonReader;

import static java.lang.System.*;

public class JSONPDemo
{
   public static void main(String[] args)
   {
      if (args.length != 2)
      {
         err.println("usage: java JSONPDemo jsonfile " +
                     "pointer");
         return;
      }
```

```
      try (var fr = new FileReader(args[0]))
      {
         JsonReader reader = Json.createReader(fr);
         JsonObject o = (JsonObject) reader.read();
         JsonPointer ptr = Json.createPointer(args[1]);
         out.println(ptr.getValue(o));
      }
      catch (IOException ioe)
      {
         err.printf("I/O error: %s%n", ioe.getMessage());
      }
   }
}
```

Index

A

add() method, 226
Advanced XPath
    extension function, 156–161
    function resolver, 159–161
    namespace contexts, 154–155
    variables and variable
        resolver, 161–163
Annotation types, 267
    changing field names, 272–273
    contexts, 276–279
    exposing and hiding fields, 268–271
    generics support, 279–287
    JsonFactory, 398–401
    JsonGenerator, 398–401
    JsonParser, 398–401
    pretty printers, 390–398
    read-only annotation
        JacksonInject, 358–361
        JsonAnySetter, 354–356
        JsonCreator, 356–358
        JsonDeserialize, 361–363
        JsonProperty, 356–358
        JsonSetter, 351–354
    read-write annotation
        JsonAutoDetect, 387–390
        JsonIgnore, 380–384
        JsonIgnoreProperties, 380–384
        JsonIgnoreType, 384–386
    versioning, 273–275
    write-only annotation
        JsonAnyGetter, 369–371
        JsonGetter, 366–369
        JsonInclude, 364–366
        JsonPropertyOrder, 371–373
        JsonRawValue, 373–374
        JsonSerialize, 377–380
        JsonValue, 375–377
Attribute node, 68

B

boolean getFeature(String name), 38
boolean isClosed() method, 327
Byte-order-mark (BOM), 6

C

Character data (CDATA) section, 11, 69
Character references
    character entity reference, 10
    numeric character reference, 10
Chicago contacts
    DOM API, 147–149
    XPath API, 150–152
Comment node, 69
Compound paths, 141
ContentHandler, 42
CouchDb, 187